General-At-Sea

General-At-Sea

Robert Blake and the Seventeenth-Century Revolution in Naval Warfare

MICHAEL BAUMBER

John Murray

© Michael Baumber 1989

First published 1989
by John Murray (Publishers) Ltd
50 Albemarle Street, London W1X 4BD

British Library Cataloguing in Publication Data
Baumer, Michael
General-at-sea: Robert Blake and the 17th century
revolution in naval warfare.
1. Great Britain. Royal navy. Blake, Robert, 1599–1657
I. Title
359.3'31'0924

ISBN 0–7195–4706–7

Typeset and Printed by
Butler & Tanner Ltd, Frome and London

Contents

Contents

Illustrations

All illustrations are by courtesy of the National Maritime Museum, Greenwich, with the exception of the portrait of Edward Popham, which is by courtesy of the Victoria & Albert Museum.

Maps and Battle Plans

Preface

Robert Blake is the least known of the great trio of English admirals of the age of sail – Drake, Blake, and Nelson. He is also the most misunderstood, because his career contradicts some of the most cherished myths about the English Navy. Drake and Nelson were both seamen born and bred. Blake was not. If he had been to sea at all before his appointment as one of the first three Generals-at-Sea, it was as a merchant, and there is no evidence that he had commanded a ship of any sort, never mind a man-of-war. Nor had George Monck or Edward Mountagu, two of the later Generals. Richard Deane may have commanded a merchant ship, but the only one with any experience of the Navy was Edward Popham, and he was dead by the time the First Dutch War broke out. Yet under the leadership of these men the Navy won smashing victories first over the Dutch and then over the Spanish. The Commonwealth inherited a fine battle fleet and then doubled its strength. The main obstacle to its efficient use was the reluctance of the seamen to accept the methods which were necessary. It was the contribution of the soldier admirals, Blake pre-eminent among them, to recognise what needed to be done and to force the captains who served under them to adapt.

It has been the tradition that the Navy is above politics, but Blake was a political admiral. He joined the Parliamentary army in 1642, not because he wanted to make soldiering his profession, but because he wanted to destroy the Church of England and replace it with a national Presbyterian Church. He was a republican and, though he seems to have preferred the deposition to the execution of the King, he embraced the Commonwealth with enthusiasm. No one did more to bind a reluctant Navy first to a republic, which was supported by only a small part of the nation, and then to the only military dictatorship this country has ever known.

The true nature of Blake's greatness does not lie in his ability as a seaman: Tromp, de With and de Ruijter all outmanoeuvred him in the First Dutch War. Nor does it lie in his tactical pre-eminence: broadside firing was already standard practice when he was appointed; fighting in line evolved while he was on shore sick. It must be sought elsewhere: in his determination never to give up once he had begun a task; in his ability to profit from his own mistakes and the discoveries of others, and to turn them into a new system which led to the shattering victory at Teneriffe. Above all it lay in his ability to inspire all those who served under him with his own vision of what needed to be done. Though he bullied them into serving governments for which they had little enthusiasm and imposed on them a novel and very irksome discipline, the only time the captains rebelled was at the Battle of Dungeness.

The seamen would follow him anywhere for he was the man who had turned down the lucrative post of Major-General of Foot to stay with the fleet and who had declared after Dungeness that he would not go to sea again until their pay was increased. Everyone who met him was impressed with the integrity of his character. He wanted nothing for himself and his last thoughts were for the men in the ships off the coast of Spain who had been left behind when the main fleet had sailed for England. No one else represented the virtues of the Puritan warrior in the way he did.

The work which has led to this book has been spread over a great number of years and it is difficult to single out all those who have helped me. I owe a great debt to those who guided my footsteps in Civil War history: Donald Pennington who was my tutor at the University of Manchester and who supervised the early years of my thesis on the Navy in the English Civil Wars, and Professor Brian Manning under whose guidance I eventually completed it. I was also very fortunate to have my first steps round the Public Record Office guided by Mr E. K. Timings and to benefit greatly from his knowledge of seventeenth-century Naval History. Like every writer on history I am indebted to the staffs of the different repositories in which the documents are kept: to the staffs of the Somerset and Dorset Record Offices, the Bodleian Library at Oxford, the Public Record Office and both the manuscript and printed book divisions of the British Library. I would also like to thank the National Maritime Museum which has been the source of all the illustrations except the portrait of Edward Popham, which was unearthed for me originally by David Piper at the Victoria and Albert Museum over twenty years ago. In quoting contemporary letters I have tried to retain the original spelling and punctuation wherever possible. The Julian calendar was still in use in Civil War England. I have used the Old Style Julian dating, but I have begun the year on 1 January as in the Gregorian calendar, not 25 March.

Part I

Soldier of God

Before the Civil Wars

ROBERT Blake was baptised on 27 September 1598.[1] He was the eldest son of Humphrey Blake, a merchant of Bridgwater in Somerset, and his wife, Sarah. The ceremony took place at the parish church of St Mary the Virgin, just round the corner from the family home off Dampiet Street. The house, now host to the Blake Museum, had six bays, with a servants' wing at the back.[2] Downstairs, the three bays at the north end were taken up by the Hall, the principal room of the house, where all the meals were eaten. The southern two bays were occupied by the Parlour. The main doorway was set in the remaining bay, at the Parlour end of the Hall, and probably opened onto a cross passage, separated from the Hall by a wooden screen.

Robert may have been the first born but he was certainly not the last. He was followed by Humphrey (baptised, 17 January 1600) and by William (28 February 1602). They were then joined by George (29 June 1606), Samuel (16 February 1608), Nicholas (31 August 1609), Benjamin (7 November 1614), Bridget (17 May 1616) and Alexander (13 April 1619). These were the children who successfully negotiated the hazards of a seventeenth-century infancy. There was an Edward, a John, another George and another Benjamin who did not.[3] Mrs Blake must have been continuously pregnant, or weaning babies, from the day of her marriage until shortly before the death of her husband.

Even if Humphrey and his wife slept downstairs in the Parlour, as was the medieval custom, space must have been more and more at a premium as the family grew. Privacy, in our sense of the word, was enjoyed by few in the Tudor age. When the pressure of those around you got too great you escaped, not to your own room, but out into the streets and the countryside. That is what Robert must have done and he had much to attract and amuse him. If the young man turned his steps westwards, he would have soon been treading the gentle eastern slopes of the Quantock Hills, where he would have found many of his relations to greet him. His great grandfather, Humphrey Blake, had been a prosperous yeoman farmer of Overstowey and his uncle William owned the manor of Tuxwell.[4] There were also his mother's relations. She was born Sarah Williams and she had Welsh blood. Her ancestor, Sir Henry Williams, had rendered Henry VII valuable service, at the time of the Perkin Warbeck rebellion, and a grateful monarch had bestowed on him a valuable estate of which the manor of Plainsfield, hard by the Blake manor of Tuxwell, was the most important part. Sarah inherited Plainsfield and land at Puriton, Woolavington, Catcot and Bawdrip, which abutted onto another Blake manor, that of Crandon cum Puriton, bought by Robert's grandfather.[5]

Alternatively, Blake could have wandered down to Bridgwater quay, to look at the ships and listen to the talk of the mariners. This has been the favourite staple of earlier biographers, who detected the first stirrings of an interest in the sea by imagining him listening to stories of Drake's voyage round the World and the Spanish Armada. Perhaps he did, but if he wanted such stimulation he did not need to go down to the river. His grandfather, another Robert, died six years before his birth but the servants would certainly have told him stories of the founder of the family fortunes. How he had left his inheritance, the manor of Tuxwell, and set up in Bridgwater as a merchant. How, by 1580, he had got four ships trading with foreign parts: the *Mayflower, Nicholas, James* and *White Hart*. How he had been elected Mayor of Bridgwater in 1574, 1579 and 1587, and how he had represented the borough in the Parliaments of 1584, 1586 and 1588.[6]

Yet the odds are that, if any of the ships the young Blake saw down by Bridgwater bridge attracted his attention, it was not the seagoing ones but the little 'troughs',[7] which flitted about between the bigger vessels. The one piece of evidence we have about Blake's youthful activities suggests that what interested him was neither the hills to the west nor the open sea to the north, but the marshes and moors to the east, which fringed the rivers Brue and Parret. In his book *Fasti Oxoniensis*, Anthony Wood records that, at college, Blake's favourite recreations were fishing, fowling and the snaring of swans.[8] It seems likely that these pastimes predated his Oxford days, because it is difficult to imagine a better place for such pursuits than the Somerset levels. Even if he did not meet the fishermen and fowlers at Bridgwater market, he would have done when he visited the family property at Puriton, which lay at the tip of the thin tongue of high land that separates the Brue estuary from that of the Parret. Perhaps we can be permitted to imagine Blake, poling his 'trough' along the many drains and watercourses, in search of game.

Blake received his early education at the free grammar school in Bridgwater and he proved a sufficiently good scholar for the master, Henry Attwood, to suggest that he might profit from a University education at Oxford.[9] Robert was entered at St Alban's Hall. The earliest evidence of his presence there is his attendance, on 27 December 1614, at the induction of the new principal, Anthony Morgan.[10] To go to University at the age of sixteen was quite normal in the seventeenth century. Blake may well have found himself one of the older members of his year, since fifteen was the median age and youths as young as thirteen were not uncommon.

While Blake was at St Alban's Hall, he tried for a scholarship to Christ Church but failed to obtain it.[11] He matriculated on 20 January 1616 and shortly afterwards moved to Wadham College as a Fellow Commoner.[12] Wadham was a new college, founded in 1610 by Nicholas Wadham, a rich Somerset merchant. By the time of its first intake of undergraduates, Nicholas had died but his widow, Dorothy, was as interested in the foundation as her husband had been and she often sent gifts of money, over and above what had been provided at its inception.[13] Blake made steady progress in his studies and was admitted to the degree of BA on 10 February 1618.[14] The following year his academic career sustained a fatal blow, when he failed to get himself elected a Fellow of Merton College.[15]

A number of attempts have been made to explain Blake's rejection. John Oldmixon, one of Blake's earliest biographers, claimed that the Warden of Merton, Sir Henry Savile, rejected him because of his lack of aristocratic connections and his lack of inches.[16] At 5 foot 6 inches, Blake was not short by seventeenth-century standards but he does seem to have had a rather squat and unprepossessing figure. Modern biographers have, understandably, found this explanation very hard to swallow and have preferred to lay the blame on his religious and political views.[17] Clarendon wrote of Blake during his time at Oxford, 'He was of a melancholic and sullen nature, and spent his time most with good fellows, who liked his morosity, and a freedom he used in inveighing against the license of the time and the power of the Court; and they who knew him inwardly discovered that he had an anti-monarchical spirit, when few men thought the government in any danger.'[18]

Those attributing Blake's rejection to prejudice against Puritans, draw attention to the Walter Durham case, which was the subject of much controversy the year Blake graduated and must have been fresh in the minds of the Merton Fellows. A vacancy occurred among the Fellows at Wadham and King James I tried to compel the College to award the place to a Scottish protégé, Walter Durham. The College statutes stated quite clearly that Fellows could only be elected from among the Scholars of the college, so there was united and, ultimately, successful opposition to the King's wishes.[19] If, as Clarendon claimed, Blake had inveighed against the power of the Court, he would certainly have had something to say about the Durham affair and his views might well have made him unpopular.

This Puritan prejudice view presupposes that Jacobean Oxford was identical with the Oxford which was to become the centre of Royal influence in the First Civil War. This was not so. Men with strongly Puritan views could be found among the fellows of practically every College and the Durham case showed that the University was quite capable of defying the King. Nor did the fact that he was treading in the steps of such an overtly Puritan elder brother seem to have prejudiced the chances of William Blake, Humphrey's third surviving son, who was made a Fellow of Wadham in 1629. He was sub-warden of the College in 1637, and again in 1642, and bursar in 1641. In 1640, he was given an honorary degree, of Doctor of Laws, by the University of Padua.[20]

An examination of William's career shows why Robert did not succeed. William won a scholarship to Wadham in 1620. The Wadham statutes confine the choice of Fellows to Scholars of the college. Robert did not qualify for his own college because he was not a Scholar, only a Fellow Commoner. Presumably Merton did not confine the selection of its Fellows to its own Scholars, but Blake must have been at a disadvantage, competing with men who were Scholars. William matriculated on the 20 November 1620, graduated BA on 4 December 1622, was admitted MA on 7 July 1625, and was only elected a Fellow in 1629, a time scale which was quite common. Robert did not bother to take his MA and tried for a Fellowship only a year after his BA. When these facts are taken into account the surprise is, not that he failed, but that he had the temerity to apply.

All the evidence suggests that Blake was a capable and intelligent man, but that he was not cut out for a life of scholarship. Why, then, did he try for a Fellowship? No conclusive answer can be given but the nature of University society may have influenced his course of action. Undergraduates could not marry while at the university and Fellows were forbidden marriage, so long as they held office. Oldmixon called Blake a 'woman hater',[21] though he produced no information with which to back up his claim. The Rev. J. R. Powell's efforts, writing in 1972, to provide Blake with some sort of social pretensions, based on the routine civilities he made to the wives of his fellow Generals-at-Sea, Mountagu and Disbrowe, are equally unconvincing.[22] What is true, is that Blake never married and women play no part in the records of his life.

Blake's upbringing would have reinforced any initial reluctance he may have had in establishing relations with the ladies. He had seven brothers but only one sister, who was two years old when he left for Oxford. The spectacle of his mother's repeated pregnancies and the seemingly unending sequence of squalling babies was unlikely to have convinced him that any intellectual stimulation or true companionship was to be found in associating with the opposite sex in marriage. Puritan society did not encourage association outside it. Dances and festive occasions were frowned on. Even in Bridgwater church, by the time Blake was old enough to attend, the men were seated according to their social precedence, the more important at the front, the less regarded at the back, and the women separately.[23]

Blake was not a hermit but he preferred an all-male society, which shared with him a common interest or purpose, whether it was the fishermen and fowlers of the marshes, the Fellows of a college, his comrades in the Parliamentary Army or his captains in the Navy. This was why he could later endure, with more equanimity than his fellow Generals-at-Sea or his subordinates, the long months away from home. There was no wife and family waiting for him. He had no home but the fleet.

Humphrey Blake must have observed the behaviour of his eldest son with growing exasperation. For William, who was a genuine scholar and only a third son, an academic career was not only appropriate, it relieved his father of anxiety about the future of one of his large family. Robert was different. He was the eldest son and would succeed Humphrey when he was gone. No doubt, he was proud that Robert had got his degree, but that was not the prime aim of going to University. What Humphrey must have hoped was that Robert would meet other young men, who would provide contacts, which would help him rise in county society.

To show what might have happened, it is interesting to look at the careers of two men who were Blake's near contemporaries at Oxford and who were to cross his path on a number of occasions in the future. John Pyne was the son of Thomas Pyne, of Curry Mallet, near Taunton. He was entered at Hart Hall on 16 February 1610, at the age of thirteen, and graduated BA on 16 November 1612. He took his MA in June 1615,[24] and he may still have been in residence while Blake was studying for his degree. In view of Pyne's later career, it is, perhaps, not too far fetched to cast him as the leader of the group of students with whom Blake habitually consorted, according to Clarendon. On 4 February 1619 Pyne was admitted to the Middle Temple, one of the four main Inns of Court. He was eventually called to the Bar ten years later, in 1629.[25] The delay in qualifying was caused by Pyne's absorption in politics. He represented Poole in the Parliaments of 1625, 1626 and 1628.[26]

The Pynes were a legal family, but it was not necessary to have as thorough an education as John Pyne to achieve the desired result. Edmund Wyndham was the eldest son of Sir Thomas Wyndham of Kentisford, which is between Williton and Dunster, some fifteen miles west of Bridgwater. The Wyndhams of Kentisford were a cadet branch of one of the most important gentry families of West Somerset. Edmund matriculated at Wadham on 16 April 1619, at the age of eighteen.[27] He did not bother to study for a degree. After a stay of not much more than a year, he left for London and, on 15 June 1620, he was entered as a student at Lincoln's Inn.[28] He was never called to the Bar and had no intention of devoting himself to serious study. Most of the sons of country gentlemen simply wanted enough law to enable them to understand cases about their own property, but Wyndham was to put his smattering of legal knowledge to a rather different use, as the next chapter will show. Like Pyne, Wyndham went into politics and represented Minehead in the 1625 and 1628 Parliaments.[29] Five days after Wyndham was admitted to Lincoln's Inn, he was joined by Pyne's cousin, William, one of the sons of Sir Hugh Pyne. This was the link which led Edmund

Wyndham to marry Christabella Pyne, William's sister and John's cousin.[30]

The course that Pyne and Wyndham had followed was the one that Humphrey Blake had planned for his own son – University, Inn of Court, advantageous marriage and a seat in Parliament for Bridgwater, like his grandfather before him. Robert would not conform. He did not attend an Inn of Court, he did not marry and he remained on the sidelines during the political convulsions of 1624–9. The Biography written by a Gentleman in the Family early in the eighteenth century says that he stayed on at the University. The author is not infallible – he attributes some verses written on the death of William Camden to Robert, which were actually written by William. But no one has been able to suggest any plausible alternative.

Humphrey Blake died towards the end of 1625, and was buried at Bridgwater on 19 November.[31] The family assembled to read the will and examine the state of their father's finances. What they found was not encouraging. When Humphrey's father, Robert, died, he had divided his existing property between his two sons. William, the elder, got the manor of Tuxwell, leaving the manor of Crandon cum Puriton for Humphrey.[32]

In 1597 Humphrey improved his position by marrying Sarah Williams, a considerable heiress, but none of the land she brought with her is mentioned in Humphrey's will. When a woman married in the seventeenth century, everything she owned passed to her husband. Consequently, the wife could be left destitute if her husband died before she did. The usual way round the difficulty was for land to be set aside, as a jointure. The widow would enjoy the income during her lifetime but the property would pass to the designated heir at her death. The properties at Puriton, Woolavington, Catcot and Bawdrip were earmarked for this purpose and, to make sure that they were not sold or mortgaged, they were tied up in a marriage trust.[33] The result was that the Blakes still retained the ultimate control but Sarah enjoyed the income, until her death in 1638.[34]

The question of Plainsfield is more difficult. The assumption has been that Humphrey sold the property in order to pay off debts but the Close Rolls reveal no sales of any sort by him. There is another problem. Sarah was a widow when she married Humphrey and it seems very unlikely that her first husband would have willed all the property she brought him to her, cutting out his own children. There was at least one son; he is mentioned in Robert Blake's will.[35] Relatives of her first husband figured in the marriage trust and they would not have co-operated had she ignored them completely. Whether or not Sarah brought the Plainsfield estate with her to her first marriage, there must be grave doubts about whether Humphrey was ever able to lay his hands on it.

Grandfather Robert's other bequest to his sons was his business, which seems to have been in difficulties at the time he died. The outbreak of open

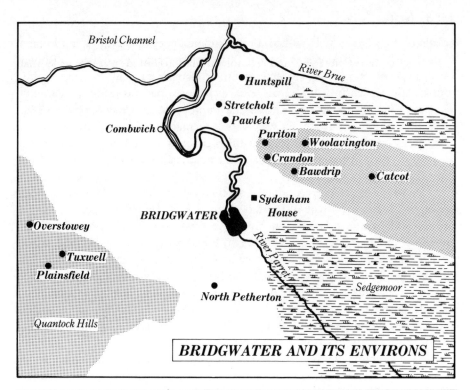

Bristol Channel

River Brue

Huntspill

Stretcholt

Pawlett

Combwich

Puriton

Woolavington

Crandon

Bawdrip

Catcot

Sydenham House

BRIDGWATER

Overstowey

Tuxwell

Plainsfield

River Parret

North Petherton

Sedgemoor

Quantock Hills

BRIDGWATER AND ITS ENVIRONS

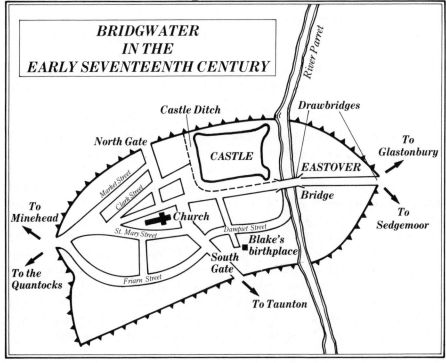

BRIDGWATER IN THE EARLY SEVENTEENTH CENTURY

River Parret

Castle Ditch

Drawbridges

North Gate

CASTLE

To Glastonbury

EASTOVER

To Minehead

Market Street

Clark Street

Bridge

St. Mary Street

Church

Dampiet Street

To Sedgemoor

Blake's birthplace

South Gate

To the Quantocks

Friarn Street

To Taunton

hostilities with Spain in 1585 had a catastrophic effect on Bridgwater's foreign trade.[36] In 1591 the burgesses, Robert Blake among them, apologised to Robert Cecil, Elizabeth's Secretary of State, for their inability to provide a ship of fifty tons for the war effort, because no vessel as large as that was using the Parret.[37] The peace of 1604 brought only a marginal improvement. Whereas, before 1585, the entries in the Bridgwater Customs book averaged twelve to thirteen pages a year, they shrank to a single page in the war years and never rose above five afterwards, even in peacetime.[38] The effect on the finances of the Blake family must have been considerable.

In 1623, the Heralds conducted a Visitation of Somerset. Humphrey does not figure in the main part of the report but a brief family tree does appear in the Appendix. This indicates that Humphrey was not on their original list but submitted a claim in person, while the two Heralds were holding hearings at the Bear Inn in Bridgwater, which was then accepted.[39] One of the prerequisites for gentility was that the claimant should be living on income and not be directly engaged in agriculture, industry or commerce. Humphrey is listed as a member of the French Company in 1611.[40] He served as Mayor of Bridgwater in 1614[41] and retained his burgage land but he may well have sold his interest in the business to his brother or simply become a sleeping partner.

That Humphrey was anxious to get into county society is confirmed by his nomination as one of the Commissioners of Sewers, in the year of his death.[42] The Commissioners were responsible for the care of all water-courses. Inclusion among them placed an aspiring gentleman on the first rung of the county administration. If he gave satisfaction he might go on to positions of greater responsibility and ultimately secure the coveted appointment of Justice of the Peace. Humphrey's resources must have been stretched to breaking point by his social aspirations, the strains of providing for a large family, and the decline in his income from commerce.

The result was that the only one of Humphrey's children who was assured of an income was Robert. He inherited the manor of Crandon cum Puriton, the income from which was to provide as much as he wanted for the rest of his life.[43] He bought a house in St Mary Street, from Widow Coxe, and settled down, for the moment, to a comfortable bachelor life in Bridgwater. He is registered as living there in the Subsidy list of 1628.[44] The position was very different for the others. They had to earn a living. Humphrey, the second son, also remained in Bridgwater. The prospects for foreign trade were even more gloomy than they had been. England went to war with Spain again in 1625, and blundered into one with France the following year, a combination which emptied the Bridgwater quays of ships. Pinning down how Humphrey made his money is difficult but the best guess is that he involved himself in the textile trade because, on 10 April 1632, he married Sarah Ceely, the daughter of William Ceely, the most important mercer in Bridgwater.[45] The case for a Blake involvement in the cloth trade is increased by the later marriage of Bridget to Robert Bowdich, a wealthy clothier of Chardstock.[46]

William had embarked on an academic career but he did not get his Fellowship until four years after his father's death. The College had found him a job as a sub dean, and that, together with some land at Huntspill and £40 left him in his father's will, was enough to cover his expenses. George is not mentioned in his father's will. He would have been nineteen at the time of Humphrey's death and he may have left home already. If that was the case, he may have had what money was coming to him. Early stories relate that he went to London to train as a goldsmith. His mother's first husband, Smithes, had been a goldsmith. George did not take to it and went to sea, the earliest of the Blake brothers to do so, eventually settling in Plymouth. Samuel was seventeen and must have been setting up as a farmer because Humphrey left him £20 with which to buy horses, cattle or sheep.

Nicholas, Benjamin and Alexander stayed at home until they were old enough to be found a trade. Each was left £100, which for the moment was invested and the income used to further their education. Tradition has it that Nicholas moved to Minehead and traded with Spain from that port.[47] The story does not make sense. Minehead was an outport of Bridgwater but its foreign trade was larger than that of its parent, thanks to the enterprise of the Luttrell family, of Dunster, in building a new harbour there.[48] An examination of the Customs books for the 1630s shows that Youghall and Cork in Ireland were the most frequent destinations. There were a small number of ships trading with France, but not one with Spain.[49] In May 1641 Parliament imposed an oath in defence of 'the true Protestant religion', the king, parliament and the 'lawful rights and liberties of the subject'. This became known as the Protestation. All adult males were supposed to sign and copies were distributed around the country. In practice Parliamentary supporters signed with enthusiasm. Royalist sympathisers were not so keen. There is no Nicholas Blake in the list for Minehead, but there is one at Luxborough.[50] The most important item of trade at Minehead was Irish wool and Luxborough was the heart of the west Somerset sheep country. The conclusion must be that, if Nicholas was involved in trade with Spain, he did not go to Minehead. If he did go to Minehead, the odds are that, like Humphrey, he was engaged in the textile trade in some way. Alexander does not enter our story and eventually died at Eaton Socon in Bedfordshire. Of Benjamin, there will be much to say, but later.

Some time between 1629 and 1632, Blake left Bridgwater and may have left the country as well. In March 1629, Charles I dissolved his third Parliament and did not call another one until 1640. The chief drawback for the King, to ruling without Parliament, was that he could not raise money by way of Subsidy. Instead, he tried a whole variety of fund-raising devices, in an attempt to make himself independent of Parliamentary subventions. The first of them was knighthood fines. During the Middle Ages, it had been usual for the eldest son of a gentleman to begin his education by going as a page in a noble household, where he would learn manners by waiting on the lord. Next he would become an esquire and learn the profession of arms. At the end of his training, he would become a fully fledged knight, after paying an appropriate fee to the King as his feudal overlord.

By the seventeenth century, everything had changed. The gentry sent their sons to University and an Inn of Court. Few bothered to put them through the business of becoming an esquire or a knight. Even if the son intended to make a profession of arms the method was to trail a pike, as a volunteer officer, in the regiment of some well-known soldier. Yet, technically, they were still supposed to give their eldest sons the old training. In 1629, the King's Attorney-General had the bright idea of compelling all those who had neglected it, to go through the process of becoming a knight. The King was not interested in the training, which was out of date. What he wanted was the fee.

The Somerset list of Knighthood Fines is dated 1630–2, so it is impossible to ascertain the exact date when each man paid. The list includes Humphrey Blake, who paid at the lower rate of £10–10s–0d, but not Robert.[51] This is very odd because it was usual for the eldest to pay. Even if Robert had paid in another county, it should have been sufficient to exonerate Humphrey. The way in which the Collectors dunned Humphrey suggests strongly that they could not get at Robert, because he was out of the country. Why he had left home can only be a matter of conjecture. Perhaps he had indulged in such open criticism of the Crown, during the 1628 election campaign, that he feared he would be arrested once Parliament was dissolved. Such behaviour would go far to explain his popularity with the Country opposition, at the time of the Short Parliament in 1640. He would have been in good company: Sir Hugh Pyne had indulged in such strong language in opposing another of Charles's money-raising devices, the Personal Loan of 1626, that he was never again selected as a Justice of the Peace. At one time it was thought that he would be committed to the Tower on a charge of high treason. The young George Monck was shipped off to the United Provinces by his father in 1625, after his rash criticism of the Duke of Buckingham. Even Edmund Wyndham was to be found in opposition to the Court in 1627.

Where Blake went, is as much a puzzle as why. C. R. Barrett did discover a Robert Blake who spent ten years, from 1629, as a merchant in Morocco, after commanding the merchantmen, *Phoenix* and *Golden Hind*, of London. This Robert Blake secured the release of fifteen captives, at the time of Captain Rainsborough's visit to Sallee in 1637, and subsequently acted as factor for the Barbary Company.[52] There are a number of objections to the identification of this man with the later General-at-Sea. Why he should pay Subsidy money, in

Bridgwater, when he was sailing ships out of London, was one. Another was provided by the late Admiralty librarian, W. G. Perrin. He compared the signature of the Moroccan Blake, on a letter in the Coke manuscripts, with that of the General and found them to be quite different. The demolition of Barrett's thesis was completed by the discovery that, on 2 November 1643, Prince Rupert hanged a Robert Blake near Abingdon, 'a fellow who had been a merchant in Barbary – releasing English'. He had become a groom of the King's bedchamber and had been caught plotting to betray the King and his two sons, into the hands of the Earl of Essex.

A second Robert Blake was discovered by C. D. Curtis. On 30 July 1629, a Robert Blake, merchant, was admitted to the Company of Freemen at Dorchester, on the payment of £20.[53] The size of the sum indicates that he was not a local man. They were admitted for around £2 a piece. There is a second reference to him under the date 23 December 1629, when he was one of four men who were to petition the Privy Council about the privileges of the town concerning musters.[54] The following year there is a petition, from Robert Blake of Dorchester alone, to the Privy Council. He had freighted the *Tessal*, or *Texel*, of Medemblick, at Middleburg, in the United Provinces, with masts, deal and other timber, for Dorchester. Unfortunately, the officers of the port of Weymouth refused to allow the boat to unload, by reason of 'His Majesty's late proclamation prohibiting the importation of such commodities in any other than British bottoms'. Blake pleaded ignorance of the proclamation and Dorchester's great need of the commodities.[55] Blake's £20 fee, paid to become a Freeman the previous year, was put towards the £70, charged by the Crown, for the issue of a new Charter to the Dorchester Freemen in 1630. All the Freemen had to take the oath afresh and enroll their names. Blake did not do so, which suggests that his petition was unsuccessful and that he saw no reason for prolonging his association with Dorchester. There is no further mention of his name.[56]

Curtis's theory, that this man was the later General-at-Sea, is an attractive one, but no document has survived bearing the signature of this Robert Blake, so that it is impossible to determine the matter. This is a pity, because the Dorchester Blake would fit in beautifully with the famous Schiedam story. The following extract comes from the *Hollandische Mercurius* of August 1652. 'When a certain fisherman (amongst others) fell amongst his [Blake's] fleet with his buss from Wijk-op-Zee, Admiral Blake made the skipper come on board, and amongst other discourse asked him where he was born. He replied. "At Schiedam". To this Blake said, "I lived at Schiedam in my youth, five or six years. Come into my cabin and let us drink a glass of wine to the welfare of the town." '[57]

Another intriguing piece of information is provided by the High Court of Admiralty Book of Examinations for 1637–8. One of the cases dealt with the fate of a quantity of tobacco. A certain Thomas Read deposed, 'That two hogsheads and one barrel were to be transported to Dunkirk and delivered to

Baptist Goodall an English merchant living there. They were laded, on the *Bridget* of Plymouth, George Blake, master, and consigned to John Barnard an English merchant there and to Goodall.'[58] There is a strong likelihood that this Blake was Robert's brother, George, because of the name of the ship – the same as their sister's – and because he was known to have settled at Plymouth.

If we put the information about George Blake, the Schiedam anecdote and the Dorchester story together, a pattern begins to emerge. Blake is living abroad, working as a factor. At first, he tries to freight ships in his own name but loses money over the Weymouth affair. He does not give up but instead acts in the name of other English merchants trading out of West Country ports like Weymouth, Lyme Regis and Plymouth. (A hypothesis of this nature would account for the failure of Blake's name to appear in the Schiedam archives because the goods would bear the name of the owner.)[59] While Robert is building up these connections, George is serving his time at sea. By 1637, when he is thirty-one, George has built up enough experience to be a master. The name of the ship suggests that it is owned either by him or by some other member of the family. Around 1638, Robert Blake returns to Bridgwater, possibly to consult about family affairs on the death of his mother, leaving the goodwill he has acquired to George. George builds on what Robert has begun and is enabled in the fullness of time to abandon the sea and become a merchant of Plymouth.

Whatever the reason, Blake did return to his native country, in time for the meeting of the Short Parliament in 1640.

The Nation Divides

*T*HE Civil Wars really began in Scotland, not England. During 1636 and 1637, Charles and his Archbishop of Canterbury, William Laud, attempted to force the Presbyterian clergymen of Scotland to use the Book of Common Prayer. There was widespread resistance, which Charles tried to suppress by force. In what became known as the First Bishops' War, he met with an humiliating and expensive military defeat at the hands of the Scots. It destroyed his position in Scotland and undermined the financial basis of the Personal Rule in England, forcing him to turn to Parliament for aid. In April 1640 the King called an election for the first time in eleven years.

The electoral situation at Bridgwater was complicated. In 1628 the borough had elected as its burgess M.P.s Sir Thomas Wroth and Thomas Smyth, of Long Ashton, near Bristol.[1] Wroth was the Recorder of Bridgwater and, since early Tudor times, it had been the accepted practice for the Recorder to occupy one seat or to nominate someone in his stead.[2] Smyth was the son-in-law of Lord Poulett, the most powerful magnate in Somerset. He was a free burgess of Bridgwater but he was only eighteen. The Mayor and Corporation were worried about his immaturity and they wrote to Poulett begging him to use his influence with Sir John Stawell of Cothelstone, one of the County M.P.s, to persuade him to look after the town's interests.[3]

Neither Wroth nor Smyth was available in 1640. Wroth was serving his year as Sheriff of the County.[4] The Sheriff was the Returning Officer and therefore ineligible. So wide was the disenchantment with the Crown, that a radical group emerged known as the 'Robins', led by Alexander Popham, which put up Popham himself and Thomas Smyth for the prestigious County seats. In the end, Sir Ralph Hopton beat Popham but Thomas Smyth was elected. His success was due partly to securing the second votes of the 'Robins' and partly to the influence of his father-in-law.[5]

The Bridgwater corporation followed its usual policy of choosing as burgess Members a local gentleman with influential court connections, and a townsman.

The gentleman was Edmund Wyndham. When Wyndham realised that both Bridgwater seats were vacant, he resigned his interest at Minehead in favour of his brother, Francis, and stood for Bridgwater instead. Since 1628, Wyndham had become a courtier and his wife was the confidante of the Queen, Henrietta Maria.[6] The second seat went to Robert Blake. His election was evidence that anger at Laudian Church innovations was far from confined to Scotland. In England too, Puritans had reluctantly accepted episcopal rule in return for liberty, at local level, to modify the services in the Book of Common Prayer and to impose their own social and moral codes. They had been outraged at the attempt by Charles and Laud to make them conform to the new Arminian theology, which emphasised the sacramental aspects of the service at the expense of its teaching functions. One of Laud's closest supporters was William Piers, Bishop of Bath and Wells, whose diocese included the whole of Somerset. Typical of his approach was his attack on the forms of worship at Bridgwater, in November 1636.

The Bridgwater churchwardens were summoned by the diocesan court to explain why they had not presented members of the congregation, at the last visitation, for a variety of religious offences.[7] One of the churchwardens was Humphrey Blake. Many of the omissions with which they were charged, related to the church services. Puritans tried to remove all the elements which seemed, to them, to smack of superstition. William Day, the schoolmaster, and William Ceely, Humphrey Blake's brother-in-law, were accused of failing to bow at the name of Jesus, during a baptism service. Many members of the congregation refused either to bow their heads at the name of Jesus in the Creed, or to stand up during its recitation. A large part of them sat during the whole service, with their hats on their heads, and refused to kneel during prayers. Nor had the churchwardens presented the vicar, John Devenish, for omitting some of the set prayers on Sundays and holy days and for leaving out other unitemised parts of the services.

A common way for Puritan ministers to avoid being contaminated by the ritual aspects of the service, was to have someone else conduct it and only appear when it was time for the sermon. Devenish may well have adopted some such device, leaving the ritual parts of the services to his colleague, George Wootton. This would explain why the two most common complaints against Puritan ministers, failure to wear a surplice and failure to have the communion table railed off at the east end of the church, do not appear in the indictment. Laud and Piers tried to plug this hole by insisting that the preacher take the service and by stopping sermons or lectures being preached without the appropriate ritual accompaniment. Indirect confirmation that this was what Devenish was doing is provided by other charges against the churchwardens. They were accused of failing to report that Devenish was holding conventicles in his own house and in other places. At these gatherings, the sermon had only been preceded by a few prayers or by the singing of a psalm. Humphrey Blake was charged with attending the conventicles himself.

Puritans did not like the Litany with its 'vain repetitions' and Devenish had neglected to recite it in church each Monday, Wednesday and Friday. Puritans were insistent on the need to observe Sunday properly and were outraged by the issue of the *Book of Sports* in 1618, and its confirmation by Charles I in 1633. The Book itemised the pastimes permissible, once divine service had been completed. They also did not recognise Saints' days as holidays. The Bridgwater churchwardens were called to account for not reporting a man who worked on Michaelmas day. The churchwardens were also asked why they had not presented a man who had been excommunicated at the last visitation, and why they had failed to see to it that the midwives in the borough were properly licensed by the church courts.

If this was not enough, the churchwardens were again presented, six months later, for failing to ring the church bells on the King's birthday.[8] For the Crown, recognition of the monarch's birthday in this way emphasised that the King was Head of the Church. To Puritans, it was a misuse of religion for secular purposes. This time the Puritans could not argue that they were going back to the days of Queen Elizabeth, for she had been even more insistent on the proper observation of her birthday than Charles.

The proceedings caused great offence, even though they may have been only partially successful because of the way in which the Bridgwater rectory was arranged, the peculiar nature of which will be examined later in the chapter. There can be little doubt about what Robert Blake thought needed to be done. The hierarchy of bishops must be swept away and replaced by some sort of Presbyterian system. He may already have contemplated the necessity for more drastic measures. James I had coined the aphorism 'no bishop, no king'. If Charles refused to abandon the bishops then the monarchy must be abolished too. The Dutch burghers of Schiedam got on quite happily without a King, so why not the English?

For the time being, if he had them, Blake kept his republican thoughts to himself, in the interests of unity against Arminian innovation and arbitrary taxation. Bridgwater was far from the only place in Somerset to be harassed by the determination of Bishop Piers to make everyone conform to the Laudian pattern of church worship. A sense of outrage permeated the entire county and there was widespread agreement that something must be done, at least to limit the powers of the episcopacy.

Blake's candidature would have been endorsed by a number of different interests. Political considerations suggest that he could have counted on Wroth's support. The Recorder was one of the radical faction and was to serve the Commonwealth later. He would also have had the support of the Pophams, whose views were very similar to his own. In Tudor times, two members of the family had served as Recorder of the borough.[9] A branch of the family still lived there and their property adjoined Blake's in St Mary Street. Blake may well have had his own following too. Under Elizabeth, it had been the custom to elect to the second seat either the current mayor or a past mayor.[10] Blake had not been mayor but his father and grandfather had both graced the office. He may have enjoyed the support of Smyth as well.

The Short Parliament lasted just three weeks. The King's aim was to get money with which to finance a second war to bring the Scots to heel, without making any concessions to the opposition in the Commons. The strategy planned by the King's minister, the Earl of Strafford, depended on securing the support of the House of Lords for the grant of sufficient money. With their support, he believed that he could push the Commons into agreeing to vote the money too, before debating grievances. This would enable the King to dissolve Parliament without making any concessions. When the Lords voted to consider grievances before supply, the strategy collapsed and the King dissolved Parliament.

Foolishly, Charles went to war with Scotland again without any grant of subsidies, relying on his right as feudal overlord to call out his principal tenants and their dependants, to serve him without payment. This Second Bishops' War was a total disaster. The army disintegrated and the Scots invaded England. They had no wish to occupy the country but they were determined to make sure, this time, that Charles could not embark on a third war, and that England should be made to pay the expenses of the Scottish army. When the inevitable peace negotiations opened, at Ripon, the Scots insisted that Charles call Parliament again. They were certain that Parliament would be sympathetic to their cause and they knew that it was the only body which could produce the money they were demanding.

When the elections for the Long Parliament took place, in November 1640, the general position of those who wanted reform was even stronger than in April, but Blake's personal prospects of retaining his seat were not good. Sir Thomas Wroth was still serving his year as Sheriff, but this time he used his influence in favour of his younger brother, Sir Peter Wroth. His decision seems to have caused a good deal of heart burning. Sir Peter lived at Bexley, in Kent, and this was the first time in living memory that Bridgwater had elected a burgess from outside the county. To be fair to Wroth, Sir Peter was the brother-in-law of Sir Edward Dering, who was to lead the attack on the bishops in the opening months of the Long Parliament. He could be forgiven for thinking that a man with such connections would serve the cause better than Blake, who was little known outside Bridgwater.[11]

Thomas Smyth found his position undermined too, because his father-in-law decided to use his influence, in the county election, in favour of his own son,

Sir John Poulett, instead of his son-in-law. Smyth reactivated his interest in Bridgwater, as an insurance against the loss of his county seat. The re-emergence of Smyth as a competitor, combined with the loss of the Recorder's support, made it unlikely that Blake would retain his seat. In the end, Smyth was not chosen either and instead Wyndham was returned for a second time.

Wyndham was the only courtier elected in the whole county and the reason why the Corporation preferred him to both Blake and Smyth gives us a fascinating insight into the way the Crown could make its influence felt in local politics. The rectory of Bridgwater passed under the control of the King at the Reformation, but in 1571, the Mayor and Corporation obtained an 81-year lease of the tithes. In return they agreed to support a preacher at £20 a year, a priest or minister at £13–6s–8d a year and a schoolmaster at £6–13s–4d a year, making a total of £40. The tithes, itemised in the deed, add up to £39–15s–4d but there is reason to believe that they only related to a part of the property and that the rectory was worth much more.[12] It was valued at £120 per annum in 1647.[13] What appears to have happened is that half of the remaining income went to the Crown and half to Bridgwater, to be devoted to charitable uses. The deal was an excellent one for Bridgwater. Not only did the borough secure a nice little income, it also got two clerics plus a schoolmaster instead of just one priest. The bargain was good for the Crown too. In the normal way, all the money would have gone to the rector, except when there was a vacancy.

The corporation seems to have been worried that the arrangement might be upset. The members were particularly apprehensive about action taken against them under the Statute of Mortmain. This forbade religious organisations from alienating property to individuals or groups, such as burgesses of towns, who could pass it on to heirs, so that the property was lost to the church for ever. In 1614, the lease was turned into a trust in order to circumvent the Statute. The deed laid it down that the trustees must be members of the Corporation of Bridgwater and the original list was headed by the Mayor for that year, Humphrey Blake, Robert Blake's father.[14] The way in which such trusts worked seems very odd to our eyes. It lasted until all the trustees had died except one or two. Then those remaining were responsible for naming a new group of trustees, which could include themselves, to whom they handed over responsibility. The Bridgwater trust was renewed in this way in 1628.[15] Maybe the lawyers, who advised the change, thought that the peculiar way such trusts worked got over the 'inheritance' hurdle.

Arrangements of this sort were anathema to Archbishop Laud. To the Puritans of Bridgwater, it was offensive that the entire income of the rectory should be monopolised by one priest. What Laud saw was that two-thirds of the income had been lost to the church and he tried to break such trusts, wherever he found them. In addition, the way in which the money was split between one minister, whose function was to preach, and another, who was responsible for the services, was just the sort of thing he was trying to eradicate. However, in the case of Bridgwater, he was forced to go carefully because one of the parties was the Crown.

Sniping began in 1634. The Earl of Suffolk had obtained a warrant from the Crown, entitling him to investigate all cases in which the Crown appeared to have been unjustly deprived of income. He would be allowed to keep three-quarters of any fines imposed. An examination of the Bridgwater trust revealed that the value of the rectory was larger than the trustees had stated and that the Crown was receiving £2 a year less than it should have done. The trustees were compelled to pay the proper amount in future and the sum the Crown had lost for the past thirty-five years, a total of £70. Suffolk pocketed £52–10s–0d and the Crown got £17–10s–0d, plus an enhanced income.[16]

The attack was renewed in 1640, by Edmund Wyndham. After the dissolution of Parliament in 1629, Wyndham had embarked on a career at court. Using the influence of his wife with the Queen, Wyndham tried to make money by getting grants, like the one to Suffolk, which has already been mentioned. In 1632, he was granted an income from proceedings concerning Writs of Error, despite the opposition of the Judges. Wyndham was one of the leading figures in the establishment of the Soap Monopoly, though he sold his interest in 1635. The grant of monopolies, in return for a fee or a cut of the profits, was one of the ways in which the King endeavoured to raise money without the sanction of Parliament, and caused great offence throughout the business community. Another of Wyndham's speculations was the Great Bedford Level in East Anglia, the biggest enterprise in fen drainage in the seventeenth century, but this time he miscalculated and lost a lot of money.[17] In an attempt to compensate him for his losses, Charles seems to have given him a warrant to investigate, and profit from, violations of the Statute of Mortmain.

As we have seen, the Bridgwater trust deed of 1614 was drawn up especially to protect the borough against proceedings under the Statute of Mortmain, but Wyndham must have found a way in which he could circumvent it and prosecute the borough. The usual way in which the Crown could break such arrangements, was to demonstrate that they were a conspiracy to deprive it of revenue, an offence which was, technically, high treason. A prosecution of this sort, over the Hatton inheritance, was the immediate cause of the fall of the Lord Chancellor, Sir Edward Coke, from power in 1616. Possible imprisonment was not the only thing that worried the trustees. Bishop Piers may have attacked the churchwardens in 1636 because he could not get at Devenish. It was difficult to prosecute a man for preaching without an accompanying Anglican service, if that was what he had been appointed to do. The position would be quite different if the trust was broken as a result of court proceedings. It would then be possible to reconstitute the rectory, as it had been before 1571.

Sir Thomas Wroth, the Recorder, soon convinced himself that, if the case came to trial, the borough would lose, so he advised the trustees to try and settle out of court.[18] This was just what Wyndham wanted. He agreed to use his influence with the King and Queen, to get the borough a special pardon, in return for payments to himself. The accounts of Humphrey Blake, the Receiver (Treasurer) of Bridgwater, for 1639–40, contain the payment to Wyndham of £21 in cash and the presentation of plate and a box worth £43–15s–0d. The special pardon had not been enrolled when the election took place, so the burgesses did not dare unseat Wyndham.

The Bridgwater rectory case may well have played a part in the tactics adopted by the Somerset M.P.s, when Parliament met. They began by sponsoring a petition from the churchwardens of Beckington, which they used to spearhead an attack on Bishop Piers. The Bridgwater pardon was enrolled in December 1640[19] and, as soon as the Commons reassembled after the Christmas break, the religious offensive was suspended temporarily, in favour of an attack on monopolies. They were denounced as illegal. On 21 January 1641, Wyndham was expelled from the Commons for his part in the soap monopoly.[20] The following day, a writ was directed to John Hippisley, Sheriff of Somerset, and Humphrey Blake, the new Mayor of Bridgwater, instructing them to hold a fresh election.[21]

This time there were three candidates: Robert Blake, Thomas Smyth and Sir Thomas Wroth, whose year as Sheriff was now over. In a letter written by John Pyne to Thomas Smyth, on 2 February, Pyne describes consultations he has had about filling the vacancy. 'Noble Sir,' he began, 'I have purused your joint letter directed unto my cosen Popham and myselfe, and thereuppon we have both together had discourse with Rob: Blake whom we finde to stand unto his firste principles which was that if it lay in the compasse of his power he would and yet will conferr the place att Bridgwater on your selfe ...' If insufficient support was forthcoming for Smyth, Blake would put himself forward, so that 'a serviceable good member should be placed there, and not such a one as Sir Thomas Wroth who would prove but disserviceable unto the publicke.'[22]

That both Pyne and Blake were prepared to support Smyth, who was to become a Royalist, in order to keep Wroth out, is an interesting reflection on the state of politics in Bridgwater during the early months of the Long Parliament. Some of the hostility to Wroth was due to the way he had used his influence in favour of his brother the previous November, and this was allied to an unwillingness to see both of the seats in the hands of the same family, but the letter hints at other reasons. The pre-election manoeuvres took place against the background of a switch in tactics in the Commons. The Beckington petition had been introduced by M.P.s angry at Arminian practices and had been paralleled by similar ones from many parts of the country. In January 1641, the campaign had been transformed into an attack on the bishops themselves, by a petition from London demanding their removal, 'Root and Branch'. The London Petition had inspired similar ones from many counties, the most important of which came from Kent. The Kentish petition was introduced by Sir Edward Dering, Sir Peter Wroth's brother-in-law.

Pyne informed Smyth that Blake was 'hot against the bishops' and the coming debates 'did much stir upp R:B: to make the place sure for yourselfe as him'. Sir Thomas Wroth was as hot against the bishops as anyone could wish but, even at this early stage, he was known for his sympathy with those who opposed a national church and supported freedom of worship for all protestant groups.[23] This was not what Pyne and Blake wanted. If they had their way, everyone would be forced to become members of the new bishopless Church, in the same way as they were now compelled to be members of the Church of England. As a result, Thomas Smyth was elected the new member for Bridgwater.

For the first half of 1641, the Somerset M.P.s adopted a common front on the issues of the day. They cooperated in denouncing the different forms of taxation that Charles had devised during the Personal Rule, such as knighthood fines, forest law and ship money. They worked together in the debates about the dismantling of the prerogative courts, by means of which Charles had ruled between 1629–40. Among these courts was the ecclesiastical Court of High Commission, whose abolition effectually clipped the wings of the bishops. Laud himself, together with his two closest coadjutors, Matthew Wren, Bishop of Ely and William Piers, Bishop of Bath and Wells, were consigned to the Tower. Only two Somerset M.P.s voted against Strafford's attainder. By the end of July, the demolition was complete and the question arose of what should happen next. About half the M.P.s were satisfied that the King had learned his lesson, that he could now be relied on to listen to advisers approved of by the majority of M.P.s, and to govern through the institutions Parliament had left him. The remainder, led by John Pym, believed that some restraint must be placed on the King's authority, so that the abuses of the period of Personal Rule could not be repeated. A minority wanted the Church reformed, Root and Branch.

The crisis, which led to war, began in October 1641. A rebellion broke out in Ireland. King and Parliament were united in a determination to suppress it, and money was quickly voted for an army. The question then arose of who should appoint the commanders. Many members of the House of Commons believed that if the King controlled their nomination the army might be used, not against the Irish, but against his opponents in England. A Militia Ordinance passed the Commons which, if it became law, would give Parliament the right to nominate the principal field officers. The Ordinance was rejected by the Lords but an analysis of the division list showed that, if the votes of the bishops were subtracted, there was a majority of secular peers in favour of the measure. This forced John Pym, the organising genius of the Parliamentary opposition, to consider first, curbs on the bishops, and eventually their abolition.

The Puritan opposition had, hitherto, maintained that it was the King and Laud who had changed both the constitution and the church from what it had been, in the palmy days of Queen Elizabeth. No such excuse could be found for the removal of the Crown's right to nominate the field officers of the army, or the ejection of the bishops from the House of Lords. Passions increased as the division deepened, between those whose reforming zeal was confined to a return to an idealised past and those who believed that effective new limitations on the monarchy were needed. Of the Somerset M.P.s, only Sir Francis Popham and his son, Alexander, were to prove active Parliamentarians. Smyth was well on the way to being an out-and-out Royalist, declaiming against the numerous libels being 'thrown up and down in abuse of the best in parliament'. Even Sir Peter Wroth had become disillusioned with what he regarded as Pym's dictatorial methods, remarking that he ought to write 'R' (for *Rex*) after his signature.[24]

The botched attempt to arrest the Six Members of Parliament in January 1642, and Charles's withdrawal to Hampton Court, mark the point at which the rift became unbridgeable. The sundering of the united front, which had existed in Somerset at the beginning of the Parliament, was dramatised by the appearance of two rival petitions. When the London Petition had been presented at the beginning of the year in favour of 'Root and Branch', Somerset had not responded with either a supporting or a hostile petition, suggesting that there was a wide measure of agreement on the need for moderate reform. The belated appearance of a petition from the County, on 10 December 1641, supporting the bishops, with 14,350 signatures, 200 of them gentry, 221 divines and none of them Papists, marks the end of the consensus.[25]

The party in the County hostile to the bishops seems to have been caught napping and hasty measures were taken to organise a counter petition. This was published on 18 January 1642, but it was not presented to the Commons until 25 February.[26] The petition was introduced by Sir Peter Wroth but the main speech in its support was made from the bar of the House by Sir Thomas Wroth. He had to apologise for the 'paucity of hands' and the small attendance of gentlemen to support it.[27] After Sir Thomas had withdrawn, there was a short debate on the petition, during which an attempt by Sir John Poulett and Edward Kirton to get the petition in favour of bishops introduced, was scotched.[28]

We can be certain, whatever the differences between Blake and Wroth at the time of the elections, that Blake would have been one of the 'Hearts and Hands as zealous and ready to maintain whatsoever is contained in our Petition, as any of the preceding Counties'.[29] He may well have been one of the gentlemen who helped Wroth carry the petition up to London and present it to Parliament. The whole thing has the appearance of being hastily engineered from Bridgwater, without consultation with the much more Puritan eastern end of Somerset.

*   *   *

The time for talking was running out and both sides were making preparations for war. On 5 May, Pym reported news from Somerset that two M.P.s were framing a petition supporting the King's authority.[30] One of them was Sir Francis Doddington and he was expelled from the Commons on 21 June.[31] By the beginning of July, both sides were busily recruiting soldiers. Sir Ralph Hopton and Thomas Smyth were both expelled for obstructing the Parliamentary Militia Ordinance and attempting to put the King's Commission of Array into effect.[32] The expulsions signified little. Royalist M.P.s had already joined the King at York and the lines of battle had been drawn.

When Blake made his first appearance in the Parliamentary ranks has been a matter for much argument among his biographers. In view of the almost complete lack of reliable evidence, all that can be done is to measure the numerous speculations against what is known of the war in Somerset. As an influential inhabitant of Bridgwater, his natural course would have been to raise, and equip, an infantry company from among his neighbours. This is what so many merchants, who sympathised with Parliament, were doing up and down the country. Yet other evidence, such as it is, seems to contradict this assumption. There is a traditional story that an attempt by Henry Byam, the Royalist minister of Luccombe, to put the King's Commission of Array into execution, was upset by the interference of a troop of dragoons under Blake's command.[33] This would appear to suggest that he was among those who responded to the Parliamentary Propositions, of 20 July 1642, for the raising of 1000 horse in the county of Somerset.[34]

Where and when Blake took part in his first battle is, similarly, in doubt. Logic dictates that he would have been among the men raised in west Somerset, by the combined efforts of John Pyne and Edward Popham. Edward was the younger brother of Alexander and lived at Wellington, a fiercely Puritan weaving community, south-west of Taunton. Blake may have been with Pyne and have had Pyne's ignominious rout at Marshall's Elm as his introduction to warfare, but it is more likely that he was with Edward Popham, who was to command the cavalry attached to his brother's regiment.

Mercifully for the Parliamentarians, Pyne's reverse was of only marginal importance. The recruiting initiative had been taken by the Royalists. The Marquis of Hertford had arrived from York with a body of soldiers, and had joined Hopton and Smyth, who were trying to put the Commission of Array into operation. The people of northern Somerset were strongly Parliamentarian and this attempt to levy men, with the aid of soldiers from outside the county, was regarded as outrageous. Thousands rallied to the Parliamentary call to arms. Soon, Sir John Horner and the Parliamentary Deputy Lieutenants could muster an army six or seven times the size of the Royalist force in Wells. Hepworth Dixon, in his 1856 biography of Blake, states categorically that Blake was present at the general rendezvous called by Horner. None of the accounts mention him by name, but Edward Popham was there. If Blake was with him, he would have been there too.[35]

After a tense confrontation, the Royalists evacuated Wells and retired on Sherborne. The Parliamentary forces followed them and were reinforced by 300 horse, under the Earl of Bedford, from the main Parliamentary army. Once again, pressure of numbers, rather than any skill shown by the Parliamentary commanders, forced the Royalists to abandon their position and retreat. They retired, through West Somerset, to Minehead. There one part, which included both Hertford and Thomas Smyth, took ship for South Wales, in search of reinforcements. The remainder, commanded by Sir Ralph Hopton, covered the embarkation before retiring into Devonshire.

The Parliamentarians were determined to exploit their success. Bedford returned to the main army but his men remained, under the command of Colonel William Ruthen. To this core were added contingents from the militias of Somerset, Dorset, Devon and Wiltshire. The Somerset forces were under the nominal command of Colonel William Strode. Hepworth Dixon claims that Blake fought in all the actions of the long and fluctuating campaign that followed and particularly distinguished himself at a sharp encounter outside Bodmin in Cornwall.[36] There is no reason why he could not have taken part, at least until the truce of February 1643, and still have returned to play his documented part at Bristol, but there is no positive evidence to support Dixon's account. None of the pamphlets mentions his name, nor does he figure in the fairly complete accounts of the Plymouth commissary, preserved in the Commonwealth Exchequer Papers.[37] He may have served as a volunteer, but it is more likely that he remained in Somerset with the portion of the county militia under the command of Alexander Popham. After seeing the Royalists off the premises at Minehead, Popham turned his attention to Bristol. It is in connection with the operations around that city, that we get the first incontrovertible evidence of Blake's presence.

Bristol and Lyme

*T*HE population of Bristol was sharply divided. Many of the wealthier merchants were Royalist in sympathy. Some farmed taxes, such as the Customs, and feared to lose their concessions. Others were bitterly jealous of the predominance of London. They supported the King because London was for Parliament. Ranged against them were the smaller merchants and tradesmen, especially those whose livelihood was dependant on the patronage of the great clothiers of north Somerset and Wiltshire, who were solidly Parliamentarian.

Alexander Popham played a part in all the moves which secured Bristol for Parliament. When the Earl of Essex, the Parliamentary Commander, sent a regiment under Colonel Thomas Essex to occupy the city, Popham moved 500 men of the Somerset militia to a threatening position at Bedminster. He orchestrated the publicity campaign, which culminated in his attendance at a Bristol Council meeting with Sir John Seymour, on 18 December 1642, at which the two men presented Parliament's demands. The result was that sympathisers were able to admit Essex's men.[1] Similarly, when doubts began to be expressed about the competence and loyalty of Colonel Essex, Popham was instrumental in persuading the Lord General to send Colonel Nathaniel Fiennes to Bristol and he supported Fiennes when he had Essex arrested and committed to Berkeley Castle, on 29 February. When Fiennes marched into the city, a fortnight earlier, he was accompanied by Popham's regiment of Somerset foot and some troops of horse.[2] This was, almost certainly, the point at which Blake's service in Bristol began.

The men of Colonel Essex's regiment were too disgusted with their commander's behaviour to cause any disturbance but there was trouble from another quarter. The Cavalier party was planning to admit Royalist soldiers into the city, and were in communication with Prince Rupert, who was at Oxford. The plan was for Rupert to march swiftly and secretly to Bristol, reaching Durdham Down, to the west of the city, during the night of 6–7 March. On a prearranged signal, the plotters would admit the Royalists through the Frome gate into the city, but their plan was discovered and the leaders arrested in the nick of time. Rupert returned, thwarted, to Oxford. The principal plotters were tried and condemned to death for treason. Among those signing the sentence was a 'Robert Baugh'. This may well be Blake because his name was sometimes spelled 'Blaugh' in documents of the time.[3]

During April 1643, the Pophams conducted a raid, which took them through Somerset and into Dorset. Blake may have been with them but he is not mentioned, nor does his name appear in the long list of officers who signed the document, summoning Weymouth to surrender. Soon after the Pophams returned to Bristol, the war in the west turned very sour for the Parliament. At the beginning of May, news arrived that the Parliamentary army, now commanded by the Earl of Stamford, had been defeated by the Cornish Royalists, under Sir Ralph Hopton, at the battle of Stratton. Hopton lost no time in exploiting his victory. He advanced across Devonshire and at Chard linked up with the Royalist horse sent from Oxford under Prince Maurice and the Earl of Caernarvon. The Somerset militia tried to make a stand outside Taunton but they were no match for the triumphant Royalists. Their best men were either away at Bristol or had been among the rout at Stratton. The resistance was of the briefest. Taunton capitulated after a short siege; Bridgwater cravenly yielded to the Royalists without a fight and the Luttrells' surrender of Dunster castle completed the débâcle.

When Parliament heard of the disaster, orders were sent to Sir William Waller, who had been conducting a most successful campaign in the Midlands, to march into the West Country, picking up on the way such forces as the local commanders could provide. Waller was engaged in the siege of Worcester but he rode to Bristol to consult with Fiennes. Fiennes was reluctant to weaken the garrison of Bristol but, under pressure, agreed to release 1500 men. Waller arranged for them to concentrate at Bath on 22 May but a week later he was still before Worcester. There is no mention of Blake, but the opening move of the campaign fits in very well with the story of a dashing attack on Bridgwater, made by him at some point in 1643. A pamphleteer wrote later in the war that Blake raised a troop of horse for Waller which 'is with him even now'.[4] John Fiennes wrote to his father on 26 May, 'I perceive Sir Will. Waller's designe is somethinge altered, he would have Coll. Popham with your horse and Sir Edw Hungerford's and the rest of the horse in Somersetshire to march strayt towards Bridgwater togeather with Coll. Popham's foot, and himselfe wil eyther come after or march on the other way, but it will be some time ere he will be ready to march.'[5] Whether elements of the force reached Bridgwater must be open to doubt, but it is not impossible because over a month elapsed between the letter and discomfiture of the Parliamentarians at Chewton Mendip about half-way between Bristol and Bridgwater, on 4 July. There are no references to Blake in the accounts of the drawn battle at Lansdown on 5 July nor in those of Waller's defeat at Roundway Down on 13 July.

The wreck of Waller's army retired on Bristol and a grim council of war

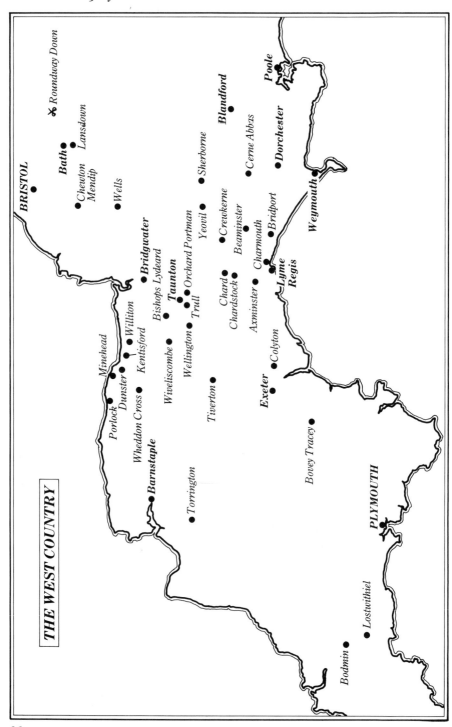

THE WEST COUNTRY

Roundway Down

BRISTOL

Bath
Lansdown
Chewton Mendip
Wells

Minehead
Porlock
Dunster
Wheddon Cross
Williton
Kentisford
Wiveliscombe
Barnstaple

Bridgwater
Bishops Lydeard
Taunton
Orchard Portman
Trull
Wellington

Yeovil
Sherborne
Crewkerne
Beaminster
Chard
Chardstock
Axminster
Charmouth
Bridport
Lyme Regis

Blandford
Cerne Abbas
Dorchester
Poole
Weymouth

Colyton
Exeter
Tiverton
Bovey Tracey
Torrington

PLYMOUTH

Bodmin
Lostwithiel

was held in Sir William's tent, outside the city. One option was for him to throw what remained of his army into Bristol. Waller rejected this course of action. Most of what had survived was cavalry, which would be wasted in a siege, so he proposed instead to ride off in search of forces, which could come to Bristol's assistance. The local commanders did not like this solution. Blake seems to have accepted that cavalry were no use to Bristol but he was not prepared to abandon the city. He left his men with Waller, but offered his services to Fiennes. The Governor appointed him to the command of Prior's Hill Fort, the most exposed point of the defences.

Since he had superseded Essex, Fiennes had worked hard to improve Bristol's defences but the task had been heavy and costly. When the Royalist army, now under the command of Rupert, arrived outside the city, the works were not complete. The heart of Bristol lay in the angle between the River Frome and the River Avon. The line of the Frome was amply defended by a thick wall and the gap, at the eastern end, was closed by Bristol Castle. Fiennes had made some improvements to the castle but it was not in as good a state of readiness as he would have liked. The main part of Bristol was connected with a suburb on the Somerset side by Bristol Bridge. This southern side was also defended by a good, solid wall and ditch.

The main problem that faced the garrison lay outside Bristol. The city was overlooked from the west and north by Durdham Down. An enemy who placed his guns there, could fire over the walls into the city, causing untold havoc among the population. In order to overcome this problem, a second line of defences had been constructed, consisting of a wall and ditch protected at intervals by forts. This was the part which was, rightly, worrying Fiennes. All the forts had palisades but some of them lacked proper footbanks and other outworks. Prior's Hill Fort was typical. It had two tiers of loopholes and had been built for thirteen guns. There were only three in position and the outworks were not complete. The wall in between the forts was not high enough and the ditch not deep enough. To make matters worse, the attempts to assist Waller had cost Fiennes over half his foot and most of his horse. The numbers had been partly made good by recruitment from the local militias, but he could still only dispose of 1500 foot and 300 horse, which was not really enough to man the whole perimeter adequately.[6]

The Royalists arrived outside Bristol on 23 July. As soon as the army was in position, the principal officers made a thorough inspection of the defences and then held a council of war, where the decision was taken to try an immediate storm. Prince Maurice and the Cornishmen were to attack the southern suburb. The rest of the army was to attack the western defences. Rupert and his engineer, Bernard de Gomme, had spotted the weakness of the wall. Lord Grandison was to attack between Stoke's Croft and Prior's Hill Fort, Sir John Belasyse between Prior's Hill Fort and Colston Fort, and Colonel Wentworth between Colston

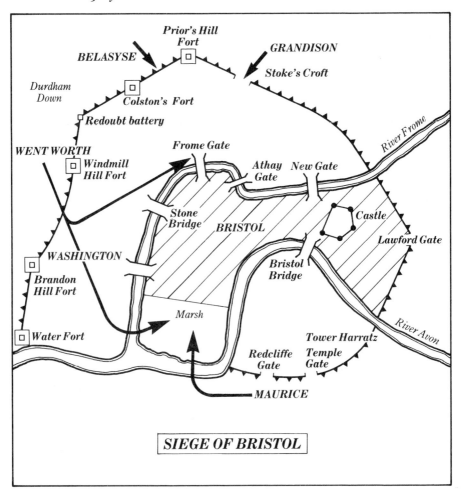

SIEGE OF BRISTOL

Fort and the Windmill Hill Fort. Blake was to be in the eye of the storm.

The assault was timed for the early hours of 26 July and to begin with, it did not go well for the Royalists. Though a Captain Fawcett got close enough to fasten a petard to the gate of Prior's Hill Fort, the attack was repulsed with loss. This was a particularly good piece of service because Blake had to contend with the men of Colonel Lunsford as well. They had been unable to penetrate Stoke's Croft and had turned their attention to Prior's Hill Fort instead. Grandison led a second charge which got into the ditch, only to find that no scaling ladders had been brought, a curious error. The Royalists found themselves cut off and it was only with difficulty that they extricated themselves. For a third time, Grandison led his weary men back to the fray. Blake did not wait for them to mount the hill, but sallied out. First Grandison and then Colonel Owen, who replaced him, were wounded and their men scattered in all directions. Grandison died later of the wounds he received.[7]

At first, Wentworth had no better luck but one of his officers, Colonel Washington, probing round the south side of the Windmill Hill Fort, found a part of the wall, where a spur of land protected him from the view of the fort. The Royalists began to infiltrate over it into the space between the inner and outer defences. To begin with, the numbers were not great, and if the Parliamentary cavalry had charged, they might well have bundled the Royalists back over the wall, but Fiennes hesitated. His view of the situation may have been confused by Royalist refugees from Blake's counter attack, many of whom, too frightened to recross the outer wall, were milling about between the two lines of defence.[8]

Rupert seized the opportunity. He redirected Grandison's and Belasyse's men to the gap Washington had created. The Cornish attack had also been repulsed by the defenders, so Rupert urged Maurice to transfer 1000 men to the north bank of the Avon, to draw off defenders from the breach. Maurice was only able to send 500 but they were enough to cause the defenders severe embarrassment. Astute soldier that he was, Rupert did not bother to try and take the outer forts, once he was over the wall in strength, but bent his energies on breaching the inner wall along the Frome.

Blake found himself isolated from the main conflict. How much he knew about, or could see, of the futile charge of the Parliamentary cavalry, far too late to be of much use, or of Rupert's fierce but unsuccessful attack on the Frome gate, or of the way in which the Cornishmen almost penetrated into the city by way of the marsh and College Green, we do not know. In the circumstances, it is hardly surprising that he was not at the council of war, which took the fateful decision to surrender. After the council, no one remembered to inform either Blake or Captain Husbands of the Brandon Hill Fort, of what had been resolved.[9] In the end it was from the Royalists, not from Fiennes, that they received notification that terms had been agreed on for the capitulation of Bristol. As the smoke cleared, Blake and Husbands could see that the inner defences were still intact, and it was some time before the two men could be convinced that their opponents were not just indulging in a ruse de guerre.

After the siege of Bristol, Blake disappears from view once more, and does not resurface until the siege of Lyme Regis, in April 1644. The fall of Bristol after only four days caused great anger and Fiennes was court martialled. Many Bristol refugees went to London to give evidence. Blake may well have been ordered to attend the trial, as the twelfth charge in the indictment dealt with the Governor's failure to inform himself and Husbands of the capitulation. Fiennes was found guilty of gross negligence and dismissed the service, only to be reinstated by the Earl of Essex. Another reason for Blake gravitating to the capital is that, once his employment at Bristol was over, he would naturally have wished to accompany the other homeless Somerset officers who were helping Waller raise a new army. No less than four of the regiments were commanded by colonels from the west: Alexander Popham, James Carr, Edward Henley and Edward Cooke.

For the moment, there was no chance of a renewed campaign in the west, because London itself was threatened. After the fall of Bristol the Royalists, under Hopton, advanced across Hampshire into Sussex. Waller was given a commission, as General of the Army of the South Eastern Association, to raise soldiers in London, Kent, Surrey and Sussex. By December 1643, he was again confronting Hopton, this time outside the walls of Farnham. Blake may well have taken part in the series of actions, which went a long way towards repairing Sir William's reputation. Before the winter closed in, Waller surprised the Royalist vanguard at Alton and then recaptured Arundel. When campaigning resumed, in the sprin of 1644, Sir William gained his revenge for Roundway Down, defeating Hopton at Cheriton on 29 March. In the weeks after the battle, Waller's forces ranged far and wide, capturing Winchester and beating up Royalist quarters at Christ-church.

To Blake, it must have seemed that the foundations had been laid for Sir William to return to the West Country, as he had promised he would at the time of the siege of Bristol. It was not to be. The battle of Cheriton was hardly over before Waller was ordered to transfer the bulk of his cavalry to Essex's army. Worse was to come. The heart of his army was the London Trained Bands. They would not consider a campaign in the West and, now that the capital was safe, they marched back home. His powerlessness was a particular disappointment to the ports of Poole and Lyme Regis. All Waller could do was to send 120 horse to supplement the garrison of Lyme, which lay in the most exposed position. The commander of these men is not known but may well have been Blake.[10] This is the most plausible explanation of the way in which he reached Lyme, just before the port became the focus of the war in the south.

During the winter, the Parliamentary position had improved dramatically in the north. The defeat of the King's Irish army at Nantwich in Cheshire, and the march of the Scottish army into England to Parliament's assistance, threatened to overturn the whole Royal position there. Prince Rupert was sent from Oxford, with all the forces Charles could spare, and with instructions to recruit as he went. The King hoped that the reinforcements Rupert brought would be enough to enable the Royal commander, the Marquis of Newcastle, to defeat the Scots and the northern Parliamentarians, under Fairfax.

The drawback to the scheme was that the King was left in a very exposed position at Oxford. Rupert advised him to sit tight and hope that his ring of garrisons would be able to hold out, until the position was restored in the north. That was not to the King's taste and, as soon as his nephew was safely on his way, he proceeded to put a very different plan into operation. First of all, he evacuated Reading and Abingdon, which added 2500 men to his army. Then letters were sent to Prince Maurice, ordering him to turn the siege of Plymouth into a blockade and march to Oxford with as many of the men he had been raising during the winter as he could. Maurice duly mustered 6000 men and marched, as ordered, but he did not reach Oxford.

When the Prince arrived at Exeter, he was greeted by a deputation of Dorsetshire Royalists, who pleaded with him to turn aside and attack Lyme Regis. Before Blake's arrival, the port had as garrison a regiment of Dorsetshire militia under the command of its Mayor, Thomas Ceely. In addition, since the fall of Exeter, Lyme had become the headquarters of 200 Devon militia, under the command of Colonel John Were. Together, their men were harrying Royalist positions throughout the western end of the county. Axminster, Colyton and Bridport had all been plundered and burnt by raiding parties, under the command of the irrepressible Captain Thomas Pyne. The local Royalists misled Maurice into thinking that the town would be overcome easily and that, once it was in Royalist hands, Dorsetmen would volunteer in large numbers. He would then be able to join the King with an increased army. Seduced by their arguments, Maurice altered his intentions and marched on Lyme, arriving outside the port, on 20 April.

A Royalist writer described Lyme Regis as a 'little, vile fishing town defended by a dry ditch'. That it was not. Lyme was a prosperous port whose customs books reveal that the chief commodity was cloth, not fish. Entries show that cloth was exported mainly from the region around Chard, but some of the Taunton clothiers used the port as well. Blake would have found three times as much shipping there, as in his own home town of Bridgwater. Like nearly all the communities dependent on the cloth trade, it was fanatically Puritan. Mary Tudor had called it that 'heretic town' and Charles I referred to it as 'ye rebellious town of Lyme'.[11]

Whether you go out onto the artificial breakwater, called the Cobb, and look up at the hills which surround the town, or labour up the main street, the impression that Lyme Regis must have been well nigh indefensible is overwhelming. Contemporary accounts also stress the weakness of the defences. There were four forts, connected by a curtain wall and with a surrounding ditch. The forts were made of turves and the wall was an earthen rampart, about six feet high; obstacles which, one might think, would not have caused many problems for an attacking force of 6000 men.

Yet Lyme had its strengths too. At the beginning of the siege Ceely, Were and Blake mustered about 1000 men between them.[12] Compared with Maurice's estimated 6000 men, this does not seem much, but it was an extraordinarily large defensive force for such a small place and it was to rise to 1500 later. Fiennes had only 1800 men with which to defend the great city of Bristol. The walls could be manned adequately, and men be left over for sorties. Blake was to remember from his Lyme days that, when fighting was over a narrow front, numbers were far less important, especially when an obstacle, however slight, protected you from enemy muskets.

One of the strengths of the Royalist army was supposed to be its artillery, though descriptions of the guns are lacking. If so, the siege of Lyme provides yet another instance of how weak this arm was, until the appearance of the New Model Army. One commentator has surmised that the correct placement of the besiegers' guns, in the broken ground around Lyme, must have been very difficult, because they were heavy and cumbersome to move. Another factor may have been that the cannon balls tended to sink into the turves of the forts and the earthen ramparts, instead of shattering them. Whatever the reason, the number of Parliamentary casualties was derisory. Only when it fired red-hot shot, with the aim of setting the thatched roofs of the houses on fire, did the Royalist artillery come near to justifying itself.

Another important advantage was that Lyme was a seaport. Unlike Bristol and Exeter, which were up rivers that could be blocked, the town could be supported directly by the Parliamentary fleet, a consideration which was to be vital for Lyme's ultimate survival. The Royalists were never able to cut off the flow of men, ammunition and supplies which sustained the garrison.

Yet it is arguable that the decisive difference between the two sides lay in the quality of the leadership and the attitude of the soldiers. The Royalists were a motley band. The best part of their army were the battle-hardened Cornishmen, who may well have wondered what they were doing trying to protect Dorsetshire Royalists from the Lyme Parliamentarians, when their own homes were still being threatened by the garrison of Plymouth. Then there were the men from the Irish Army. They had enlisted to fight Irish papists, not fellow Englishmen. Most had little heart for the struggle and some actively sympathised with the Parliament. The numbers were made up by forces newly levied from the estates of Lord Poulett on the Somerset–Dorset border. They were raw and of low quality. Prince Maurice lacked the charisma, which made his brother such an inspiring leader, but he was experienced and capable. Unfortunately, he was ill for most of the siege and no one else had the vision, or drive, needed for success.

Contrast this with the Lyme defenders. The official commander was Thomas Ceely, the town's Mayor. Wisely, he realised that he did not possess the necessary credentials. He was content to be the nominal commander, confining himself to ensuring that the garrison was fully supported by the inhabitants. In this, he was totally successful. Every man was prepared to fight for his home and every woman turned out to assist, by doing the fetching and carrying which was necessary, even under fire, so no potential soldiers were wasted on non-combatant tasks. They were urged on by no less than twenty-five preachers. The quality of the officers was outstanding. Thomas Pyne has already been mentioned. Colonel Were was one of the many competent officers that the county militias were throwing up all round the country. And there was Blake.

From the moment he set foot in Lyme, Blake was accepted as the main protagonist on the Parliamentary side, even though both Ceely and Were officially outranked him. So great was the grip that he exerted on the imagination, of friend and foe alike, that Were was to complain that his own considerable exertions had been totally forgotten. By this time, Blake must have been experienced in all the arts of war, but that was not what distinguished him from his colleagues. For him, the war was a struggle for the soul of the country. If any man was the personification of the 'church militant here on earth' it was Blake. In the stern puritans of Lyme, he found a community just waiting for such a leader. As he stumped round the walls of the beleaguered town, animating and encouraging, he kindled such a fire in their hearts, that they would have gone anywhere and done anything for him.

The first week of the siege was occupied by the Royalists investing the town and probing for weaknesses.[13] Attempts, in turn, to storm West Fort, Gaitches Fort and Davie's Fort were repulsed and followed by sallies, which did considerable damage to the Royalist batteries. The only minor success the Royalists achieved, was the capture of Newell's fort, which appears to have lain outside the main defences. Piecemeal attacks having failed, the Royalists decided to try and storm the town. The assault took place on 28 April, and was a total failure. The Royalist foot had no stomach for the fight and when they came under fire from Lyme's guns, they were only prevented from running away by the horse in the rear, beating and slashing at them. The fight was hot, but never in doubt, and the Royalists drew off discomfited.

By this time, events at Lyme were beginning to cause ripples. George Skutt, the Mayor of Poole, wrote to the Committee of Both Kingdoms, informing them that he had sent three ships to Lyme's assistance as a temporary measure. He asked for action to be taken for the security of the town. One of the ships was a privateer, the *Achilles*, commanded by Captain Mann, which reached Lyme on 26 April. He does not seem to have stayed long. The other two may have been the 5th rate, *Mary Rose*, commanded by Captain William Somaster and the armed merchantman, the *Ann and Joyce*, commanded by Captain Thomas Jones. They were attracted by the gunfire of the general assault two days later. Their arrival proved to be of crucial importance. Powder was running low, so the captains provided supplies from their own stores. The unusually large number of people had emptied the town of food. According to Edward Drake, the ships landed beef, pork, dried peas, butter, cheese, bread, beer and wood.

The next day the Royalists tried a new tactic, shooting fire arrows into the

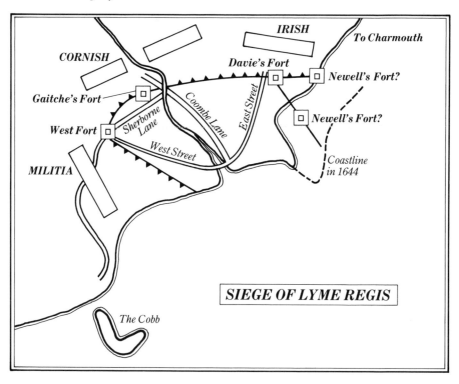

SIEGE OF LYME REGIS

town, but the inhabitants were ready with water and wet hides to put out the flames. The garrison's response was not slow in coming. On 30 April a sally in force was organised against a battery to the west of the town. Somaster and Jones landed a hundred seamen to help in the attack. The fight was fiercely contested. They 'clogged' (spiked?) one of the guns and killed or captured a number of men. Drake observed that the water, which served the town, ran red with the blood of the Royalist soldiers.

There followed a week of inaction, while the Royalists licked their wounds and decided what to do next. The passivity of the besiegers lulled the garrison into a false sense of security and the next Royalist assault, during the usual evening mealbreak, caught them unawares. The besiegers swarmed over the walls in three places, and some of them reached the town centre. The defenders were quick to recover, rushing to man the walls so that more men could not enter. Furious hand-to-hand fighting took place before the ramparts were recaptured. Power of numbers then overwhelmed those Royalists cut off inside. Some 400 were killed or wounded, others captured and the remainder forced back out of the town.

The booty included the colours of Maurice's own regiment.

Among the killed was a Colonel Blewitt. When a Royalist deputation came, under a flag of truce to collect his body, we get our first real glimpse of the characteristics which so endeared Blake to his men. He is reputed to have taunted the Royalists, 'Here you see and behold how weak our works are: they are not things wherein we trust; therefore tell the Prince that, if he desires to come into the town to fight we will pull down ten or twelve yards, so that he may come in in a breast, and we will fight with him.' The view that tactics were of minor importance compared with morale was to be the hallmark of Blake's approach to military affairs for most of his career. If you believe that your cause is right and you obey the orders of a godly commander, victory is assured. The Royalists seem to have been rather irritated and refused to exchange Harvey, Ceely's brother-in-law. Nor were they prepared to pay for Blewitt's coffin. Blake is reputed to have remarked, 'Take it, we are not so poor but we can give it to you.'[14]

The Royalists now resorted to artillery bombardment again, which proved as ineffectual as in the past. Meanwhile there was a steady procession of ships, bringing succour and reinforcements to the garrison. On 8 May an armed merchantman, the *Mayflower*, commanded by Captain Cock, arrived, escorting a supply ship. Three days later, the *Achilles* returned, accompanied by the 5th rate, *Expedition*, and six transports, carrying 300 soldiers. These had been shipped at Portsmouth, and came from Waller's army. A further 150 arrived on 15 May, all of them, presumably, being added to the men under Blake's direct command. The ships also landed guns. The *Mary Rose* gave a culverin and the *Mayflower* a demi-cannon.[15]

It is indicative of the paralysis in the Royalist command that, although the officers must have watched the unloading of the ships day by day, two weeks elapsed before they realised what the real weak point of Lyme's defences was. Unloading took place within the artificial breakwater, the Cobb, which lay outside the line of the town walls. If the little harbour could be rendered untenable, the garrison's supplies could be cut off. Guns were shifted from Colway Meadow to the cliffs above the Cobb. At first, the garrison did not realise the significance of what was happening and took advantage of the weakening of the works to beat up Fort Royal and other batteries. When they did spot the new works, they attacked them in turn, but they were only able to delay, not stop, the construction. On 22 May the Royalists opened fire on the barges in the Cobb, burning several of them. Sallies were organised from the town, but they were driven back and, even worse, Captain Thomas Pyne was so seriously wounded, that he died five days later, mourned by the whole town. Had this happened earlier the consequences would have been very serious.

Blake's major worry was not the town's defences, or its garrison, which was more than adequate. The main problem was one of supply. The very activity of the garrison consumed powder and match at a great rate. Every soldier who was landed had to be clothed and fed from Lyme's very limited resources. The Royalists realised this vulnerability too late because next day the provider of the supplies, the Lord High Admiral, the Earl of Warwick, reached Lyme in the powerful 2nd rate, *James*, accompanied by the *Constant Reformation, Dreadnought* and *Warwick*. Lyme had never seen such a powerful assemblage of ships. Warwick immediately went on shore to consult with the defenders and he was appalled at the state of the garrison. The seamen generously provided some of their own rations, together with 30 pairs of boots, 100 pairs of shoes and 160 pairs of stockings.

The Royalists were far from giving up and, despite the full power of the fleet, supplies could only be ferried in at night. On 27 May, the Royalists shifted their guns again. They had realised, at last, one of the reasons why their artillery was so ineffective. Due to the nature of the ground, they had not been able to depress the muzzles of the guns low enough to do real execution. They now had the idea of placing the guns at the western side, so that they fired on the eastern part of the town, and vice versa. The Royalist barrage became much more effective. On the day of Thomas Pyne's funeral the Royalists attacked again. Blake and Were were both wounded, one in the thigh and the other in the stomach, though neither wound was dangerous. Blake was able to return to duty immediately but Were was immobilised for a period. With each new consignment of extra troops from Waller, Blake's authority had increased and, with Were temporarily hors de combat, he took full command. From this point, until the end of the siege, he directed all the operations.

The Royalist artillery's battering of the town was beginning to have a serious effect. A conference, on board the *James*, resolved to land 300 seamen to reinforce the garrison, and to try and create a diversion. Two ships and six or seven shallops full of soldiers were dispatched towards Charmouth, in full view of the besiegers. The idea was to decoy part of the Royalist force away from Lyme, so that the garrison could sally out and destroy the batteries. Events did not follow the course planned. Maurice was not fooled by the expedition and seized the opportunity, provided by the absence of some of the defenders, to launch a full-scale attempt to storm the town.

The hottest fighting took place round the West Fort. A breach was smashed in the wall and the fort was assailed by 1000 Royalists with scaling ladders. Seamen were prominent among the defenders, led by one of Warwick's own men, Edward Moizer. Though the fighting lasted eight hours, the Royalists were repulsed everywhere. Their casualties were so heavy that they had no stomach for another effort and resorted to more attempts to burn the town down. On 31 May, four houses were burnt, and the following day another twenty. The men had to stay on the walls, so the firefighting force was mainly women. They stuck grimly to their task, despite Royalist attempts to stop them putting out the blaze by firing small shot at them. Fortunately, fire-raising tactics could only be used effectively when the wind was favourable. This may have been the reason why another attempt to burn the town was not tried for ten days. Royalist morale was not improved by the constant procession of ships using Lyme Bay. They could stop supplies entering by daylight, but not after nightfall. Today, the Cobb is connected with the shore but this was not the case in 1644, so attempts to capture and hold it were impossible in the face of Parliamentary seapower. Maurice should have cut his losses and abandoned the siege after the failure of 28 May, but injured pride led him to linger another fortnight. What finally forced his withdrawal was the approach of Essex's army. News of the Lord General's movements reached the garrison via Royalist deserters on 13 June, and two days later Maurice retired to Exeter.

The losses the Royalists sustained are not accurately known but they were considerable. Essex estimated their army at 5000, which suggests a loss of about a thousand men as casualties, from disease and from desertion. This may have been an underestimate as it was in Essex's interest to exaggerate Maurice's strength. The garrison's losses were so small that the diarist Edward Drake was able to itemise them. When Warwick and his officers came on shore to inspect the siege works they were astonished. 'They found those of the besiegers' contrived with so much skill and strength and those of the townsmen's so slight,' wrote William Jessop, Warwick's secretary, 'that it was a miracle how they could hold out so long against such a resolute foe ... The truth is the courage and honesty of the officers and soldiers were in a manner, their sole defence.'

Taunton

*T*HE relief of Lyme Regis was the first move in a totally misconceived Parliamentarian campaign, which had its roots in the violent jealousy harboured by the Earl of Essex against Sir William Waller. In obedience to the orders of the Committee of Both Kingdoms, Waller had abandoned his cherished design to return to the West, and had taken his army to join that of Essex near Abingdon. The King was in a difficult position. His rash evacuation of Abingdon and Reading had exposed Oxford and, with Maurice absorbed in the siege of Lyme Regis, Charles was much inferior in numbers to the Parliamentarians. The King's Council even contemplated surrendering Oxford itself. Essex threw the chance away. While he was bickering with Waller the King slipped past and made off into the Cotswolds. For two days Essex and Waller lumbered after him but the Lord General soon tired of the chase. At Stow-on-the-Wold, on 6 June, he declared that the best way of taking advantage of the weakness of the Royalists was to destroy their position in the West. Waller's task would be to hold the King in play while he did it.[1]

A course of action which divided the superior Parliamentary army into two smaller armies, each inferior to their opponent, is difficult to explain on rational grounds. Essex's excuse was a letter from the Committee of Both Kingdoms, asking him to relieve Lyme Regis. All that was wanted was a brigade powerful enough to force Maurice to abandon the siege, a pattern which was later, twice, to drive the Royalists from before Taunton. The Earl of Warwick had suggested that 1500 horse would do the trick.[2] The correctness of his estimate was quickly demonstrated. Essex did not need to go to Lyme Regis. As soon as news arrived of Essex's presence at Dorchester, Maurice abandoned the siege and retreated to Exeter, leaving Essex to reduce the Royalist garrison of Weymouth at his leisure, before marching after him. The real reason for the Lord General's behaviour was an obstinate determination to prove that he could succeed where Waller had failed.

The irrationality of Essex's behaviour was not long in manifesting itself. He hoped to recruit more men in the West and divided his army up for the purpose.

Three regiments of foot and two of horse were sent to Barnstaple. Another regiment of foot and a troop of horse were left at Weymouth. Most of the remainder stayed with Essex at Tiverton, where recruitment was combined with keeping a wary eye on Exeter. He had little success. Even in areas which were predominantly Parliamentarian in sympathy, he could get no one to volunteer while the Royalists held the local garrison towns.

There was one solitary exception. Sir Robert Pye was sent with a party of horse to see what he could do in the countryside around Taunton. After a siege of less than a week, the Royalist governor, Colonel Reeve, surrendered Taunton Castle, upon Pye promising to allow him to march away with his men to Bridgwater. Essex was surprised. He wrote that 'only their panic fears' could have induced the Royalists to surrender. Perhaps the hostility of the inhabitants and the removal of a large part of the garrison had something to do with it.[3] Yet the eighty men left could have held the castle for a long time. The chagrined Royalists agreed with Essex. Reeve was court-martialled, found guilty of cowardice, and executed.[4]

Still Essex got no volunteers. The local people would only serve under men they knew and there were none in Essex's army. All the Somerset officers were serving with Waller, evidence if any were necessary that the man who should have campaigned in the West was Waller, not Essex. The only man within reach, with the influence necessary, was Blake. When he and Were joined the army with their men from Lyme, he was sent to recruit in the Vale of Taunton, with Pye providing the necessary cover. Blake set to with a will. He concentrated his attention on Wellington, where he must have been well known. He proclaimed that he was raising a regiment in the name of the brother of their local landowner, Edward Popham. The Popham name, combined with Blake's enthusiasm, soon had the desired result. The men Blake raised were a valuable addition to the Parliamentary strength, but Blake did not march with them.[5] In Essex's mind, Blake was associated with Waller and the Lord General did not want any such tainted men around him. Blake was left behind, as Governor of Taunton.

The calm did not last long. Ominous news was filtering through from the East, even as Blake was assembling men for the Lord General. After chasing the King's army around the Midlands in the pouring rain for three weeks, Waller forced an engagement at Cropredy Bridge on 29 June. Militarily, the action was indecisive but the failure to get a definite result was the last straw for an army whose morale was already very low. A couple of days later there was a mutiny and Waller's infantry melted away. For a second time Waller was forced to return to London to try and raise more men. The King was now free to pursue Essex, who had been marching steadily westwards. The reluctance of men in Somerset and Devonshire to volunteer should have warned Essex that he was not likely to get a good reception in Cornwall, which was solidly Royalist, but he pressed on, regardless. In the end, the Parliamentary army was surrounded at Lostwithiel.

The cavalry broke out but the infantry was forced to surrender. Essex himself escaped to Plymouth by boat, leaving his Major-General, Philip Skippon, with the unpleasant task of agreeing terms.

The stream of bad news must have caused Blake to think hard about his course of action. There were sound reasons for abandoning Taunton. Taunton Castle was strong and could hold out for a long time, with adequate supplies. The town was not overlooked by hills, like Lyme Regis, but it had no walls or forts around it and, being twenty miles from the sea, there was no help to be had from the Parliamentary navy. Perhaps the men he commanded would be better employed in the field army. The crucial period was the first week in September. Taking advantage of the King's absence in Cornwall, Waller had once more gathered a small army and taken the field. Hearing that Essex's cavalry had broken out, he sent some of his own men to meet them. The junction took place, on 6 September, between Taunton and Bridgwater.

Blake could have reached the rendezvous without much difficulty, but he decided to stay and fight it out. Taunton was an important road junction and the presence of a Parliamentary garrison would create problems for the Royalists when they tried to recruit men in west Somerset. He was not without hope that his isolation would be of only short duration. The Scots and the northern Parliamentarians, reinforced by the Army of the Eastern Association commanded by the Earl of Manchester and Cromwell, had defeated Rupert and Newcastle at Marston Moor. Since the victory Manchester had been marching steadily southwards. If he could unite his forces with the army under Waller's command and the remnants of Essex's men, a decisive battle could yet be fought before the winter closed in. The battle did take place. The King's army, returning from Cornwall, met the combined forces of Manchester, Waller and Essex outside Newbury on 29 October. The Parliamentarians mishandled the attack but still forced the Royalists to retreat. Despite the urgings of Cromwell and Waller, Manchester failed to order a pursuit. His pusillanimous conduct led to arguments, which paralysed the Parliamentary leadership, and left Blake dangerously exposed at Taunton.

The siege had begun even before the result of the battle at Newbury was known. The King's army had stopped at Chard for a week, between 23 and 30 September, on its way back from Cornwall. The delay was caused by shortages of supplies and the need to settle the affairs of Somerset, in which the problem caused by Blake's garrison played a large part. Charles ordered Blake's old political rival, Colonel Edmund Wyndham, now the Governor of Bridgwater, to blockade it with 3000 men drawn from his own garrison and the Devonshire militia. This diversion of men who might otherwise have supplemented the Royal army was, by itself, a justification for the maintenance of a garrison at Taunton.[6] Clarendon believed that the precious week wasted at Chard had a big effect on the course of the campaign.[7] The town was invested at the beginning of October, and

Wyndham must have been confident of success. Blake had about 1000 men, mostly townsmen or Parliamentary sympathisers from the countryside who had sought refuge in Taunton. They were stiffened by a few regulars, and a troop of horse, which had come with Blake from Lyme Regis. The western side of the town was defended by the castle and the River Tone, but to the east, the defences were limited to a ring of palisades and hedges, with barricades blocking the main streets.[8]

The chief resource of the defenders was the spirit with which they set about their task. Blake's first action was to put before the inhabitants, in a graphic fashion, what they were fighting for. Everyone was summoned to the parish church where they were exhorted to sign the Solemn League and Covenant, if they had not already done so. This was the agreement by which the Scots undertook to send their army to Parliament's assistance, in return for a promise that, when the war was won, Parliament would replace the Church of England with a national Presbyterian Church, modelled on the one in Scotland. The people responded with enthusiasm. Like Lyme, Taunton was fiercely Puritan. The open commitment by each man to the cause, before his neighbours, was important psychologically. Anyone who refused could be branded as an enemy and any subsequent backslidings, by those who had signed, would expose them to public humiliation. Nor would a person who had taken the Covenant be able to pretend to a Royalist from the surrounding countryside that he had remained neutral.

Blake had learned at Lyme Regis that the best form of defence was attack and, for the first month of the siege, he organised frequent sallies, which hampered the efforts of the enemy. The most successful one broke up the besiegers' quarters on the north side of the town, causing the Royalists many casualties and capturing eighty prisoners, including some high-ranking officers. The exploit was not repeated because the prisoners proved something of an embarrassment. There appear to have been about 5000 people in the town and providing for them was already causing difficulties, without extra mouths to feed. Blake had to threaten to allow them to starve if Wyndham did not send provisions.[9]

The failure to follow up the success at Newbury intensified the pressure on Taunton. The sallies became less frequent and the food problem got worse. Two attempts by the Royalists to break into the town were repulsed, but a third was successful and, after heavy fighting, Blake was forced to retire to the castle, retaining only an entrenched position in the market place, which was covered by the castle's guns.[10]

The townspeople, outside the castle, were in a most unpleasant position and Blake seems to have been prepared to allow them to surrender, if Wyndham would pledge himself not to exact reprisals. Wyndham rejected the idea because he had come to realise that starving the inhabitants was the strongest weapon he had. Instead, he tried to pressurise the Parliamentarians into surrendering the castle as well, by offering honourable terms and by threatening to put all to fire and sword, if his offer was refused.

Blake was unmoved. A letter signed by himself, his brother, Samuel, John Coleborne and Samuel Perry, bade him do his worst, declaring 'we neither fear your menaces nor accept your proffers', adding that they had no intention of making themselves 'odious both to God and man by quitting a fort so wonderfully delivered into our hands at first, so mightily preserved ever since, and for the future so strongly provided'.[11] Wyndham soon found that his idea of using the civilian population as a kind of hostage was double edged. The pressing need for food forced the besieged into daily forays in search of supplies, which had the effect of putting the Royalists on the defensive. One detachment after another was withdrawn from the town to protect potential targets, until the siege degenerated, once more, into a blockade.

For the Parliamentary generals Taunton was the least of their problems. Divided councils led to pointless marches, which exhausted the soldiers and allowed the King to receive a reinforcement of 5000 men, without any hindrance from his opponents. The King's strength was then used as an excuse to fall back on Reading, but the garrison far away in the west was not forgotten. The Parliamentary press needed a hero. Manchester, Essex and Waller had all failed them, in their different ways. Cromwell was too much identified with the sectaries and Fairfax's time was yet to come. Blake was the man of the moment. At Lyme Regis he had won such golden opinions that the pamphleteers attributed the capture of Taunton castle in July to him alone, disdaining any mention of Sir Robert Pye.[12] In October praise was showered on him for the efforts he had made in raising men for the armies of both Waller and Essex.[13] On 14 November Waller wrote, 'I am under a persecution from the perpetual clamour in the west, concerning the distressed condition of Taunton.'[14]

The clamour had its effect. Instructions were sent to Waller, to detach 1000 horse for Taunton's relief, only for them to be cancelled, when the King's advance on Donnington Castle near Newbury became known.[15] The cancellation provoked a row behind the scenes, which produced a compromise proposal from Waller. He offered to send 500 horse under his Major-General, James Holborne. To them should be added 1000 foot from the Dorsetshire garrisons, under the energetic leadership of Sir Anthony Ashley Cooper. There was a snag. The Dorsetshiremen would not move without a fortnight's pay. Waller dispatched Holborne to Westminster, with orders not to leave town without the money.[16]

A valuable fortnight was consumed in haggling, before a supply was finally voted at the beginning of December.[17] The force was stronger than Waller had envisaged. Holborne had under his own command the cavalry regiments of Ludlow and Fitzjames, together with some of Waller's own men under Commissary Vandruske, a total of 1200. Among the men marching with Holborne were several Somerset officers who had helped the successful lobby of Parliament, one of whom was Colonel Edward Popham. They left Chichester during the first week in December, linking up with the foot of the Dorset militia soon afterwards. According to newspaper reports, the combined force was not far short of 3000 men.[18]

Holborne's route lay through Chard, where there was a Royalist force of about 500 men covering the siege. An officer described how the Parliamentarians made ready to fight,

> but the enemy discovering our Forces drawing nigh, fled out of the town in great hast and left above 100 Armes which they had thrown away in the flight behind them and dispersed themselves in a disorderly retreat: but our Forces pursued them, and took a whole Troupe of horse, the Captaine, Lieutenant, Cornet, and all, both Officers and Souldiers, Horse, and Armes, besides 20 other Prisoners, whereof 5 Officers and all their hay, oates and other provisions, which they brought with them for their relief there.[19]

The relieving force reached Taunton, without further opposition, to find the townspeople on the brink of starvation, but the castle capable of enduring a long siege, being only short of salt and powder. Sir Anthony Ashley Cooper reported, 'The enemy on Friday last have quitted their garrisons in Wellington, Wycraft, and Cokum houses. The last two they have burnt, and, as I now hear, they have quitted Chideok house, whether it be out of fear or to make a body able to encounter us we cannot yet under stand but Sir Lewis Dives coming up with his horse to the Bridgwater forces argues the latter.'[20]

Wyndham certainly tried to pretend that that was his aim and in a letter to Prince Rupert, he wrote that 'I stayed until the enemy came within two miles of me and then I rose from my quarters and brought off all my guns and carriages without the loss of a man.' He went on to claim that he had been 'absolute master of the field' and 'resolved to attack the enemy in his headquarters at Taunton'.[21] Yet he was forced to admit that the ease with which he disengaged was due, more to the chief priority of the besieged being the search for food, than to any skill he had shown. Cooper's letter suggests that the Parliamentarians would have welcomed an encounter which, if the Royalist behaviour at Chard was anything to go by, could have had only one result. The King thought so too, and decided on a complete overhaul of the command.

A new Royal Council for the West was created, with the young Prince of Wales at its head and Lord Hopton prominent among his advisers on military affairs. Hopton would have liked to preserve good relations with Wyndham but, as soon as his appointment was known, Wyndham retired to Bridgwater in a huff.[22] Sir Edmund had not forgiven Hopton for advising the King to appoint Sir Francis Doddington to command the Taunton operations, the previous September.

For the moment changes in the Royalist command made little difference.

Holborne and Blake were in control. They made life miserable for the Cavaliers in Bridgwater. Under the date, 8 January, the *Parliament Scout* reported that 'the Plymouth regiment and some others, hath fallen upon the enemies quarters, about Bridgwater and took 200 horse at least and had within a little taken Bridgwater had we not unhappily been stopped in our conjunction'.[23] A week or so later, the Parliamentarians surprised Wyndham, as he and Colonel Hawley were quarrelling in their quarters near Taunton. Sixty horse and prisoners were taken, together with 100 arms and the two colonels only escaped by precipitate flight.[24] To complete an unpleasant month, a wagon train with supplies for Bridgwater, guarded by ten musketeers, fell in with Colonel Pyne and four companions. The five Parliamentarians overpowered the ten Royalists and diverted the wagons to Taunton.[25]

Nowhere around Bridgwater was safe. A surprise attack, on Sydenham House, led to the capture of the Royalist High Sheriff of Somerset. Part of Hopton's forces on their way to Devonshire were waylaid and 200 prisoners taken.[26] Blake led the garrison of Taunton Castle even further afield, descending on Tiverton while Sir John Culham and the other Commissioners of Array for Devonshire were trying to recruit men for the Royal cause.[27]

This could not have gone on for much longer without some Royalist reaction and, from the beginning of February, the position began to change. On 8 February the Royalists surprised the upper town of Weymouth and, with Lord Goring's army ready to take a hand, a crisis appeared to be developing in Dorset. This may have been the event that led to the withdrawal of the Dorset militia under Cooper. At least, no more is heard of them in the actions taking place round Taunton.

The greater confidence among the Royalists was reflected in their first attempt to take the offensive. Reports of what happened are conflicting, but they all agree that the Parliamentary forces came out on top. The *London Post*, for 11 February, informed its readers 'that the enemy did fall upon our Quarters about Taunton but were bravely received and repulsed, we are certified that the enemy lost many brave Men in that bold service and that many of them are taken Prisoner and carried into Taunton. The number of them is said to consist of about fourty-four men, in which list, eleven are said to be Commanders.' The Parliamentarians only admitted to two killed, Colonel Luttrell and a common soldier.[28] The *Diary or Exact Journal* has a different version, in which the prisoners were taken in an attack on Bridgwater, by Vandruske, while the Royalists were occupied at Taunton.[29] According *Mercurius Civicus*, Luttrell was killed in fighting at Wiveliscombe.[30]

March 1645 brought a further worsening of the situation around Taunton, due, oddly, to a Parliamentary success. Much to the fury of Goring, who had been vainly trying to take the lower town of Weymouth, seamen from ships under the command of Vice-Admiral Batten recaptured the upper town right under his nose. This unexpected reverse forced the Royalists to revise their strategy. Goring was recalled westwards and instructed to deal with Taunton, before any further operations were undertaken. This was just the sort of development that Cooper had feared, when he had written back in December: 'However we are in a very good condition if they receive no assistance from the King's army, which we most fear, this county being of so great import to the enemy that it will be worth engaging their whole army.'[31]

The Committee of Both Kingdoms had been well aware of the possibility. At the time Holborne was dispatched, letters had been written to Manchester to watch the movements of the Royal army closely and send assistance to Holborne, if Wyndham was reinforced.[32] Subsequently, Holborne had sent Major Okey to represent his exposed situation and Parliament had duly earmarked extra forces to go to his assistance.[33] Only when Waller, under pressure from Goring's superior numbers, ordered Holborne to leave Taunton and rendezvous with him at Cerne Abbas, did the Committee wake up to the fact that the reinforcements had not reached him and that Cooper's men had returned to their native Dorset.[34]

Even now, little happened. As Waller was preparing to obey peremptory orders to march to Taunton's assistance, his small force was attacked by Goring and sustained a humiliating reverse. This was the last straw for Sir William, who had become disillusioned with the war. His men were deserting for lack of food and pay. Holborne had resigned, rather than accept the army reforms going through Parliament, and Waller knew that he was shortly to be superseded. He would leave the thankless task of relieving Taunton to his successor.

Fortunately for the defenders of Taunton, the dissensions were even worse among the Royalist commanders. The new attempt to subdue Taunton was to be conducted by Sir Richard Grenville. He was to have under his command 3300 of his own Cornishmen, all of Goring's foot, 200 of his horse and some local levies, about 6000 men in all. Goring was to remain, with the bulk of his cavalry, on the borders of Wiltshire and Dorset, to prevent the garrison being relieved. Goring obeyed what had been his own suggestion originally, but in a sullen manner and, instead of staying on watch himself, went off to Bath, to take the waters.[35] Grenville was slow to take up his command and spent much of his energy quarrelling with Sir John Berkeley. As late as the end of March, the garrison was able to sally out and attack Sir Hugh Wyndham's house. The expedition missed its main object, which was to capture Colonel Francis Wyndham, the Governor of Dunster Castle. He was not in the house, but immediately he heard what had happened he set out in pursuit of the raiders. Francis was a much more capable man than his brother and he so harassed the Parliamentarians that they were glad to shed most of their booty and escape into Taunton.[36]

There were no more forays because Grenville was tightening his grip on the situation. His first aim was to eliminate Parliamentary posts outside Taunton, of which the most important was Edward Popham's house at Wellington. As Grenville was reconnoitring the position he was seriously wounded in the thigh by a musket shot from one of the garrison. The way their leader had been felled angered the Cornishmen so much that they pressed the siege with vigour and part of the house was blown up.[37] Accounts disagree as to whether the explosion was due to a mine planted by the Royalists, or whether it was a ruse to cover a break out. Whichever it was, the attempted escape was frustrated and, in the ensuing fighting, the Cornishmen slaughtered fifty of the garrison of 200, before they could be stopped. The news must have been a bitter blow to Blake because many of those who lost their lives were men who had followed him from Lyme. The Royalists were very embarrassed and attempts to allot blame for the carnage added to their dissensions.

The success at Wellington could not make up for the wounding of Grenville, who was forced to surrender command to the much less capable Berkeley. To him fell the task of trying to storm Taunton itself. Blake had not been idle during the winter. He strengthened the barricades and trenches in the East Reach. Pope's almhouses and other nearby buildings were drilled with loopholes, so that they could be used by musketeers. Some houses, which impeded the field of fire or could provide cover for the enemy, were knocked down. The Vicar's House was heavily fortified and a new defensive work, called the Maiden Fort, was built. Some guns had been shifted from the castle and placed so that they could sweep East Street.

The Royalist attempt was made on 25 April and was a ghastly failure. The assault foundered on the valour of the defenders, sustained by Blake's forethought and inspiring leadership. One of Goring's best men, Colonel Ballard, was killed in the fighting.[38] The Royalists retired to rethink their strategy and Berkeley resorted to Wyndham's tactics of trying to starve the town out; there were now as many as 7000 people inside. But the policy required time and time was running out for the Royalists.

Meanwhile disputes in the Parliamentary ranks had led to the passage of two very important ordinances. The first, the New Model Ordinance, created a new army, independent of the local associations, whose officers and men would be appointed and paid by the Parliament at Westminster. The second, the Self Denying Ordinance, required every officer, who was a member of either House of Parliament, to surrender his commission within forty days. Parliament would then decide which, if any, should be reappointed. All the senior commanders were affected except Sir Thomas Fairfax, who was the man that the majority wanted to command the new army. Essex, Manchester and Waller all had their military careers abruptly terminated.

By the time Grenville reached Taunton, Fairfax was well on with the organisation of his army and there was universal agreement that its first task must be the relief of the town. There does seem to have been an attempt to make the

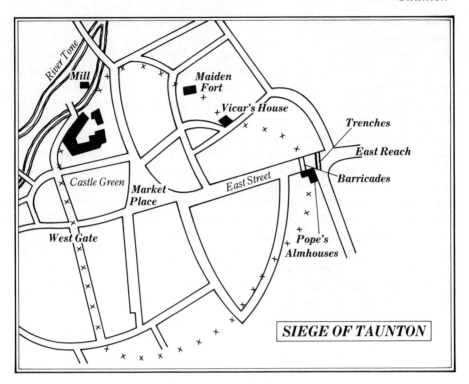

SIEGE OF TAUNTON

expedition part of a wider campaign. The minutes of the Committee of Admiralty show that preparations were being made for a large fleet, which was to relieve Plymouth and then sail round Land's End to combine with the Army in an attack on Bristol. But strategy by this time was of secondary importance in the popular imagination. Blake's resistance had become the symbol of the Parliament's cause. If he were to perish on the walls of Taunton, like some seventeenth-century Gordon, the authority of the Parliamentary leadership would be undermined and the hard-fought reforms compromised.

Yet the unthinkable nearly happened. When news of the westward march of Fairfax's army reached the Royalists, Hopton went to the trenches to galvanise the besiegers into one last great effort to take the town and castle, before the Parliamentarians got there. On 6 May the Royalist artillery opened up a devastating bombardment on the Vicar's House, which made it completely untenable. The next day, it was the turn of the defensive work across the East Reach to take a battering, but this time the defenders held on and repulsed the Royalist efforts to drive them from their trenches, supplementing bullets by a hail of stones and showers of scalding water.

There was a lull during the morning of 8 May. Rumours were circulating in both camps about the approach of Fairfax. In the afternoon, Hopton organised a 'sham' fight to try and tempt the defenders outside the walls, under the misapprehension that the Parliamentary army was near. The ruse did not work. Blake remembered what had happened at Lyme and refused the bait. His vigilance forced Hopton to make another effort to break down the defences. The assault began at 7 pm. This time the whole of the town was attacked, except the castle. The East Reach was lost as far as the Almshouses and the Royalists got a footing on the western side, though they failed to take the West Gate. During 9 May the Parliamentarians were pushed back, street by street and house by house. The Royalists fired a number of houses in an attempt to smoke the Parliamentarians out, but the wind was in the wrong direction and the tactic contributed little to the battle.

Nonetheless, when night closed in the position appeared to be desperate. Most of the town was in the hands of the Royalists, only the castle, the church and the Maiden Fort remaining in Parliamentary hands. Supplies of match had run out and bed cords were being used as a substitute. Inhabitants and soldiers alike were short of food and water because the Royalists had cut off the flow to the mill. Undeterred, Blake declared obdurately, to the cheers of his men, that he had four pairs of boots and he would eat three of them before he would think of giving in.[39]

Hopton sent a message, under a flag of truce, demanding that the garrison surrender, otherwise only seven people to be named by him would be spared. Blake retorted that if he would name the seven people, he would send him their heads. Hopton's demand was a bluff, because information had arrived that Fairfax was not far away. The next morning, he began drawing off his guns. Before the evacuation of the soldiers could follow, fresh news contradicted the previous day's reports: Fairfax had retreated, because of threatening moves by Goring. Hopton urged on his men to one last effort, telling them that Goring would soon bring reinforcements.[40]

The reports were only partly correct. Fairfax had begun his march towards Taunton on 30 April, but on 3 May Cromwell, riding to join him, had fallen in with some of Goring's troopers in the dark, and had suffered some loss. This showed that Goring was not coming to help the besiegers, rather he was marching in the opposite direction. On 7 May Fairfax reached Blandford where he received new orders.[41] He was to detach a force strong enough to relieve Taunton, but with the rest of the army he was to countermarch into the Midlands. Rupert and the King were moving north from Oxford and it was feared that they would fall on the Scots. Colonel Ralph Weldon was put in charge of a brigade some 6000 strong. He was given four regiments of foot: his own, and those commanded by Colonels Lloyd, Fortescue and Ingoldsby. In addition, there was the cavalry regiment of Colonel Graves and an unstated number of local militia horse under Colonel Morvill.[42]

Weldon left Blandford on 8 May, and made forced marches in order to reach Taunton in time. The Parliamentarians quartered around Bridport and Beaminster during the night of 8–9 May and the next day moved swiftly via Pellesden Pen to Chard, where they saw their first Royalist scout. The following morning, Weldon began the last stage of his march. The Royalists seem to have been totally unaware of the existence of Weldon's brigade until after they launched their last attack. This was the reason why Weldon encountered no opposition until after he left Chard, when a party of 300 Royalist horse tried to disrupt the advance by repeated charges. The Parliamentarians refused to be deflected and moved steadily on until, when darkness fell, they were between Trull and Orchard Portman, only a mile short of Taunton.

Meanwhile, Hopton was making his final attempt to capture the town. It was a desperate affair on both sides. By now, the real nature of the approaching force was known to the Royalists and that, combined with the limited gains of the two previous days, must have sapped their morale. All the accounts agree that the fighting on 10 May did not have the scale or intensity of the two previous days. The most dramatic part was the systematic firing of many of the houses by the Royalists, to try and produce enough smoke to cover a last attack. That night, the glare of the burning town illuminated the sky for miles around. A Cavalier travelling from Exeter to Bristol, reported that all Taunton seemed to be on fire. Sir Edward Nicholas, writing to Digby, hoped it presaged a Royalist success.[43] He was to be disappointed. The smoke was only serving to cover the besiegers' failure to break the will of the inhabitants. Even had they taken the remaining parts of the town, which did not look likely, there was never any chance of them capturing the castle, which Blake would have defended to the end. It was the knowledge that Blake would never flinch that sealed the fate of the Royalist operation.

During the first two days of fighting Blake seems to have been as much in the dark about the movements of the Parliamentary army as Hopton, but he knew of Weldon's approach. A messenger eluded the besiegers and got into Taunton, with the information that Weldon would fire signal guns when he got to within three or four miles of the town. Eye witnesses describe how, when the guns were heard, Blake took 'a perspective glass' and went to a high place, where he encouraged the defenders by describing what he could see of the approaching relief. It was enough. The Royalists were again driven back.[44]

The night of 10–11 May was a tense one. The defenders lay to arms and Weldon surrounded his camp with a strong guard. As soon as it became light, the Royalists abandoned their trenches and withdrew in the direction of Bridgwater. Their disengagement was effected more quickly than usual, because their guns had been removed the previous day. There was a delay before Weldon's men were able to join hands with the gallant defenders of Taunton, because the Royalists had felled large numbers of trees to slow down the progress of the relieving force. Besides the devastation in the town, there is general agreement that the defenders lost 50 killed and had 200 wounded. Weldon's men estimated that the Royalists lost 300 men killed. Culpepper admits that 320 sick and hurt men returned to Bridgwater but says nothing of the number of men killed.[45]

11 May was a day long remembered by the inhabitants of Taunton but Blake had to persuade them that they could not relax their vigilance yet. The main Parliamentary army was marching into the Midlands and Weldon's brigade was smaller than the army which Goring commanded. The Committee of Both Kingdoms kept a careful watch on the position. A letter was written to Blake, instructing him to send all of the garrison of Taunton who were not townsmen, to join Weldon. An extremely tart letter was dispatched to the Governor of Poole, drawing his attention to the failure of the Dorset garrisons to send the reinforcements to Weldon that had been promised and pointing out that, if Taunton were to fall, Poole would be one of the next targets.[46] Major-General Edward Massey was appointed as commander of the new army for the Western Counties, which was being assembled at Romsey in Hampshire by Colonel Popham.[47]

All these measures would take some time to come to fruition and Taunton was only saved from a third siege by the mismanagement of Lord Goring. He returned to the West, shortly after the relief of Taunton by Weldon, with a commission to command the army there. *Mercurius Civicus*, for 15–22 May, reported that Goring had 5000 men and Hopton 4000.[48] Weldon posted himself at North Petherton where, according to Clarendon, 'Goring fell so opportunely upon their quarters that he did them great mischieve, and believed that in that disorder he had so shut them up between narrow passes that they could neither retire to Taunton nor march eastward.' Two parties were sent out different ways, under Colonel Thornhill and Sir William Courtney, to fall upon the Parliamentarians, but their orders do not seem to have contained proper recognition signals because 'they fell foul of each other, to the loss of many of their men; both of the chief officers being dangerously hurt, and one of them taken, before they knew their error'.[49]

On 24 May orders came from the King to Goring, instructing him to march with his men to the main army.[50] Goring stalled as much as he could, giving the resistance of Taunton as a reason why he could not bring the forces the King required. Clarendon even went so far as to maintain that Goring deliberately neglected the siege because, if the town were taken, he would have no excuse for staying in the West. Despite this, the position was very threatening and there were some grounds for the Royalist claim, on 10 June, that the King's position in the West was better than it had been for a long time. No assault had been made on Taunton but the town was again blocked up.[51]

The victory of Sir Thomas Fairfax and the New Model Army over the King at Naseby, on 16 June, intensified the crisis, because the remnant of the Royal forces retreated westwards. Parliament was alert to the developing situation. By 21 June, Massey had assembled 3500 men at Blandford and rumours that he intended to march via Lyme to join Weldon, led Goring to detach 3000 men to block his route. From information received, the Committee of Both Kingdoms understood that Goring was expecting 2500 extra men, under Grenville, so the forces of Massey and Weldon were not enough to make certain that a third attack on Taunton would not be successful. Orders were sent to Fairfax to return to the West and execute the design which had been proposed earlier: a relief of Taunton, followed by an attack on Bristol.[52]

Fairfax moved with exemplary speed. When he received his orders, five days after Naseby, the army was encamped outside Leicester. A week later he was at Marlborough in Wiltshire and had already decided on his course of action. The direct route was barred by Royalist garrisons at Devizes, Bath, Bristol and Bridgwater so, like Holborne and Weldon before him, he decided to take the southern route, drawing his supplies through Lyme and Weymouth. An added advantage would be that he could link up directly with Massey's forces and summon Birch's regiment from Plymouth, without the danger of them being exposed to attack. The New Model left Marlborough on Monday 30 June, and billeted the next night at Amesbury, twenty miles away. The following day, the army passed Salisbury Plain and reached Blandford. From there Fairfax followed Weldon's itinerary, camping successively at Beaminster and Chard. The junction with Massey was effected without hindrance. Nor was the New Model's approach to Taunton opposed because Goring broke up from before the town and retired in the direction of Yeovil. This time the deliverance was final and it must have been a mightily relieved Blake who rode out to meet Fairfax and his officers.

The Victors Quarrel

*T*HE war was entering its last phase. On 10 July, Fairfax defeated Goring at Langport, then he laid siege to Bridgwater. The only reply to the Parliamentary summons to surrender was a musket shot aimed at Fairfax himself and fired by Christabella Wyndham, the wife of Edmund Wyndham. At a council of war, it was decided to attempt to storm the town. The Parliamentary attack on Eastover was successful and drove the defenders back across the Parret bridge. Parliamentary troops also broke into the town from the north and penetrated as far as the market place. A second summons was rejected but, when the assault was resumed the next day, Royalist opposition collapsed and Wyndham surrendered upon promise of quarter.[1]

Blake did not take part in the battle of Langport and he does not seem to have commanded any formation at the siege, but both Pophams were present and this seems to be the appropriate place for the story of the death of his brother, Samuel, misdated by earlier biographers to the beginning of the war. The story tells how Samuel was 'diverting himself' at the Shoulder of Mutton Inn at Pawlett, four miles north of Bridgwater, when he heard that a Royalist officer was levying men for the King, close by at Combwich. Blake, who seems to have taken too much to drink, gave chase. He caught up with the Royalist officer at Stretcholt, only to find that he was accompanied by a party of soldiers. Common prudence suggests that he should have beaten a hasty retreat, but Samuel charged into the Royalists and was cut down.

Samuel's death was soon known among the soldiers of Popham's regiment, but it was some time before anyone could pluck up courage to tell his brother. When the bad news was broken to him, Blake said stoically, 'Sam had no business there.' Then he retired to his room to grieve, privately, for the only one of his brothers to die in the fighting. When asked about Samuel's death later, he remarked sadly, 'Died Abner, as the fool dieth.'[2]

There is a traditional story which may relate either to the end of the siege of Taunton or the siege of Bridgwater. It relates how Sir John Stawell of Cothelstone retreated through Bishop's Lydiard closely pursued by Blake's cavalry, frightening the inhabitants so much that they heard ghostly horsemen for many years after, clattering through the darkened streets.[3] After the fall of Bridgwater, Fairfax turned his attention to Bristol. Massey was left to keep a watch upon Goring. It was a tense time at Taunton. Massey had less than 4000 men under his command. All through August Goring was mustering a new army, rumoured to be 11,000 strong. The threat never materialised. Bristol surrendered on 10 September and by the end of the month the New Model Army was back in the West.[4] On 23 October, Tiverton was taken and shortly afterwards the Parliamentary vanguard reached the east side of Exeter. There Fairfax halted. The weather was deteriorating and his men were badly in need of a rest. The only activity for the next two months was to be in the west of Somerset.

At the beginning of October, while Fairfax was still on his way from Bristol, Goring attacked Minehead. He plundered and burnt the town without opposition, Massey being too weak to stop him.[5] This provocation could not be ignored and once Fairfax was ensconced in his quarters at Tiverton, a force of 600 men under Colonels Blake and Sydenham was sent to lay siege to Dunster Castle.[6] Now Blake was to receive a taste of what he had meted out to others. Dunster Castle lay on a lozenge-shaped hill, to the south of the town. The sides of the hill were steep, the castle had its own water supply, it had been reprovisioned as a result of Goring's raid and, in Colonel Francis Wyndham, it had a governor of a very different stamp from his brother.

With the number of men Blake had, there was no question of an immediate storm and his guns were not sufficient to batter down the walls, but he was not content to just sit and starve the garrison out. Mining operations were started. Anyone who has stumbled about the gardens, which now adorn the slopes below the castle, will be aware of the problems digging under the walls posed. It was late December and Sydenham had departed, before the saps had reached the point where the walls could be undermined. The results of his efforts must have disappointed Blake greatly. One of the mines exploded without doing any damage. The second was neutralised by the defenders countermining under it, so that the trenches collapsed. The third did blow a hole in the wall but the slope was so steep that an attempt to storm was impracticable. There was small consolation in the report that the Royalists had to do double duty to protect the breach.[7]

Further frustrations were in store. During the lull in the fighting, Hopton had been reappointed commander-in-chief in the West by the Prince of Wales, and he had managed to gather together a small army. Early in January 1646, he advanced towards Exeter but Fairfax was on the alert. On 6 January, his cavalry, under Cromwell's command, made a night attack on the Royalist quarters at Bovey Tracey, throwing the whole army into confusion. Hopton's retreat exposed Dartmouth to attack. The port was besieged and surrendered on 18 January.[8]

Fairfax's southward move against Hopton left Blake very isolated. To make matters worse, Massey had moved eastwards to deal with some Royalists around

Crewkerne. Fairfax was aware of the problem and had left 1500 men posted at Wheddon Cross on Exmoor, above Dunster. Despite this precaution, a Royalist force of 1500 foot and 300 horse under Colonel Finch managed to relieve Dunster. They may have evaded the Parliamentary covering force by marching from Barnstaple, via the coast road through Porlock. Blake was not caught off his guard but Finch's force was too strong for him and he had to abandon his trenches. He managed to save his ammunition and retire to a prepared 'strong house'. The Royalists levelled the siege works and, after giving the garrison much-needed supplies, set off on the return journey. This was much more difficult. Blake's men were still intact and one of his first actions must have been to alert the Parliamentarians at Wheddon Cross. The retiring Royalists were harried the entire way and more than fifty prisoners were taken.[9]

Meanwhile the Parliamentary advance continued. As they retreated, the Royalists became more and more dispirited. At the beginning of February, Hopton's little army was again defeated at Torrington. The Prince of Wales left for the Scilly Isles, and on 14 March the whole Royalist army laid down its arms outside Truro.[10] The only question left was how quickly the remaining strongholds could be reduced. Fairfax decided to concentrate on Exeter. A blockading force was left at Dunster under Captain Burridge. Blake was ordered with his regiment to Barnstaple, where his arrival enabled Sir Hardress Waller to reinforce the besiegers of Exeter. The effect of Blake's presence was immediate. The defenders abandoned the town and took refuge in the castle.[11]

The Governor of Exeter knew that the position was hopeless. Negotiations began on 1 April and, after somewhat protracted haggling, Exeter surrendered twelve days later.[12] As soon as news of Exeter's surrender reached Barnstaple, terms were agreed and the castle was in Parliamentary hands the following day.[13] Dunster was so isolated that, since Finch's raid, the garrison's only source of information was from the besiegers. When rumours began to spread that Barnstaple had capitulated, a message was sent to Captain Burridge, asking for permission for two representatives to go and find out the truth. If the castle had surrendered, they were prepared to agree similar terms. In the end there was no need for such a mission. Blake reached Dunster with his own regiment and that of Major General Skippon the next day; evidence, if any were needed, of the truth of the rumour.[14]

Terms were concluded quickly. They were very liberal. In return for the surrender of the castle, all the Commissioners, officers and men were to be allowed to march away with their horses and arms. As many of them as wanted to could join the King at Oxford and they were given twelve days to get there.[15]

Blake played his part in binding up the wounds. The Committee for the Advance of Money fined John Question, surgeon of Dunster £100, because of his service to the Royalists. He appealed against the assessment, claiming that he had atoned for his behaviour by attending wounded Parliamentary soldiers at the siege of Dunster. His claim was endorsed by a certificate to that effect from Blake, and the assessment was reduced to £10.[16]

Blake's political fortunes had risen in step with his increasing military reputation. When fighting started he was little known outside his native Bridgwater, despite his election as an M.P. to the Short Parliament. He was not on the list of Parliamentary Commissioners for the Propositions, of 20 July 1642. Nor did he figure on the list of Somersetmen, dated 27 January 1643, who were to collect the contribution money for the maintenance of their own forces. The first reference to him was on 27 March 1643, when he was named on the Somerset Committee for Sequestrations.[17] The Committee's task was to administer the Royalist estates under Parliamentary control, so that the income could be used to support its armies. The timing suggests that it was his activity at Bristol that brought Blake to the notice of the Parliamentary managers.

Blake's name does not appear among the men who were to levy contributions from those who had not lent voluntarily. At the time the ordinance was passed, 7 May 1643, he had his hands rather full, but his name does appear on 3 August, among those charged with raising money to maintain the Army.[18] The honour was purely nominal, as Somerset was under Royalist control at the time. Much more important was his inclusion among the Somerset members of the Western Association, on 1 July 1644.[19] These men were to form the committee which ruled the county when the fighting ceased. His heroic defence of Taunton prevented Blake from taking any active part in the deliberations of the committee until the war was almost over, but the reputation he built for himself ensured that another honour would come his way.

At the beginning of the war, Parliament had expelled all the M.P.s who had supported the King, but holding elections to fill the vacancies was impossible while fighting continued, so the seats remained empty. In the autumn of 1645, with the victory of Parliament practically assured, elections to 'recruit' new members began. Both Bridgwater seats were unoccupied. Thomas Smyth had been expelled and had subsequently died. Sir Peter Wroth had adhered, rather hesitatingly, to the Parliament but he, too, died in 1644. There could have been little doubt about the two men who would replace them. Sir Thomas Wroth, the Recorder, was a staunch supporter of the Parliamentary cause and he would have been an M.P. already, if it had not been for the accident of his shrievality in 1640. With Smyth dead and Wyndham disqualified as a Royalist, Robert Blake would have been the natural choice for the second seat, even without his military exploits. With the support of his brother, Humphrey, who was Mayor once more, and Edward Ceely, Humphrey's brother-in-law, who was Receiver, his election as a Recruiter M.P. was a foregone conclusion.[20] The writs for Bridgwater were issued on 24 September, but Blake did not take his seat until the following year, presumably after the surrender of Dunster.[21]

As a member of the County Committee, Governor of Taunton and M.P. for Bridgwater, Blake assumed the rank to which his military exploits entitled him. He was one of the most important men in West Somerset, but politics held little intrinsic interest for him. The positions he held were a means to an end, not ends in themselves. The end was the godly reformation of the country and of Somerset in particular. He must have greeted the execution of Archbishop Laud in 1645, together with the passage of the ordinances abolishing bishops and providing for the sale of their lands, with grim satisfaction. The replacement of the Book of Common Prayer by the Presbyterian service book, the Directory, would have had his hearty concurrence. So would the ordinance establishing a Presbyterian class system. Each county was to be divided geographically into a number of classes which were to nominate equal numbers of ministers and lay elders to be responsible for church discipline.

In 1640, the possession of such views put Blake among the religious radicals, but by 1646 the picture had changed. Since the death of John Pym in December 1643, the influence of the Independents within the Parliamentary movement had grown steadily. The title 'Independent' covered many different groups, from those whose services differed very little from the Presbyterians, to Baptists, Levellers and Quakers; but they all had one thing in common. They rejected the idea of a single national church, whether Church of England or Presbyterian. Many of the groups supported a system of 'gathered' churches, instead of one which was parochially based. Some of them encouraged lay preachers, a practice regarded with horror by the Manchester presbytery. Worst of all, the most radical sects advocated the abolition of tithes, the minister being supported by the voluntary contributions of his congregation.

Independents could be found among Blake's own men. A pamphlet, printed a short time later, describes a series of exchanges during the siege of Dunster between one of Blake's officers, a Captain Francis Freeman, and the Royalist Governor of Dunster, presumably while Blake was absent at Barnstaple. Freeman propounded a number of questions to Colonel Francis Wyndham. His seventh query to Wyndham was – 'What think you of the Parliament, what religion are they of?' To which the Royalist Governor replied, 'I must confess I think they are Protestants, but there are a great many Sects and Schisms among them which makes them far worse than any Papist or Irish Rebels; there is the Puritane alias Round head, there is the Brownist, the Anabaptist, the Separatist, some Antinomians and some Independents.'[22]

Blake would not have agreed that the Sects were worse than Roman Catholics but, equally, he would not have supported Freeman's definition of a true Gentleman, as being one who fights God's battles and defends the Sects. To Blake, their ideas were anathema. If a country was to remain at peace with itself, the people must belong to the same church as their rulers and the rulers must be able to control that church. How could they exercise discipline, if the people could choose which church to go to and if they controlled directly how much the minister was paid? Holding such views, it is hardly surprising that when a sectarian meeting house made its appearance in St Mary Street, Taunton, it was quickly suppressed on Blake's orders. 'Our governor', one of the congregation told Thomas Collier, 'doth labour to beat us down', attributing their ideas to 'damnable pride'.[23]

Even before the end of the war, the growing influence of the sects was making many Parliamentary supporters believe that some sort of accommodation with the King needed to be made before they became too powerful. After fighting ceased, Charles exploited the fear to such great effect that many Presbyterians began to think that his restoration was the lesser of the two evils. Blake was not one of them. For him, they were the faint hearts, who had never wanted a root-and-branch change. Most of them had been quite prepared to retain bishops and had only abandoned them at the insistence of the Scots. Their ideal was a return to the church of Elizabeth and James I, shorn of the Court of High Commission and purged of the Arminianism of Laud and his followers.

For Blake, too, there was no logical place for a monarch in his scheme of government. When he came to this conclusion is difficult to determine, as we have no positive declaration from him on the subject until 1650. He may have adopted republican views simply because of the behaviour of Charles I, but the likelihood is that his republican roots were put down much earlier. If Clarendon is to be believed, Blake was a republican even in his University days.[24] His residence at Schiedam, among the burghers of the United Provinces, may well have shown him that dispensing with a monarch was not necessarily a recipe for disaster. Thus, as he surveyed the political scene Blake had little doubt in his mind that, if concessions had to be made, it was far better to allow some latitude to 'tender consciences' within a national Presbyterian church, than to compromise with the King. The events of 1646–8 were to prove a severe test of his resolve.

It is very easy to paint the siege of Taunton in a romantic light, but for the whole of western Somerset it was an economic and social disaster, whose ripples spread far and wide. Blake had conducted the siege with vigour. Hardly a hamlet had escaped the garrison's attentions. The Royalists had replied in kind. Their inability to take the castle forced them to try and starve the Parliamentarians out. At the height of the first part of the siege, Wyndham swept the whole area clear of food, not because he was short himself but in a vain effort to prevent supplies reaching Blake, with appalling consequences for the countryside. Blake's obduracy led to a repeat performance the following April and May. The Parliamentarians accused the Royalists of rounding up any men with known Parliamentary relatives, and forcing them to serve in the front line at Taunton, in the hope that the defenders would be reluctant to fire on their kinsmen. Wives and dependents of men who had served in Lyme or Taunton were evicted without ceremony and their property plundered.

Such behaviour was highly distasteful but it could be argued that it was the inevitable outcome of the fighting. The same could not be said of the depredations of the field armies which operated within the county. Maurice's Royalist cavalry plundered far and wide during the campaign against Waller in May and June 1643, and there was a second visitation when Maurice was recruiting men from Lord Poulett's estates. Nor were the Parliamentarians spotless. Attention has already been drawn to the way in which Waller had to use a species of blackmail to screw money out of Parliament for the Dorset militia. The troopers of Holborne and Vandruske were not paid properly either and resorted to free quarter. However, the behaviour of Maurice and Holborne paled into insignificance beside that of Goring. They might be excused, on the grounds that they were forced to do what they did, by the failure of their leaders to make proper provision for payment. Goring, on the other hand, seems to have believed that the murder, plunder and rape, of friend and foe alike, were perquisites which his men should enjoy by right. The result of his depredations was to reduce the countryside to a desert. When Weldon's men marched to the relief of Taunton, in May 1645, it was through a wilderness. The villages they passed were empty. All the inhabitants had fled. One writer remarked, 'You would suppose the great Turk and his Janissaries and Armies rather than their Natural Prince his Souldiers had been there.'[25] So extreme had the situation become, that groups of Clubmen had appeared, dedicated to defending their property against both sides.

For the common people the most pressing need was the disbandment of the soldiers. So long as they remained in arms, they would have to be paid. To begin with, matters got worse, not better. The civil war in Ireland still continued and Parliament was determined to send in reinforcements to the beleaguered Protestant forces there. In July 1646, Colonel Jephson's regiment marched into Somerset and was quartered around Bridgwater, ready to embark at Minehead.[26] First, there were delays in the arrival of embarkation orders; then there was a wait due to unfavourable winds and, all the time, the burden of supporting the men fell on the local populace. Jephson was followed by Townsend and Long. The procession of soldiers, drinking, whoring and demanding food and quarters, seemed never ending. The Petition of the Grand Jury to Parliament, drawn up at the Taunton Assizes in March 1647, detailed the outrages committed by Townsend's men, many of whom appear to have been disbanded Royalists.[27]

More ominously, the discontent was turned into an attack on the County Committee, which was accused of exempting its friends and victimising its political opponents. Men who had the temerity to complain, endured a tirade from John Pyne, the dominant man on the committee, but got no redress, and the most pertinacious found themselves in prison. The opinion soon began to spread that the county's sufferings would only be ended when the Committee was abolished and the old system, of Deputy Lieutenants and Justices of the Peace, was restored. The Committee's opponents were encouraged by the Presbyterian majority at Westminster, prominent among whom were two Somerset men, William Prynne and Clement Walker.

Blake's attitude to disbandment was ambiguous. No one was more aware of the devastation that Somerset had suffered and the need for a reduction in the taxation burden. As a soldier himself, he was keen to see that the men were paid off in an orderly fashion. He was only too pleased to play his part in the disbandment of the forces under Major-General Massey. The soldiers were a direct burden on the Western Counties, their pay was in arrears and their behaviour disorderly. Their disbandment was suggested in July 1646 but the process was not completed until February 1647. The reason was that Massey was prominent among those who wanted some sort of a compromise with the King. The Presbyterians tried to delay the disbandment as long as possible. The Journals of the House of Commons record that when it was found that the money allocated was not enough, it was resolved to raise the extra out of Royalist compositions. Blake was selected to go to Massey with £500 which was immediately available.[28]

Disbandment did not stop there. Early in 1647, Parliament began considering how many garrisons should be kept. A petition from Bridgwater was lying on the table, which proved a convenient starting point.[29] The corporation complained of the amount the borough had to pay of the assessment of the hundred of North Petherton, and asked that the proportion be reduced from a third to an eighth.[30] It was resolved to knock down Bridgwater's fortifications and pay off its garrison. Taunton castle was to retain a reduced garrison of 100 men. Blake was replaced as Governor, by Lieutenant-Colonel Samuel Perry.[31] The Journals give no reason for the change but there were two quite adequate ones. 100 men did not warrant a full Colonel and Blake was an M.P. The idea behind the Self Denying Ordinance had been that a man could not be in two places at once. If Blake was in London, attending the affairs of Parliament, he could not be functioning effectively as Governor of Taunton and vice versa. Yet, there can be no doubt that those who engineered Blake's removal intended it as a blow at the authority of Pyne and the County Committee.

We can only guess at what Blake thought about the turn events were taking. Unlike Pyne, local politics held no interest for him and he never appears as a principal. Being the sort of man he was, Blake would have been quite prepared to step down if it was in the interests of the country as he saw them, especially for a man such as Samuel Perry who had fought bravely at his side throughout the siege of Taunton. But he must have been disturbed at what was happening. He did not like the sects but the authority of the County Committee had to be maintained, otherwise the Godly Reformation, on which he had set his heart, would be jeopardised. Blake knew only too well the strength of the opposition that existed in Somerset. In July 1645, he and Pyne had been sent by Fairfax to try and negotiate an agreement with the West Somerset Clubmen, so that they could form a united front against the Royalists.

Blake was peculiarly fitted for the task. The spokesman for the Clubmen was Humphrey Willis.[32] Willis came from Woolavington, where Blake's family owned property and which was next door to Puriton, the manor Blake had inherited from his father. The two men must have known each other and many of Willis's followers may well have been the men Blake had gone fowling and fishing with, in pre-Civil War days. Despite this, the mission was a failure. The Clubmen refused to be bound by Parliamentary Ordinances and neither Fairfax, Pyne nor Blake could accept the Clubmen's programme. Blake stalled at the very first clause which ran – 'Imprimis. We stand for the true, Protestant Religion as it was used and observed in Queen Elizabeth's time.'[33]

Now this same Willis appeared as the scourge of the County Committee and Blake could see what was going to happen.[34] He and his allies would undermine the Committee, aided by Presbyterians like Prynne who were frightened of the sects, and then destroy the Presbytery itself, once an agreement had been made with the King. Even as it was, the good work was in difficulties. Blake had watched London draw up its plan of classes, complete with ministers and elders, in the autumn of 1645. Essex and Lancashire had established Presbyterian systems before 1646 was out. In Somerset, the work proceeded on leaden feet. The arrangement of classes was not completed until March 1648 and even then, the framers of the plan had to confess that there were not enough qualified ministers and competent elders to fill up the number they had originally intended. Blake eventually figured as an elder in the Taunton classis,[35] but in the spring of 1647 he could have been forgiven for wondering whether the work would ever be completed.

Fortunately for Blake and those who thought like him, the folly of the Presbyterian majority in Parliament came to their assistance. The desire to promote the Protestant cause in Ireland, combined with a wish to reduce taxation and suspicion of the New Model Army, led them to make a crucial blunder. A loan of £200,000 was raised from the City of London. The money was sufficient to equip an army for Ireland but not to pay off those officers and soldiers who either did not volunteer or were not selected for the service. Soon rumours began to sweep the army that all those who did not volunteer were to be disbanded, without the payment of their considerable arrears. Nothing could have been better calculated to give the army militants widespread backing among the rank and file. Parliament then compounded its mistake. Instead of trying to defuse the situation, its members began to try and organise a rival army, based on a combination of the London militia, Presbyterian elements in the Eastern Association, the Royalists and the Scots. The whole thing was orchestrated by the French Ambassador.

Blake took little interest in his own arrears of pay. He was voted £1000 in March 1648[36] for the repayment of money spent in 1644, but he did not petition for his pay until he was making his will in 1656! He was paid £3815–16s–0d 'for his personal pay for his land service in England'.[37] Blake could wait because he had an independent income. Ordinary soldiers could not, and he must have been scandalised at the behaviour of M.P.s over the matter of arrears. Among the reduced officers in London, petitioning for their pay on 19 June 1647, were Thomas Adams, who had served with him at Lyme Regis and his own brother, Benjamin.[38] Where Blake was when the Army finally occupied London on 6 August, is difficult to determine. He was not among the 57 M.P.s who went to Fairfax and asked him to restore Parliamentary liberties by occupying the capital. But he did make a rare appearance, on 18 August, as a member of the committee which examined the ordinance annulling all Parliamentary acts between the flight of the two Speakers, on 26 July, and their return, under the Army's wing, on 6 August. Only an M.P. who was in sympathy with the Army would have made such an early return to his seat.[39]

The autumn of 1647 brought Blake heartaches of a different sort. He must have become very worried at the increasing influence of the extreme sectaries and the open way in which such issues as one man one vote and complete toleration were being debated at Putney by the Army. Two events must have determined his course of action. The first was the suppression of the Levellers by Cromwell, at Corkbush fields, on 15 November 1647. This would have given Blake confidence that the Army leadership would not give in to the demands of the extremists. The other was the attempted flight of the King, followed by the revelation of his intrigues. While he had been negotiating one set of terms with the Army and its Parliamentary supporters, Charles had also been conducting separate secret talks with the Scots, in which he offered a totally different and contradictory set of concessions. Parliament's fury at the King's double dealing knew no bounds and in January 1648 it passed the vote of No Addresses, in which the M.P.s pledged themselves never to negotiate with the King again. There is no direct evidence of Blake's attitude but one of the first places to send a Petition, in support of what the Parliament had done, was Taunton.[40]

Blake's movements during the Second Civil War, which broke out in April 1648, are equally difficult to determine, but he seems to have taken little part in the fighting. Alexander Popham believed that Royalism was widespread in Somerset. When news of a rebellion in Pembrokeshire arrived he used its existence to justify his demand that he be allowed to raise a regiment. The analysis given earlier in the chapter suggests that his fears were well grounded, but it is equally true that the restoration of the local forces would enhance the prestige of the County Committee.[41] The rebellion in Kent and the Fleet mutiny added to fears of a revolt in Somerset. On 23 May Popham was sent down to raise a troop of horse 'for seizing, securing and suppressing Malignants'.[42] Blake did not accompany him. He was in London on 10 June, because he was named to a committee investigating the shooting of the Sheriff of Caernarvon by Sir John Owen.[43]

The rebels in Kent were defeated at Maidstone by the New Model Army under Fairfax but there was another scare at the beginning of July, when an abortive revolt took place in Middlesex. Evidence came to light that parties had been sent to raise the Western Counties. Again nothing happened but fears became acute when negotiations with the Scots broke down and they invaded England. Popham put forward a scheme for associating all the Western Counties for their defence. Blake must have been reappointed to look after Taunton as part of these plans because he is listed as Governor, in a document of 19 August.[44] In the event he was not called on to perform heroic deeds. Indeed there is no positive evidence that he ever left London. There is no record of him being excused attendance at the House of Commons and his name does not appear as being either excused or absent without leave when the House was called on 26 September.[45] Not that it mattered. The Scots were defeated by Cromwell at Preston on 11 August and Somerset remained peaceful throughout the war. Blake was in his place on 1 November because he was named to the committee which considered the Ordinance for Essex Sequestrations.[46]

Part II

Fighting the Royalist Fleet

Ireland

O NE of the major imponderables faced by the leaders of the New Model Army during the Second Civil War, was the attitude of the Navy. In July 1647, feelers put out by the agitators to Trinity House, the merchant captains' guild, met with no response. The following September, after the occupation of London, Vice-Admiral Batten was removed from his command for plotting with the Royalists and Presbyterians. Great exception was taken to his replacement, Thomas Rainsborough, partly because of his Leveller politics and partly because of his obnoxious personality. A mutiny occurred in the Downs squadron in April 1648, in which Rainsborough was turned off his flagship, the *Constant Reformation*. She was one of eleven ships which joined the Royalists, with Batten in command. Parliament restored the Earl of Warwick to his office of Lord High Admiral. He was able to contain the revolt but not to reclaim the ships which had rebelled. Late in August, lack of food forced the Royalists to abandon their station in the Downs and retreat to Helvoetsluis, in the United Provinces. Warwick followed them and there began a long and wearisome blockade, which lasted three months.[1]

The atmosphere of suspicion about the Navy's intentions, which had been fuelled by the mutiny and Warwick's inability to crush it, steadily poisoned relations. Warwick could not do anything without political motivation being seen as the mainspring. His initial move to the Downs was seen as reluctance to engage the Royalists, not as sound if a little unimaginative strategy and a desire to ensure that Walmer, the last remaining Downs castle in enemy hands, was reduced as quickly as possible. When the Parliamentary fleet did go to the United Provinces, the decision not to sail straight into Helvoetsluis harbour was attributed to similar influences, instead of the well-grounded fear that the Dutch shore batteries would open fire on them, with catastrophic results.

Warwick's motives in opening a secret correspondence with Batten and accepting the Dutch offer of shelter inside Goree, in return for a pledge not to begin hostilities with the Royalists, were similarly misconstrued. The one plotting treason was not Warwick, but Batten. They agreed that if the negotiations between the King and the Parliament in progress at Newport failed, Batten would bring his ships to join Warwick. The presence of Warwick's ships in the harbour would make it easier for Batten to overpower any Royalists who objected. Warwick came within an ace of success. At first, he was thwarted by the appearance of a squadron of Dutch men-of-war under Tromp, sent by the Stadtholder. By patient diplomacy, Warwick managed to get them withdrawn. Then, at the crucial moment, the Prince of Wales dismissed Batten and appointed Prince Rupert in his place. Even so three ships were recaptured, before Rupert got the rest up the sluice, where Warwick could not get at them.

After lingering another month, Warwick sailed for home, reasoning that there was little mischief Rupert could do before the spring, if a strong squadron held the Downs. Once more his motives were misinterpreted. While he had been away the crisis had been deepening at home. The Army leaders had decided to cut the Gordian knot. On 5 December 1648, Pride's Purge saw the removal from the Commons of all those M.P.s who had supported the negotiations with Charles. By the time the fleet reached the Downs, preparations for the King's trial were far advanced and the Army Council feared a Navy plot to stop it. Warwick was ordered up to London and the fleet dispersed, so that the events of April 1648 could not be repeated.

Warwick had deserved well of his political masters, but he could not be kept. He had supported the Newport negotiations, he was opposed to the trial and execution of the King, and he was disinclined to serve a regime that had beheaded his egregious brother, the Earl of Holland. The Committee of the Navy of the purged House of Commons (usually known as the Rump), which controlled naval appointments, decided not to replace him. The M.P.s wanted to divide his responsibilities. Naval appointments they would keep in their own hands. The administration was entrusted to a committee of Merchants, who promised to root out corruption and reform the whole system.[2] A renewed attack was planned on the High Court of Admiralty, on the grounds that it was a prerogative court, like the Court of High Commission.

One of the most awkward decisions was about the command of the fleet. Three Generals-at-Sea were to be appointed. This would make sure that no one man could carry the fleet off, as they believed Warwick had planned to do. The three men were all to be soldiers. There was no seaman whom the Army, the Committee's masters, was prepared to trust and anyway there was no precedent for appointing a seaman. Even Warwick, the so called 'tarpaulin' Admiral, had only commanded one rather unsuccessful expedition, before his appointment as Vice-Admiral in 1642. The two determining factors were loyalty to the new Commonwealth government and proven military ability.

The three men selected were Robert Blake, Richard Deane and Edward Popham. The one who fulfilled the political criterion best was Richard Deane. He had signed the King's death warrant and was wholly committed to the new regime. Both Blake and Popham were M.P.s. Every M.P. who wished to serve the Commonwealth had to sign a declaration, in which they dissented from the repeal of the Vote of No Addresses of 3 August 1648, the Newport negotiations and the vote of 4 December 1648 to continue them, the event which precipitated Pride's Purge. David Underdown, in his study of the Purge, divides the M.P.s into three. Those who signed before the King's execution, he regards as the real revolutionaries. Those who signed during February and March 1649, he labels Conformists. They would not take part in the trial but accepted what had been done. Those who signed later, he calls Abstainers. They wanted nothing to do with what had happened, but wished for some place or preferment, under the Commonwealth. By that yardstick Blake and Popham were Conformists. Both men entered their dissent during February 1649. Blake's attitude to the King's trial is unknown but, like Sir Henry Vane, he may have believed that the King should have been deposed not executed.

Deane comes top of the poll on the second count too. A campaign in Ireland was under consideration and it was expected that Cromwell would be appointed to command it. The most influential man on the Committee of the Navy was Colonel Valentine Walton, Cromwell's brother-in-law.[3] He knew that Cromwell would want someone he could trust in charge of the transportation of the men across the Irish Sea. Cromwell was also planning to carry his siege train by sea because of the bad Irish roads. Deane was the ideal man. He was one of the best of the younger officers of the New Model Army and he had commanded its artillery. Cromwell was deeply attached to him and was very upset when he was killed at the battle of the Gabbard in 1653.

Deane may have been responsible for suggesting both Blake and Popham. All three were west-countrymen and they would have met during the 1645 campaign. But the evidence suggests that Deane might have proposed Blake for the second vacancy and that Blake then suggested Popham for the final place.[4] John Pyne entered his dissent on 1 February, Blake followed on 5 February. Alexander and Edward Popham waited until 12 February.[5] The inference is that Pyne persuaded Blake to throw his lot in with the new Commonwealth. He was then offered the post of General-at-Sea. Blake in his turn proposed Popham who had to enter his dissent to qualify. This explanation is consistent with the military criterion too. Blake's reputation was far greater than that of his friend and former patron.

There are other straws which point the same way. The evidence suggests that Popham did not really want to go to sea. He had been included as a captain in the list for the Summer Guard of 1648,[6] but he had not gone to sea then. He was named as one of the two civilian commissioners to go with Warwick to Goree but he had declined the honour and Walter Strickland had replaced him.[7] In a letter written to Popham in September 1649, Blake declared that he would not have accepted the post of General-at-Sea without Popham's presence at his side.[8]

Blake valued Popham as an old friend and he had the seagoing experience Blake lacked. He was flag lieutenant to Sir John Pennington in 1636, and commanded the *Fifth Whelp* in 1637. The vessel sank off Guernsey, but Popham was not held responsible, and in 1639 he commanded an armed merchantman. This suggests that Blake was at least partly responsible for persuading Popham to accept the appointment. Another factor may well have been monetary. The Popham estates were in a very embarrassed position. A Captain in the Navy got less than a Colonel but a General-at-Sea got more.

Finally, there is the possibility that Deane and Blake knew each other before the Civil Wars. Deane was a Plymouth merchant, who traded in mast timber and deals with Sweden.[9] He would have known George Blake and if Robert did spend several years in Schiedam as a factor, they might well have done business together. The Dorchester Blake traded in the same commodities and it was quite usual for English merchants to use a middleman in the United Provinces.

The first task was to re-establish confidence. What the Generals-at-Sea would have really liked was the grant of martial law, so that they could discipline officers on the spot. The Council of State was prepared to support them but Parliament was not. Fortunately the captains were nowhere near as disaffected as the heated imaginations of the republicans had led them to believe. With the exception of Batten, no captain voluntarily deserted to the Royalists. Their greatest worry was the threat to their professional prospects from the wholesale importation of army officers. Soldiers continued to be appointed from time to time, but the enormous expansion in the size of the fleet created openings for capable men from all backgrounds. Such was the shortage, that the Commonwealth sanctioned promotions from among the non-commissioned officers. The few malcontents were easily removed. Captains were appointed for the duration of a cruise. The list of captains for the Summer Guard, which stayed out for eight months, was selected in February or March. A smaller fleet, known as the Winter Guard and which stayed out for six months, replaced it in October and its captains were selected in August or September. All that had to be done was to take their names from the list.

Another calming factor was the presence of Blake and Popham as counterweights to the regicide, Deane. Both were moderate republicans and their Presbyterian views coincided with those of the majority of the officers. Their confidence was increased by the determination of all three men to make merit the sole criterion for promotion, and to stamp on all outside political interference. The Committee of the Navy was proving to be a severe embarrassment and its attempt to interfere in the appointment of the officers of the fleet soon brought its members into conflict with Blake and his colleagues. The disagreements came to a head, when instructions were sent to imprison the master and crew of the

Elizabeth hoy, because the ship had been with the Royalists. The Council of State was quick to override the Committee, when Deane and Blake recommended that all the men detained at Plymouth should be released because they had voluntarily deserted Rupert's fleet.[10] The Generals asked for, and were granted, the right to veto the appointment of captains, of whom they disapproved.[11]

Fears of a sectarian witch hunt were finally laid to rest when the Council of State ordered that the Committee of the Navy should leave the fleet alone in future and confine its activities to the Customs. The Council gave authority to the Generals to reinstate any suspended officers whom they thought had been victimised.[12] It was as well it did so. John Hollond in his *Discourse* characterises the Committee's behaviour as venal and corrupt. He wrote, 'the game was played that one should have an office in the excise another in the navy and a third in the customs, all able to pleasure a fourth, a merchant as occasion might require.'[13]

The experiment of having a Navy Board of Commissioners combined with merchants proved as counter-productive as it had done on the last occasion it had been tried, in 1642. There is no evidence that its activities influenced the efficiency of the dockyards or victualling one way or the other. The reforms of the ordnance saved a small amount of money but the economies may have been partly responsible for the department's slowness in 1652. The Committee had nothing to say about the crucial problem of whether the supply of guns for the Navy should be separated from those for the Army. All in all it gave an unimpressive performance and few tears were shed when the Committee was dissolved in March 1650, and the Navy Commission returned to its old pattern of professional administrators responsible to the Committee of Admiralty.

Efforts were made to conciliate the other ranks as well. On 19 March, Sir Henry Vane reported to the Council of State from the Committee of Admiralty, that the Navy Commissioners had declared Lent a superstition and that no distinction should be made in the distribution of meat. They recommended that the abatements on Fridays should also be abolished, 'being begotten by the covetous desires of the contractors for victuals, though coloured with the specious pretence of abstinence and religion'.[14] The suggestion had originally been made in a letter from Deane and Popham. Perhaps Popham recalled some bleak pre-Civil War Lents, from his earlier service at sea. A great cheer must have gone up round the Fleet, when the alterations to the meal schedules were announced.[15]

The realisation that promotion prospects were good and that the Generals would support the interests of both officers and men was enough to ensure that the Leveller rebellion in the Army, of April 1649, would gain no support in the Fleet. The dangers were on the other flank and the officers must have been reassured by the drastic way in which Cromwell dealt with the rebellion. When Hugh Peters came down to preach to the seamen about the need to destroy Prince Rupert's fleet, the battle for their minds and hearts was already won. Blake drove the advantage home, as he had done at Taunton, by preparing an 'engagement the better to discover the mariner's affections which we the officers have subscribed'. The 540 men on the *Triumph* offered to sign, without being asked, and it was received with enthusiasm in the other ships. The engagement was then sent to Popham, who was already at sea, and to the ships in the north.[16]

The real threat to naval discipline was not political at all. It was the question of prize. Even after the pay rises of 1642 and 1647, navy rates were low and it had been usual to try and supplement them, by taking and selling prizes. So much so that the lust for prizes, among both officers and crew, often distorted and sometimes totally destroyed campaigns.

The Commonwealth moved quickly to tighten control and update the legislation. The use of privateers was phased out and new regulations were introduced. Under the old system, when a merchant prize was captured, the ship and its cargo would be sold by the Commissioners of Prize Goods. After expenses had been deducted, one third of the remaining money would go to the captain of the capturing ship, the second third would be divided among the crew. If the capturing ship belonged to the government, it would take the remaining third. When it was an armed merchantmen or a privateer, the third would go to the owners. In each case one tenth of the value would go to the High Court of Admiralty, which was responsible for condemning the prize. That money would go to the Lord High Admiral, when there was one; if the office was vacant it swelled the government's third.

By 1649 the regulations had been extended. Men-of-war were less valuable and more difficult to attack, so the rules laid down that thirds would also be paid on them, according to the number of guns they carried. The great flaw which remained, was that money was only paid on ships taken: there was nothing for ships sunk. The regulations of 1649 went some way towards remedying this omission. Rupert possessed three large capital ships, the *Constant Reformation*, the *Swallow* and the *Convertine*. These were regarded as the Admiral, Vice-Admiral and Rear-Admiral of the Royalist fleet. If any of these three were sunk, the ships concerned in the action would be paid prize money, as though they had been captured. It was also laid down that the tenth, which had previously gone to the Lord High Admiral, was to be set aside to establish a fund to help the sick and wounded and to provide pensions for widows of men killed at sea.[17]

Deane and Blake showed considerable interest in the problems of the Prize Goods office. They were worried about the delays in condemning prizes, caused by the political crisis. They pushed hard for payments to be made to Captain Gilson, Captain Chappell and others, who had had to wait a long time for the ships that they had taken to be condemned.[18] They were concerned that the small number of Commissioners appointed would make it difficult to get perishable goods condemned quickly enough to be sold, before they deteriorated. Their concern was such that the Council of State asked them what changes they thought should be made in the Principal Prize Commissioners. They recommended that

Thomas Smith, who was one of the Navy Commissioners, should be kept but that John Hill should be replaced by John Sparrow.[19] Parliament preferred to adopt the spirit of the Generals' criticism, rather than their precise recommendations. The Act passed on 17 April, removed the name of Thomas Smith as well as that of Hill, probably because it was felt that the former could not do two jobs at once. The Generals would not have objected because the Act named three Commissioners not two, one of whom was John Sparrow, the man they had nominated, while another was Blake's brother Humphrey.[20]

Yet the Generals were either not consulted or took little interest in the drafting of the legislation itself, because on the day the bill was introduced into Parliament, they were writing a letter pointing out that, although the act clearly allowed ships carrying corn, ammunition and contraband of war to Ireland to be confiscated, the position regarding their cargoes was left very vague.[21] If they had been consulted earlier such a mistake presumably would not have occurred. The Generals certainly approved of a change which would encourage captains and crews faced with a pitched battle against Rupert's biggest ships, but their failure to take the initiative is an early indication of their blindness to the revolutionary potential of the prize issue. It was to be left to Monck, a man of a very different temperament and outlook, to open Blake's eyes.

Warwick had left the Royalists in bad shape but it was essential to keep the fleet concentrated in the Downs, so that any move by Prince Rupert could be countered immediately. Unfortunately Parliament's panic action in dispersing the fleet at the end of 1648 destroyed most of his good work. When the Royalists made their bid for freedom in January 1649, Vice-Admiral Moulton did not have enough ships in the Downs to stop them, with catastrophic results for English shipping. With Rupert ranging the Channel and privateers of all nationalities bringing English shipping to a standstill, immediate action was needed. Moulton had hardly stepped on dry land before one of the Navy Commissioners, Colonel William Willoughby, arrived at Portsmouth with orders for him to go to sea again. His flag was in the *Leopard* and he had with him the *Bonadventure* and the *Elizabeth*. The *Adventure* soon followed, giving him a compact and effective squadron with which to stabilise the position in the Channel, though not sufficient to take on Rupert's full force.

The next move was to get as many ships to sea, as quickly as possible. For once money was no object. The Generals consulted about what to do and decided that Popham should go to sea with the first batch of ships to emerge. This was a sensible decision. Popham was the most experienced of the three of them in fleet operations. Deane needed to stay in London to organise the convoys carrying vital supplies for Ireland. Blake, with his merchant background, was the right man to see through the excuses of suppliers and dockyard officials and to galvanise them into activity.

The Commonwealth inherited thirty-nine ships of different sizes. Since at least 1642, and possibly earlier, it had become usual to divide them into six rates roughly according to size and, from 1648, the ship's rate was regularly entered along with its name, number of guns, total of ship's crew and tonnage. The purpose seems to have been to fix appropriate establishments and wage rates for the different sizes of ships. There is general agreement that the 1st or largest rate contained the *Sovereign of the Seas*, the *Resolution* (renamed *Prince Royal*) and the *Naseby* (launched in 1655). The boundaries of the other five rates vary from list to list and attempts to categorise them either by number of guns or tonnage throw up anomalies. The rating system is therefore a useful but very rough guide to size. The Council of State was determined to equip for sea all the ships it had except for the two 1st rates, but there were serious delays, caused by the late decision to make such a large effort which strained the dockyards to breaking point. Despite the attempts of Deane and Blake to drive up the work rate, it was to be late in the campaign before many of them got to sea.

Moulton's squadron could not be everywhere and there was great pressure to speed ships out. When news of the capture of five rich merchantmen south of the Scilly Islands arrived, Popham ran up his flag in the 2nd rate *Charles*, and sailed for the Downs.[22] His arrival there released Moulton's ships to move westwards and guard the approaches to Plymouth. Popham spent eleven days in the Downs, organising convoys to the United Provinces, dispatching the *Nonsuch* to block up Ostend and providing protection for the North Sea and Iceland fisheries. Satisfied that there was at least minimum protection, he sailed to join Moulton, with the *Constant Warwick* and *Assurance* in company. Off Portsmouth, he picked up the armed merchantman, *Increase*. Once the two squadrons joined, there would be a real chance of tackling Rupert successfully.

Meanwhile Deane and Blake were driving on the dockyards to get ships to sea. Sir George Ayscue was given a commission, as Admiral of the Irish Seas, and rode off to Chatham to get the *St Andrew* out. With him went James Moulton, who was to convey the *Victory* out to his father and then take over the *Leopard*. Penn was made Vice-Admiral of the Irish Seas. He was given Ayscue's former ship, the *Lion*, and posted down to Portsmouth, where Willoughby was preparing it for sea, together with a powerful armed merchantman, the *Hercules*. By the middle of April, the two Generals had done all they could at Westminster and the focus of their activity shifted to Tilbury Hope, where they hoisted their flag on the *Triumph*, and assembled as large a number of warships as they could. As the Generals were preparing to sail, they received welcome news. Moulton and Popham had rendezvoused forty leagues off Lundy, on 20 April. Moulton had encountered a detachment of Rupert's fleet, in poor visibility, and had managed to capture the *Thomas*. After a game of blind man's buff in the fog, Popham's squadron surprised another ship, the *Constant Charles* (the Guinea Company frigate lost in 1648).[23]

Preparations were now in train and it was time the Generals left the Thames. Deane would be more use to Cromwell at Plymouth or Milford, and Blake had done all he could to increase the administration's efficiency. His formidable presence was needed to inspire the men in the firing line in the difficult months ahead. The *Triumph* reached the Downs at the beginning of May. Richard Badiley, the captain of the *Happy Entrance*, was appointed to command there and, on 5 May, Blake and Deane followed Moulton, Popham and Ayscue down the Channel.[24] The *Triumph* was accompanied by the *Garland, Nonsuch, Phoenix* and *Satisfaction*. The passage was long and frustrating. Another fortnight elapsed before the Generals could take counsel together off Plymouth. Once Ayscue's convoy was safely on its way to Dublin, the three men were free to concentrate on Rupert. The decision was taken to head for his base at Kinsale in Southern Ireland. If Rupert were at sea, it might be possible to intercept him when he returned from his foray. If he was at home, he could be bottled up so that he could not interfere with the projected invasion. Landfall was made on 21 May, and the forest of masts indicated that Rupert was indeed in residence.[25]

Masthead observations and other intelligence showed that the *Constant Reformation, Swallow* and *Convertine*, the three really powerful ships that Rupert could call upon, were all there. With them were most of his smaller ships. They identified the *Ark, James, George, Culpepper, Roebuck, Blackmoor Lady, Ambrose* and *Charles*. In addition there were two unnamed ships referred to as the 'Washford' and 'Scots' frigates together with three smaller vessels. After a thorough discussion of the options available, the three men decided to separate once more. One General was to stay with the squadron blockading Prince Rupert in Kinsale, because it was essential to keep him there, during the crucial phase of the invasion. A second was needed to organise the convoys of troops and equipment. Wisdom dictated that the third General should return to London to make sure that efforts did not languish. Out of sight was often out of mind too, especially with the victuallers. There was also the consideration that the transportation of such a large proportion of the Army to Ireland might leave the South East dangerously exposed to a descent from the Continent, so the Council of State had a right to expect that one of the Generals would look after the Downs. Badiley was a competent commander but he did not possess the necessary authority.

Logic might suggest that, as Popham had been the first to go to sea, because of his previous experience, he should have stayed out, either at Kinsale or at Plymouth, but the Generals decided to obviate all chance of dispute by drawing lots.[26] Their action shows the trust that existed between them. The result was that Popham went home, Deane drew Plymouth and Blake stayed off Kinsale. Hindsight suggests that this was the right arrangement. Deane was ideally placed at Plymouth to push forward preparations for the Irish campaign, as Cromwell would have wished, and Blake was to demonstrate that he had the tenacity to conduct a long blockade.

Blake welcomed the challenge. Though he was not immune from the common human frailties, he felt the frustrations of long months tossing on the stormy waters of the Atlantic much less than his colleagues. The prospect of a lengthy blockade produced in them longings for their homes and their families. Blake had neither. Soon the fleet was to become the community for which he cared above all other. When the pressure mounted, he did not look for a shoulder to cry on and a home where he could forget his cares for a while. Instead he retired to his cabin and walked in his own private world: a habit which grew on him as he got older.

The ships left off Kinsale were the *Triumph, Charles, Garland, Leopard, Adventure, Hercules, Elizabeth, Nonsuch* and *Rebecca* ketch and Popham was to use his homeward voyage in collecting as many reinforcements as possible.[27] Popham embarked on the *Adventure*. His first task was to find Sir George Ayscue and instruct him to send his two best ships to Kinsale, because the major threat which he had to guard against was now removed. He was then to head for Plymouth and contact Vice-Admiral Moulton. Moulton was to post the *Phoenix* and the *Constant Warwick* in the Western Approaches to protect the shipping lanes and then to sail, with any remaining ships, to Kinsale. Finally Popham was to find other transport at Plymouth so that the *Adventure* could return to Blake.[28] How effective Popham's mission was is hard to gauge. Fleet lists suggest that the two ships Ayscue sent were the *Lion* and a powerful armed merchantman, called the *John*. The *Adventure* was back by the beginning of July, but there is no mention of either the *Victory* or the *Bonadventure*, the other two ships in Moulton's squadron.

Blake soon had his first taste of the Atlantic in an angry mood. There must have been a typical English summer, because June blew in with a violent westerly gale, which forced the blockading squadron to run for the cover of Milford Haven in Wales. Worried that Rupert would use the opportunity to escape, Blake took his ships out as far as Lundy Island on 6 June, but bad weather forced him back to Milford again and it was 20 June before the Commonwealth squadron regained Kinsale. His relief must have been considerable when he found Rupert still there, imprisoned by the same storm which had forced him to take shelter.[29]

The return of the *Adventure* brought news that preparations were sufficiently advanced for Deane's presence to be required at Plymouth and he departed in the *Charles*, leaving Blake to his lonely vigil. At first there was some action to keep the men happy. Rupert brought his ships down the river from the town and seemed to be about to make a determined effort to escape. One frigate, the *Sta Theresa*, was unwise enough to make a run for the open sea at night early in July and was snapped up by the *Adventure*.[30] On board was Sir Hugh

Wyndham, which must have brought back memories of the raid on his house in 1645. Then a Dutchman ran into the welcoming arms of the squadron. He claimed to be a peaceful merchant wanting to trade with Kinsale, but investigations showed that his last port of call was the Scilly Islands, so his ship was sent to Plymouth as prize. As the summer wore on such opportunities became fewer as privateers and legitimate traders alike learned to steer well clear of Blake's frigates. In the words of Robert Coytmor, naval affairs progressed like 'the Egyptian cavalry in the Red Sea'.[31]

The next three months were frustrating. The action was taking place just over the horizon but it was, perversely, reluctant to progress in Blake's direction. Letters from Deane would have told him that the delay caused by the Leveller rebellion had forced Monck to surrender what remained of his position in Ulster, but that the help brought by Ayscue had kindled new hope in Dublin. He would have kept him posted about his consultations with Cromwell at Bristol, and the revised ship dispositions required by the progress of the vital convoy with the all-important siege train from the Thames, round to Portsmouth and on to Plymouth. Perhaps he even detached ships to reinforce Moulton, so that there would be no trouble from the Royalists in the Scillies, on the most dangerous leg of the voyage to Milford.

Then came the momentous news from Dublin. Reinforced by two regiments, shipped from Chester under Ayscue's protection, the Parliamentary Commander Colonel Michael Jones had sallied out from Dublin and totally defeated the besiegers at Rathmines, on 2 August 1649. Dublin could do without the relief Cromwell was preparing at Milford and Jones recommended him to begin his campaign in the south, in Munster.[32] For the next fortnight, Blake must have eagerly anticipated the appearance of Deane's armada, but Nature dashed his hopes. The winds were so persistently adverse, that Cromwell lost patience and the expeditionary force landed in Dublin on 23 August.[33] From there the army turned north and besieged Drogheda.

Cromwell and Deane were disappointed that the change of plan left Blake in lonely isolation. Their original scheme had envisaged a major role for him, a remarkable testimony to the impression he had created. Even now they were reluctant to see him kicking his heels. The very day that the transports were redirected to Dublin from Munster, Deane wrote to Popham, 'I perceive that my Lord Lieutenant will write to the Council of State to move for Colonel Blake to be Major-General of Foot. I wish we may have as honest a man in his room if it be so.'[34] The offer did not reach Blake for another three weeks. Blake informed Popham, in a letter dated 16 September, that Cromwell had invited him 'with much affection to be his Major-General of his foot and telling me that he had written to some friends in London to obtain it'.[35]

Blake's surprise at the offer was genuine. So was his embarrassment. It was an honour that he did not want and he told Popham that, rather than accept the post, he would retire into private life. Faced with such a firm stand, the Council of State left the choice to him. If he did not want to become Major-General of Foot, they were happy for him to stay on as General-at-Sea.[36] The refusal of the honour offered him by Cromwell marks a turning point in Blake's career. He knew that he had found his life's work. At last the Lord had shown him what he must do and he must be constant to the end. When news got out that he had turned down a lucrative army appointment, the effect on the Fleet must have been considerable. Here was a man who really cared for them. This incident shows why Blake was the most popular, if not the most uniformly successful, of all the Generals-at-Sea. Blake was to make heavy demands on those under him, but they responded, because they knew he would never let them down.

There were also negative factors. Blake must have realised that service in Ireland could be a poisoned chalice. Later, when news came of Ireton's death, worn out sweeping up after Cromwell, he must have reflected that, if he had accepted Oliver's offer, he could have been the sacrificial lamb instead. Blake's attitude may well have made Cromwell wonder about the Fleet. Ayscue had done marvellously well in supporting Jones at Dublin but, despite all Cromwell's persuasive power, he had insisted on resigning for personal reasons and returning to England. And now here was Blake spurning one of the most valuable appointments in his gift. Were there political considerations which made Blake want to keep him at arm's length? As his reputation and popularity grew, Cromwell may well have reflected uneasily that Blake owed nothing to him and that he would merit careful observation.

Meanwhile, the war progressed. Drogheda was stormed and at last the focus of the conflict shifted southwards. It was high time. Victuals were running short and for a second time an equinoctial gale forced Blake to raise the blockade. Rupert failed to capitalise on his absence again, but the worsening weather forced Blake to send his older and larger ships home, increasing the likelihood of a Royalist escape in the near future. By 26 September he had been forced to shift his flag to the *Lion* and he had only four other ships with him, the *Garland*, *Elizabeth*, *Nonsuch* and *Guinea*.[37] Careful watch would have to be kept for any ships crossing their yards or beginning to warp down the river from the town towards the sea.

On 3 October, Cromwell reached Wexford and four days later Deane was able to announce the arrival of the siege train. After a bombardment the castle was betrayed into English hands. The repercussions of the swift conclusion to the siege were immediate. On 16 October the English garrison at Cork declared for the Commonwealth and the possibility that Blake's long vigil would be rewarded by the capture of Rupert's entire fleet began to take shape. At the critical moment the weather intervened and Blake was forced to fly for refuge to Milford yet again. Rupert knew that there was no time to be lost and put to sea immediately the weather let up.[38]

When Blake heard of the escape of the Royalists is not known, but he did not hasten back to his station. On 30 October he was conferring with Cromwell at New Ross, about the position at Cork.[39] He sailed from Waterford with the *Nonsuch* and *Guinea* and on 5 November reached Cork, despite being fired on by a fort at the harbour entrance, which was still in Irish hands. Colonels Townsend and Reeves were brought out by water, so that they could give Cromwell first-hand information about the position. Meanwhile, the *Garland* had come into Waterford bay with a valuable prize, and Cromwell took the opportunity to put on board 500 foot, under Lieutenant-Colonel Phaire, to stiffen Cork's garrison. They were hardly under sail, when news came that Youghall had declared for the Commonwealth. Phaire was diverted to Youghall, because it was more exposed to an Irish counter-attack, and Blake promised to fill the void at Cork by providing ships of force to lie there instead.[40]

The campaign was nearing its end. Blake's squadron dispersed. The *Lion* was told off to watch the Shannon and the remainder turned their attention, once more, to the question of Prince Rupert. When the news of his escape became known, Popham had sailed westwards, so that any attempt to repeat the raids of the spring would be countered. Rupert made no such attempt. Instead he made for Portugal so that he could play on the sympathy of the Portuguese for the Royal cause and use Lisbon as a base for further attacks on English shipping. The Council of State had no intention of tolerating such a situation and began preparations for sending a fleet to deal with him once and for all. This time there was no drawing of lots. Blake was named as the General to go south.[41] Deane was sick and Cromwell made it clear that, when he recovered, he wanted him in Scotland. Popham's behaviour suggests that he would not have opposed his friend's selection. Blake would have been content too. He was no doubt eager to try conclusions with Rupert again.

When Blake reflected on his first year at sea his feelings must have been rather mixed. He would have been pleased at the way the ships under his command had responded to his leadership. The captains and seamen had not only submitted to the Commonwealth, they had performed so well that it was difficult to remember how, only a year earlier, there had been a serious mutiny. Much of the credit for the change of heart must go to the Generals, with Blake pre-eminent among them. Already he was repeating, in the naval sphere, his ability to motivate the men who served under him that he had shown in the Army during the Civil Wars. If he viewed the long blockade of Rupert in Kinsale with less satisfaction, yet the operation had played a major part in the success of the campaign. The experience of both Blake and Deane as soldiers had ensured that none of those hitches occurred which so often blighted amphibious operations when soldiers and seamen were expected to function together, who were ignorant of each other's problems. But, in the end, Rupert had got away. The Royalists had braved weather that the Commonwealth's experts had deemed too dangerous.

Blake still had too little experience to question the advice he had been given. Yet he was already beginning to show an unrivalled capacity to finish the tasks allotted to him without being distracted by side issues. Prince Rupert might have escaped him in 1649, but Blake would not be content until his power to make mischief had been completely neutralised.

Portugal

*B*Y the beginning of 1650, King Charles had been almost a year in his grave, a long time in politics. When the news leaked out that the Commonwealth was preparing a fleet to pursue Prince Rupert to the Iberian peninsula, there was much fluttering in diplomatic dovecotes. It was rumoured that the Spanish government was about to recognise the Commonwealth and that the representatives of any country which refused to follow suit would be expelled.

The reports were rather premature but they did reflect the political realities. The Thirty Years War was over, but the Spanish conflict with France continued, and Spain still refused to recognise the independence of Portugal, which had rebelled after eighty years of Spanish rule in 1640. The Spanish government might well be thinking that, if the Commonwealth were recognised and Spanish help offered against Rupert, the embarrassment to Portugal could be serious. There was the prospect, too, that the English would be embroiled further with the French, who were allied to Portugal and who had consistently allowed Royalist privateers to sell their prizes in French ports. The Venetian Ambassador thought that Blake might use his fleet to support the opponents of the French Crown at Bordeaux.[1]

Blake left Cowes Road with fifteen ships on 1 March 1650, rather later than the Council of State had hoped.[2] His flag was in the 2nd rate *George* (56 guns), with Charles Thorowgood as captain. There were two 3rd rates, the *Leopard* (56 guns) and the *Happy Entrance* (46) commanded by his Vice-Admiral, Robert Moulton and his Rear-Admiral, Richard Badiley, respectively. In addition there was another 3rd rate; the *Bonadventure* (42). The Council of State hoped that these four ships would be more than a match for the three powerful vessels Rupert was known to possess.[3] They were supported by five 4th rate frigates. Three of them were from the post Civil War building programme. One of them was the *Assurance* (32) commanded by Benjamin Blake, the General's brother. When he exchanged the Army for the Navy is unknown but he made his first appearance as a captain in 1649 in command of the 5th rate

Paradox.[4] For intelligence and scouting purposes Blake was given the best two 5th rates from before the Civil Wars. The fleet was completed by two fireships and two ketches.[5]

For once Blake was favoured by fair winds. The whole voyage to Portugal took only ten days. The first move was to spy out the land. His lieutenant was sent with a message for the King. He was accompanied by Charles Vane, the Commonwealth agent to Portugal, and Captain Thorowgood, whose task was to see what ships were in port. Thorowgood and the lieutenant were soon back with the news that Rupert's whole fleet was there. In number, the Royal fleet was approximately the same as Blake's, but it was inferior in the power of its individual units.[6]

Blake immediately convened a Council of War. With Rupert present, it was considered unlikely that the King would agree to allow the Commonwealth fleet the free use of the port of Lisbon. A Royalist agent reported that 'Blake has gone to sea with 14 sail besides fireships and resolves to act once more the business of Helvoetsluys, in any Prince's harbour.'[7] All the captains present would have been aware of the precedent too. It was widely believed that Warwick had made a mistake in not attempting to force his way into the port immediately. Blake would not make the same error. The council of war decided to try and sail the fleet up the Tagus and destroy Rupert's ships as they lay at the quays.

The fleet formed up, in line ahead, with Blake leading in the *George*, Moulton in the middle and Badiley bringing up the rear. As soon as the English came within range of Fort St Julian, the Portuguese opened fire. Coastal forts were made of stone, ships of wood. Shore-based batteries were usually more powerful than the guns mounted on ships because solid ground can take more weight. Finally, land-based gunners almost always enjoyed an altitude advantage, so there was the danger that heavy shot would plunge straight through a wooden ship, while the ship would find it very difficult to elevate its guns sufficiently to strike back. Once the Portuguese had made their intentions clear, there was only one thing to do and Blake did it. The English fleet slunk back to sea with its tail between its legs. Perhaps Warwick had been right after all.[8]

The damage that land-based guns could do to his ships was not the only reason Warwick had refrained from an immediate attack. He knew that, in the delicate situation which existed in the United Provinces, outrage at a Parliamentary attack could have played into the hands of the Stadtholder, who was friendly to the Royal cause, and damaged the republican friends of Parliament. There were similar considerations which suggested that a 'softly softly' approach might have borne more fruit with the Portuguese.

The arrival of Rupert in Lisbon had been the last thing King John IV of Portugal wanted. However much sympathy he had with the Royalist cause, he was engaged in a life-and-death struggle with Spain. He needed any allies he could get and it was vital to avoid offending potential enemies. Rupert's action, shortly after his arrival, in sending his brother Maurice to sea to capture any merchant ships he could lay his hands on, called forth anguished protests to which Rupert paid no heed. The Portuguese wanted him to confine his depredations to states hostile to them, which would have limited him to attacking Spanish shipping. They were particularly sensitive to attacks on English shipping, because Portugal depended for its financial existence on the Brazil trade which was largely carried in English bottoms.

The position soon reached impasse, because Rupert could only pay his men as long as he captured prizes, so he could not afford to be choosy. He was not going to keep his hands off the shipping of those who had executed his uncle. Only two days before Blake put in his appearance, the King's secretary had been pointing out to Rupert that he had agreed not to attack the shipping of countries which were in amity with Portugal or those which were neutral; that he had only been guaranteed use of the port for fifteen to twenty days and for four ships not twelve.[9] The attempt by the English to force their way in, played into the hands of the Queen and her friends. They were fervent supporters of Rupert and of the Roman Catholic Church, to whom the religious views of the Commonwealth were anathema.

Perhaps it is too harsh to call the attempt to force the Tagus a blunder. Warwick got no credit for his dextrous handling of the Dutch and Blake's action was what the Commonwealth government would have expected of him, especially in view of the rumours that four French frigates were on their way to reinforce the Royalists. Equally the Council of State would not have been happy with the suggestion of King John, commended by Vane, that if Blake would take the fleet out of sight of the river mouth, the Portuguese would force Rupert to leave. In fact, that was to be the ultimate solution and it would have saved a lot of time and money, if it had happened in March instead of November.[10]

Whatever the rights and wrongs of the attempt to force a way into the Tagus, Blake came to believe, in retrospect, that his next move was a mistake. Vane's support for the King's proposal, that the fleet disappear over the horizon, had commended itself to the English community as little as to Blake, and had undermined his position. In addition, Vane and Rupert were indulging in a slanging match. Rupert accused the Commonwealth fleet of being 'nothing else than a tumultuous, factious soldiery', who were 'the sworn enemies of settled government in Church and State'. Vane replied by calling Rupert a 'vagabond German'.[11]

At a council of war on 13 March, called to consider the King's request that a person of quality should be sent to confer with him about Rupert, it was resolved to send the Vice-Admiral, Robert Moulton. He was instructed to demand the surrender of Rupert's ships on the grounds that they were the property of the Commonwealth of England, which had been stolen. If this were denied, Moulton was to request that Blake's fleet should be allowed to seize them, wherever they should be found. In other words, instead of the Portuguese handing them over, they should allow the Commonwealth fleet in to do the job instead. If that were not acceptable, Moulton was to ask that Rupert be ordered to sea, presumably while the Commonwealth ships were still at the entrance. Finally, if none of these courses of action appealed to the King, he was to ask for permission to use Oeiras Bay for taking on water and as shelter in bad weather.[12]

There was little hope that King John would agree to any of the first three proposals, but he was willing to allow the English the use of Oeiras Bay on the understanding that, while they were in Portuguese waters, they would make no hostile moves against Rupert and that measures would be taken to ensure that no clashes took place between the rival groups of sailors.[13] Blake accepted the offer. The nearest Spanish port was Cadiz and the weather experts in the fleet were forecasting a major storm.[14] Blake feared that, if he were forced to seek cover so far away, Rupert would get out again, as he had from Kinsale the previous October. What he only came to see slowly, was that as long as he accepted favours from the Portuguese, he was in no position to tighten the screw. At Helvoetsluis, Warwick had accepted a similar arrangement but with the difference that he was able to get alongside the Royal ships, so that when the crews of some of them decided to change sides, he was on hand to help. Blake was kept carefully segregated in Oeiras Bay. When the crew of the *Swallow* rebelled, Rupert was able to crush the rising without too much trouble.[15]

Even after the storm had passed and Blake's fleet regained its station, the English were still drawing fresh water from the streams round Oeiras Bay, so that when two French frigates anchored among his fleet, mistaking it for Rupert's, Blake was in a quandary. The political situation made it as logical for France to support the Royalists, as it was for Spain to help the Commonwealth, so Blake did not take seriously the disavowals of the French captains. If he let them go, Rupert would receive valuable reinforcements. If he detained them, King John might well use his action as an excuse for denying him the facilities of Oeiras Bay. With considerable reluctance, Blake released the ships, on the grounds that he was empowered only to attack the shipping of countries actively helping Rupert.

The Royalists were not slow to take advantage of Blake's embarrassing position and King John abetted them. He made no attempt to discipline the Royalists who molested Blake's water parties. Instead he adopted their claim that the need to get water had been used as a cover for an attempt to murder Rupert and Maurice while they were out hunting. Nor did he reprove Rupert for sending an explosive device in a boat disguised as a trader, hoping to get it on board the *Leopard*. A letter from on board the *Happy Entrance* described it as '. . . a small cask fitted with fireworks at one end and oil at the other end; and it went with such a device, that at the handing into the ship, they in the boat pulling at a string which was fast to the spring of a pistol within the cask, it should take fire and burn the ship'.[16] Prince Rupert was to retain an interest in chemistry until after the Restoration, and he was reported to be in a rage when he was told of the failure of his scheme.

The incident convinced Blake that the Portuguese were preparing to support Rupert openly. Charles Vane advised caution. He was worried that English merchants would have their goods expropriated and their ships seized, if Blake made any overt hostile moves. Although Blake was continually urging Vane to get a straight answer from the King, he was reluctant to make the move himself, which would commit him to riding out the blockade in the open sea.[17] In the end Blake wrote home to England for further instructions.

While Blake waited for an answer, relations deteriorated steadily. The attitude of the King of Portugal hardened and, by the end of April, he was imprisoning English merchants of known Commonwealth sympathies, despite the remonstrances of Vane. Blake, now back in the open sea, became less punctilious. Ships were not only stopped but seized, yet the General so steered his course that it was difficult for the King to find an excuse for a complete break.

Towards the end of May, Blake was faced with the tricky problem of what to do about the outward-bound Brazil fleet. If he stopped it, he gave a pretext for a declaration of war, because ships going to Brazil could be of no conceivable assistance to Rupert. After a bit of thought, he held the nine English ships, on the grounds that he needed them for the blockade, but released the nine French and Flemish ones.[18]

Meanwhile Blake's first dispatches had reached England. The parts about the possible reinforcement of Rupert by four French frigates particularly alarmed the Council of State, as it had received information of French attacks on English merchant shipping in the Mediterranean. The decision was quickly taken to send reinforcements, in the form of eight ships commanded by Colonel Edward Popham. Popham had his flag in the *Resolution* (68). With him went the 2nd rate *Andrew* (42), sister ship to the *George*, two 4th rates and four armed merchantmen.[19]

Popham left Plymouth Sound on 15 May and, after a quick passage, joined Blake in Cascais Road on 26 May.[20] He brought his own instructions together with additional ones for Blake. They were quite clear: the Council of State ordered them to destroy Rupert's ships, wherever they were found. They were to attack them in Portuguese ports, if they thought it practicable, because they were pirates with no right of protection by neutral nations. If they were hindered by the King of Portugal, they could attack his trade.[21] After this there could be no further room for parley, and messages were sent recalling Vane. Vane was horrified by the consequences for English merchants. He should have come off on 29 May, but he did not leave his post until two days later, and only then because the Portuguese were seeking to arrest him.[22]

The King of Portugal arrested the goods and ships of English merchants in Lisbon and the fleet was forced to think of ways of sustaining itself in the open sea. Popham wrote gloomily that there was no immediate prospect of capturing Rupert's fleet and that it looked like being a repeat of Kinsale. They would ride out the summer and Rupert would wait until the autumn gales forced them to return home, giving him an opportunity to escape, a remarkably accurate prognosis.[23] The sending of the eight extra ships deprived King John of his best excuse for pushing Rupert out, unless events forced the Generals to weaken their fleet. It was no accident that all the events of the summer happened when the fleet was not at full strength, for one reason or another.

The first problems which Blake and Popham had to face were logistical. With Oeiras Bay closed to them, there would be the ever-present problem of water supplies and there was the looming difficulty of victuals. When Blake left in March his ships had six months' victuals on board. The Council of State, realising that they would expire at the end of July, took the precaution of sending victualling ships with Popham. Unfortunately, when the victuals were examined, they were found to be bad.[24] On 11 June, all hopes of an accommodation being at an end, Vane decided to return to England and two days later he embarked on the *Constant Warwick*. At the same time, Badiley was dispatched with eight ships – the *George, Entrance, Leopard, Adventure, Assurance, Merchant, Tenth Whelp* and one of the ketches – to revictual at Cadiz. At the beginning of July the *Tiger* and the *Providence* were sent to Vigo. The effect of these dispositions was to reduce the Commonwealth strength by half.[25]

King John was increasingly desperate to find some honourable way of getting rid of Rupert. According to Venetian reports, Popham's arrival had forced the Portuguese to recall a large part of their army to Lisbon, leaving the frontiers exposed to Spanish attack. The King's position would be made even worse if the Commonwealth fleet seized the incoming Brazil fleet, whose cargo was needed to provide money for his soldiers.

Blake's and Popham's difficulties gave the King room to manoeuvre. His first move was to try for a compromise. His hand is clearly visible in the scheme put forward, on 22 June, by William Rolles, an official of the Brazil Company. Rolles came to Blake and Popham with an offer from the Company to buy all the Royal ships. In return, Rupert and Maurice were to be allowed to leave freely and none of the shipping using the Tagus was to be molested. The Generals listened politely but rejected the plan firmly. Their instructions specifically enjoined them to attack anyone who bought the ships and they were probably sceptical that Rupert could be brought to accept such a solution, unless the sale was a purely cosmetic transaction.[26]

Negotiation having failed, King John tried a different tack. He collected together as many ships as he could and offered them as a shield. The idea was that the ships would hold off the Commonwealth fleet, while Rupert made a run for the open sea. With Badiley still absent at Cadiz, this was a gambit that the

Royalists could not reject out of hand without losing face. The lookouts in the Commonwealth ships began to note a build-up of ships in Oeiras Bay, beginning on 22 July, and Rupert made his first bid for freedom four days later. The exact odds are hard to calculate. The core of Rupert's fleet were the three powerful ships, the 2nd rates, *Constant Reformation* (52) and *Convertine* (46), and the 3rd rate *Swallow* (40), together with an assortment of frigates, totalling in all 12 ships and 372 guns. Counting the two French frigates and the other ships the King had collected, the total fleet numbered somewhere between 44 and 47 vessels.[27] Of the ships which had remained on guard, Blake and Popham had the *Resolution, Andrew, Phoenix, John, Satisfaction, Expedition, America, Great Luke* and *Cygnet*, plus the *Tiger*, which had returned from Vigo. The total number of guns was about 320. In addition, the Generals could call upon the nine Brazil ships.[28] This still left a considerable disparity on paper.

Despite their numerical superiority, the allied fleet intended to avoid a battle if possible. Rupert was under no illusions about what would happen in a conflict between the Commonwealth ships, manned by experienced seamen hardened by months at sea, and his own men who had been rusting in port. King John did not want a fight either. A defeat would be disastrous and a victory would bring down the wrath of the Commonwealth on his head. Brito de Freire, the captain of the *Na Sa. da Candelaria*, confirmed this analysis. He declared that the plan was for the whole fleet to sail with the morning tide. The Portuguese were to interpose themselves between Rupert and the Commonwealth ships. At dusk, Rupert's squadron was to dowse all lights and steal away, while the Portuguese carried extra lights to deceive the enemy. He does not mention any intention to engage, which would have been contemplated only if no other course remained.[29]

At first, with the wind at ESE, there seemed to be a reasonable chance that the Royalists would make it to the open sea, but soon it turned southerly, forcing them to tack towards the Commonwealth fleet if they wished to weather Cape Espichel.[30] This was just what the Commonwealth Generals wanted. They tried to bring on an engagement because their smaller numbers would be less of a liability in the river mouth than out at sea. The allied fleet attempted to keep their opponents at arm's length, planning to disrupt the Commonwealth fleet by sending in fire-ships. There were two obstacles to success. They needed to wrest the weather gauge from their opponents and they needed to draw them inside a shoal, called the Catchops, which divided the two fleets and made the release of the fire-ships difficult. With this plan in mind, Rupert tried to play a game of cat and mouse. Every time the Parliamentary ships tried to get at the large French frigate and the *Constant Reformation*, which led the Royalist line, they bore away and their manoeuvre was imitated by the rest of the fleet. This happened so many times, that in the end they were facing back up the river.

Blake and Popham and their advisers were not fooled. Use of fire-ships was a well-known strategem and the *Phoenix* had been told off to keep a watchful eye on them. The Generals were also wary of risking a ship like the *Resolution*, which drew so much water, among shoals on a lee shore, so when the leadsman reported only 10 fathoms of water, the chase was called off. 'We finding the night draw on, and Indraft there,' wrote Popham to Sir Henry Vane, 'and ourselves like to be engaged within the Catchops, and upon a lee shoare, were advised by all that were acquainted with the place to stande off againe; and they came to an anchor some within the Catchops and some betweene them, and we stood off to sea under short sail all night . . .'[31]

When the next day dawned, the wind came up easterly, the most favourable quarter for an attempt at escape, but the allied fleet made no move. All the Generals could do was send the *Assurance* snapping at their heels, but even this irritant was not enough to move them. The *Assurance* had rejoined the fleet the previous evening. Rupert may have known that it was one of the Cadiz squadron and guessed that Badiley was not far away. The other seven ships of the squadron arrived the next day and the allied fleet straggled back to Lisbon.[32]

After this failure Rupert was not keen to try again while the whole fleet was there. He was confident that, if he was patient, the Commonwealth would have to raise the blockade, or at least weaken the forces off the Tagus, letting him out and the Brazil fleet in. His confidence was far from misplaced. The need to ride at sea had damaged the fleet of Blake and Popham very severely. The victuals crisis had only been partially solved by the month-long absence of Badiley at Cadiz. Worst of all was the water situation. Badiley reported that one third of all the supplies which he had taken on board at Cadiz had been lost due to leaky casks.[33]

On 14 August, a dispatch arrived from England on board the *Constant Warwick*, which now rejoined the fleet. The Council of State was getting restive over the lack of action. It complained of the loss of a valuable carrack to privateers. It bemoaned the excessive cost of keeping so many ships off Portugal and suggested that, as rich ships from Brazil were known to be rendezvousing in the Azores, part of the fleet should be sent there.[34] The Generals rejected the scheme because the shortage of drinking water made it impossible. They used the Council's complaints about cost as a justification for Popham's taking home the *Resolution, Andrew, Entrance, Satisfaction, Great Lewis, Tiger, America* and *Cygnet*.[35] Blake shifted his flag back to the *George*. He too was to come home, if nothing happened within a month.

Popham left on 3 September, to load supplies at Cadiz for his voyage home. His ships had only just disappeared over the horizon, when Rupert made his second bid for freedom. Blake's own account is in his usual laconic style. Prince Rupert's fleet, thirty-six strong, was sighted at 4 pm, in misty conditions.

> I had only with me the *Phoenix* and *Expedition* having lost the rest in the fog. By God's good providence, the enemies fleet was all to the leeward of

us, so we keeping the wind made toward them being resolved to encounter Prince Rupert, who was the headmost of the fleet. Coming within reach, we gave him a broadside, so did the two frigates, which the Lord was pleased so to Direct that his foretopmast was shot off by the cap. Whereupon he bore up into the midst of the fleet and the thick mist taking them again out of our sight, we stood off to seek the rest of our squadron, which we met with the next day.[36]

Richard Gibson in his account turned the affair into a game of 'chicken'.

Prince Rupert in the *Constant Reformation* with his fleet and several French ships of war quits Lisbon, and in a fog meets with General Blake in the *St. George* and they stand stem to stem, endeavouring to weather one the other. Captain Arkinstal, master under the General, tells him that he believed they could not weather Prince Rupert, advised him to tack in time. Says the General, 'Can you stem him?' 'Yes', says the Master; 'but then we shall hazard both ships.' The General replied, 'I'll run that hazard rather than bear up for the enemy.' Upon which Rupert was forced to bear up.[37]

This was the sort of story which began to build Blake's legendary reputation as it circulated round the fleet. Gibson claims to have been on board the *Tenth Whelp* fire-ship, so he would have been on the cruise but not actually present. His description fits Blake's own account but significantly misses out the fact that Rupert was forced to bear up because his foretopmast was shot away, not because he lost his nerve. Nonetheless, Rupert had had enough and, being unable to see how far away the remaining ships in Blake's squadron were, retreated to the safety of the Tagus again. It says much for the impression that the Commonwealth fleet had made under Blake's leadership, that in July over forty ships had run away from nineteen and now thirty-six refused to engage just three, because the mist might obscure one or two more.

Just a week later, the financial pay-off for the long wait took place. Early on Saturday morning 14 September, the English sighted the incoming Brazil fleet. A chase took place and over half the ships failed to make it to the safety of the Tagus. The haul included 4000 chests of sugar and 4000 prisoners. The Admiral managed to get away to Setubal. Benjamin Blake was in the thick of the fight. The *Assurance* took on the Vice-Admiral but, after the English boarded her, she caught fire and sank. Blake, in the *George*, engaged the Rear-Admiral. The battle lasted three hours. Portuguese galleons were notoriously tough and the rolling sea made it impossible for the English to run out the bigger guns in the ship's lower tier. According to Portuguese sources, ten ships out of twenty-three reached Lisbon. In addition to the ship sunk by the *Assurance*, the English claimed seven prizes. What happened to the other five is not quite clear. They may have taken refuge in some of the smaller ports outside the estuary. The bad state of the prizes suggests that those which were attacked put up sufficient resistance to absorb the entire energy of Blake's ships, thus allowing the remainder to escape.[38]

The decision of the Portuguese Admiral to try and evade the blockade must be accounted an extremely rash one. Only the previous month the *Constant Warwick* had intercepted a big East Indiaman off the Rock of Lisbon, and captured her after a five-hours fight. If a 4th rate could force their biggest East Indiaman to strike, in ship to ship combat, the Admiral must have known that he had little chance if his ships fell in with the English fleet. Popham's departure may have misled him into believing that the whole English fleet had gone. Or perhaps he reasoned, as Blake did when arguing with Mountagu in 1656, that if the wind was right and the ships scattered, most of them would make it to the Tagus.

Now that the worst had happened, Blake had to recognise that there was no further way in which he could pressure the Portuguese into allowing him to get at Rupert. Early in October, the extra month being up, the entire Commonwealth squadron sailed for Cadiz in order to get supplies and effect repairs before embarking on the journey home. It was almost ready to sail when dispatches arrived from England in the *Hopewell*, ketch.[39] Their contents are unknown. The Council of State was worried about French attacks on English shipping in the Straits of Gibraltar, as well as about Rupert. The orders seem to have instructed Blake to send home most of the ships under Badiley, but to remain out himself, with half a dozen of the fittest, until he could be replaced by a new fleet under Penn, which was preparing for sea. Badiley took his own ship, the *Happy Entrance, George, Assurance, Hercules* and *Merchant*, and the four prizes, which were fit enough to make the voyage. The *Leopard* was to follow as soon as necessary repairs to her masts had been completed. This left the *Bonadventure, Phoenix, Elizabeth, Expedition, Constant Warwick* and *John.*[40]

Blake wasted no time in carrying out his new instructions. Badiley had hardly left on his homeward voyage than he shifted his flag to the *Phoenix*. Leaving the other frigates to complete their careening, he put to sea in search of a squadron of four French frigates, which had been destroying English shipping in the Straits. The details of this short cruise are obscure but Blake succeeded in capturing a powerful French frigate, commanded by the Chevalier de Lalande. Lalande surrendered without a fight even though his ship had 40 guns to the *Phoenix*'s 32; yet another indication of the awe in which the English ships were held.[41]

As soon as Blake returned to Cadiz, news reached him that Rupert had been out since 12 October. He had cruised off the Tagus for a few days, before deciding that the Mediterranean held out the best prospects for merchant prizes. Rupert and Badiley must have passed close to each other, suggesting that Rupert believed the entire fleet had returned to England. Blake put to sea immediately with his entire squadron, without waiting to complete the fitting out of the French frigate which he had just brought in.

At first Blake was uncertain about where Rupert had gone but, on 28 October, he heard that Rupert's fleet had been seen off Malaga, inside the Straits of Gibraltar, and the chase was on. Two days later Blake was at Malaga, where he was told by indignant merchants that Rupert had sunk four merchantmen off Veles Malaga, after promising not to molest them, and then shaped his course for Alicante. Blake wasted no time; he was in and out of Malaga in two hours. On 2 November, a Frenchman was captured from whom he learned that the Royalists were just to the northward.

Shortly afterwards, four Royalist ships with two prizes were sighted. Watchers on the Spanish coast were treated to the rare spectacle of the Commonwealth ships in full cry, crowding on all sail after the Royalists who were trying desperately to reach the safety of Carthagena harbour, before their pursuers closed with them. The *Henry* was overhauled and captured off Cape de Paulo on 3 November. The next day the leading Commonwealth ship, the *John*, began to gain on the *Black Prince* so rapidly that its captain, John Goulding, was obliged to run his vessel on shore and then burn it to prevent Saltonstall's men landing and taking it. The other four managed to make the harbour just in time.[42]

At first it seemed that Blake was to be frustrated at Carthagena, as he had been at Lisbon. When he attempted to follow the Royalists into the harbour, the forts at the harbour entrance fired on him, but Spain was not Portugal. At Blake's insistence, the Governor sent to Madrid for instructions. To make doubly sure, Blake himself also wrote to the King.[43] Spain was about to recognise the Commonwealth and the mere fact that the Royalists had been helped by the Portuguese was enough to ensure the enmity of the King of Spain, who was anxious to do something for the Commonwealth in reparation for the murder of their agent, Anthony Ascham, by a Royalist, a short time before.

The Royalists decided to make a dash for freedom while they still could. They chose to make their attempt during the night of 6–7 November, hoping that darkness and the stormy weather would cover their exit. Their chances of escaping the guns of Blake's squadron, even in darkness, could not have been high. In the event, he did not have to do anything. Navigating an unknown harbour at night is not easy at the best of times. The Royalists made such a hash of it that, in their attempts to evade Blake's squadron, all of their ships were wrecked. Everything was lost, wrote the disconsolate officers to Cottington and Hyde, 'but 46 packs of cloth and 16 bags of pepper', and even these had been impounded by the Alcalde.[44]

The only disappointment was that the *Constant Reformation* and the *Swallow* were not present. Blake learned from the crew of the *Henry* that Rupert had gone off with four ships, appointing a rendezvous at Formentera, one of the Balearic Islands. Blake kept the rendezvous but, forewarned perhaps, Rupert did not put in an appearance. Instead he left written directions for another rendezvous at Cagliari, which Blake treated with great suspicion, because he could just make out another place scratched out underneath. After a fruitless cruise round Majorca, he abandoned the search on 23 November, opining that Rupert had gone to Villafranca or Toulon. He was right: Rupert had gone to Toulon. Blake wrote, 'I should have accounted it my greatest outward happiness if in recompense for all the charge this Commonwealth hath been at, I could have put a final conclusion thereto by the total destruction of that Piratical crew, but the will of God being otherwise I must acquiesce in it.'[45] They were never caught. The *Swallow* was lost with all hands in a storm off Terceira in 1651, but Rupert and the *Constant Reformation* survived an adventurous cruise, which took him to the West Indies and ended at Brest in 1653, where he sold his prizes and the ship was broken up.

Despite this, the task Blake had been sent to do had been effectively completed off Carthagena. Though only four of Rupert's eight ships had been destroyed, the Royal fleet ceased to exist as an entity. Even more important, the Mediterranean nations now had to reckon that the Commonwealth's power to retaliate, if they assisted Rupert, was formidable. Spain at last took the step that the Venetians had been prophesying all year. An Ambassador was despatched to London, with instructions to apologise for the murder of Ascham and offer suitable compensation. Supporters of the Stuarts were to be expelled and Commonwealth ships offered the facilities of Spanish harbours. In the longer term, the expedition laid the foundations of a policy which was to last for three hundred years. 'Wafters' had been appointed to convoy English ships as far as the Straits of Gibraltar for two hundred years but the successive fleets commanded by Blake, Penn, Hall, Appleton and Badiley were the first concerted attempt to extend protection to English ships trading in the Mediterranean.[46]

Yet one senses a growing dissatisfaction in Blake's mind about the way the blockades of 1649 and 1650 had been handled. The conventional wisdom, by which he had been guided, was insufficient. His conduct of the blockade showed no original tactical features. What distinguished him from his predecessors was the tenacity with which he stuck to his task. It was imperative to find ways of making the blockade more rigorous and everything pointed to the need for steps, which no council of war of captains would willingly accept. His captains needed firm handling if they were to be welded into the fighting machine he needed. Six years were to elapse before Blake had to put his mind to the problems of blockade again, but the events of 1656–7 were to show that he had learned the lessons of 1649–50.

Blake started for home in the early days of the New Year and presented his account to the House of Commons on 13 February 1651, having been away over eleven months.[47] The Journals record that the M.P.s thanked him and voted him £1000. It was largely due to his efforts that the Royalists ceased to be a naval threat and became no more of a nuisance than any number of other privateers that swarmed out of Ostend, Dunkirk, Jersey and the Scilly Islands. To do something effective about them was his next task.

The Scillies and Jersey

*T*HE fleet dispositions for 1651 reflected the belief of the Council of State, correct as it proved, that no pitched battles were to be expected. Neither of the 1st rates was to be made ready and only four 2nd rates, but every ship of 4th rate or lower was to be sent to sea.[2] Colonel Deane was to command in the North Sea, as he had done the previous year, assisting the army in Scotland wherever possible. Colonel Popham was to remain in the Downs, keeping an eye on the international situation and the position in the Channel Islands. Blake was destined for the Irish Sea. The Commonwealth government was worried about the possibility of a combination between the Scots and the Irish, which if allowed to develop unchecked would hamper the operations of Ireton and paralyse merchant traffic in the Irish Sea. The focus of the trouble was the Isle of Man, still in Royalist hands, and Blake's task was to capture it.[3]

The ships Blake was given reflected the operations he was expected to undertake.[4] There was one 4th rate of post-war vintage, the *Phoenix*, commanded by John Taylor, which Blake used as his flagship. She was supported by the *Constant Warwick* and the *Providence*, both classed as 4th rates but smaller than the *Phoenix*. All three were ships known to handle well and ideal for catching privateers. The remaining capital ships were two armed merchantmen and the *Crowned Lion*, a Royalist prize captured during the Lisbon blockade. The squadron was completed by a number of small vessels suitable for inshore work, scouting and carrying dispatches.

Blake was not destined to reach the Isle of Man, because events forced the Commonwealth to deal with the Scilly Islands first. The Royalist governor of the islands, Sir John Grenville, had been behaving in exactly the same way as Prince Rupert. In order to get money to pay his garrison, he had been equipping privateers and sending them to sea, to attack merchant shipping in the Western Channel. His captains had not confined themselves to Commonwealth shipping. Everything was grist to their mill. On 27 December 1650, the deputies of the State of Holland complained in the States General that in recent months twenty-eight Dutch ships had been captured by Royalist privateers operating from the

Scilly Islands. They moved that Charles II's resident ambassador, McDowell, be summoned and presented with a demand for the return of the ships and their cargoes. The States General agreed and instructed the Lieutenant Admiral of the United Provinces, Martin Harpertszoon Tromp, to confer with representatives of the Provinces' ten Admiralties, about the dispatch of a squadron of ten ships to the Scillies. This proved difficult to implement immediately, but in January the Amsterdam admiralty sent Captain Evert Anthonissen to sea and he was quickly followed by Captain Cornelis Evertsen of the Rotterdam admiralty.[5]

Meanwhile efforts were made to defuse the situation. The Duke of York intervened and wrote to Grenville. Grenville in his turn dispatched his personal envoy, the Bishop of Down, to the United Provinces. These diplomatic exchanges were to no avail because Grenville was not prepared to admit that he had done anything wrong or to make any reparation. He maintained that the ships were all taken by Royalist privateers regularly equipped with letters of marque issued to merchants who had lost ships and goods to Dutch privateers. For sheer effrontery, impertinence and stupidity, Grenville's attitude is hard to rival. The Dutch had given the Royalists supplies during the First Civil War; had sheltered their fleet during the Second Civil War; and were now giving asylum to the Prince of Wales and the Duke of York. Sir George Carteret, the Governor of Jersey, could make a handsome profit out of privateering, without stirring up international incidents, and there seems no reason why Grenville could not have done so too.

The Dutch were, not unnaturally, furious. Tromp was ordered to sea to seek restitution, by force if necessary. He was off the Scilly Islands by the end of March, but due to sluggish preparations he had with him only the ships of Captains Uyttenhout and Dorrevelt, which had relieved Anthonissen as guards for merchant shipping using the Western Channel. The three ships entered St Mary's Road on 30 March, and demanded reparation. All Tromp got was a letter, delivered by an English nobleman, containing 'inopportune compliments'. A captain was sent on shore to get a straight answer. Grenville allowed him to negotiate the release of two groups of Dutch prisoners but again evaded the issue of compensation.

Tromp's growing belief that nothing was to be gained from Grenville without the use of force, was confirmed by a report from Captain Uyttenhout who had just recaptured an Enkhuisen ship from a Scilly privateer. The rescued men had informed Uyttenhout that many of the disputed ships had already been condemned and sold, together with their cargoes, for sums well below their real value, so that Grenville was in no position to return the ships or to pay full compensation. Grenville did not fear a blockade. There were six or seven different exits, three of which had deep water right up to the cliffs. He calculated that Tromp would be unwilling to commit himself to an all-out assault. In the short run he was right. Tromp could do nothing until he had his full squadron with him, and even then he would need soldiers to mount an attack. When the three

Dutch ships disappeared over the horizon, he must have congratulated himself on the success of his intransigent attitude. What he did not realise was that Dutch activity would inevitably attract the attention of the Commonwealth.

The Council of State was finally stirred to activity by a letter from Colonel James Disbrowe, who held general responsibility for military security in the West Country, detailing the close interest Tromp was taking in the Royalist stronghold and containing the news of the interception, by Royalist privateers, of a ship carrying Colonel Sadler, Colonel Le Hunt and Lieutenant Colonel Axtell on their way from Waterford to London to report on the situation in Ireland.[6] On 1 April, the Council wrote to Blake, instructing him to 'repair with speed to Scilly and there meet with the squadron, under Sir George Ayscue, and put into effect the instructions annexed.' These ordered him to

> require of van Tromp what he intends in the Scillies. If it is prejudicial to the Commonwealth, you are to make him desist, by force if necessary, but it is not the intention of this commonwealth to protect those who are now in possession of Scilly, in the wrongs they have done the Dutch, or to hinder them from righting themselves upon them, so that they act nothing to the prejudice of the commonwealth.[7]

The arrival of the orders cut short a brief rest in Somerset. On 24 March, Blake was the guest at a public reception in Taunton, where 'for his faithful service to the commonwealth by Land and Sea, he was entertained with much love and affection by the inhabitants of the town and also by the officers and soldiers of the Army.'[8] The orders, to Captain Taylor of the *Phoenix*, to take his ship from Portsmouth to Plymouth and there report to General Blake, if he was present, and to Sir George Ayscue, if he was not, suggests that Blake wasted no time and travelled directly to Plymouth.[9]

The exact composition of the forces at Blake's disposal are difficult to sort out as the only ship mentioned in the accounts is the *Phoenix*. Tromp estimated the English at sixteen when he saw them on 18 April. Other accounts give between fourteen and twenty-two, the variation probably being accounted for by troop transports. The core of the force was the expedition under Sir George Ayscue, intended ultimately to bring Barbados back under the control of the mother country. Ayscue had a compact force of six ships. He flew his flag in the 2nd rate *Rainbow* (52) supported by the *Amity* (34), a prize bought into the Navy, and four armed merchantmen.[10]

How many of the ships of Blake's Isle of Man squadron were present, besides the *Phoenix*, is more problematical. All but three of them can be shown to be elsewhere so the balance may well have been made up by the five ships under Captain William Brandley in the *Portsmouth*, one of the brand new frigates just launched.[11] They are mysteriously listed as on special duty, somewhere in the Irish Sea, and it is conceivable that the special duty was an attack on the Scilly Islands.

The number of soldiers carried is similarly difficult to assess. Tromp gave the total as 2000 and so did the Bishop of Down.[12] English newspaper reports mention 900–1000 foot, many of them newly raised, under the command of Lieutenant-Colonel William Clarke.[13] The arms listed for the Barbados ships seem to envisage a force of 500 men.[14] Tromp may well have included the seamen who took part in the fighting in his estimate.

The little armada sailed from Plymouth on 12 April and was off the Scilly Islands three days later. Blake was fortunate to have Ayscue as his subordinate, not just because he was a most capable officer. The first service he did that history has recorded, was to take a leading role, as captain of the *Expedition*, in the capture of the Scilly Islands in 1646. His sage advice led Blake to concentrate his attention on the islands of Tresco and Bryher, instead of making an immediate direct assault on St Mary's. Ayscue wrote, 'the two islands command the road, as well as St Mary's and the gaining of those Islands would render St Mary's useless to the enemy ... so that the men-of-war belonging to those piratical rocks, will be like mice that run from a falling house, and must be forced to seek a new rendezvous: neither can St Mary's exist without them.'[15]

Grenville was well aware that Tresco was his Achilles heel. The main harbour of New Grimsby was protected by two frigates, the *Michael* and the *Peter*, and the island was garrisoned with as many men as he could spare. Careful reconnaissance and an attempt to probe the harbour defences convinced Blake, Ayscue and Clarke, that New Grimsby was too strong to be attempted but there was an abandoned harbour called Old Grimsby, on the other side of the island, which was only defended by earthworks and which was too large to be covered by crossfire.[16] A landing there looked more practicable. Once ashore, the defences would be turned and the superior numbers of the Parliamentarians would ensure that the whole island would soon be theirs.

At a Council of War on 16 April, it was decided to attack early the following morning. One half of the force was to land in the harbour and the remainder, a short way down the coast at Stony Bay. The assault got off to a bad start, when the men in the Old Grimsby contingent came under fire and in their eagerness to get out of the vulnerable boats, landed on the island of Northwithiel, which their pilots, disoriented by the morning mist, mistook for the mainland.[17] The pilots of the Stony Bay half made an even worse hash of it. The boats wallowed about in choppy seas for hours, so that the soldiers became seasick and were then carried by the tide into Old Grimsby harbour.[18] All chance of surprise was lost, many of the men were ill and there was no diversion to draw the defenders' attention. Subjected to a hail of shot, most of the boats turned and fled. One party did manage to land but the defence was ably conducted by Colonel Wogan and, despite the brave personal example of Colonel Clarke, it was forced to

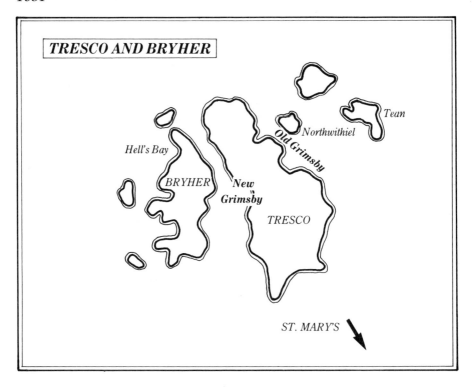

TRESCO AND BRYHER

Tean

Northwithiel

Old Grimsby

Hell's Bay

BRYHER

New
Grimsby

TRESCO

ST. MARY'S

withdraw and row off. The result was a repulse and the attackers, retreating in confusion under the covering fire of the fleet, were lucky to get off with the loss of only six men and one shallop.

The rival accounts produced later suggest that there were recriminations between the soldiers and seamen about the failure, and the camp on the small island of Tean cannot have been very cheerful that night.[19] Blake was not the man to give up easily and immediately began planning a second attempt. He probably realised that the real culprits were the guides and that raw recruits, who had been once broken, needed careful nurturing before their confidence could be restored. This time the leading boats were to be filled with seamen. Seamen made good soldiers, if the fighting was short or plunder was in prospect. They could also sound their way in, so that guides would be unnecessary.

A stretch of shoreline was chosen about three-quarters of a mile from the site of the earlier repulse. Once again the attack took place in the early morning. Eighty men were posted on Northwithiel and fires were left burning on Tean to mislead the Royalists.[20] They gained the attackers only a short respite, because this time there was no mist and the Royalists sighted them before they were half way across. Fortunately there was a flat calm, so the two frigates at New Grimsby were unable to interfere.[21] The initial landing was hotly contested but the advanced guard of seamen under Captain Lewis Morris stood their ground long enough for sufficient soldiers to be landed, to drive the enemy back. According to the Bishop of Down, a fierce charge took place 'even to the club musket ... they overpowered our men with multitudes and the strength of their pikes.' The Royalists lost between 4 and 12 killed and the Parliamentarians took 167 prisoners. One further disaster took place. That night Grenville and his remaining men made their way secretly to boats, which would convey them back to St Mary's, but such was the mad rush that forty men were drowned. The island of Tresco surrendered the next day and both frigates fell into Parliamentary hands. They were added to the Navy and renamed *Tresco* and *Bryher*.

At this point Tromp reappeared with his full squadron of ships, and sent Captain Cornelis Evertsen, on board the *Phoenix*, to inquire about the position of affairs. Some commentators have related a later letter from Tromp to Blake, of 2 June 1652, in which he asks for the return of a ship for 'our former friendship sake', to the Scilly Islands encounter, and have suggested that Tromp offered his assistance in their subjugation. If any such offer was made, it was politely refused and Evertsen was able to report to Tromp that the Commonwealth had the situation well under control. The Dutch squadron sailed away and did not return until after Grenville's final submission.[22]

That there was no immediate surrender was largely owing to the obstinacy of Grenville, who may have hoped that some Scottish miracle would enable him to survive. After a month of haggling and hesitating, even he was forced to agree with the Bishop of Down that they had not a friend left in the world and that they had best close with the terms being offered by the Commonwealth, before they were withdrawn. The capitulation, when it came, was far more generous than a man of Grenville's rapacity had any right to expect. The garrison was to march off with drums beating and flags flying. If they did not have enough transport of their own, Blake undertook to provide them with one ship of 300 tons to take them wherever they wished to go. The officers could go in peace and they were allowed up to nine months to settle their affairs in the islands. All the inhabitants were to have liberty of person, immunity of property and all their former privileges. There was to be an act of indemnity, a moratorium on all debts and Blake and Clarke were to pay Grenville £1000 for the ordnance left in the castle.[23] Appropriately, the agreement was carried up to London by Colonel Sadler, Colonel Le Hunt and Lieutenant-Colonel Axtell, who had been freed from their confinement in St Mary's Castle cellar.

The Scilly Islands agreement is a monument both to Blake's humanity and to his good sense. The conflict was terminated without further bloodshed, the population was conciliated and there was little left for the Royalist soldiers to do wherever they went. The Bishop of Down wrote dismally that their probable destination would be Ireland and he felt less safe there than he did at St Mary's, even when under Commonwealth attack, which suggests that he had little love of his see.[24] The Council of State endorsed what Blake had agreed in its name. The Commonwealth was magnanimous to all fallen foes – except when the fighting was in Ireland.

Blake got back to Plymouth on 28 June, after shepherding the last of the Irish from the Scilly Islands to Kinsale. If he had hoped to turn his attention to the Isle of Man, he was destined to disappointment. The war in Scotland was on the move again. Cromwell had cleverly exploited his command of the Firth of Forth by using Deane's ships to land men at Inverkeithing, getting between the Scots and the Highlands and making their position untenable. They had no choice but to retreat southwards into England. When the Council of State understood what was happening, it took measures to deal with the unwelcome guests. Major-General Disbrowe was ordered into the Midlands, to organise a warm reception and to liaise with Cromwell's army, which was hot on the heels of the Scots. So Blake was ordered to go on shore and fill Disbrowe's shoes, while he was away.[25] All he could do was dispatch the *Little President* and the *Nicodemus* to reinforce the ships already on the station.[26]

The emergency made it impossible for Blake to refuse the land appointment thrust upon him, though he must have made it clear, privately, that he wanted to go back to sea as soon as the crisis was over. His return was quicker than he could have expected, though the reason must have filled him with great sadness. On 22 August, after only twelve days in command, and with the Scots marching through Warrington, he received a letter from the Council of State with new orders. 'General Popham having lately died, you must forthwith go to sea in person to keep those affairs in good order, and to prevent an impression which may be made on the seaman by misrepresentation of affairs.'[27]

Popham is a shadowy figure and his influence on Blake is difficult to ascertain. A warm comradeship had developed during the Civil Wars, and Blake no doubt valued his friend's experience of the sea but it is difficult to identify anything with his personal imprint on it, except for the decision to abolish the observation of Lent and Fridays in the food allowances. His journals do not help as they are just a log of ship movements. He did his job conscientiously but without evident enthusiasm. He was only too willing to leave Kinsale to Blake and to go home, as soon as he decently could, from Lisbon. Perhaps his attitude was conditioned by a growing distaste for his political masters or perhaps he was ruing the day that Blake had thrust greatness upon him. He was not an old man and neither his journal nor his letters suggest bad health. In one of his own letters, Blake says that he died of a fever, which could happen to anyone in the seventeenth century. Deane was superintending affairs in Scotland and was soon to be commander-in-chief there. Colonel George Monck, who was appointed General-at-Sea in Popham's place, showed so little interest in his new honour, that he did not go to sea until February 1653. So the result of Popham's death was to leave Blake the only General-at-Sea still active.

Blake was instructed to proceed with all haste to the Downs.[28] The chief danger, as the Council of State saw it, was that Continental states might try and capitalise on any confusion caused by the march of the Scots and land an expeditionary force to help restore the monarchy. He ran up his flag on the *Victory* in Plymouth Sound, and reached his new station on 2 September.[29] The crisis he was sent to handle lasted one more day. On 3 September, the whole Scottish army surrendered after the battle of Worcester.

The final defeat of the Scots released Blake from the Downs and made possible the capture of Jersey. As usual the ships for the Winter Guard came out in penny numbers, making the dispositions laid out in the fleet list impossible to arrange immediately, so the Council of State decided to utilise those which got to sea first for the Jersey operation, while they were waiting for their consorts.

The *Victory* went in to Chatham and Blake shifted his flag to the *Happy Entrance*. He was given four ships which were ultimately to go to the Mediterranean, headed by Richard Badiley in the 2nd rate *Paragon*, and one of the two ships destined for Virginia. To them were added two new frigates, fresh off the slipway, and the *Tresco*, which were intended for the Western Channel. The fleet was completed by three smaller vessels, one of which, the *Hart*, should have been guarding the North Sea fishery. The other two do not figure in the fleet list at all.[30]

Blake sailed west and reached Weymouth on 27 September.[31] Preparations for the invasion were put in hand immediately. The soldiers to be used were the infantry regiment commanded by Colonel James Heane, six companies of Hardress Waller's foot and two troops of horse, commanded by Captains West and Magerum; in all about 2000 men.[32] The embarkation took place on 15 October and the expedition, which numbered eighty sail, most of them transports, left Weymouth two days later.

Blake knew that time was not on his side. Nearly all the ships he had were earmarked for other tasks and the Council of State would not want them to be kicking their heels off Jersey for long. There was the weather to consider too. Winter was approaching and the season of the equinoctial gales was upon them. The Channel Islands, with their strong tides, were no place to be in bad weather. Blake would have remembered Popham telling him about his mishap off Guernsey. As if to underline the problems he faced, the expeditionary force was only two leagues from the shore, when gale force winds blew them back. A second effort, two days later, was more successful and the task force arrived off Jersey on 20 October, after having spent the hours of darkness anchored off Sark.[33]

Blake cast anchor in St Ouen's Bay about noon, and an officer went on shore, with a flag of truce, but Sir George Carteret, the Royalist commander, had it fired on.[34] The delay off Sark had given him time to call out the militia, which gave him a force of infantry 2000 strong. He also managed to augment them with 300 horse and six small field pieces. It looked better than it was.[35] He did not dare let the Parliamentarians talk with representatives of the militia. If they were offered terms like those given to the Scilly Islands, they would accept them immediately. Carteret hoped against hope that winter would come to his assistance, if he could hold Blake off for a short time, and that the respite would enable him to get reinforcements from France. As if to confirm the correctness of Carteret's calculations, high seas during the afternoon prevented Blake from attempting a landing. The Commonwealth commanders had to confine themselves to taking their ships inshore and bombarding the Royalist positions.[36] The militia were so scared that they hid behind the sand dunes, but the officers put a brave face on it by showing themselves to the Commonwealth ships as though nothing was amiss, which did much to restore their men's courage. Next day, to Carteret's disappointment the weather improved and Blake began the game of cat-and-mouse that finally broke the Royalist resistance.

Blake's first move was to sail round the south-west of Jersey to St Brelade's Bay, to attempt a landing there. Once Carteret was sure that the move was not just a feint, he marched his men across the neck of rock, which separates the two bays, and was in position long before the ships could round the dangerous Corbière Rocks.[37] The natural fortifications of St Brelade's Bay were much stronger than those of St Ouen's, so no landing was attempted. For the whole of 22 October, Blake remained cruising off St Brelade's Bay, sending the smaller frigates into St Aubin's and St Clement's Bays to shoot up the shipping and alarm the islanders, so that they would force Carteret to disperse his troops.

Carteret was an old campaigner, not easily deflected by civilian complaints, and Blake realising that time was short, called a council of war. The result was that, on 23 October, the fleet sailed back round the Corbière Rocks to St Ouen's Bay. The idea was to attempt a landing there and the soldiers were put into the boats at 5 am, ready for action. Unfortunately, with the weather deteriorating again, the ships were forced to give such a wide berth to the underwater hazards off the Corbière Rocks that Carteret had countermarched his men across the neck of land before the ships were in position. High tide had passed and the bay shelved only gradually so that the boats would ground a good way out on a falling tide. Reluctantly the landing was called off, but Blake was far from beaten and he was determined to try again on the evening tide.

The day was occupied by the fleet sailing towards Grand Etaquerel, at the north end of St Ouen's Bay (L'Etac of the accounts), and then back again. The manoeuvre had to be executed carefully, because there were rocks just under the surface there too, and a dangerous sandbank to seaward. The movement was

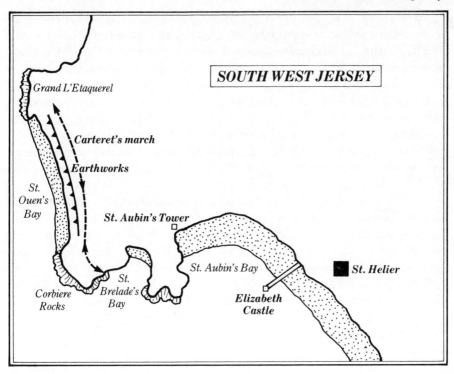

SOUTH WEST JERSEY

more than a time filler. St Ouen's Bay had earthworks for its entire length, but they were only useful if occupied by defenders, and there were practicable landing points all the way along. Carteret was forced to march his men, through the whole of a wet and stormy day, parallel with the Commonwealth fleet to make sure that any attempt at a landing was opposed. By the time they arrived back at their starting point, the militiamen were exhausted, soaked to the skin and in no condition to oppose a determined assault.[38]

Carteret was alive to the danger of a landing during the evening but when high tide, at 9 pm, passed without incident, the Royalists relaxed. Carteret sent the horse inland to forage and bivouacked the foot on the foreshore. An hour later he discerned a large ship working her way in by putting out her anchors and then hauling on the cable. All the local seamen assured him the ship could not get close enough inshore at that state of the tide but the appearance of other ships through the gloom convinced him that the long awaited attack was upon them, so he recalled the horse and tried to muster the local militia.

The timing of the attack was quite deliberate. Either side of high tide the currents in St Ouen's Bay were very strong and the boats might have ended up anywhere in the dark. There was the added consideration that the Royalists would not be prepared for such a late attack. Blake anticipated the difficulty Carteret's seamen had foreseen. Some of the transports drew as much as seven feet of water and would ground a good way out, so he put a large number of smaller vessels in the vanguard of the assault. They did not carry many men but they could get closer in. According to a Royalist account they were connected by 'great bridges' to the larger transports behind. Even so, many of the infantry had to swim the last stretch. Mindful of what had happened on Tresco, the forlorn hope which led the way was composed of seamen, commanded by Captain Dover of the *Eagle*.

Carteret's attempt to assemble the foot was a miserable failure. They all fled. He managed to muster only about a third of the horse by the time the first Commonwealth troops were disembarking, though that was a full hour after he had spotted the ships. They immediately charged the men coming ashore and for half an hour a furious fight raged at the water's edge. Dover and his lieutenant were both wounded and the accounts show that Captains Coppin, Reeves, Taylor, Blake, Cuttance and Gething all took part. The conflict was decided by the death of the Royalist commander, Colonel Bosville, after which the horse recoiled, disheartened. Even so, had the foot supported, the result might have been different.[39]

The following day the Commonwealth troops consolidated their position and captured St Aubin's Bay, which secured their communications. They were only just in time for the weather became so bad that Blake and Heane lost contact with each other. Only four or five men were lost in the landing and it was left to the weather and the dangerous Jersey coast to exact the highest toll. Attempting to enter St Aubin's Bay, the *Tresco* struck a rock and sank with the loss of all its crew. The captain of the *Tresco* was William Blake, the General's cousin.[40]

Badiley could now begin what turned out to be his ill-fated voyage to the Mediterranean and Dennis could leave for Virginia. There was just one more piece of clearing-up to be done. Guernsey was generally staunchly for the Parliament but the Royalists had managed to barricade themselves in Castle Cornet. Only the previous year an attempt to storm the castle had been defeated. Colonel Burgess, the Governor, was reluctant to come to terms and Blake was not prepared to waste men's lives so he left it to the Lieutenant-Governor of Guernsey, Colonel Bingham. He went on shore at Portsmouth on 19 November, the earliest for three years. Heane needed another month to complete the subjugation of Jersey. Mont Orgueil Tower quickly surrendered but Carteret withdrew into Elizabeth Castle and a wearisome siege resulted. Still hoping for relief from France, the Royalists resisted to the bitter end. It was not to be. The Commonwealth was too powerful at sea to be trifled with and the castle surrendered to Heane on 19 December 1651.

The campaign of 1651 had been a most successful one for Blake. It can be argued that the capture of the Scilly Islands and of Jersey were simply mopping-up operations. Yet the closer they are examined, the more they reflect great credit on Blake for the manner in which they were achieved. In the Scilly Islands campaign, there was the sound decision to concentrate on Tresco. That was followed by the skilful revision of the tactics and the revitalisation of the men after the initial failure. Finally there was the patient way the negotiations were pursued which avoided further bloodshed. They all show Blake at his best and the conquest a model in the conduct of amphibious operations. Jersey, too, was a witness to Blake's growing confidence. There is nothing which shows the master more than the way he wins a won game. Sooner or later Jersey would have fallen, but the night attack must rank high among his exploits. On the surface, the whole concept was a horrible risk and it is difficult to imagine anyone else attempting it. The cruise around the Corbière Rocks and then up and down St Ouen's Bay, with dangerous rocks at each end, in bad weather, in October, must have had the heart of each captain in his mouth. Then there was the landing itself. If it was executed at high tide, there was the hazard of strong currents; if he chose any other time the boats would ground a long way out. Carteret's seamen believed a landing impossible. Blake calculated that the Royalists would be taken by surprise, if the landing was a couple of hours after high tide, and that they would have been weakened by the softening-up process. He was proved quite correct.

Blake never did get to the Isle of Man which, since the collapse of the Scots at Worcester, had become of little moment except as a centre for privateers. While he was engrossed in attacking Jersey, Colonels Thomas Birch and Robert Duckenfield organised their own expedition and the island surrendered during December 1651. Sir George Ayscue was still on the high seas but the Council of State was soon to learn that Barbados too had reluctantly accepted the authority of the Commonwealth.

Part III

The Dutch War

Reputation and Reality

*I*N 1652, the Commonwealth went to war with the United Provinces. The political and economic reasons for the decision will be noticed, briefly, at the beginning of the next chapter. The purpose of this one is to examine the strengths and weaknesses of the two nations when fighting began. Neutral observers had little doubt that the Dutch would emerge the victors. England had had a fine fleet in the days of Queen Elizabeth, but forty years rotting in port under the Stuarts, followed by the strains of civil war, led the continental powers to regard it as a spent force. The Dutch, on the other hand, had emerged victorious from a long war with Spain in 1648, and the maritime world rang with the exploits of Heemskerk at Gibraltar in 1607, Piet Hein at Rio de Janeiro in 1628, and Tromp in the Downs in 1639. There was universal astonishment when the English came out on top.

The Commonwealth started off with a number of advantages, some of which were apparent to onlookers and others which were not. England was still, predominantly, an agricultural country. She could be seriously damaged by the destruction of her trade, but not brought to her knees. Such a stoppage was not likely, as only the North Sea trade was really vulnerable to attack. Informed commentators believed that the English need to import naval stores from the Baltic would put them in serious difficulties but, in the event, this did not happen. The war proved relatively brief and the shortfall was made up by tapping resources in Scotland and the New England colonies.

The Dutch, on the other hand, relied for the money with which they financed their war effort, almost entirely on trade. Most of it went by sea and used three main routes. One of these passed through the Sound into the Baltic. The second went down the Channel to France, Spain, the Mediterranean and the Indies. The third, not much used, but an alternative to the second, took their ships round between the north of Scotland and Norway.

The vulnerability of two of the three main Dutch trade arteries to English attack, was the reason for the large number of pitched battles which characterised all three Anglo-Dutch wars. All the English had to do was to threaten one of the

Dutch merchant fleets and the United Provinces had to respond or see their trade strangled. The result was that the English could force a fight whenever, and wherever, they chose. This conferred a number of advantages. If battle was offered close to English ports and away from Dutch ones, English ships badly damaged in the engagement might limp home and live to fight again, while Dutch ones could well sink at sea. Dutch energy was also dissipated in trying to protect convoys. At Dungeness and Portland, Tromp's ability to manoeuvre was circumscribed by the presence of large numbers of merchant ships.

In 1649, England had thirty-nine ships, of different sizes, which was not much more than half the Dutch fleet. Between 1649 and 1652, the Commonwealth increased the strength of the fleet by new building, by buying every suitable ship which came on the market, and by keeping prizes. At the outbreak of war, the number of ships had risen to eighty-six. During the same period, the Dutch had only added twelve, so the combatants were roughly equal in numbers.[1] In practice the Dutch still had a considerable edge. Both sides supplemented their numbers with armed merchantmen and the Dutch had a much larger mercantile marine from which they could recruit ships, whose size and gunnery establishments were similar to the States' men-of-war. In most of the battles, the English were in the minority by anything between ten and twenty ships.

To contemporaries this was not the relevant factor. What mattered in their eyes was the relative calibre of the leadership. Two of the three senior pre-Civil War officers, Pennington and Carteret, were Royalists. The Parliamentary leadership had been decimated, too. Warwick had been forced out of office, Batten deserted to the Royalists, Owen disappeared, Swanley died in 1650 and both Moulton and Hall had been pensioned off. Of the three soldiers appointed in 1649, Popham was dead and Deane occupied in Scotland. Blake was winning golden opinions but he had only three years in command, had never fought a pitched battle, and probably had had no experience of the sea, prior to 1649. His Vice-Admiral, William Penn, was considered a most promising rising star but he had much to learn. And who was this man, Nehemiah Bourne? He was another soldier, who had first commanded a ship in 1650, and was now appointed Rear-Admiral, after two years at sea! There could be only one explanation for such a promotion: the Council of State could not find another trustworthy seaman. It was confidently predicted that the pressures of war would produce political disturbances in the Navy, which the Dutch could exploit.

Contrast this sorry state of affairs with the galaxy of stars on whom the Dutch could call. At their head was the famed Lieutenant Admiral of the United Provinces, Martin Harpertszoon Tromp. Tromp went to sea at the age of nine, and he had worked his way up the service, reaching the rank of Lieutenant-Admiral, in 1636. By 1652, he had had sixteen years in command during a period of almost continuous conflict with Spain. The high point of his career was the destruction of the Spanish fleet in the Downs, in 1639. Tromp was supported

by many other fine seamen. There was the Vice-Admiral of Holland, Witte Cornelis de With, as brave as a lion and as astute a tactician as Tromp himself. There
was Jan Evertsen, the Vice-Admiral of Zeeland and his brother Cornelis, vastly
experienced, who could read Tromp's mind and divine instantly what he wanted.
There was the up-and-coming Commodore Adrianszoon de Ruijter, who was
to prove the greatest of them all. In 1652, he could not match the experience of the others. He had only commanded States' ships for twelve years. How
could the likes of Blake, Penn and Bourne stand comparison with such men?

In an important sense the contrast was illusory. The English fleet was not
united, politically, as the later disgrace of both Penn and Lawson was to prove,
but it was capable of sinking its differences in the face of the foreign foe, whether
Dutch or Spanish. The Dutch may not have suffered the trauma of civil war but
divisions, similar to those which had brought civil conflict to England, fissured
Dutch society. The dispute between the Stadtholder, William II, and the State
of Holland, was reflected by a similar dispute within the fleet. The Evertsens
were outspoken supporters of the Stadtholderate. Tromp, though less vocal, was
identified with the Orange cause as well. De With on the other hand was a
violent republican. Only de Ruijter avoided identification with either party. The
overwhelming feeling of the fleet lay with the Standtholderate, so the death of
William and the collapse of his party, in 1650, had serious consequences.

Tromp's reputation was so great that the new republican regime did not
feel strong enough to remove him. The result was a lack of confidence between
politicians and seamen. For too long the republican regime believed that the war
could be won by some cosmetic rearrangement of the command. Without the
division, it would have recognised much earlier that, despite a superiority in
numbers, the Dutch fleet was very inferior to the English one, and the war only
kept going at all by the skill and dedication of Tromp. In order to understand
how this disparity had come about, it is necessary to survey what had been
happening, in England and the United Provinces, between 1588 and 1652.

The popular view of the defeat of the Spanish Armada represents the English
David achieving a famous victory over the Spanish Goliath. The truth is rather
different. Under the impulse of Henry VIII, the English had embarked on a
policy of building up their maritime strength, with the State playing an important
role by itself building a core of ships. The same policy was followed by Elizabeth,
so that by 1588 England was the strongest naval power in western Europe. Spain,
by contrast, was not an Atlantic power at all before the reforms instituted by her
far sighted Minister of Marine, Pedro Menendez, in 1574. Her experience had
been confined to the Mediterranean, where conditions were quite different. Not
until she acquired the Portuguese fleet in 1582 did Spain become any sort of
threat. The attempt of Philip to invade England was one of the biggest gambles

in naval history. The surprise is, not that it failed, but that it came so near to success. In the succeeding half century, the conclusions drawn from the Armada campaign dominated thinking, in naval circles, in Western Europe.

Henry VIII had built his fleet round a central premise which was quite revolutionary. For him, the object of a battle was to sink as many of the enemy ships as possible, by gunfire. This was quite different from the orthodoxy of the day, which aimed at getting the ships alongside each other and fighting an imitation land battle across the decks. Powerful iron guns called cannons and culverins replaced the brass sakers and minions, which were the usual armament and which were designed more for protection against boarding than for damaging enemy ships.

Drake's attack on Cadiz, in 1587, revealed to Philip the power of the English guns and he scoured Europe for heavy weapons to put on his ships. The reputation of the new guns stood the Armada in good stead to begin with, as it sailed up the Channel the next year. One of the reasons why the English fought such an ineffective battle, at long range, was fear of the possible effects of the new guns. Not until the Spanish fleet was nearing Calais did they realise that the Spaniards were having difficulty in using them. Modern marine archaeology has revealed that many of them burst when they were fired.[2] This was no new problem, but the haste with which the Spaniards collected the guns may have led to neglect of the usual practice of test firing them beforehand. While the Spanish fleet lay off Gravelines fire ships were sent in, which caused a panic. The English were able, at last, to destroy the cohesion of the Spanish fleet and isolate individual ships, which could then be attacked in overwhelming force. Even when the English closed the range not a single Spanish ship was sunk by gunfire.

For the Dutch, watching from the sidelines, the conclusions were obvious. The Spanish heavy guns had been worse than useless. Nor had the English tactics met with any success until the fireships were sent in. The big gun was not the answer. They were encouraged in this view by the change in the nature of the sea war, caused by the Armada's defeat and the failure of the second Armada of 1597. The war became a commercial one, with the Spaniards attempting to destroy the trade which was the lifeblood of Dutch resistance. Over the next half century the Dutch evolved a very effective tactical system. Their ships were built for speed, so that they could catch the privateers which swarmed out of Dunkirk and Ostend. Guns were heavy and slowed the ship down, so their numbers were cut to a minimum and confined to the lighter calibres. Instead the Dutch ships carried as many men as they safely could. In a ship-to-ship combat, the Dutch employed their superior speed to catch up with their opponent. Then they used their guns to destroy their sails. Once the quarry was sufficiently slowed down, it was boarded and the crew overpowered by superior numbers.[3]

In their search for greater speed the Dutch copied a style of building from the Spanish, which was called frigate building. Both sides used oared frigates in the canals around Ghent and Bruges, and sailing versions quickly followed. Soon the design was adapted to larger ships to increase their speed. The essential features of frigate design were: an increase in the length of the ship relative to the breadth; a cutting down of the unwieldy superstructure, which was a feature of sixteenth-century ships; and the construction of flush decks. Olde ships were divided into three compartments: the forecastle, waist, and aftercastle o poop. Each section was divided by bulkheads and the decks were at different levels. In the new designs, the bulkheads were done away with, and the decks were built continuously from stem to stern.

The ultimate in frigate building was the *Aemilia*, praised for its speed and handling qualities throughout the maritime world. From its launch in 1632, until the First Dutch War, the *Aemilia* was the prototype for all Dutch warships. The list of 100 Dutch ships to be sent to sea, in June 1652, illustrates the extraordinary uniformity of their fleet. The *Brederode* mounted 54 guns. Of the remainder, twenty-six had between 31 and 40 guns, and fifty-two between 21 and 30 guns. Three had between 11 and 20 and there were six smaller ships.[4] A similar pattern appears in the squadron of thirty ships already at sea, under the command of de Ruijter.[5]

The English drew quite different conclusions from the Armada campaign. The ships they built got bigger, not smaller. The *Prince Royal*, launched in 1610, could mount 102 guns and was the biggest ship in Western Europe, until the launching and brief career of the *Gustavus Vasa* by the Swedes in 1628. The *Sovereign of the Seas* was even bigger, having three decks and room for 120 guns. These two ships were only the tip of the iceberg. Between 1618 and 1623, the Navy Commissioners constructed a series of capital ships which survived the Civil Wars and many of which have already figured in the narrative – the *George, Andrew, Victory, Constant Reformation, Triumph* and *Happy Entrance* among them. Then there were the Ship Money fleets of the 1630s. At the top end of the range were the 2nd rates: *Charles, James, Henrietta Maria, Unicorn* and *Garland*; but the best one, such as the *Bonadventure, Lion, Leopard* and *Swallow*, were 3rd rates.

By the outbreak of the Civil Wars, England had a battle fleet that was second-to-none in Western Europe, but it was little use because there was no money to pay the seamen, never mind fight a war. At the very time all these ships were being built, English commerce was being plundered by other nations because the smaller ships speedy enough to capture privateers were not there. True, a handful of smaller ships, such as the *Whelps* of 1628, and the *Providence, Expedition, Nicodemus* and *Greyhound* of the late 1630s, were constructed, but they were nowhere near enough.

The cry for smaller, swifter ships became even more vociferous, as a result of experiences in the First Civil War. Every suitable prize was bought and, once the war was over, a programme of convoy frigates was begun. We are fortunate that the great marine artist, van de Velde, sketched many English ships and his drawings show, that the English idea of convoy frigates was not that of the Dutch. The drawing of the *Tiger*, of 1647, shows 20 ports broadside and 2 in the stern.[6] If it is assumed that 2 were mounted on the forecastle heads, this gives a total of 44. Fleet lists show that the *Tiger* rarely carried its full complement of guns, presumably to reduce the weight and make the ship more weatherly. What is striking is that the idea of a 4th rate frigate in the minds of the English Navy Commissioners was a ship, which could carry more guns than any ship in the entire fleet that the Dutch sent out in June 1652, bar one. The massive building programme of the Commonwealth shows the same emphasis on heavily gunned ships.

A comparison between the list of Dutch and English ships equipped for sea, at roughly the same time, is quite startling. The largest English ship had 62 guns. There were six between 51 and 60; ten between 41 and 50; twenty-four between 31 and 40; fifteen between 11 and 20 and seven less than 10.[7] The English fleet had ships spread through the entire range, seventeen of which could outgun all the Dutchmen but Tromp's flagship, the *Brederode*. This does not take into account the *Sovereign* and the *Resolution* (the renamed *Prince Royal*) which, after remodelling, could still mount 100 and 88 guns respectively; and three other 2nd rates, which had between 51 and 60 guns.

The two fleets were even more unbalanced than these figures suggest. The English had not only been true to the big ship, they had remained true to the big iron gun as well. Oppenheim prints a table showing the standard gunnery establishment of the six different rates in 1655.[8] Of the 86 guns carried by a 1st rate, only the 5 sakers were brass guns; 19 of the remainder were cannon, 9 demi-cannon, 28 culverins and 30 demi-culverins: all iron guns. 2nd rates were to have 64 guns. Only 4 were brass sakers but there were no full cannon. The 3rd rates were to have 60 guns of which 8 were sakers. Only the 6th rate with 8 guns each had no iron guns. The numbers for ships of each rate appear to be more than were carried in the equivalent rates in the First Dutch War but it is possible that the gun sizes were less. The guns ordered for the new frigate at Woolwich, in March 1652, were 20 demi-cannon, 4 culverin, 20 demi-culverin and 2 sakers, a total of 46.[9]

According to Sir William Monson a cannon could fire a ball of 60 lbs weight, a demi-cannon one of 30.5 lbs, a culverin one of 17.5 lbs.[10] Contrast this with the Dutch strength. The table included in Johann Elias's book *Vlootbouw in Nederlands* shows that the heaviest Dutch gun was a 24 pounder and that, even after the new programme of building of 1654 had been in progress for a year, there were only 44 of them. They had 157 18 pounders, similar to the culverin; just enough to equip seven English 4th rates.[11] The firepower of the English fleet was enormous but the question was, could it be used to good effect? If Drake had failed to use the big gun properly in 1588, against the Spanish, were the likes

The first Generals-at-Sea: Major-General Richard Deane (above), by R. Walker, Colonel Edward Popham (left), by R. Walker and Robert Blake (below) by S. Cooper.

The *James*. Described as 'a paragon of ships', and launched in 1637, she was flush decked and frigate built. By

Prince Rupert, in command of the Royalist Fleet from
1649 to 1653. By Lely.

Martin Harpertzoon Tromp, Lieutenant-Admiral of Holland.
The scene below at Helvoetsluis in 1648 depicts the Earl of
Warwick's Fleet in front with the Royalist Fleet to the right
and Tromp to the left. (see p. 67)

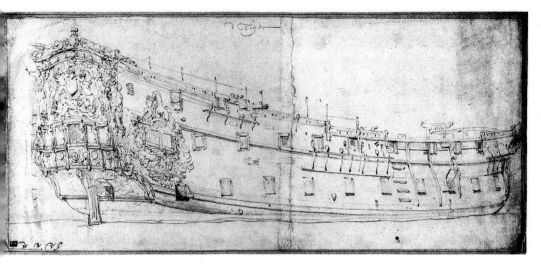

The *Tiger*, a typical English convoy frigate, 4th rate, launched in 1647. By W. van de Velde the Elder.

The *Aemelia*, launched in 1632, was the prototype of all Dutch warships until 1651. Engraving by C. J. Visscher.

The *Vrijheijt*, ◻
rejected Dutch◻
prototype of 1◻
based on Engl◻
models. By W.◻
de Velde the ◻

Captain William Penn,
the first seaman to be made a
General-at-Sea. By Lely.

Captain Richard Stayner, one of
Blake's outstanding captains.
Mezzotint by C. Turner.

Michel Adriaenzoon de Ruijter, one of the greatest seamen of all time who learnt his craft in the hard school of the First Dutch War. By H. Berckman.

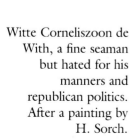

Witte Corneliszoon de With, a fine seaman but hated for his manners and republican politics. After a painting by H. Sorch.

The Battle of Scheveningen, 31 July 1653. The view is from the rear of the Dutch Fleet and shows the English breaking through. A grisaille by W. van de Velde the Elder.

of Blake, Penn and Bourne going to fare any better against a nation, which had just given those same Spaniards a beating and who possessed incomparably the best seamen in Europe?

The key to the mystery was the truck carriage. Every aficionado of the sailing-ship Navy will be so used, in their mind's eye, to the picture of the iron guns on their wheeled carriages, secured to the sides of the ships by their breeching ropes, that they will find it difficult to realise what a revolution such carriages caused in naval warfare. The first shipboard guns were made of brass and were cast in two pieces, the barrel and the breach, but brass was only suitable for the smaller pieces, such as sakers and minions. Larger guns, such as cannons and culverins, had to be made of iron which, due to the limitations of sixteenth-century metallurgy, had to be cast in one piece. The consequence of this restriction was that the guns had to be loaded down the muzzle.

The use of iron guns, on cumbrous artillery mountings, created serious problems. At the beginning of the action, the guns had to be dragged forward until their muzzles projected out of the gunports. Only the first round could be loaded inboard. After that the gunner had to get out over the side to swab out the barrel and reload the gun, presenting a sitting target to marksmen in the rigging of the enemy ship. Philip II tacitly admitted the uselessness of his big guns, for anything other than a preliminary to boarding, by instructing that they should not fire more than one round per engagement. Worse, the guns could only be used in a flat calm, otherwise there was great danger of the ship being flooded through her open gunports. This happened to the *Mary Rose* in 1545, and the *Gustavus Vasa* in 1628.

The new carriage solved both the major problems of the big gun. At the beginning of the action, the gun was attached, by ropes, to the side of the ship and was loaded inboard. The crew then pushed the gun, on its wheeled truck, until the muzzle projected through the port. When the gun was fired, the recoil sent it running backwards inboard until brought to a halt by the ropes. There was no longer any need for the crew to go out over the side and the ports could be closed after firing, if it was thought necessary.

At one time it was believed that the truck carriage did not come into use in the English Navy until after the Armada campaign, but the finds on the *Mary Rose* have included guns on truck carriages. What happened during the Armada campaign therefore needs to be reinterpreted. Analysis of the gunnery establishment of the Armada shows that the Spanish had 112 very powerful guns, which were twice the calibre of the largest English ones. Unfortunately Philip did not realise the crucial importance of the truck carriage and they were all on artillery mountings. Even if the guns had not burst, they would have been to all intents and purposes useless.[12]

Recent research has shown that many Spanish ships were seriously damaged by the English guns and Spanish reports of the battle off Gravelines emphasise the firepower that guns, mounted on truck carriages, gave to their opponents. Nevertheless no Spanish ship was sunk simply by the iron guns alone. There may be a number of reasons for the failure. There is evidence that English gunfounders increased the power of their guns in the early seventeenth century, and the use of breeching ropes does not seem to have been standard practice, until the period of the Dutch Wars.

The most important reason may have been that the ships were not suitable for use with the guns. The years which followed the Armada were dominated by an argument about the best way to build ships of war. The debate culminated in the report of the Naval Inquiry of 1618, which decreed that, in future, all ships should be built flush decked (i.e. the decks should be continuous from stem to stern) and that their superstructures should be cut down.[13] These were both elements of fast frigate building but, in the hands of English shipwrights, the new style was given a different purpose: the creation of a stable gun platform. If all the guns were fired at once, the strain on the ship's timbers would be enormous, so it was essential that as many joints as possible should be done away with. Similarly the recoil from firing a large number of guns could capsize a top-heavy ship, so the superstructure was cut to a minimum. At the same time, English gunfounders were modifying the design of their guns to limit the effects of recoil and to enable them to take greater charges of powder.[14]

Rival navies did not adopt the truck carriage until much later. So little did they understand what was happening, that continental gunfounders rushed to buy English iron ordnance, melt them down, recast them as lighter pieces and sell the surplus iron. Such contemporary blindness has been paralleled by subsequent misconceptions among naval historians in England itself, stemming from the belief that frigates were fast lightly armed ships. English seventeenth-century frigates were not: they were massive floating gun platforms. After 1641 all English ships built for the State, large and small, were frigate-built.

In order to use the magnificent weapon that the shipwrights and gun-founders had forged for them, the seamen had to find the right tactics. The first element of these tactics was the broadside: that is the firing of all the guns on one side of the ship together. When broadside firing began is still a matter of debate. In 1625 an Anglo-Dutch squadron, commanded by Captain John Weddell, engaged a Portuguese squadron off Gombroon. The master's mate of the *Jonas*, one of the two big East Indiamen involved, describes his ship not only firing broadsides, but firing them three times as fast as the Portuguese. 'We gave them East India profit, three for every one.'[15] The captain of the *Jonas* was Richard Swanley who entered the Parliamentary navy at the outbreak of the Civil Wars and served as Admiral of the Irish Seas, so the regular use of broadsides could well be pushed back to 1642, or earlier. Weddell's own ship fired broadsides at Gombroon and he commanded the *St George* in 1627, in the ill-fated La Rochelle expedition. Indeed, the new evidence of the antiquity of the truck carriage suggests that broadside firing may already have been in use during the Armada campaign.

The logic behind the changes was that the battle was to be a gunnery duel and that boarding, if it took place at all, would only come when the opponent was battered into submission. This was something that seamen found hard to accept. The Dutch closed their minds to it. In 1651, in response to the demands of Dutch seamen that the Admiralties should embark on a building programme similar to the one in progress in England, a competition was organised for an appropriate design for the new ships. Two were submitted. One was based on the *Aemilia* and the other, known as the *Vrijheijt*, was very similar to English designs. It was the *Aemilia* design which was adopted.

Despite the way in which one administration after another, whatever its political complexion, espoused the big gun, there was a bitter dispute in English naval circles too. The arguments are laid out by Sir William Monson, in his description of the *James*, a 2nd rate, launched in 1637.

> I will make a comparison of the James Regis of his Majesty's of which I will say that, for her mould and condition, she is a paragon of ships and not to be equalled. But in her, built with a flush deck, and her close gallery abaft, she is to be excepted against in a defensive part . . . The only strength of the James at this present is in her broadside, where she hath two brave platforms of ordnance to overdare any ship to board her; nor no enemy in discretion will do it if he can find a weaker part in the ship to attempt. But suppose she be boarded in her prow, or abaft at the poop, and be entered by more men than the company can resist; she neither having forecastle ahead or close fight abaft, all must rest upon the valour of a few men; which, if they be overcome, both ship and they must fall into the hands of an enemy in the manner I have shewed.[16]

That there was some truth in what Monson suggested is demonstrated by an incident involving the *Phoenix* in 1652. The *Phoenix* had been impounded by the Grand Duke of Tuscany and handed over to the Dutch. The ship was recaptured by a cutting-out expedition, which gained control of the upper deck while the prize crew was asleep, and battened down the hatches. This was only possible because the *Phoenix* had neither poop nor forecastle.[17] Where Sir William betrays his lack of comprehension is in his next paragraph where he asserts: 'Fighting further off is like a Smithfield fray in times past with sword and buckler, which is nothing but the wasting of powder to little purpose.' (In such market disputes there was much noise, but few people got hurt and fatalities were rare.) The idea that the attacking ship might be sunk or totally wrecked before coming within pistol shot was something that he could not or would not consider.

The arguments surfaced again, in 1646, in relation to the new building programme. The ship builder Andrew Burrell wrote a pamphlet bitterly attacking the record of the Navy Commissioners in the First Civil War.[18] Burrell's hostility was a by-product of his rivalry with the Pett family who had, he believed, been responsible for his getting far fewer Navy contracts than he thought he deserved, so everything he says has to be treated with care. Nonetheless the answers of the Navy Commissioners to the charges he brought are most instructive.[19]

Burrell complained that many of the ships were too big and spent most of their time in harbour. The remainder were so sluggish that they could not catch the fleet-footed Royalist privateers, with the result that merchant shipping friendly to the Parliament was destroyed and few or no prizes taken. He believed that the bigger ships could be made more useful by removing one of the gun decks, because the reduction in weight would lessen their draught and increase their speed. When it came to new building he maintained that he could build speedier ships, if he were allowed to substitute his own design for the one laid down by the Navy Commissioners. He was prepared to test his ships against those of other builders, by racing them around the Isle of Wight.

The Navy Commissioners were able to show that the Parliamentary Navy was catching the privateers and their answer includes a long list of prizes. They rejected the idea of a race round the Isle of Wight, remarking that such a contest would only prove who had the best pilot, because of the peculiarity of the tides. Much the most interesting part of their rebuttal related to the cutting down idea. For Burrell speed was the key. For the Navy Commissioners speed was important, but so was strength. To illustrate the weakness of ships with only one full gun deck, they described the battle in the Downs, between Tromp and the Spaniards.

> In Anno 1640, Don Antonio de Kendo came into the Downs with a fleet of ships from Spain, and having rid there sometime, the Admiral Van Trump, with six of the best ships in Holland, attended the motion of Don Antonio, his Ship; the rest of his Fleet consisting of eighty Sail, attended the Spanish Fleet. Don Antonio when he had refreshed his men & fitted himself, weighed Anchor out of the Downs; the Admiral of Holland did the like with six Ships; & coming without the Goodwyn Sands, the Admiral of Holland came up with the Admiral of Spain, as far as his transome; but received such entertainment, that he durst never more come up with him, nor any of the other ships in his company, notwithstanding the Admiral of Spain stayed for them with his top Sails down, & main yard a crosse; such great force had this great Ship with two Tire and an half of Ordnance, that the Hollanders durst not deal with her. The Admiral of Portugall, being another great Ship of that Fleet with two Tire of Ordnance, fought with sixteen States [Dutch] Men of War almost a whole day yet could never take her, [until] two of their Men-of-War desperately ran aboard of her with two Fire-Ships, where they burned together until they were consumed.

Just as the Dutch had examined the Spanish Armada campaign and found the English tactics wanting, even though the Armada had failed, so the English watching from the Kentish cliffs had drawn unexpected lessons from the great Dutch victory.[20] The difficulty facing the naval administration was convincing the seamen that they were right. In their hearts, the seamen wanted to believe Monson, Burrell and the Dutch because sinking or wrecking vessels would rob them of the prize money with which they supplemented their pay. The captains, too, came to look sourly on the new ideas when they realised that broadside firing alone would not win the day against the adroit Dutch. The method of fighting in line, which evolved during the war, robbed the captains of their prized independence and forced them to submit to a discipline that many of them found unendurable. Consequently the new ideas would have to be imposed from outside the fleet.

The catalyst which precipitated the vital change in attitude was the appointment of soldier admirals. The original reason for their selection was political but, as luck would have it, two out of the three had had detailed acquaintance with the use of guns on land. Richard Deane had commanded the artillery of the New Model Army, and practically all Blake's fighting had been connected with sieges, so he must have acquired a detailed knowledge of their capabilities. The odd one out was Popham. It is a curious trick of fate that the only one of the soldier admirals who had previous seagoing experience, turned out to be the one least fitted to initiate the revolution in tactics.

In a general sense Blake must have realised from the beginning the tremendous power of the fleet which he commanded. He would have grasped the principles of broadside firing immediately and made certain that his ships had regular firing practice. The accounts of the 1650 campaign show that warships of other countries would not face Commonwealth ships in equal combat. Appreciation of the strength of individual English ships, throws new light on the failure of Rupert to get out of Lisbon. On the first occasion, all the Flemish and Portuguese ships bore away as soon as they came within range and on the second, a whole fleet turned and ran from just three English ships. Their terror became far more understandable in the context of the battle in the Downs where, according to the Navy Commissioners, the Portuguese Admiral had taken on sixteen Dutchmen. Only Rupert was prepared to stay and fight. His ship the *Constant Reformation* was equipped with iron guns at the time of the mutiny and presumably still had them.

A story told by Richard Gibson, a petty officer, confirms all this. It concerns the capture of the French privateer, commanded by the Chevalier Lalande, in the autumn of 1650 off the Straits of Gibraltar.[21] Blake was alone in the *Phoenix* which, according to the fleet list, had 32 guns. Lalande's ship had 40 guns. Despite his superiority Lalande made no attempt to fight, presumably because his crew were too frightened of the *Phoenix*'s powerful iron guns. Yet doubts must have remained in Blake's mind, as another famous story, about that legendary captain Christopher Myngs, indicates.[22] In the early days of the war, according to Gibson, Myngs took on three Dutch warships, single handed, and captured them. He returned to Blake to report his success, confidently anticipating his General's approbation. Instead what he got was a dressing down, in front of the officers of the flag ship, for unnecessarily risking his ship. The curious side to this story is that, as the war unfolded, Blake was to accept battle at odds not far different from those of Myngs himself, for instance at Dungeness. The only conclusion that we can come to is that Blake did not realise the full extent of English superiority at the time of the Myngs incident, but that by the time of Dungeness he did. What had opened his eyes was the Skirmish off Dover.

The Skirmish off Dover and the Shetland Expedition

*F*ROM the beginning of 1652, the political temperature began to rise rapidly. The fleet list for the summer, reported by Blake from the Council of State on 14 January,[1] contained fifty-nine ships of various shapes and sizes to be employed in home waters. In addition, there were eight ships under Penn, expected home shortly from the Mediterranean; seven under Ayscue, in the West Indies; seven more employed in convoy duties, between England and the Levant; and two in Virginia: a total of eighty-three, the largest fleet England had ever put to sea. Even this enormous fleet did not satisfy some members of the Rump and it was debated whether the *Sovereign of the Seas* should be taken out of its mothballs, for the first time since the beginning of the Civil Wars.

There was only one enemy such extraordinary measures could be directed against and that was the Dutch. The cause of the quarrel was commercial. The conclusion of the long war between Spain and the United Provinces was the prelude to a sharp decline in English trading fortunes.[2] While the war was in progress, Dutch merchantmen were banned from the Iberian peninsula and from trading with all Spanish possessions. Much of the vacuum was filled by English ships. The attacks on Dutch shipping by Spanish privateers resulted in a sharp rise in freight rates. Merchants found it cheaper to lade their goods in English ships which were less vulnerable. As a result practically the entire trade of the Mediterranean with northern Europe fell into English hands. The East India Company also found itself with a protected market for its spices in southern Europe.

The return of peace exposed the hollowness of the English position. The Dutch were much more efficient and made rapid progress in recovering their lost trade with Spain and Portugal between 1648 and 1652. In the Mediterranean, too, the English were exposed to the blasts of competition, when Genoa offered its services to the Dutch as an *entrepôt*. Perhaps the worst affected was the East India Company; access to the Amsterdam money market gave its Dutch rivals a considerable advantage.

The English merchants responded aggressively. In 1650, a Navigation Act was passed, with the aim of keeping Dutch ships out of the trade with English colonies. To show that it intended to enforce the act, the Commonwealth dispatched Sir George Ayscue to Barbados with instructions to arrest any Dutch ships found there. Seventeenth-century economic theory taught that the volume of trade remained static. It followed, therefore, that force was the only way to increase a country's share if it was unable to compete commercially. In 1635, John Selden had written a book, entitled *Mare Clausum*, in which he claimed that a country owned the seas around it. In any disputed cases, the country with the longest continuous history had the prior claim. In Western Europe, according to Selden, that honour fell to England. He claimed that the North Sea, the Channel, the Irish Sea and the Atlantic as far west as Cape Finisterre belonged to England. Everything in those seas belonged to England and ships could only use them with English permission. To show that they accepted the English claim, all foreign merchantmen should strike their flags when in the presence of English men-of-war, and submit to being searched for contraband of war. As England was hostile to some nation or other practically all the time and the Dutch carried the goods of every nation in Europe the English were, in effect, claiming the right to stop Dutch merchantmen, when and where they liked, and to remove what they considered to be contraband of war. No self-respecting nation could allow that.

The pro-Dutch faction led by Cromwell and Sir Henry Vane, who believed that the ties of religion were more important, tried its best to advocate an alliance with France against Spain but, faced as he was with enemies within and without, Mazarin was not yet prepared to pay the English price, which was the expulsion of the Stuarts, compensation for English losses to privateers using French ports and the ceding of Dunkirk.[3] The only pressure that the English could bring to bear was by attacking French seaborne trade but, as most of that was being carried in Dutch merchant ships, all considerations led to the same conclusion.

A stream of cases came before the High Court of Admiralty, in which Dutch ships had been stopped by English privateers and searched, under the rules about contraband of war. Goods of French origin were then removed. In each case, the privateer carried letters of marque, entitling him to recover the value of ships and goods lost to Royalist ships and sold, as prize, in French ports. Matters were made worse by news that Sir George Ayscue had been successful at Barbados. He had found a large number of Dutch merchant ships in Georgetown Harbour. They were all arrested, and ships and goods condemned as prize, because they had been trading with an English colony under Royalist control. The States General was furious and demanded that a squadron be sent to intercept Ayscue on his homeward voyage, to repossess the ships by force.[4]

The Dutch faced a situation where the alternatives were war or complete humiliation, which was just what the war party in England wanted. The Dutch reaction was to begin energetic preparations for war, while still trying to preserve the increasingly fragile peace. A scheme was set on foot to equip 150 ships,[5] and three plenipotentiaries were dispatched to try and effect a compromise.[6] Any chance of success they might have had, was extinguished by the Skirmish off Dover.

At first it looked as if the Commonwealth had bitten off more than it could chew. The English naval administration cracked under the strain of preparing such a large fleet for sea. There were delays in victualling the ships and there was a shortage of prime seamen, but the worst problems were at the Ordnance office. Gunners' stores were in short supply and there were not enough guns to equip all the ships. The Dutch won the race to be the first to get their fleet to sea. By 30 April, when Tromp was given his instructions, eighty-eight of the 150 ships were ready. Of these, ten were to reinforce the squadron under Jan Evertsen, Vice-Admiral of Zeeland, already on convoy duties in the Channel and the Western Approaches, four were added to the squadron under Cornelis Witte de With, the Vice Admiral of Holland, which was looking after the Baltic trade. Nine were added to the eleven already earmarked to escort the East and West India fleets home. Fifteen were assigned to guarding the North Sea fishery. This left fifty under Tromp's immediate command.[7]

Tromp sailed from the Wielings on 10 May, and for the next four days cruised off the Flemish coast until he had forty-two ships with him. His original intention was to wait for the eight stragglers before he made any move, but the idea was disrupted by the weather. The next day was so stormy that many of the ships dragged their anchors and he was forced to seek shelter under the South Foreland. The Dutch reached the 'backside of the Goodwins' about 10 am on the 18 May.[8] Already at anchor there were nine English ships, under Rear-Admiral Bourne. They were the *Andrew, Triumph, Fairfax, Entrance, Centurion, Adventure, Assurance, Greyhound* and *Seven Brothers*, a handy collection of ships which could give a good account of themselves. Nevertheless Bourne was rather alarmed at the appearance of a Dutch fleet of over forty ships. Tromp was quick to reassure him. Captains Thyssen and Aldertszoon were sent on board the *Andrew* to explain that they were taking refuge from the weather and would sail as soon as it improved.

Bourne also reported, rather ominously, the Dutchmen as saying that Tromp would have come himself but he was not prepared to strike his flag.[9] Bourne decided to take no chances. That night he had two frigates patrolling the water between his squadron and the Dutch, and all nine ships lay with their anchors apeak. Tromp's determination was underlined the next day, when he occupied the time in gunnery practice which alarmed the good people of Dover. The Governor sent to him to strike his flag, an instruction which he contemptuously ignored, even though the castle fired some shots to draw attention to his omission. The weather was now much improved and true to his promise to Bourne, Tromp set sail for the French coast soon after midday.[10]

Meanwhile Blake was being kept abreast of events by Captain Brandley of the *Portsmouth*, which was in Dover Road when the Dutch appeared.[11] Brandley found him in Rye Bay, with thirteen ships, where he had been investigating a Dutch merchant fleet anchored off Fairlight. Blake had his flag in the *James*, and the other members of his squadron were listed as the *Victory, Garland, Ruby, Sapphire, Centurion* (this is clearly a mistake for the *Worcester*), *Star, Marten, Mermaid* and an unnamed merchant ship.[12] As soon as Blake had heard what Brandley had to say, he put his ships in motion towards the Downs. At 10 am, a ketch reached Bourne from Blake, with orders to join him. Bourne immediately weighed anchor and started cautiously southwards. He must have seen the departure of the Dutch with great relief because he would have had to pass close by them, which would have raised the question of the flag again.

By the time Blake was beating across the bay from Dungeness, the crisis appeared to be over. The Dutch were only dimly visible on the opposite side of the Channel near Calais and, in two or three hours, all the English ships would be reunited. As the wind was NE, Blake could not join Bourne directly. Instead, he put his ships on the port tack and headed out into the Channel. This had two advantages. Bourne, who had the wind at his back, could sail out of the Downs towards him, without changing course, and the Dutch could be kept under observation at the same time.

Up to this point, Tromp seems to have had no intention of provoking a fight. Indeed, his departure from Dover Road may well have been to avoid the two English squadrons, both of which were in sight, but he now received what appeared to be very alarming news. Two Dutch warships joined him from the west, one of them very much the worse for wear. The senior man, Commodore Huyrluyt, reported that he and two other men-of-war had been escorting a large convoy of Dutch merchant ships, inward bound from Genoa, when they had encountered three English warships.[13] They were the *Great President*, commanded by Anthony Young, the *Paradox*, Jacob Reynolds and an armed merchantman, the *Recovery*, Edmund Chapman. They were on their way to meet Ayscue, who was expected back in the Channel very shortly. They carried much-needed supplies and Young had instructions to warn him about the unpleasant reception planned by the Dutch.[14]

Young ordered Huyrluyt to strike his flag, which he did, but the other two refused and a fight developed in which the Dutch got the worst of it. Van der Zaanen, the second-in-command, fled rather than be seen condoning the search of Dutch ships. The other two followed, leaving the merchantmen under Young's control.[15] Huyrluyt and van der Zaanen had then sailed up the Channel, and reported seeing Dutch merchant ships surrounded by English frigates off Fairlight.

Blake had not molested the Dutch merchantmen. He had no letters of marque and as far as he was concerned they were law-abiding merchant ships going about their business. They, like Tromp himself, had taken shelter from the weather under the English coast. The tension had so far relaxed that when a boat from Dover came alongside the *James* with forty volunteers Blake found time to meet them at the gangway and give each man a glass of old Malaga, with his Lieutenant Thomas Adams, who had served at Taunton, looking on. The wine was poured out by Richard Gibson, who had missed the boat to take him to his ship, the *Assurance*, which was with Bourne in the Downs. The scene shows why Blake was so popular with the common seaman: the hero admiral, who had time for even the least of the men who served under him.[16]

Tromp was not to know that Blake had left the ships alone and Huyrluyt's report led him to fear that they were being searched for contraband, which he was specifically instructed to oppose by force.[17] He reacted promptly. He put the Dutch fleet onto the starboard tack and headed back across the Channel. When Blake observed the change of plan, he realised that Tromp would have to pass him if he continued on his present course. Blake tacked his own ships, until they faced towards the Sussex shore, which had the odd effect of making the *James* the last ship in the line, not the first. The purpose was to prevent Tromp passing between him and the English coast. He then ordered his ships to heave to, furl the main sail and clear for action: a wise precaution, which any commander in charge of a fleet would take, when in the presence of a possible enemy over twice his numbers.[18]

Tromp's flagship, the *Brederode*, came within musket shot of the *James* about 4.30 pm. Blake ordered two shots to be fired across the Dutchman's bows, to remind him about striking his flag. Tromp ignored them, hung out the red battle flag and replied to a third shot, fired at the flag itself, by a full broadside. At the same moment, Bourne made contact with the rear of the Dutch fleet.[19] Basing themselves on Gibson, some historians have tried to see in this battle the germ of the line formation, but Blake seems to have had no intention of fighting the sort of battle familiar from accounts of the eighteenth-century Navy. He had only thirteen ships, but he was determined that Tromp was not going to pass him without striking his flag, so he spread his ships out as far as he could, without risking them being cut off from each other.

Once battle was joined Blake changed his formation. Gibson says the General 'put his ship before the wind, hauled his foresail half up the brails and lowered his topsails about half mast down and this was done to bring the two leeward ships into service and give way for Major Bourne's division to come in to the windward of the Dutch.'[20] An interesting, but risky manoeuvre, which prolonged the separation of the two halves of the English fleet.

The Dutch played into Blake's hands. They adopted the old charge tactics, which badly misfired. After a considerable struggle which lasted for the rest of the day, some of the Dutch ships broke through Blake's squadron, the fight raging fiercely around the *James* in particular. After the battle over seventy shot holes were counted in the hull and superstructure of the flag ship.[21] Once

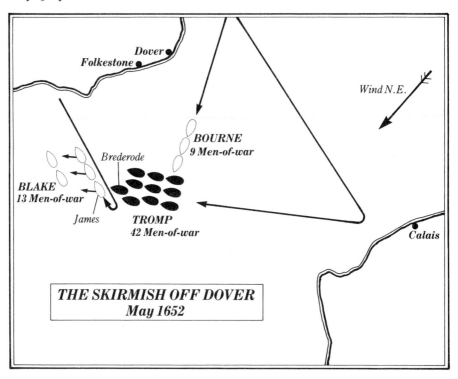

THE SKIRMISH OFF DOVER
May 1652

through, the successful Dutchmen found themselves to leeward. The remainder were trapped between Blake and Bourne.

Bourne describes the Dutch tactics as an attempt to get away from him which, in a sense, they were.

> They did their utmost to decline us and avoid our coming near, which we endeavoured by all means; but their Admiral leading the van, they made all sail after him, and so shot themselves to leeward and so left the rear of the fleet to us, which we endeavoured to sever from the rest, and accordingly did in part break the body; and some of us who were the nearest and had the advantage of the wind, fell upon the sternmost, who, I suppose, found it hot work.

He went on to describe how they divided the Dutch into two or three clusters isolated from each other.[22]

The English did not have enough ships to hold their opponents indefinitely, but it was the Dutch who were the first to recoil. The English lost no ships and the Dutch one, the *Sta Maria*, commanded by Captain Tuynemans. It should have been two. Captain Sipke Fokkes surrendered his ship, the *St. Laurens*, to the *Fairfax*, commanded by John Lawson but the English abandoned her, believing her to be so badly damaged that she would sink. The Dutch repossessed the ship and managed to get her back to the United Provinces.[23] Bourne was sure that, if his ships had not been foul and heavy sailers, he could have done even better.[24]

Investigations were launched into the circumstances by both sides. Cromwell and Denis Bond were dispatched to Portsmouth where they met a jubilant Blake. With the advantage of the wind, and almost twice the English numbers, Tromp had failed to capture a single English ship, while he had a trophy to exhibit. There was only one sour note. Captain Thorowgood of the *Worcester* and Captain Gibbs of the *Garland* were accused of not supporting Blake as they should have done. There is a report that the *Garland* and another ship, which may have been the *Worcester*, had fallen to leeward, even before the battle began.[25] A defence of Thorowgood's conduct and a petition for his reinstatement by his crew was forwarded to the Council of State by Blake, without comment. They were too late. Anthony Young had already been promoted, from the *Great President*, to replace him. [26] As Thorowgood was Blake's flag captain in 1650, he was serving notice that he expected the strictest obedience and that seniority would be no defence.

Blake's attitude to naval warfare comes out clearly from the Skirmish and its aftermath. It was the same heroic mode of leadership that had characterised the defences of Lyme Regis and Taunton. He appealed to the heart, rather than the head. Blake would set the example and he expected that, as a matter of duty, his captains would imitate him, even if that entailed immolating themselves and their ships, against their better judgement. One thing Blake would never forgive, was failure to support either him or the other captains, in action. The Skirmish only reinforced his conviction that the emotional approach was the right one. The superior quality of the English ships and guns made sophisticated tactics of secondary value. All the English had to do, was to be of good courage and put their trust in God.

Tromp's reaction was to try and pretend that Blake had begun the engagement. He claimed that Blake had fired the first broadside, not the Dutch. Complaints had also been made that the Dutch had gone into battle in no sort of order, which Tromp adduced as additional evidence that he had no intention of fighting.[27] Nobody likes to be branded as the aggressor, but the logic of the situation suggests that Tromp began the fighting. If he believed that the merchant ships had been searched, his instructions were quite clear. He was to use force. Tromp himself had been responsible for adding a clause to them which said that the ships conducting the search, should be pursued and captured.[28] If the ships off Fairlight had been searched then it was Blake who had searched them, and he was the guilty party who should be punished.

The truth was that Tromp was spoiling for a fight. He disliked the Commonwealth, he knew Dutch commercial supremacy was at stake and he had twice the number of ships that Blake had. If he could teach the English a sharp lesson, a larger conflict could be headed off and the trading position preserved. He got a shock. Blake proved a far more formidable adversary than he had bargained for, and the power and discipline of the English gunnery must have come as a most unpleasant surprise.

Whatever the rights and wrongs of the matter, it would be unfair to brand Tromp with more than a tactical misjudgement. The English were the real aggressors. They intended to compel the Dutch to honour their flag, their right to search for contraband, and the Navigation Act. The Skirmish off Dover was the occasion for the war, not the reason.

Blake's success destroyed what chance there had been of a compromise. The English knew now they could force their views on the Dutch. Those who, like Cromwell and maybe Blake himself, wished to turn English naval might in a different direction, found themselves in a quandary, which was to persist throughout the war. If they proposed negotiations when the war was not going well, they could be accused of betrayal. If they proposed to quit while the war situation was favourable, they could be accused of passing up a golden opportunity of enforcing measures such as the Navigation Act with which they agreed. If the war was to be stopped, the Dutch had to make the first concession. They tried hard for a compromise, sending out the experienced Pauw to join their plenipotentiaries in London, all to no avail. They gave up and went home on 30 June, Pauw remarking plaintively, 'We are attacking a mountain of iron, they are attacking a mountain of gold.'[29] The formal declaration of war followed on 8 July.

The unbounded confidence the Council of State now felt, led them to take the war to the Dutch. The best way to do that was to attack Dutch trade. Information had reached London that the Dutch West and East India fleets were on their way home, round the north of Scotland. As early as 7 June, the decision had been taken to send a squadron northwards to intercept it, but problems in victualling the ships delayed their departure.

The original proposal was that the expedition should be commanded by Sir George Ayscue, now safely back in England.[30] What the Council of State had in mind, was a squadron powerful enough to deal with the merchant ships and their escort, but too small to merit putting a General-at-Sea in command. That was logical. The pivot of all operations was the Straits of Dover, which was where the main fleet should be. Blake should only move when it became clear what Tromp would do.

Yet when the instructions were brought down to the fleet three days later the plan had been changed. One reason may have been the time-lapse involved in getting Ayscue from Plymouth to the Downs, but if that had been the only consideration, logic suggested that some other officer, perhaps Penn who was now with the fleet, should be substituted. What happened was quite different. Blake was put in command and it was left to him to select the ships he would take.[31] It is difficult to resist the conclusion that Blake himself was responsible for the change. The exact composition of his fleet has not come down to us. At the end of June, the Council of State estimated that it had 110 ships ready for sea, some of which were still in the Thames. According to Tromp, Blake had eighty-three ships with him, so he must have taken practically every available ship,[32] leaving Ayscue with a purely nominal force to look after the Straits of Dover.

This extraordinary decision, which left the whole of southern England open to attack, tells us a good deal about the nature of the war. The war was about commerce not about territory. A formal invasion of each other's country was considered at no point by either side in any of the three Dutch wars. Yet, even when this unspoken assumption is taken into account, the decision contradicted all the tenets of sound strategy and left Ayscue exposed to attack. Ayscue had reached Plymouth sometime between 15 and 30 May.[33] After refitting and receiving the supplies by Young's squadron, he was ordered to the Downs. He arrived on 21 June and Blake left for the North four days later, without waiting to see what Tromp would do.[34] Ayscue had the seven ships which had accompanied him to Barbados – the *Rainbow, Amity, Success, Increase, Malaga merchant, Ruth* and *Brazil* – plus three other ships: the *Paragon, John and Elizabeth* and the *Mary* flyboat. The Council of State was rapidly preparing more ships for sea and planned to send them to the Downs as they became available. They included some of the most powerful units in the fleet: the *Sovereign* and the *Vanguard*.

The whole arrangement was fraught with danger. Tromp's fleet was off the Dutch coast and was reported to be increasing every day. Yet ships were dispatched, singly, from the Thames to the Downs, round the North Foreland, by a government happily oblivious to the enormous Dutch fleet only just over the horizon. Nor did it appear to be aware what a tempting morsel Ayscue's small squadron represented. This happy-go-lucky attitude was shared by Sir George himself. His best policy was to lie low and hope that the Dutch would not notice him, until Blake's voyage was sufficiently far forward to draw Tromp after him. That was just what Sir George did not do. On 2 July, he sallied out and attacked a Dutch merchant convoy of thirty to forty vessels. After a sharp engagement with the four escorting men-of-war, seven were taken and the rest dispersed, most of them running on shore near Calais to avoid capture. The fight was not without its cost. the *John and Elizabeth* had to be towed back to Dover and its captain had his leg amputated.[35]

This was too much for Tromp and, on 5 July, he appeared off the Downs with his entire fleet, numbering 102 vessels. When the Dutch arrived Ayscue was on shore taking physic and the prospect looked black.[36] He sent orders to Captain Harrison of the *Vanguard*, which was in Margate road, to stop ships coming out of the Thames, and then hastened back on board the *Rainbow*. Accounts differ, but none of them places his strength at more than twenty. The ships huddled under the guns of the Downs castles and their companies were reinforced with 200 soldiers.[37]

Yet Tromp did not attack. A plan was drawn up at a council of war which divided the fleet into two. Tromp and Evertsen would command seventy-five ships which would make the main attack via the northern entrance. De With would remain outside the Goodwins with the rest to make sure Ayscue did not escape around the South Foreland. For success the Dutch required a favourable wind. According to Tromp, his efforts on 6 and 7 July were thwarted by calms.[38] The next day, there were favourable north and north-west winds, but they were very strong and a storm was brewing. Two very stormy days followed but, by the morning of 11 July, conditions had moderated and the Dutch prepared to attack.

The wind was too light to make it worth putting much sail on the ships but, using the tide, the Dutch crept towards Ayscue's little squadron. By the time the ebb forced him to anchor, Tromp was between the Quern and the Goodwins, a league from the English ships, and all seemed set for a grand finale. Around midday, the wind swung round to the south and south south east. The shift in direction spoiled Tromp's plan, 'making it impossible for our ships to beat up against it through the Narrows', but it was a favourable wind for the North Sea and the Dutch streamed away northwards, out of the Downs, to Ayscue's great relief.[39]

The whole incident is very curious. Tromp's failure to press home his attack against an enemy a fifth of his size for an entire week is difficult to understand, even when the superior nature of the English guns is taken into account. One possible explanation relates to the state of the tide. The ebb is a west-flowing tide in the Channel and Ayscue might have been able to attack de With's smaller squadron before the main force at the northern end could get into action. De With's situation could have been complicated by the light airs which might have stopped his ships supporting each other properly. But the most likely explanation is that the Dutch Admiral was really only filling in time until he got a fair wind for the north. Ayscue was not really important enough for Tromp to risk disabling part of his fleet in order to destroy him. Tromp's orders did require him to pursue Blake, as soon as there was a favourable wind,[40] and he knew that his part in the Skirmish off Dover had made him unpopular in some republican quarters. He could not afford to exceed his orders again. Nevertheless it was a lucky escape and there were those who would have laid the blame at Blake's door, if Ayscue had been destroyed.

Meanwhile Blake was ploughing northward. Progress was slow. The same adverse winds which pinned Tromp in the Downs, forced the English to beat about off the East coast for over a week. Not until the wind came about southerly, on 11 July, was Blake able to begin fulfilling his instructions. As soon as the latitude of Shetland was reached, a powerful squadron under Penn was sent in search of the Dutch fishing fleet. The next day the fleet, guarded by twelve men-of-war, was sighted by the leading frigates. The English had the wind and the first to come within range was the *Laurel*, commanded by John Taylor. He fired a broadside but then lay by and waited for the other frigates to come up. The first seven to arrive were all 4th or 5th rates and battle was not joined until they were supported by the *Speaker*.

The action was sharp while it lasted, but the result was never in doubt. Though the Dutch had the advantage of numbers, they were outgunned and eleven of the twelve were forced to surrender. Nine hundred prisoners were taken. Another ship was captured by the *Nonsuch* the next day, but it is not clear whether this ship was the lone survivor of the earlier action. Three of the prizes were so badly damaged that they were sunk, three Blake sent to Deane at Inverness. The remaining six were added to the fleet.[41] The most notable English casualty was Captain Brandley, of the *Portsmouth*, who had to have a hand amputated.[42]

'Lying by' was not an attitude Blake was trying to instil. The responsibility of the 4th rate frigates, in particular, was the same as Beatty's Battle Squadron's in the First World War. The enemy must be held in play, whatever the cost, until the big ships could get into action. Blake would not forgive a captain who let the enemy escape, because he was unwilling to sacrifice his own ship. A month earlier the *Laurel*, in company with the *Tiger* commanded by Captain James Peacock, had chased two Dutch men-of-war off the Flemish coast. Peacock had managed to board and capture his enemy ship, but Taylor could do no more than run his quarry on shore. This was not good enough for Blake and when the Council of State received his report, it issued a formal statement admonishing Taylor to do better for the future.[43]

The whole fleet held its breath, waiting on Blake's verdict. There must have been great relief when Taylor was not disciplined a second time. Richard Gibson served on the *Assurance*, commanded by Benjamin Blake, which also took part in the action. He comments, 'I observe none of the English capts were blamed for lying still until the *Speaker* began.'[44] That he thought such a comment necessary, when the entire enemy force was captured, is most revealing of the relations which existed in Blake's fleet. Penn, who was Taylor's immediate superior, may have defended his subordinate's behaviour by reasoning that there was little chance of the Dutch escaping. They had to stand their ground while the fishermen scattered. Taylor's success in subjugating three Dutch frigates and making a fourth to strike may have played a part in justifying his tactics. Privately, Blake may have been glad that the delay allowed most of the busses to get away. Contemporary accounts stress that he and Tromp treated kindly any fishermen they captured. Both men showed distaste for making economic war on the defenceless. With those he did capture, Blake limited himself to taking the tenth herring the Commonwealth claimed as its due and then released them.

Blake was now free to concentrate on finding the Dutch East and West India fleets, but information about his movements is scanty. The Council of State itself complained about lack of information. What happened has been reconstructed from Dutch accounts, supplemented by an assessment of what a commander in Blake's position would be likely to do. Ships working their way round the north of Scotland were often separated by the weather. They needed a rendezvous point of known latitude, where they could link up again, and which would tell them their position. The almost universal rendezvous point was Fair Isle, which lay midway between the Orkney and Shetland Islands. Blake reasoned that if he stationed his fleet within striking distance of the island, he could not go far wrong. If the India fleet arrived first, he would be able to snap it up. If Tromp arrived first, he would get his battle.

His reasoning was sound. Tromp's destination was Fair Isle, but foul winds made his passage slow and tedious, so he did not reach its latitude until 24 July. During the afternoon Dutch lookouts spotted five ships. Visibility was poor and, with darkness approaching, they could not be identified before contact was lost.[45] The next morning Tromp sent Captains Kempe and van der Veere, to seek information on the whereabouts of the English fleet. They returned, later in the day, with the news that Blake was either between Fair Isle and the Shetlands, or at anchor in Bressay Sound.[46] Confirmation was not long in coming. At 4 pm, English ships were seen from the masthead. Six were spotted, bearing west-north-west, and another three, to the north-east, indicating that the main body of Blake's fleet was just over the horizon.[47] Scenting battle, Tromp got his fleet under sail and started in pursuit, but he had no sooner set course for the Shetlands, than the wind began to rise. By 5 pm the wind was already at gale force and the unfortunate Dutchmen found themselves in one of the worst storms ever encountered by a battle fleet at sea.

One Dutch writer described the storm in graphic terms. 'The fleet being as it were buried by the sea in the most horrible abysses, rose out of them, only to be tossed up to the clouds; here the masts were beaten down into the sea, there the deck was overflowed with the prevailing waves; the tempest was so much mistress of the ships they could be governed no longer, and on every side appeared all the forerunners of a dismal wreck.'[48] To make matters worse, the winds were blowing the Dutch straight towards the sharp rocks of Sumburgh Head, the southern cape of the Shetland Islands. By the afternoon, conditions were as bad as many of the Dutch had experienced in a lifetime of sea faring. It was every one for himself and the fleet scattered, each captain seeking his own salvation. As the Chief Officers wrote, the only escape was by tacking but the wind was so strong, that it would tear the sails to shreds and they would lose control of their ships.[49]

For all that terrible night and the next day, the Dutch captains were at full stretch, trying desperately to claw their way out to sea, away from the devouring rocks. Not until the morning of 27 July, did the weather let up sufficiently to allow Tromp a chance to assess the situation. A count revealed thirty-four ships out of a fleet of over a hundred.[50] What had happened to the rest he did not know, and he had no means of finding out.

Six weeks were to elapse before the Admiralties were able to form a complete picture of what had happened. Those who remained with Tromp had managed, either through good seamanship or because they had well-found ships, to beat off Shetland. One or two pushed far out to sea and ended up in Norway. Most of the captains decided to take refuge among the islands. Guessing correctly, that attempts to shelter in the main anchorage would lead them into the open arms of Blake and the English fleet, they decided to risk weathering Sumburgh Head and taking refuge in the western fiords.

Twenty-three ships came to rest off Scalloway, five in 'South West Bay', by which the Deeps near Skelda Ness appear to be indicated. The 'West Bay', in which seven more took refuge, is probably St Magnus Bay. Another seven ended up in what the Dutch author called 'Buyshaven,' which may have been Burra Voe. The nine ships which used the inlets of Northern Shetland to shelter from the storm, brought the total to fifty-one.[51]

Some of them did not make it. According to an English account, ten Dutch men-of-war were wrecked on the Shetlands, and six more foundered at sea.[52] Whether this number included the ship of Isaac de Jongh, which sank in Tromp's own sight, is not clear.[53] The storm engulfed the ships of the India fleet too, which was approaching Fair Isle when it broke over them. Two were wrecked on the Shetlands, the *Orangie* and the *Breda*. Two more, the *Lastdrager* and the *Salamander*, together with four West India ships, were among those with Tromp, when the weather finally moderated. Another, the *Coning David*, joined him on 29 July. Two more made it into 'South West Bay'.[54]

The English had not suffered as badly as the Dutch, but they had not got off scot free. When the weather began to deteriorate, they made the best of their way into Bressay Sound, on the east side of Shetland. This enabled Blake to keep his fleet together, but the English ships received a severe buffeting. All the extra victuals were lost and when the storm was over not a ship remained undamaged, some being rendered almost useless for fighting purposes.[55]

Realising the pointlessness of staying in the Shetland area any longer, and worried about what might be happening further south in his absence, Tromp started for home. He left two galliots to tell any stragglers who came in to follow him. Blake, too, realised that, now the India ships had arrived, remaining in the Shetlands was a waste of time. The two fleets sailed on more or less parallel courses. They came in sight of each other briefly but neither Tromp nor Blake had any stomach for a fight.[56] For Tromp his reduced numbers are a sufficient excuse but Blake's reluctance needs more explanation. The English ships were generally slower sailers than the Dutch, so Tromp could only be brought to battle if there was commerce to defend. The effect of the storm had been to slow down the English further. Blake may have thought chasing Tromp a pointless exercise. His knowledge of the extent of the Dutch disaster may have been very limited and he was only too well aware of the difficulties of his own captains.

Though the majority of the Dutch ships reached the United Provinces safely, the successful reassembling of most of Tromp's fleet should not be allowed to obscure the extent of the Dutch reverse. Without striking a blow, the English had won a major victory. Sixteen ships was the exact number the Dutch were to lose at the battle of Portland. The episode was a remarkable demonstration of the strategic advantage the position of the British Isles conferred on the Commonwealth.

Another even more serious consequence was that most of the fifty-one who scattered, were not available for the next phase of the campaign. They shaped course for Norway and were reported off the Nase in early August. They straggled home during September, which was too late for most of them to be refitted in time to take part in the autumn's dramatic manoeuvres in the Channel or the battle of Kentish Knock. The Hand of Providence had presented the English with an unparalleled opportunity. How effectively Blake and his colleagues exploited their advantage will be the subject of the next chapter.

De Ruijter in the Channel and Kentish Knock

*T*HE departure of Tromp northwards in pursuit of Blake on 11 July, had left the initiative in the Channel in the hands of the English. Ayscue already had twenty ships and, now that the way was open, more joined him every day. English East India ships were expected shortly, together with rich merchantmen from the Mediterranean. Sir George was ordered westwards to shepherd them through the Western Approaches. He was to damage as much Dutch and French trade as he could, at the same time. Ayscue's orders show that the Council of State had learned from his lucky escape. He was to leave one good ship and one 'nimble of sailing' to secure the Straits of Dover, and take all the rest with him. As long as Tromp was absent, there was little chance of an attack on the Thames.[1]

Ayscue sailed from the Downs on, or about, 19 July. The size and constitution of his fleet is difficult to discover. A correspondent at Portsmouth, where Ayscue anchored inside Bembridge Point on 20 July, put his numbers at fifty.[2] Dutch reports made him forty-five, of which two ships mounted 60 guns and eight, between 36 and 40.[3] The two 60 gun ships were his flagship, the *George*, and the *Vanguard*, which his Vice-Admiral William Haddock, had taken over from Captain Harrison.[4] The English fleet was off Plymouth, on 21 July. The merchant ships arrived right on cue and the Council of State could relax, knowing that the next fleet of any importance was not due for another two months.[5]

There was no such security for the Dutch. Tromp was hardly out of sight before the States General was preparing another fleet under Commodore de Ruijter. He was to escort out merchant ships, waiting in the Texel, and bring back the West Indies silver fleet, which was off Spain considering whether to go round Scotland or wait for a convoy.[6] De Ruijter was in the Straits of Dover by 31 July,[7] but he did not sail down the Channel for another fortnight because a jittery States General held eight of his men-of-war in the Texel, until the remnants of Tromp's fleet arrived back from the north.[8]

De Ruijter must have known that his task was difficult, if not impossible. He would have to fight Ayscue. Even if he beat him, there was the problem of getting back. He had talked to fellow Zeelander, Jan Evertsen, so he was only too well aware of the disaster which had overtaken the main fleet and the ominous possibility that Blake would be in control of the Straits of Dover, by the time he returned.[9] As strong north easterly winds blew the Dutch rapidly down the Channel, de Ruijter must have hoped that he could get rid of his merchant ships before having to deal with Ayscue. He was doomed to disappointment. Ayscue sailed from Plymouth early on 15 August. Guessing that the Dutch would keep to the French side, Sir George shaped course for the Brittany coast and was rewarded by sighting the Dutch, between 1 pm and 2 pm the following day.[10]

The accounts of the battle agree that the English strength was about forty. The most circumstantial gives them thirty-eight warships and four fire ships.[11] The Dutch numbers are more difficult to gauge. According to de Ruijter, he had thirty men-of-war and sixty merchantmen. English reports reversed the proportions.[12] Strictly speaking de Ruijter was right but it is clear that many of the merchantmen were armed and took part in the fighting. There is much less doubt about the disparity in fire power. The list of de Ruijter's fleet shows two ships with 40 guns and the rest with between 30 and 24. The English had two over 60 and eight between 36 and 40. In addition, the greater power of the English iron guns must be taken into the reckoning.

The battle began auspiciously for the English. The Dutch were dead to leeward and Ayscue used his advantage intelligently. The Dutch were arranged in three divisions, the most westerly under their Rear-Admiral, Verhaeff, the middle one, under de Ruijter himself, and the easterly one, under the Vice-Admiral, den Broucke. The English directed their attack exclusively on de Ruijter and den Broucke, temporarily cancelling any Dutch numerical advantage because Verhaeff's ships would have to tack before they could take part in the fighting.[13]

Ayscue failed to capitalise on the opening he had created for himself. Descriptions of the battle show that he adopted the charge tactics, which had failed so often in the past. The English crashed into the Dutch in one compact mass and the initial impact must have been considerable. It was in this phase of the action that the desperate struggle took place over one of the largest Dutch ships, the *De Struisvogel*, commanded by Douwe Aukes.[14] At one point the crew wanted to cry quarter but Aukes forced them to fight on, by threatening to blow up the ship under them. The *De Struisvogel* survived and made an important contribution to the English repulse.

After a hard struggle the *George* broke through. One report says 'Sir George ... began the fight with great resolution, himself and six more charging through the whole body of the enemy's fleet.'[15] Unfortunately the remaining English ships did not make it. The same account shows that the Dutch were using their customary tactics. The English ships 'received very many shots in their hulls, but more in their masts, sails and rigging, the enemy's main design being to spoil them, in hope thereby to make the better use of their fire ships upon them.'

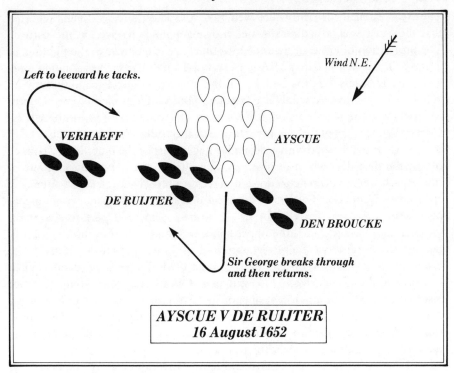

Wind N.E.

Left to leeward he tacks.

VERHAEFF

AYSCUE

DE RUIJTER

DEN BROUCKE

*Sir George breaks through
and then returns.*

**AYSCUE V DE RUIJTER
16 August 1652**

Another correspondent points up the difference in gunnery tactics, describing how the English aimed at the hulls and the Dutch at the masts and rigging.[16]

Many of the English ships were caught in the Dutch fleet and, with Verhaeff's ships coming into play, the position looked grim. The powerful ships in the English fleet just saved the day. According to the anonymous informant of the Council of State, whose letter was published in *Mercurius Politicus*, 'Sir George tacked about and weathered them, and charged them all again, and so continued still engaged in the body of their fleet until it was dark night.'[17] A particularly violent conflict took place around the *Bonadventure*, which was only rescued by the resolute conduct of Captain Smithson.[18] He set light to his fire ship, which drifting among the Dutch ships, frightened their captains enough to give the English sufficient time to tow the badly damaged ship out of the action.[19]

Darkness put an end to the battle. Each side claimed to have sunk one or more of their opponents, but the only casualty seems to have been Captain Smithson's fireship and even there, the intrepid captain and his crew escaped in the ship's boat. The Dutch lost fifty to sixty killed and forty to fifty wounded.[20]

The Rear-Admiral, den Broucke, died two days later, but de Ruijter reported that the cause was 'a natural disease' and not wounds received in the battle.[21] The proportion of killed to wounded, testifies to the intensity of the fighting. *A Letter from Plymouth*, dated 31 August, put the English casualties at ninety-one, which is a little less than the Dutch, but the writer does not distinguish between killed and wounded. Ayscue's flag captain, Thomas Lisle, died of his wounds. Michael Pack, the Rear-Admiral, had a leg amputated, and died a short time later. Captain Witheridge, of the *Bonadventure*, was also badly wounded but survived.[22]

The Dutch finished with a clear advantage. Despite the bravado of a council of war the next day, which resolved to fight again if the opportunity occurred, the English were in no state to do so and retreated to Plymouth on 18 August.[23] De Ruijter rightly claimed that he came off best and that he came within inches of a famous victory. There is an air of frustration in his report to the States General that, having gained the upper hand, he could not finish the English off, because the fireships were all to leeward and could not get into position.[24] The extent of the Dutch success can be measured by de Ruijter's behaviour. When Ayscue withdrew, the Dutch followed him. On 18 August, a council of war resolved to attack the English at anchor in Plymouth Sound, and only a providential shift in the wind preserved Ayscue from a major disaster.[25] Curiously, though Ayscue remained in harbour throughout the rest of de Ruijter's cruise, the Dutchman did not consider the plan again.

There were the inevitable post mortems. Both sides blamed the behaviour of a minority of captains, who were accused of cowardice. Attention focussed on the commanders of the armed merchantmen. It was usual for the captain of a merchant ship to have a share in the ship and cargo, to give him an incentive not to run off with it. Naturally, such men were not enthusiastic about the prospect of having their livelihood sunk under them. The outcry was greatest on the English side, a sure sign that they had got the worst of it.[26] There may be some truth in the accusation, that they did not second Ayscue as vigorously as they should have done. The trouble was, that blaming them diverted attention from the real cause of the defeat, which was faulty tactics.

Meanwhile there was a lull in the main theatre. Blake reached Southwold on 9 August[27] and a week later, used the same favourable winds which blew de Ruijter down the Channel, to shift his position to the Downs.[28] Apart from that his activity was confined to sending out a strong squadron under Penn, to reconnoitre the Dutch coast.[29] When news of Ayscue's defeat came in he did detach the *Convertine, President, Dragon, Convert, Sampson* and *Golden Dove*, to reinforce the stricken commander, at the importunity of the Council of State,[30] but he resisted attempts to persuade him to go in search of de Ruijter. The most he would do was to send Penn out on patrol again, but with strict instructions not to go west of Dungeness.[31]

There were two main reasons for the refusal of the English to be drawn down the Channel. Though Blake has not much to say on the subject, the English fleet seems to have been severely damaged by the storm which scattered the Dutch. The worst affected ships were the *Fairfax* and *Happy Entrance,* which were sent to Chatham, and the *Centurion* and *Adventure,* which docked at Deptford. An exact survey was made of the victualling position which showed thirteen ships to be very short indeed. Most of them were the smaller vessels, the only exception being the *Laurel.*[32] Another problem was that the *Nonsuch, Advice, Drake* and *Merlin* would soon be unserviceable for want of masts, yards and cordage.[33]

Blake's reluctance to move, before the wants of his fleet had been supplied, was reinforced by the knowledge that the Council of State was making a great effort to get as many extra ships to sea as possible. The aim was to extend the summer cruise, in the hope of forcing a decisive battle, before the onset of the winter. Ships were being prepared for sea with all speed. The prize fund was being raided for money for victuals for 14,000 men for an extra month. This would enable the fleet to stay out to the end of October instead of being reduced to its winter size during September as was usual.[34] Mindful of what had so nearly happened to Ayscue in July, he was determined that the Dutch would find no small squadron in the Downs, ripe for the picking, while he was away chasing an elusive de Ruijter.

By the beginning of September all was ready but, before devoting himself entirely to the destruction of the Dutch, Blake took the opportunity to show the French the folly of their ways. France was still at war with Spain. In the late summer of 1652, the Spanish took the offensive and laid siege to Dunkirk. All the French efforts to relieve the town by land failed and food began to run short. The Spanish commander summoned the garrison to surrender. The Governor replied, that he would give the town up, if no help reached it within the week.

The Duc de Vendome, who commanded the French forces, concluded that only one ploy was left and that was to run in food and extra men by sea. A relieving force of seven ships was assembled at Havre, and set out for Dunkirk on 3 September.[35] Calais road was reached, without incident, but the next day the whole English fleet appeared over the horizon. At first, the French watched it unperturbed. Only when Blake was about to strike, did they realise that they were under attack. One, more alert than the rest, cut his cable and escaped. All the others were captured and Dunkirk surrendered a few days later.[36]

Vendome was appalled and wrote angrily to the Commonwealth government, demanding Blake's dismissal. The Council of State rejected his complaints coldly. England and France were not at war, officially, but Vendome was reminded of the continuing attacks by privateers on English shipping, the refuge provided for the Stuarts and the facilities made available to the Dutch Mediterranean squadron in French Provencal ports. Blake was acting within his instructions. The English government took a good deal of quiet satisfaction in the French loss to Spain, of the town, which they had named as the price for their alliance, nine months earlier.[37]

Blake now had a difficult choice to make. If he wished to prevent de Ruijter reaching home, with his precious convoy, the simplest course would be to wait for him in the Downs. Sooner or later, he must make for home and there was no chance of him avoiding the English battle fleet. Yet the more Blake considered the option, the more he must have seen snags. The shoals of the eastern Channel made manoeuvring difficult and increased the chances of an indecisive action. The prevailing winds were from the southwest, so that de Ruijter would probably have the wind in his favour. More important, there was the possibility of being caught between two fires, when the main Dutch fleet made its reappearance.

Blake must certainly have considered the drawbacks of going in search of de Ruijter too. The Dutch were as likely to be to windward of the English in any engagement in the Western Channel, as at the eastern end. In both the battles fought there, the fleet coming from the west started with the weather gauge. There was no real reason why the Dutch main fleet should not follow the English down the Channel, as Tromp had followed Blake. Worse, the advantage of deep water was more than offset by the opportunity it gave de Ruijter to evade the English fleet. Yet there was little doubt what Blake would do. When the choice was between action and inaction, action always won and the English fleet began the painful task of beating down the Channel. Ten days were consumed in the effort.

Meanwhile de Ruijter was preparing for the return voyage. After abandoning the Plymouth plan, the Dutch had sailed to Brest, where they took on stores and one of their badly damaged ships was made seaworthy again with French aid. Within a week the Dutch were at sea once more, cruising between Land's End and Ushant. De Ruijter's timetable was conditioned by the arrival of the merchantmen he was to convoy home. Four Caribbee traders, who may have been the expected silver fleet, joined him on 21 August, but he still had to wait for the ships from the Mediterranean and southern France. His orders were strict. He must not give in to the importunities of merchants to come home early so that they could scoop the market.[38]

De Ruijter must have thought long and hard about what he should do. Eastbound fleets usually hugged the English shore. In rough weather, Torbay was to be preferred to the sharp rocks of Brittany, but de Ruijter knew that there was a strong possibility that he might encounter the English fleet. At a council of war on 2 September, he arranged rendezvous points on the French coast, off Cap Barfleur and near Havre. A galliot was left to tell any Dutch merchantmen still to come, what the arrangements were.[39] If Blake came west and the Dutch were forced to beat a hasty retreat, a meeting place as far from the point where the English had last seen them as possible, and within reach of friendly France, was very desirable. If, on the other hand, Blake stayed in the Downs, Havre was a convenient place at which to wait for information from the Hague about the movements of the main fleet, and to organise a coat-trailing manoeuvre similar to the one Tromp was to execute before the battle of Scheveningen.

The shrewdness of his dispositions was demonstrated by what happened. The most circumstantial account is provided by Penn. Blake had followed his usual habit of assigning a strong squadron to his Vice-Admiral, and sending him out on patrol, ahead of the main fleet. Just before noon on 15 September, Penn's lookouts spotted two ships to windward, one of which was immediately identified, from the cut of its sails, as a Dutch flyboat. Men were sent swarming to the mastheads for a better view, and they were soon reporting excitedly that the whole Dutch fleet was just beyond the two original sightings. Penn called a council of war. 'I told them that I was resolved to use all means I could to bring them to engage us it being their choice, they having the wind to which our commanders showed a great deal of willingness.' A ketch was sent to tell Blake what was happening.[40]

De Ruijter's numbers are given as between thirty-six and forty. He names thirty men-of-war under his direct command, the same ones which had set out with him from the United Provinces. They were probably supplemented by strong armed merchantmen from among his convoy. He puts Penn's numbers at twenty-five. Penn says he had eighteen. Twelve are named and the others can be guessed. On his return from the north Penn had shifted his flag to the *James.* He had ten other ships from the main fleet, the *Andrew, Speaker, Triumph, Garland, Assistance, Foresight, President, Nonsuch, Ruby* and *Warwick.* In addition, there was the *Vanguard* from Ayscue's fleet and the six ships sent to reinforce him.[41]

On the surface, the decision to accept battle by Penn was rash: he only had half de Ruijter's numbers. But that may not have been Penn's plan at all. De Ruijter, in his account, says that he 'chased' twenty-five English ships for most of the day, which suggests that Penn was attempting, not unsuccessfully, to draw him towards Blake.[42] Once more the weather intervened. At daybreak the wind had been West by North. It now switched to South West and increased to gale force. Penn lost contact with the Dutch about 5 pm. Around midnight, there were flashes of gunfire on his weather quarter but he could not see what was going on. When morning broke, he saw a squadron of twelve ships, sheltering under the Start, but they were English not Dutch: reinforcements sent by Blake and led by Captain Taylor in the *Laurel.*[43]

The Dutch were nowhere to be seen. Penn cast about to see if he could pick up their trail. He does not seem to have strayed far across the Channel and his orders from Blake prevented him going east of Portland Bill. The Dutch were

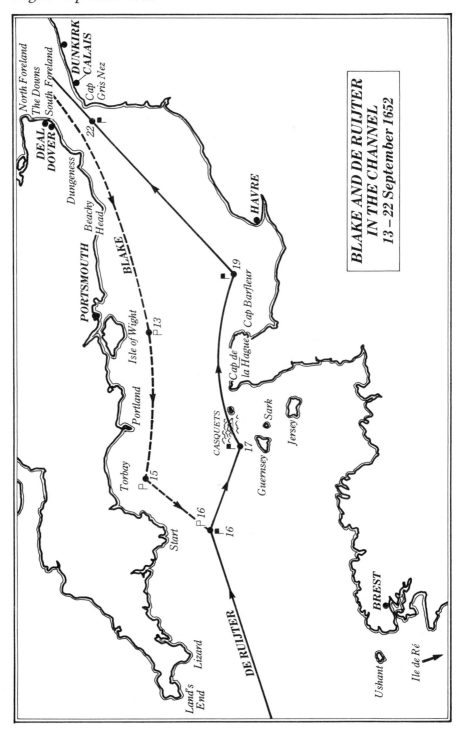

BLAKE AND DE RUIJTER
IN THE CHANNEL
13 – 22 September 1652

far away. At the time Penn was conferring with Taylor, de Ruijter was off Guernsey.[44] A council of war wisely decided not to try conclusions with the English but get their charges home. A couple of days was needed to round up the strays, but de Ruijter was soon on his way up the Channel and, on 22 September, his squadron rejoined the main fleet cruising off Nieuport.[45]

De Ruijter could be justly pleased with what he had done. He had fought and worsted Ayscue and he had avoided Blake's charge down the Channel, like a skilled matador who shows the bull his cloak and then quickly sidesteps. All this had been achieved while hampered by the need to protect convoys. The English had cause for disquiet. The advantage conferred by the storm had been dissipated, due to bad tactics by Ayscue, and bad strategy by Blake.

Once Blake realised that de Ruijter had evaded him, he gave orders for the fleet to retrace its steps. On 20 September, the English regained Portsmouth and when the Dutch scouts cautiously reconnoitred the Downs, the whole English fleet was there.[46] There was great expectancy of a battle. One report confidently predicted that the Dutch would have to fight, because they had 200 merchant ships, waiting to pass the Straits of Dover.

The Dutch fleet with which de Ruijter was reunited, was a very unhappy one. Even before Tromp's return from the north, there had been much criticism of the Lieutenant-Admiral among the republicans. When the extent of the disaster became known, Tromp was chosen as the scapegoat. He was ordered on shore to explain why he had not kept the States General regularly informed of his movements. He protested in vain that he had sent letters, before the one by Cornelis Evertsen which revealed the extent of the calamity, and that they must have miscarried.[47] Information which showed that most of the missing ships were safe in Norway availed him little.[48] Realising that he was about to be dismissed, Tromp resigned on 21 August.[49] He retired to the country to wait on events, convinced that his successsor would encounter the same obstacles as himself. The rampant republicans gleefully replaced him with Witte Cornelis de With, the Vice-Admiral of Holland.

By 2 September, de With had assembled thirty-two men-of-war at the Schooneveld, but he was nowhere near strong enough to take on Blake, who had fifty-four in the Downs.[50] Not until de With was sure that Blake was committed to the pursuit of de Ruijter, did he leave the safety of the shoals for the empty Straits of Dover. His strength had risen to forty-five by the time de Ruijter rejoined him. De Ruijter had twenty-nine, but ten were not fit to remain at sea, including his flagship the *Neptune*, and they were sent in. This left the Dutch with a fleet of sixty-four.[51] During the cruise down the Channel, Blake had picked up at least eight of Ayscue's original fleet and quite possibly more, so he had sixty-two ships at the lowest computation. The most reliable accounts gave him sixty-eight, so for the only time in the war, the English had a superiority in numbers as well as firepower.[52]

This was not the worst of it. The Dutch administration was chaotic. The ships were equipped by five different boards of Admiralty – Friesland, North Quarter, Zeeland, Amsterdam and Rotterdam (both of the last two in Holland). At the beginning of the war they had been made responsible for producing 100 ships. Another fifty were to be set out by five boards of Directors, making no less than ten different jurisdictions.[53]

Each board made its own decisions. Some boards sent their ships promptly to the appointed rendezvous, others responded very slowly. Some put eight months' victuals on board as they were asked to do, some six and some only four. The confusion caused by a group of ships appearing on time with only four months' victuals and then having to wait a month for other ships, which turned up with eight, can be imagined. The same was true of the ships' equipment. Shortages could only be replaced from among the ships of the same Board. If a ship was damaged she had to return to the ports controlled by her home Board. Each Board had its own policy for recruiting seamen. Some paid promptly, others slowly. The standard rate of pay among the regular Boards was eleven guilders a month, but the men in the Directors' ships were often paid more. Even the Directors' ships, which were the best paid, were losing men to private men-of-war, who offered increased pay and the chance of more prize money.[54]

When Zeeland ships docked after a cruise the men were allowed on shore.[55] The Amsterdam admiralty was not so liberal and confined the men on board ship. They feared desertion and justly, because they paid less than the others and their credit was not good. Two thousand came ashore on 10 September, demanding their pay and the army had to be called in to disperse them.[56] The Lieutenant-Admiral had as little control over his captains as over his men. They, too, were appointed by the Boards and unsatisfactory ones chould only be dismissed with the agreement of their Boards, which were often prepared to condone defiance of the Lieutenant-Admiral's orders.[57]

In such conditions only a man who was respected and trusted by his subordinates had any chance of welding the fleet into an effective fighting force, and that man was not de With. The unanimous desire of the officers and men was that they should be commanded by Tromp who alone had the trust of the seamen and enough authority to impose his will on the recalcitrant. If they could not have Tromp, the least that the captains expected was that his trusted subordinate, Jan Evertsen, should be appointed in his place. None of the senior officers wanted de With.

It was not that de With lacked courage. He was the bravest man in the fleet. Like Blake, he would never flinch whatever the odds. Nor was his ability to handle a large fleet in battle in doubt. As a tactician, he was Tromp's equal and beside him Evertsen was pedestrian. His trouble was that he was a thoroughly unpleasant man to work with, and he had a foul temper. To make matters worse, he was a radical republican and made no effort to conceal his views. The rest of the senior officers were Orange sympathisers. Those from Zeeland, in particular, detested their new admiral so much, that de With complained that he did not dare to walk openly in the streets of Middleburg and Flushing, for fear of assassination.[58]

The chances of a fleet, in battle, in such a state, with an enemy superior in numbers and in firepower, were poor. At a council of war, all the officers, led by de Ruijter, advised against a battle but de With, spurred on by an importunate States General worried about the effect a prolonged closure of the Channel would have on finances, overrode them. Though de With had shared the perils of the Northern Voyage, he had not been present at the Skirmish off Dover and he would not believe the evidence that they put before him of the power of the English fleet. When even de Ruijter, who had got the better of Ayscue, counselled caution a wise admiral would have listened. But de With was convinced that he could succeed where Tromp had failed. The Dutch fleet put to sea on 25 September, with the aim of driving the English out of the Straits of Dover. Blake's chance had come.[59]

When the Dutch topsails were seen, Blake called a council of war and as the captains were assembling, messages from the North Foreland confirmed that the whole Dutch fleet was in sight. The council concluded, reluctantly, that the battle would have to be put off until the following day, because darkness was approaching and the weather was rainy and blustery. Plans were laid for the morrow. If the English had the wind, they would sail out of the Downs into the North Sea, where there was more room to deploy their ships and force a decision.[60]

The next day brought a favourable south-south-west wind, but it was accompanied by rough weather and high seas, which made fighting impossible. The same conditions persisted throughout the following day as well. By the morning of 28 September, the English were becoming very frustrated. As the seas began to go down and the weather moderated, the wish to get to grips with the enemy must have been overwhelming. The decision to engage was taken as soon as it was known that the Dutch were still there. By noon, the whole fleet was streaming northwards out of the Downs. It was every captain for himself in the rush to get out of the anchorage, with those who had been badly battered by the weather getting left behind.[61]

As usual, the Dutch had suffered more from the weather, because they were riding in the open sea. De Ruijter recorded that, despite all his efforts, his anchors dragged and the other ships had similar experiences. So, when the leading English ships were seen coming out of the Downs, the Dutch fleet was much scattered. There was no time for a council of war but de With tackled the problem with his customary energy. He sent a galliot round the fleet to tell the captains how he wanted the ships ordered. After some difficulties, he managed to bring his ships into rough battle stations, in three squadrons under himself, de Ruijter and de Wildt, sailing almost due west.[62]

The speed with which the leading elements of the English fleet left the Downs caused some of the ships to get ahead of the main body. Becoming aware of what was happening, Blake ordered the pacemakers to heave to, but once his own and Penn's squadrons had closed up, the charge was recommenced, without waiting for the third one commanded by Bourne. There had not been enough room for the Rear-Admiral's squadron to get out of the Downs at the same time as the other two and his leading ships were left wallowing far behind, one account says by as much as two leagues.[63] Blake and Penn should have waited to allow Bourne to deploy his ships but the day was already far advanced and, after two-and-a-half days' waiting, Blake was determined that his cherished battle was not going to elude him again.

De With was quick to exploit the error. He waited until Blake and Penn were almost on top of him and then ordered the whole Dutch fleet to tack, from its westerly course, until it was facing south east with the wind abeam.[64] This manoeuvre brought about an immediate conflict between de With's squadron and part of Blake's, but the vast majority of the Dutch admiral's ships and all of de Ruijter's squadron bore down on the hapless Bourne. All the accounts describe the furious conflict, which enveloped Bourne's leading ships, centring on the one commanded by Captain William Badiley. *A Letter from General Blake's Fleet* described this phase of the battle very vividly.[65]

> First Major Bourne with the *Andrew* led on and charged the Hollanders stoutly and got off again without much harm. Captain Badiley with his ship also, he charged exceeding gallantly; but was in very great danger to have lost his ship, for the Hollanders were so close on both sides of him charging against him, that one might have thrown biscuits out of his frigate into the Dutch ships.
>
> All his sails were so torn and shattered that he could not sail to or fro or any more but as the tide drove him and there were about 60 men killed in that frigate and she had near a 100 shot in her hull and was in danger of sinking or taking; but blessed be God they got her safe to harbour the fighting being not above six leagues from the shore.

Bourne and Badiley were saved by two developments. Tacking a fleet, in the presence of the enemy and after riding out a severe storm, was a most difficult manoeuvre. Some ships fell off to leeward, because they were unable to point high enough into the wind, and they were only able to engage by shooting over friendly ships. Other captains took advantage of the new course and deliberately kept out of the fighting. After the battle, de With was to complain bitterly about the cowardice of many of the Dutch captains. Yet their behaviour was hardly

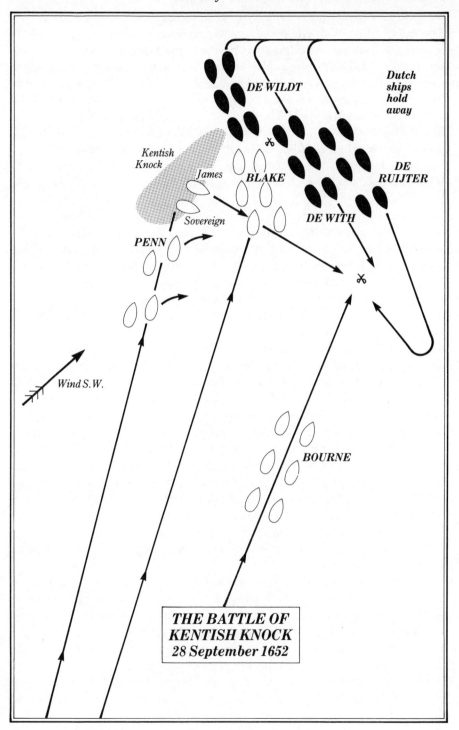

Kentish Knock

DE WILDT

Dutch
ships
hold
away

James

BLAKE

DE
RUIJTER

Sovereign

DE WITH

PENN

Wind S.W.

BOURNE

**THE BATTLE OF
KENTISH KNOCK
28 September 1652**

unexpected. None of them wanted the battle and most of them hated de With.[66] The extent of de With's unpopularity was revealed by a bizarre incident. For most of the cruise, de With had flown his flag in the *Princess Louysa*, but the ship was on the small side and, as the English fleet approached, he attempted to transfer to the *Brederode*, Tromp's old flag ship. As the most powerful unit in the fleet, the *Brederode* was the most suitable ship for the Admiral, but de With reckoned without the crew. They refused to let him on board. De With was forced into the humiliating expedient of rowing round the fleet, trying to find a ship that would accept him. Eventually he got on board the *Prins Willem*, a large East-Indiaman. Unfortunately the ship was a bad sailer and, although he fought her valiantly, de With ceased to have any influence on the course of the battle.[67]

The other development was, in its way, just as odd. The southern North Sea is full of shoals, some of which are very near the surface at low tide. The speed at which the English were sailing made it impossible to take regular soundings, with the result that Penn's own ship, the *James*, and the massive *Sovereign* went aground on a steep-sided shoal, called the Kentish Knock, from which the battle takes its name. Luckily, neither ship was holed. The boats were launched and the two ships were towed off. This took time and brought the following ships to a stop. As Blake's squadron streamed past him, Penn saw beyond them the Dutch fleet sailing in the opposite direction and ready to descend on Bourne. As Penn put it in his letter to George Bishop, '... indeed it fell out better for doing execution on the enemy than we could have cast it ourselves, for as the Dutch fleet cleared themselves of our General, he standing to the northward and they to the southward, we fell pat to receive them and so stayed by them until night caused our separation.'[68]

The entry of Penn's squadron into the fight was decisive. When Ayscue had charged de Ruijter, the effect of his heavy guns had been limited because the Dutch kept close together. At Kentish Knock, the position was much less favourable because the ships had spread out when the fleet tacked. The English ships were able to get among the Dutchmen and do considerable execution. The *Sovereign*, in particular, took on twenty Dutch frigates at once and spread death and destruction all around her, just as the great Portuguese ship had done in 1639.[69]

Battle was joined about 4 pm and was terminated by nightfall, but in the two hours of combat the Dutch received a severe battering. De Ruijter's squadron suffered least. He himself was in the thick of it and Captain Lokke was forced to limp away to Ostend, but no ships were lost. De With was not so lucky. The *Prins Willem* lost its mainmast and, when the foremast went by the board too, he had himself rowed back to the *Princess Louysa*, which gave rise to rumours that he had been killed. Then the ship commanded by Captain Gerrit Nobel received a shot in the magazine and blew up. The gunner of the *Gorcum* saved his ship from certain capture by threatening to fire the magazine, which caused a panic among the boarders.

De Wildt was the most heavily engaged because the change of course had left him facing all of Blake's squadron and part of Penn's. After violent fighting, the *Garland* took de Wildt's ship at the third attempt, but the Commodore escaped and managed to get on board the ship of Captain Sippe Fokkes. Shortly afterwards Fokkes' ship and another were both dismasted.[70] With darkness falling, the *Nonsuch*, commanded by the enterprising John Mildmay, managed to come up with Fokkes as he was attempting to tow the other damaged ship out of the action. Fokkes and de Wildt were both made prisoner. Mildmay managed to make Fokkes' ship prize but the other ship was in such a state that Mildmay dared not take her in tow with the Dutch fleet close, so he cast off the rope, believing that she would sink.[71] As at the Skirmish off Dover, the English underestimated Dutch ingenuity. They repossessed her and got her back to the United Provinces.

The next day de With called a council. He himself still wanted to renew the fight but this time he had to bow to the inevitable. Apart from the three lost ships, three more were entirely disabled and nine had disappeared. Of those who had fought stoutly, hardly any had emerged without serious damage.[72] The 30 September brought weather conditions favourable for renewing the contest. When de With proposed that the fleet should beat to windward to see if the English wished to continue the battle, he met a blank refusal. The captains, led by de Ruijter and Cornelis Evertsen, demanded that the fleet should return to the United Provinces. De With fumed and ranted and called them all cowards but there was nothing he could do.[73] The Dutch returned to port with their tails between their legs.

In his heart, de With must have known that de Ruijter was right. Though he was reluctant to admit it openly, the English gunnery had made a profound impression on him. He reported, 'We found that the guns on their smallest frigates carry further than our heaviest cannon and the English fired smarter and quicker than did many of ours.'[74] At the beginning of October, he was urging that all Dutch ships should adopt the English practice of putting the charges of gun-powder in paper cartridges. This simplified gun laying and made the performance of the cannonballs more predictable.[75]

The English had considerable cause for satisfaction, yet with the superiority they possessed they should have done better. The fleet had not been used to the best advantage and the victory had not been as decisive as it should have been. The fleet with the wind could usually pick the part of the enemy to attack. The failure of Blake and Penn to wait for Bourne allowed de With to outmanoeuvre them, with consequences which could have been very serious.[76] The advantage that the English did gain was due more to chance factors and the disorder in the Dutch fleet, than to the excellence of their tactics. Some excuse for the faulty dispositions can be found in the limited amount of daylight in late September, which made it imperative to get into action as quickly as possible. But, when everything is taken into account, it is difficult to banish the feeling that an opportunity to finish the war quickly had been missed. They would never have the chance to catch the Dutch again, at such a disadvantage.

Dungeness

THE Dutch fleet, which straggled into Helvoetsluis after the Battle of Kentish Knock, was battered and bitter. De With was boiling with rage against the captains who had failed to support him. Seven of them were committed to prison while their conduct was examined. Action against them was hampered by de With's failure to call a council of war, on the morning of the battle, and his failure to adopt a consistent attitude. One moment he was raging against all his captains, and de Ruijter in particular, because they were unwilling to re-engage on 30 September.[1] The next he was claiming that the English missed a great opportunity by failing to pursue them properly, after being heavily reinforced.[2]

The State of Holland was compelled to bow to the inevitable. Tromp must be recalled. The reinstatement of Tromp healed the rift between the senior officers and the politicians so that preparations for the new expedition went forward with fresh vigour. What it did not do was to remedy the underlying problems. The Lieutenant-Admiral was soon experiencing the same recalcitrance among a minority of captains that had been seen earlier. The manning position was, if anything, worse than it had been. There had never been enough Dutch nationals and it had long been standard practice to employ foreign seamen, including English ones. Soldiers were also being used to plug the gaps. Part of the difficulty was caused by the reluctance of the States General to sanction the pressing of merchant seamen. In the end, Tromp took the law into his own hands. He waited until his merchant convoy was assembled at the rendezvous, and then pressed as many men as he needed. Only Tromp could have got away with such high handed action but even he was powerless to sort out the chaotic victualling situation described earlier, or to prevail on the Admiralties to come to some arrangement about the repairing of damaged ships.

The reluctance to face facts was seen, at its starkest, in the argument over the new building programme. During his enforced idleness, Tromp had employed his time in drawing up a shipbuilding plan, which aimed at giving the Dutch a fleet capable of meeting the English on equal terms. The scheme which he submitted to the States General, provided for thirty new ships to be started immediately, six of which were to be 150 feet long, twelve 140 feet long and twelve 134 feet long, corresponding to the first three English rates.[3] The defeat at Kentish Knock had convinced the States General that a building programme was necessary, but there was much opposition to Tromp's proposal. Exception was taken to the large size of the ships, which would be unsuitable for operations among the shoals off the Flanders coast. Opponents claimed that they would draw too much water to enter Dutch ports. This 'conservative' faction took even greater exception to Tromp's most crucial proposal, to base the designs of the new ships, on the *Vrijheijt* and not the *Aemilia*.[4]

The centre of the opposition was Amsterdam, which put forward a rival programme of fifteen ships each 130 feet long and fifteen ships of 125 feet, based on the *Aemilia*. Both programmes were considered by a committee of three deputies of the States General and Vice-Admiral de With. All five Boards were invited to comment on the programmes. The only answer to survive is the one from Rotterdam. The Board there backed Tromp wholeheartedly, and asserted that the ports under its control could take ships of the draught he proposed.[5]

The Report was written by de With. Although the State of Holland was his sponsor and he had no liking for Tromp, the lessons of Kentish Knock were unmistakable. His recommendations were a slightly watered-down version of Tromp's original scheme. He proposed two ships of 150 feet, eight of 140 feet, eight of 134 feet and twelve smaller frigates, all to the *Vrijheijt* design.[6] Expert naval opinion was united but still could not prevail against the opposition of the State of Holland. The programme adopted in February 1653 was for one of 150 feet, ten of 136 feet and nineteen of 130 feet, with the nineteen still based on the *Aemilia*.[7] A lot more hard knocks were to be needed, before it was borne in on Holland that the only way to safeguard their precious commerce was to meet, and defeat, the English fleet.

The English had their problems too. On 4 November, Colonel George Thompson reported the total expenses of the Navy as £963,360 and the revenue voted at £515,000. These figures did not take into account £300,000 for thirty more new ships to match anything the Dutch might build nor £22,000 for 500 new guns.[8] The success at Kentish Knock induced such a feeling of euphoria, that nothing was done, either to vote more money or reduce the commitments of the Navy. The building programme went forward. Another four of the current batch, the *Kentish, Essex, Sussex* and *Hampshire*, were launched during the autumn.[9] The war was not going as well in the sideshows, as in the main theatre. An expedition sent to Denmark, under Captain Andrew Ball in the *Antelope*, had got little change out of the Danes so a second was planned to bring them to heel.[10] The Mediterranean was another problem area. One squadron under Richard Badiley had been mauled by a Dutch one of twice its size and a second under Henry Appleton was being held in Leghorn by the Grand Duke of Tuscany.

A fleet of twenty ships was planned to restore the situation.[11]

The neglect of the main fleet, which this shift of priorities implied, was made worse by the Council of State elections, which took place on 25 November.[12] They weakened the mercantile lobby, who were the most vociferous in favour of fighting the war to a finish, in favour of those, like Sir Henry Vane junior, who thought that, now the Dutch had been taught a lesson, the time had come to negotiate an end to the war, if suitable terms could be arranged. Vane was a strong supporter of the Navy and not prepared to throw away the advantage, which the superiority of the fleet had achieved, by concessions at the negotiating table. The problem was that factional infighting and the growing belief that the war was all but won, distracted attention away from the sea to social and legal reform.

The Committee of Admiralty was only a subcommittee of the Council, which rubber stamped its decisions, so the growing reluctance of Council members to take an interest in the fleet induced a growing paralysis in naval affairs.[13] A typical example occurred after the Battle of Kentish Knock. On 5 October, the Council of State resolved that Sir Henry Vane, Colonel Dixwell, Lord Commissioner Lisle, one of the Navy Commissioners and one of the victuallers should go down to the fleet off Portsmouth, and confer with Blake about its needs.[14] Two days later the decision was amended to read, 'The members of the Council formerly appointed to go with the Commissioners be dispensed with.'[15] Blake had won the battle so the details could be safely left to the professionals.

There were serious repercussions. The fleet had been victualled, until the end of October. The plan was to send in those vessels first, which were in need of repair or which were earmarked for the winter guard, leaving Blake with the remainder. Once the winter guard was ready, it would replace the ships with Blake. In theory, the changeover should not have taken long. Plans had been laid for victuals for the winter guard some months earlier, but they were not ready. The basic reason for the delay, was lack of money. The victuallers were usually prepared to supply, so long as they knew that the money had been voted, but the large gap between the revenue and the expenditure made all the government contractors hesitate.[16]

The seamen thought the same way. The crew of the *Portsmouth* refused an offer of six months' pay and demanded all they were owed, saying they would not go to sea again until they were paid in full for the summer.[17] They could hardly be blamed. The ship was earmarked for the Mediterranean, so there was no knowing when they would get their money, if they did not get it before they sailed. Similar recalcitrance showed itself among seamen in the Thames, the crews of the *Reformation*, *Fleece* and *Maidenhead* declaring, flatly, that they would not serve again, and demanding their pay.[18] The Navy Commissioners enclosed a letter to the Council of State, from Captain Young of the *Worcester*, another of the ships for the Mediterranean, saying that he was short of between thirty and forty men.[19]

While the politicians bickered and Tromp struggled to get his ships to sea, Blake rode at anchor in the Downs with a skeleton fleet. Blake's position was very exposed and the ships he had with him were not really sufficient to take on the whole Dutch fleet.[20] Many of them were short of equipment and men, and waiting to go into port for a refit, but he did not dare leave his station because the exchange of ships was taking place piecemeal. A move towards the Thames might expose reinforcements coming from Portsmouth and a move back to St Helen's Road would leave traffic in the Thames open to attack. Blake's correspondence betrays no anxiety at the false position he was in, though the Dutch preparations must have been known to him, so some of the blame for what was to happen must be laid at his door. As early as the middle of October, the newssheets were carrying details of Tromp's preparations and confidently forecasting 26 October as the date of his sailing.[21] The date was wildly optimistic and another four weeks passed before Tromp put to sea. Blake could have been in little doubt that the Dutch would try to run a convoy down the Channel as soon as it was feasible, but the prospect produced no tremors of disquiet.

As late as the morning of 24 November he was tranquilly recording, for the information of the Navy Commissioners, the positions of Tromp in Goree Gat, and other elements of the Dutch fleet at the Wielings and Texel. Nor does he seem to have been worried that his information came from a Dutch scout, trying to ascertain the strength of the English fleet.[22] The letter had just been dispatched, when a fleet of eighty sail was sighted off the North Foreland. As darkness fell, a courier came in from Margate, to announce that over 400 sail had been counted from the cliffs. Blake called a council of war. In his dispatch, earlier in the day, he had announced his intention to put to sea. This decision was reversed. The wind was South-West by South, rising, and rain threatened, so the captains resolved that the ships should remain at their moorings and that they should confer again, at daybreak.[23]

The next day proved stormy. Tromp sighted four English men-of-war off Margate, but the weather was so thick that it was impossible to see who they were.[24] De Ruijter recorded in his log that, with the wind flat against them at South-South-West, and thick drizzling weather, no progress could be made.[25] By evening, most of the merchantmen had returned to Goree and the fleet had taken refuge in the Wielings, or under the Flanders coast between Ostend and Blankenbergh.[26] As de With had finally gone off in a huff, Tromp promoted de Ruijter to command his squadron.[27] By Saturday 27 November, the weather had moderated sufficiently for the Dutch to make a second attempt and, by midnight on Sunday, the fleet lay between the North and South Forelands, with its convoy some way behind.

The council of war which met on board Blake's flagship, the *Triumph*, on

Monday morning must have viewed the immediate future with grave anxiety. Intelligence reports estimated that ninety-five of the imposing array of nearly 500 ships, were men-of-war.[28] The Dutch put their own strength at eighty-eight but this was still more than double the forty-two that the English had. After much debate it was resolved to avoid battle, if this could be done without endangering the fleet. Blake's interpretation of the decision was to leave the Downs, by the southern end of the anchorage. The Dutch quickly spotted the move and went in pursuit. The wind was South-West, so that the Dutch found it difficult to get within range. With the weather deteriorating again, both fleets anchored for the night, the English in Dover road, and the Dutch some five or six miles to seaward.[29]

That night the wind shifted to West-North-West, and rose to gale force but towards daybreak the weather improved and as soon as the light was good enough, Tromp signalled for the Dutch fleet to make sail westwards. De Ruijter's log indicates that the Dutch were determined to fight, so the manoeuvre must be interpreted as an attempt to get far enough to the windward of the English to tack upon them.[30] That was what Blake thought because, as soon as he observed the Dutch move, he imitated it and the two fleets were soon racing each other down the Channel. At first, the Dutch were unable to get to grips, because of two shoals – the Varne and the Rip Raps – which lay longitudinally down the centre of the Channel and separated the two fleets. They were so close, that shots were exchanged and the English could hear the Dutch seamen encouraging the leading ships.[31]

As the two fleets crowded on all sail, Blake tried to keep away from the Dutch, in an attempt to honour the council's resolve to avoid action, if that was possible, but he must have known that a battle was inevitable if he persisted on his course. The Rip Raps were not endless and Dungeness Point, looming on starboard bow, would force him to alter course towards the Dutch, but he pressed on regardless. Tromp viewed the developing situation with grim satisfaction. He waited until the leading English ships had cleared the Rip Raps and were passing Dungeness Point, before altering course towards them and hanging out the red battle flag.[32]

Tromp could not have timed his strike better at this Battle of Dungeness, as it came to be called. The Dutch onset caught the English at a disadvantage, because the nearness of land limited their ability to manoeuvre and use their guns to best effect. The *Brederode*, which was the most weatherly ship in the Dutch fleet, rapidly drew ahead of the rest of her squadron and made for Blake's flagship, the *Triumph*, which was leading the English gallop. Her attempt to draw alongside the *Triumph* was thwarted by the interposition of the *Garland*, the second English ship.[33] Unable to reach Blake, Tromp grappled with the *Garland* and a hot fight ensued. The balance was tipped in favour of the English by the arrival of the *Anthony Bonadventure*, an armed merchantman commanded by Walter

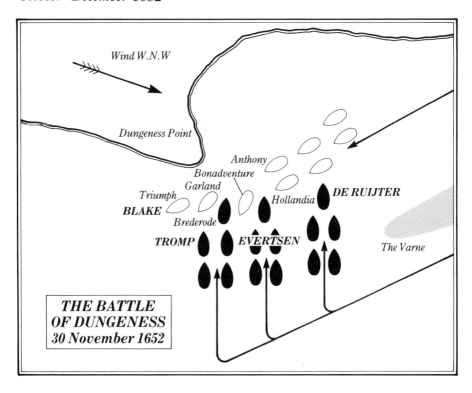

**THE BATTLE
OF DUNGENESS
30 November 1652**

Hoxton. She attacked the *Brederode* on her disengaged side and, for a while, it looked as if the *Brederode* would be captured. Disaster was turned into victory by the intervention of Evertsen in the *Hollandia*. After a gallant resistance, in which Hoxton was killed, the *Anthony Bonadventure* was captured.[34] Both Dutchmen now turned to deal with the *Garland*, which resisted bitterly. At one stage a series of explosions occurred on the ship, which made observers on the coast think that the magazine had been fired. In reality, the crew had blown up the decks, in a desperate attempt to repel boarders. The Dutch were not to be gainsaid and the *Garland* also succumbed, but not before she too lost her courageous captain, Robert Batten, killed in the final struggle.[35]

Meanwhile, Blake found himself on his own, to the west of the battle. Like Ayscue earlier in the war, he tacked about and tried to go to the assistance of his hard-pressed captains. Unfortunately he ran into the Dutch ships following at the heels of Tromp and Evertsen and was soon too desperately engaged to worry about anything other than his own defence. The *Victory*, which tried to help, was also hotly assailed, probably by de Ruijter, but she was ably supported by the *Vanguard* and one or two others.[36] The position of the leading English ships was made worse, because the attempts of the rear to engage the Dutch were, either feeble or non-existent. The author of 'A Letter from the Fleet', printed in *Mercurius Politicus*, on 1 December, wrote ominously 'and not twenty came to the engagement, the rest pretending want of men, and that they had not enough men to ply their tackle. Among these were some frigates as well as merchantmen that were so backward; and among them that did engage, not above eight stood to it to any purpose.'[37]

Battle was not joined until three in the afternoon, so nightfall robbed the Dutch of total victory, just as it had thwarted the English at Kentish Knock. The English drew off towards Dover, much torn but thankful that the reverse had not been far worse. The Dutch pleasure at the result of the battle, was marred by the loss of the ship commanded by Captain Juynbol, which blew up when the magazine was fired by accident.[38] Dutch control of the Channel brought other successes. Captain van der Zaanen surprised and captured a rich merchantman, its convoy frigate, the *Merlin*, only just managing to escape.[39] Three more men-of-war – two frigates, the *Ruby* and the *Sapphire*, and an armed merchantman, the *Hercules* – on their way to join Blake, fell in with the whole Dutch fleet. The *Ruby* and the *Sapphire* escaped but the captain of the *Hercules* was forced to run her ashore to avoid capture. The job was not done properly and Captain Contsen managed to float her off at high tide.[40]

The next days were anxious ones for the English. Blake, who had returned to the Downs, watched carefully for evidence that the Dutch intended to pursue him. For a day or two Tromp made no move. His first task was to see his merchant flock on their way. That accomplished he turned his attention to the English fleet once more. Blake did not wait for him. As soon as he had news of the Dutch approach the fleet fled from the Downs northward and took station off Long Sands Head.[41]

The disarray of the English fleet presented the Dutch with another opportunity to strike at an English port. Tromp's council of war on 10 December debated whether to sail up the Thames. There were two routes. The most direct was straight along the north Kent coast but this was shoal-infested and was not navigable at low tide. Without pilots, the Dutch were naturally reluctant to venture into such dangerous waters. The more usual course was to sail north to Long Sands Head, where Blake had posted himself, and then south-westwards into the Thames.[42] Tromp would have been happy to fight Blake for a second time, if he did not retreat. The first part of the route was well known but, again, there were doubts about navigating the fleet when it got near to the English shore. According to Tromp, £50 Flemish was offered to anyone who would pilot the fleet in, but there was no response, so the plan was abandoned. After seeing the convoys for the Seine safely to Havre, the Dutch fleet sailed down the Channel to the rendezvous, at the Isle de Rhé, off La Rochelle, where the incoming merchantmen would assemble for convoy.[43]

Before the battle of Dungeness, Tromp had complained to the States General of the dual burden placed on his shoulders, of fighting the English battle fleet and protecting trade, asking unsuccessfully that he be absolved from the latter task.[44] He knew that a mistake in the Thames would have serious consequences for Dutch commerce. Nevertheless, the bold course was the only one which held out any real hope of success. The Thames was notorious for its shoals, but it is incredible that there was no one among the Dutch captains who was confident enough to navigate a sea route, which Dutch merchantmen must have followed many times. A really determined commander would have risked the loss of one or two ships, in the interests of ultimate victory. His own questioning of the crew of the *Garland* told him that it was now or never. The English had no less than 126 ships, either at sea or in port,[45] so that if he sailed away and gave them time to recuperate his numerical advantage would disappear. Yet that is what he did, and one is left with the feeling that, superb seaman as he was, Tromp was out of his depth when amphibious operations were needed to exploit an advantage gained at sea.

The battle was scarcely over, before the English post mortem began. In his letter to the Council of State, Blake asked for Commissioners to be sent to the fleet, to establish the reasons for the defeat.[46] This time there was no procrastination. Colonel Herbert Morley, Colonel Valentine Walton and Thomas Chaloner reached Dover at the double, but not fast enough to catch the fleet before its retreat to Long Sands Head, so they were not able to begin work until 7 December.[47]

One of the tasks the Commissioners had to perform was to examine the conduct of the captains in the State's service, during the battle. Batten and Hoxton were beyond praise or blame but Lionel Lane, the captain of the *Victory*, and John Mildmay, promoted from the *Nonsuch* to the *Vanguard*, were publicly commended for the service they had rendered in helping the *Triumph's* passage back through the Dutch fleet.[48] The other side of the coin was the apportionment of blame among those who were judged to have failed in their duty. Six captains were removed from their commands. An examination of the circumstances which led to their dismissal throws a fascinating light on the battle and on Blake's relations with his subordinates.

Captain Zachary Browne of the *Hercules*, an armed merchantman, was removed for incompetence, leading to the loss of his ship. Without a more detailed account of the action, when the *Hercules*, in company with the *Ruby* and *Sapphire*, encountered the Dutch fleet, it is impossible to establish whether running his ship ashore was the only course open to him. What is certain, is that he did the job very badly.[49] The verdict of guilty, as charged, would have been returned by any court martial.

Four captains were charged with failing to support Blake properly in the battle. Little is known about Captain Edmund Chapman of the *Happy Entrance*, except that he began the war in command of an armed merchantman, so he must have performed well enough to be promoted. The incomplete ammunition return from the battle shows that the *Happy Entrance* expended 14 pounds of powder, against the 51 pounds used by the *Triumph*.[50] The *Entrance* was a smaller ship with fewer guns than the *Triumph*, and its position in the fighting cannot be established with exactitude, so the disparity, while it is suggestive, may not have been as great as it appears.

The other three captains were far from unknown and their combined prosecution raises issues greater than the individual cases. All of them have been mentioned in earlier chapters. Due to the incomplete nature of the records, it is not possible to identify the ship commanded by Captain Charles Saltonstall. We last met him commanding the *John* in 1650, when he chased the Royalist ship, the *Black Prince*, on shore near Carthagena. He was one of the most experienced commanders in the fleet. Before entering the service of the State, he had commanded ships in the East India Company's fleet of defence. In 1642, he had gone with Captain William Jackson on his famous privateering voyage, during which he seized the island of Jamaica and held it for eighteen months.[51]

It was predictable that Captain John Taylor of the *Laurel* would figure among the delinquents. He had already incurred Blake's wrath for his reluctance to risk his ship in attempting to capture a Dutch man-of-war among the shoals of Flanders. If Gibson is to be believed, the fleet held its breath to see whether he would be censured a second time for 'lying by' in the presence of the Dutch squadron protecting the fishing busses. Yet his standing in the fleet must have been high. He was Blake's flag captain during the Scilly Islands operation, in 1650. Later, when Penn informed Blake of de Ruijter's presence off the Start in September 1652, Taylor was put in charge of the reinforcements which were sent.

The last of the quartet, Captain Anthony Young, was arguably one of the bravest men in the fleet. When Prince Rupert sailed from Helvoetsluis in 1649, he did not have enough men to man his ships or guns to equip them with, so he decided to leave the *Antelope* behind, distributing her crew and guns among the rest of the fleet. Young, then Captain of the *President*, approached Richard Badiley, the commander of the squadron in the Downs, with a plan for the ship's capture. With Badiley's active support, he successfully cut the ship out from under the noses of both the Royalists and the Dutch authorities.[52] Young was also involved in the outbreak of the Dutch War. It was Van der Zaanen's report of the way in which Young made Commodore Huyrluyt strike his flag, that led Tromp to fear that the merchant ships off Fairlight were being searched. If such a man believed that the odds were too great, then Blake must have been acting very rashly indeed.

The most extraordinary prosecution of all was that of Benjamin Blake, the General's own brother. The Orders of the Council of State simply instruct that he be no more employed, without giving any reason for his dismissal. In his case refusal to engage cannot have been the reason. A careful collation of the information shows that he was captain of the *Triumph*,[53] and therefore his brother's flag captain.[54] Blake's secretary, Francis Harvey, was dismissed at the same time.[55] What are we to imagine? What happened at that critical council of war? Had Robert wanted to engage and Benjamin helped to sway the council, so that the decision taken was to decline battle, if it could be done without disadvantage? Had there been a row on the quarter deck, as Blake pressed relentlessly westward in his determination to hold the wind? Or had Benjamin defended the errant captains before the Commissioners and criticised his brother in such a public manner that his retention was impossible? Or was it a combination of all three? The Blakes were known for their formidable tempers.

There were grounds for criticising Blake's handling of the situation. The first was the way in which the appearance of the Dutch off the North Foreland, caught him by surprise. Whether this was because of bad scouting or deliberate misinformation provided by a Dutch merchantman at Tromp's instigation, he had been beaten to the punch.[56] Then there was his treatment of the decision of the council of war to avoid an engagement. At the time, any attempt to debouch from the northern entrance to the anchorage would have been fraught with danger and escape southwards was made impossible by the wind. Blake seems to have believed that the change in the wind altered the situation. His captains, on the other hand, appear to have thought that the resolution was a general prohibition, based on the English numerical inferiority, undermanning, and shortage of supplies.

After the storm, the wind shifted from South-West to North-West. Tromp's report on the earlier encounter with Ayscue shows that he considered this to be the ideal wind for an attack from the northern end of the Downs, so the English move southwards into Dover road was logical. They had the wind, which would make it difficult for the Dutch to come at them. More questionable was Blake's behaviour on 3 November. When he spotted Tromp's move westward, he became obsessed with preventing the Dutch getting so far ahead, that they could tack and gain the wind. The result was that Tromp was able to pin the English ships on Dungeness, with insufficient sea room in which to use their heavy guns to the best effect. As at Kentish Knock, Blake's impetuosity enabled his opponent to outmanoeuvre him.

What was the alternative? Let us suppose that the English had held back and that, despite the Rip Raps and the Varne, the Dutch gained the wind. The English would have had to retreat through the Downs and into the North Sea.

Tromp would have followed. All the journals of the Dutch commanders show that they were determined to fight. The advantages for the English would have been that the weather might have changed and there would have been more sea room than at Dungeness. The disadvantages were that the Dutch would have had the wind and the necessity of retreating might well have affected the English captains psychologically. That discretion could be the better part of valour was a hard dictum for Blake to accept. Before Dungeness he had never retreated in his life. Even at Bristol the surrender was negotiated without his knowledge. If it had been left to him, he would have resisted, if necessary until not a building stood in the city, as he was to do at Lyme Regis and Taunton, because that was what a revolutionary hero would do.

At Lyme Regis and Taunton, his men followed him not only because of his inspiring example, but because they did feel they were fighting for religious and political principle. That was not the case in the Dutch War. Suppose the English were to lose it, what matter of principle would be sacrificed? The answer was none at all. Nor was England's political independence at stake. The war was solely concerned with commercial advantage. In such circumstances, the hero's image starts to lose its potency and even the bravest of men begin to ask whether immolating themselves at their leader's behest, is the right course of action. The result was that Blake was forced into the retreat northwards, which he had earlier scorned.

The real sin committed by Chapman, Saltonstall, Taylor, Young and Benjamin Blake was that they thought for themselves. They knew that the fleet was outnumbered, their ships badly in need of a refit, short of ammunition and undermanned. They believed that Blake was acting against the spirit, if not the letter, of the decision of the council of war. In their eyes, that entitled them to rebel against what they thought was a senseless course of action. In the new atmosphere, that could not be allowed. If the cause alone would not make Blake's captains follow where he led, then they must be compelled by the fear of condign punishment.

The dismissal of the captains marked a significant change in the management of the fleet. The custom of appointing landsmen, with no practical knowledge of the sea, as admirals had given great authority to the council of war. There the captains could make their influence felt and the weight of their united professional opinion could usually force the Admiral to do what they wanted in tactical matters. By accepting battle, Blake defied his council and he then succeeded in persuading the Council of State to support him, despite the defeat. The precedent began a change in the functions of the council, which was to be completed when the fleet was entrusted to professional admirals, as a result of the reforms initiated by Samuel Pepys. Under the new system, the Admiral made the decisions and his council confined itself to suggesting ways of carrying them out.

Blake's approach was an emotional one and it is unlikely that he had thought out the consequences of what he was doing. An examination of his later behaviour shows that, where he was genuinely uncertain what to do, he would listen to his council, but when he knew what he wanted, he was prepared to ride roughshod over it, even if every captain opposed his wishes. His behaviour was dictated by a growing belief that a prerequisite of an efficient fleet was that his captains should do exactly what they were told. Discipline was the first essential for success. He would fulfill the heroic role and lead. They must put their trust in him and follow. It is an extraordinary testimony to his strength of character that Dungeness was the only occasion when the captains rebelled.

What the Commissioners really thought about the behaviour of the captains is not known. Four out of the five – Chapman, Young, Taylor and Benjamin Blake – were later quietly reinstated, but their careers never recovered from the setback.[57] The problem they faced was that Blake had made it abundantly clear to the Council of State that it was either them or him. Both the Council of State and the Commissioners knew that his removal would be a bad psychological blow to the fleet and they undoubtedly agreed with him that discipline had to be tightened. The captains were dismissed, as an example to their colleagues, and a series of measures adopted to make sure there was no repetition of such disobedience.

The place to start was the top. There were three Generals-at-Sea but two of them, Deane and Monck, had not taken up their commands, even though their commissions had been renewed as recently as 26 November, four days before Dungeness. The suggestion that they should take a more active role, was made by Blake himself.[58] When he was properly supported and the war was going well, Blake did not mind shouldering the burden of command, but when the political will wavered and he was left with an inferior fleet, he was determined that he should not take the blame alone. They were ordered to sea.[59]

At Dungeness, twenty out of the forty-two ships available were armed merchantmen. Their captains were criticised for not supporting Blake properly. Nehemiah Bourne wrote in their defence, that they had a large part of their personal estates invested in their ships and that equipping the ships had cost them a lot of money.[60] Many of the merchant captains in Ayscue's fleet had behaved similarly and the Dutch had even greater problems than their opponents. The Council of State quickly realised that, with such divided loyalties, a merchant captain was in an impossible position. It decreed that, in future, armed merchantmen in the service of the State should be commanded by a captain appointed by the State and not by the owners.[61] The remedy was drastic but the results justified the change.

Finally a series of Articles of War was drawn up. They defined the duties of the officers and crews and laid down severe punishments in the event of failure to fulfill them.[62] In 1649, the Generals-at-Sea believed that they had been granted the power of martial law at sea, but the commission was found to have been wrongly drawn and nothing had been done to rectify the matter. The Articles of War allowed the Generals to execute summary justice at sea.

No less than twenty-five of the 1652 articles had the death sentence as a possible penalty, and their savagery has led to much argument. No instances of the death sentence being pronounced during the Interregnum can be found, so one might conclude that they represented an expression of intent rather than a code to be rigidly enforced.[63] There is a good deal to be said in favour of this view. Despite being landsmen Blake, Popham, Deane, Monck and later Mountagu, were much closer to their men than the Admirals drawn from the society that was to evolve after 1660 with a sharpened class-consciousness, and did not feel the need to proceed to extremes to protect their authority. One of the motivations for the savage penalties may well have been fear of revolution. The war was accompanied by a number of changes, which culminated in the dissolution of the Rump by force. Ayscue resigned because he did not want to fight the Dutch and there were continual rumours of dissensions. When these proved to be grossly exaggerated, the need for drastic measures disappeared.

Reorganisation and Portland

*T*HE way in which the Commonwealth handled the naval crisis after the
defeat at Dungeness was in marked contrast to the Dutch reaction
after Tromp's disastrous Northern Voyage. The Dutch condemned the
admiral, the English fixed the blame on the politicians. They were enabled to do
so by the elections to the Council of State of 25 November. Vane was not
identified with those who made the mistakes of the autumn, so he could set
about reform with a clear conscience. A bill was introduced into Parliament,
which set up a Committee of Admiralty to exercise the powers of the Lord High
Admiral. Unlike its predecessor, the new body would not be a sub-committee of
the Council of State but an independent committee. Two of the six members
were to be on the Council of State, two were M.P.s who were not on the
Council, and the last two were not M.P.s.[1] The two members of the Council
who were elected were Vane himself and Colonel George Thompson. The two
ordinary M.P.s were John Carew and Major Richard Salwey. The two non M.P.s
were John Langley and James Russell. The whole rearrangement was a victory
for the Godly party and its allies in the army over the republican sceptics around
Henry Marten, Sir Arthur Hesilrige and Colonel Morley, who had led the
Commonwealth into the war. Only Thompson had any connections with the
previous dispensation and he was a known middle-of-the-road Puritan. Though
the Act does not define the position of the Generals-at-Sea, the Committee book
shows that Monck attended regularly until mid January. Blake and Deane also
put in occasional appearances.[2]

Blake's attitude to the new dispensation is difficult to fathom. In general
he probably welcomed the more godly outlook of the new men, though he may
have found the Fifth Monarchist, Carew, hard to stomach. They were anxious
to keep him as a General-at-Sea and that had considerable implications. In the
aftermath of Dungeness Blake had offered his resignation, but this was not an
admission of his own inadequacy or distaste for the new administration. It was
the reaction of a man who believed that he had been badly let down and not
only by his captains. By reaffirming its confidence in him, the new Council of

State more or less bound itself to do something to remedy the deficiencies of the fleet, so that the Commonwealth could recover the ground lost at Dungeness. This was an ironic position for men who were not really keen on the war at all. When they were elected, they seemed to be in a position to negotiate from strength. Now, if they opened talks, the Dutch would be able to use their victory to protect their commercial dominance. Paradoxically, the 'peace party' were compelled to step up the war effort and spend more money, not less.

For Blake the disciplining of his captains and the imposition of draconian Articles of War had been a necessity, not a solution. The hero leader should inspire his followers with devotion, not bludgeon them into obedience. One of the ways in which he could do that was by showing those who served under him that he cared for them, was aware of their problems and would see to it that the Commonwealth government satisfied their just demands. The plan for the care of the sick and wounded, adopted by the Council of State on 4 January, had his full support.[3] Their pay was to be continued until they were completely cured or a pension settled on them. Every six months, £5 per hundred men was to be laid out for necessary provisions for the sick such as old linen for their wounds. If the sick seamen had to be sent on shore, by order of the General, their tickets were to be paid by the deputy Treasurer of the Fleet, together with enough money for their travel to the place where they were to be looked after. A house was to be hired at Deal, or some other convenient place, to act as a hospital. Places in London hospitals were to be reserved, as they became vacant after January. For the duration of the war, considerable care was taken of the sick and wounded seamen, at least by seventeenth-century standards. The accounts of the war show that one of the reasons why the Rump was kept up to the mark, was the activity of Elizabeth Aikin, a seventeenth-century Florence Nightingale, known to the seamen as Parliament Joan. She was so successful that Monck and Deane complained that the sick got their wages but the fit did not.

The post-mortem on the battle of Dungeness showed that the *Garland* and the *Anthony Bonadventure* had been well defended and their loss was no fault of either the captains or the crews. Arrangements were made for the support of Hoxton's widow and for the payment of the wages of the men, as they were released by the Dutch. Good service would be rewarded.[4] But the central problem was the question of pay. Blake put the position bluntly, in a letter which appears to have been written sometime before 7 December, when the defeat off Dungeness was still very much on his mind. How could seamen be expected to enlist, when their opponents got a prize allowance and 40s a week and they only got 18s a week? He was reported as saying that he would not accept battle again unless something was done.[5]

Parliament hastened to satisfy him. The new pay scales were published on 20 December.[6] Most ranks got an increase on 1647 rates.[7] The largest was for captains. The pay for the captain of a 1st rate was advanced to £21 making it roughly equal to that of a colonel in the Army. Other ranks received more modest advances but the Committee of Admiralty did respond to the criticism that ordinary seamen were paid the same, however long their service or however well or badly qualified they were. The new pay scales provided for three ranks. A yeoman of the sheets, tackle and halliards was to be paid 32s. An able seaman fit for helm, lead, top and yard would get 24s. The rest would remain at 19s except gromets and boys who would be paid 14s 3d. Volunteers would get coat and conduct money as well as those that were pressed. This was a logical change. The old system positively encouraged seamen to hold back, in the expectation of getting money to provide for their clothing and transport to their ships, if they had to be pressed. All the arrears of the seamen were to be paid and to persuade them to transfer from the summer fleet to the winter one, they were offered an extra month's wages, in recognition of their willingness to go without a rest.[8] These improvements did not solve the problem entirely and the gaps were increasingly filled by soldiers. The regiments of Cromwell and Colonel Ingoldsby served regularly during the First Dutch War. They could be used for gun crews, releasing the skilled seamen to work the ship. They were also invaluable when the fighting came to close quarters. The position was to be regularised, after the Restoration, by the creation of the Admiralty Regiment, the ancestor of the Marines. Unlike the United Provinces, the Commonwealth had no compunction about pressing seamen and embargoing trade, until the fleet was supplied.[9]

Even more significant were the changes to the prize regulations. Attention has been drawn to the alterations of 1649, which allowed prize money to be paid on the Admiral, Vice-Admiral and Rear-Admiral of the Royalist fleet, if they were sunk, instead of being captured. Nothing had been said about other enemy ships. There was no provision for prize money for sinking Dutch men-of-war. The opportunity was taken to rectify the omission. A month's extra pay was voted for all seamen, who had been in service at least six months, in lieu of prize money which might have been earned from enemy men-of-war sunk in action. For the future, it was laid down that 'In time to come officers and men be allowed to plunder above the gun deck with 10s per ton and £6–13s–4d per gun for every man-of-war taken and if the man-of-war be sunk or destroyed £10 per gun only, to be divided according to the custom of the sea.'[10] A large part of the credit for the improvements in pay rates must go to the Interregnum fleet commanders and particularly to Blake. It was the combination of the remorseless way in which he drove his captains, with his sensitivity to the needs of those who served in his fleets, which marked Blake out from those who came after him.

Another problem which had afflicted the fleet was bad and insufficient supplies of food and drink. The inadequacies led to a violent argument between the Surveyor of the Navy, John Hollond, and the representative of the victuallers, Captain John Limbery. After an investigation, the Committee of the Admiralty came down on the side of the victuallers and Hollond resigned.[11] The victuallers claimed that the problems were created by the government. The rate they paid, per man, placed a severe limit on the quality that could be provided. Indecision about the quantities required made matters worse. Meat and beer would only keep if put into casks at a cool time of year. When the Council of State delayed making up its mind how much it required, the victuallers were compelled to slaughter, and to brew, in high summer.[12] The delays that held so many ships in port, which otherwise would have been with Blake in the Downs in time for Dungeness, were due to the failure of the government to pay their earlier bills.

On 16 December the Council of State ordered victuals for 30,000 men for the summer fleet of 1653, so that they could be prepared in the winter months.[13] The contract for victuals allowed 8d per man, per day, for ships on active service and 7d while they were in port. In 1653 the rate for ships at sea was raised to 9d.[14] The question of money for the Navy was debated at length. During the autumn the Rump had languidly explored the possibility of providing £100,000 from the sale of the Cathedral Deans' and Chapters' lands.[15] The defeat at Dungeness lent urgency to their debates and led to the realisation that £100,000 was nowhere near enough. There was a proposal to double the amount but, in the end, M.P.s opted for a rise in the Monthly Assessment. The rate was fixed at £120,000 per month, of which £40,000 was guaranteed to the Navy.[16] This was the largest sum ever levied in taxation and showed the determination of the Commonwealth to defeat the Dutch.

The complaints continued. There were some genuine grounds for concern, such as the persistent refusal of the victuallers to use iron bound casks, but the basic problem was the enormous increase in the amount they were expected to provide.[17] It has been calculated that in 1653, 7,500,000 lbs of bread, a like quantity of beef and pork and 10,000 butts of beer were supplied besides cheese, butter, fish and other necessaries.[18] A Report prepared by a group of senior Captains suggested that a better system would be to supply every ship with four months' victuals, and have special victualling ships with the fleet to carry the rest.[19] The idea was not new. The fleet seems to have taken extra supplies on the Northern Voyage. They were lost in the great storm, an experience which may well have prejudiced Blake against the idea.[20] They were to be tried again, during the Spanish War, but without any improvement in the quality of the victuals.

The resignation of Hollond left five active Commissioners: Richard Hutchinson the Treasurer, Major Robert Thomson, Captain Francis Willoughby, Captain Peter Pett and Thomas Smith. Hutchinson confined himself to money matters, Pett looked after Chatham and Willoughby's post was officially defined as Navy Commissioner at Portsmouth. This left the remaining three to handle the business of the Navy Office. Hollond's place was taken by Edward Hopkins but the position of Surveyor was abolished. An extra Commissioner was appointed. He was Nehemiah Bourne and he soon came to have the oversight of Harwich as his main task.[21] A proposal from Yarmouth that a Navy Commissioner should be located there was not acted on and Captain Henry Hatsell at Plymouth remained an agent, not a Commissioner.

The zeal for reform extended to all departments. Proposals were considered for obtaining timber, hemp, pitch and tar from Scotland and from New England. How much came from these sources is not known but the fleet was not hampered by lack of supplies from the Baltic.[22] Reform of the Ordnance office was considered yet again. The office of Lieutenant was abolished, for a second time, but there was no fundamental change.[23] The office continued to supply guns to both the Army and the Navy. It would have been more logical for the Navy to supply itself with guns but it is arguable that if they had done so in Tudor times, the iron guns might never have triumphed over professional prejudice.

While these changes were in gestation, frantic efforts were being made to get the fleet to sea before Tromp returned. The Navy Commissioners, with the exception of Willoughby, worked as a team and when a task appeared, the man available tackled it. Their efforts were seconded by the three Generals who were eager to do anything they could, and they were all commended by the Council of State for their efforts. The position became a great deal easier when Hutchinson and Bourne went down, with £25,000, to pay the seamen on the ships in the Swin.[24] Money acted as oil on troubled waters at Portsmouth too but, though the men were conciliated by the payments, Blake was complaining about under-manning right down to the day of his departure. The fleet sailed on 11 February and took on board the soldiers at Dover two days later. Much to the relief of the English, Tromp had only just rounded up the last of his merchant flock, when Blake picked up the ships prepared by Willoughby, off the Isle of Wight on 16 February. They were in time to intercept him, on his homeward journey.

Criticism had been voiced of the way in which the English fleet had dashed into battle at Dungeness all in a bunch, in contrast to the Dutch who had been divided into squadrons, each with its own leader. The difference was more apparent than real. The English fleet had been divided in three at Kentish Knock, so the lack of formal division was probably due in part to the smaller fleet and in part, to the confused way the changeover, from the summer fleet to the winter guard, took place. The increase in the number of flag officers now made would enable this problem to be avoided. There were to be three squadrons again, to be called the Red, Blue and White.[25] The Red was to be commanded by the General or Generals; the Blue, by the Vice-Admiral of the Fleet; and the White, by the Rear-Admiral. Each squadron was to have its own vice-admiral and rear-admiral, making a total of nine flag officers.[26]

The new arrangement had two effects. The first was to make control of the fleet easier and more flexible. Without it, Lawson would have been unable to execute the manoeuvre described later in the chapter. The second was to establish a hierarchy of command. The old councils of war, at which all the captains advised the Admiral freely, became less frequent. Instead, the commander would normally consult with his flag officers; full councils would just be to inform the captains what was expected of them or, at the most, to ask for advice on how to carry out a decision, taken in their absence. There would be no repeat of the disagreements before Dungeness. The process had begun in which a professional and a class structure was to replace the heroic and egalitarian forms favoured by the Revolution. Blake may well have accepted the logic of the change reluctantly. His own actions had emphasised the need for discipline but he would have regretted the move away from the comradeship of Civil War days.

When the fleet finally went to sea, the command structure was not quite the one that was laid down on 14 January. The Red squadron was commanded by Blake and Deane in the *Triumph*; the Blue was commanded as planned by William Penn, the Vice-Admiral of the Fleet but the White squadron was commanded by Monck. As a result, the new Rear-Admiral of the Fleet, John Lawson, found himself without a squadron and had to content himself with acting as vice-admiral of the Red.

There are a number of possible reasons for the arrangement. There has been speculation about the relations which existed between Blake and Monck. In both temperament and politics they were poles apart. Monck was a professional soldier who already had a long career behind him when the Civil Wars broke out in 1642. Despite his bluff exterior and jolly manner with the men who served under him, he had learned the art of dissimulation. His actions on the battlefield were determined by ruthless calculation, not revolutionary fervour. He embodied all the virtues of the good professional, while Blake had many of those of a brilliant amateur. Blake was by temperament a republican. Monck had the soldier's preference for strong government by an individual. He had served the King, before hitching himself to Cromwell's rising star, and he was later to be the architect of the Restoration. Blake became a soldier and then a seaman as a result of his political beliefs. Monck was a soldier first and foremost but, though he was a much more adroit politician than Blake, he had no wish to remake England into an earthly Jerusalem of any sort, something for which his country was to be profoundly grateful in 1660.

There was certainly a tug-of-war going on in the background, because the Council of State originally decreed that only two of the three Generals-at-Sea should go with the fleet.[27] The third was to stay in London to superintend the setting of the ships to sea. There was little doubt that Blake and Deane were the two who would go and Monck the one who would stay at home. Blake would have seen to that. He would have preferred working with Deane, whom he knew, rather than with Monck who was a stranger to him. Whether the reasons were ideological or administrative Monck would have none of it. Perhaps he suggested that Lawson, who was a radical Baptist, should not be entrusted with a squadron.

Whatever the reason, the Council of State changed its mind and all three Generals went to war.[28]

The discussions, which led to the more detailed order of seniority among the flag officers, did not bring any change in tactics. Instructions 2 and 3 from the Generals to Penn run –

> 2. At the sight of the said [enemy] fleet the Vice-Admiral ... as also the Rear-Admiral ..., are to make what sail they can to come up with the Admiral on each wing, giving a competent distance for the Admiral's squadron if there be sea room.
> 3. And as soon as they shall see the General engage and [he] shall make a signal by shooting of two guns and putting out [a red flag] on the fore-topmast head that then each squadron shall take the best advantage they can to engage the enemy next unto them.[29]

There is no hint here of a move towards fighting in line. If there is any common feature, it is an imitation of Dutch practice.

The size of the English fleet is, as usual, difficult to calculate with accuracy. S. R. Gardiner gives the names of eighty-three ships but he expresses doubts about the presence of some of them.[30] At the other extreme, one account puts the English at only fifty-two.[31] These were, in all likelihood, the ones which sailed from the Thames and they were augmented by additional ships in the Downs, from Portsmouth, and at least three from Plymouth. We would not be far wrong if we put the English strength at around seventy, which is what English prisoners told de Ruijter.[32] A report by the senior captains on 13 January had estimated that sixty well found and properly manned men-of-war would be sufficient to take on a Dutch fleet of ninety[33] so, all other things being equal, the English had the capacity to gain revenge for Dungeness. That the battle of Portland was to be so hard fought, was once more due to English errors, caused partly by the superior seamanship of the Dutch and partly by Blake's obsession with bringing the Dutch to battle, whatever initial disadvantage was incurred.

The English plan was to fight Tromp in the Western Channel, where the water was deep and the Dutch were far from home. Blake was determined that Tromp was not going to give him the slip as de Ruijter had done in the previous autumn, but the method he adopted was calculated to give the English the worst of all possible worlds. The English fleet zig-zagged backwards and forwards across the Channel, trying to cover as much water as it could. For some reason which it is difficult to understand, no attempt was made to post small fast ships in the Western Channel to report on Dutch movements. The English possessed such ships. One of the differences between the two fleets was that the Dutch ships were all of a medium size, but the English had a greater variety, from large ships which were powerful but slow moving, to small ships which could sail right away from their opponents, as the *Merlin* had done after Dungeness.

The English compounded their error by withdrawing the ships stationed in the Western Approaches. The *Ruby* and *Sapphire* had been on watch while the refitting was going on, but they rejoined the main fleet once it was at sea.[34] The *Diamond*, commanded by Roger Martin, had been posted off Land's End but, once the immediate danger of Tromp's return before the fleet got to sea was over, she was recalled, too early for Martin to be able to provide any useful information about how the Dutch were planning their voyage home. While the fleet was off the Isle of Wight, it was joined by the *Gift*, *Duchess* and *Success* from Plymouth who reported simply that they had seen no sign of the Dutch. It would have been much more sensible to instruct Hatsell to post them in the Western Approaches. They should have stayed there until the Dutch appeared and then monitored their progress. This would have enabled the main fleet to remain concentrated at some convenient location, such as Torbay, until the Dutch committed themselves to one route or the other. Blake's failure to provide for proper scouts indicates that he had not learned one of the most important lessons of Dungeness.

The result of the English omission was that the first solid news Blake got of the Dutch was not until 17 February, when the English fleet met a Spanish merchant ship commanded by an Englishman, Martin Mayes. Mayes reported seeing the Dutch fleet and its large convoy twenty leagues to the west, between Land's End and the Start.[35] The consensus of opinion was that, with the wind at North-West, the Dutch would take the English side, because to cross to the French coast would put them on a lee shore. Unfortunately the English fleet was off the Casquets near Alderney when the information was received, so it had to undertake a long beat against the wind to place itself across the path of the Dutch.

Meanwhile, Tromp was shepherding his flock of merchantmen into the Western Channel. He had hoped to be homeward bound earlier but he had been delayed at the Isle de Rhé by late arrivals and he did not get away until the first week in February. Bad weather and contrary winds further hampered his movements and at one point the sea became so rough that the fleet and the convoy was forced to heave to. The mouth of the Channel was not gained until 16 February, the day the Dutch were seen by Mayes. Progress was still so slow, that when the wind came up North-West, Tromp decided to sail through the night. So it was at first light, on the morning of 18 February, that lookouts on the *Brederode* sighted the English fleet to seaward.[36]

The contrast between the two fleets could not have been greater. Though he was looking after a convoy, Tromp had the whole of his eighty-strong fleet well in hand, while the English were scattered all over the Channel. Due south of him, Tromp could see a dozen or so ships, from one of which waved the flag of William Penn, the Vice-Admiral of the English fleet. Some two miles further east, was a compact group of a similar number. In between and dead in the wind's eye was the *Triumph*, which had Blake and Deane on board, with only half-a-dozen ships in company. The rest of the English fleet was five or six miles further to leeward.[37] Tromp knew he would never have a better chance of registering a famous victory. The red battle flag was hoisted and the Dutch bore down on the scattered advanced elements of the English fleet. De Ruijter's squadron made for Penn's ships. Floriszoon aimed at the gap between Penn and the Generals, while Evertsen made Lawson his target. Tromp, with his squadron following in his wake, made straight for the *Triumph*. This time he would get the head-to-head confrontation with Blake that he had just missed at Dungeness.

Why the English were in such disarray has occasioned much debate. 'We endeavoured that night,' wrote the Generals subsequently, 'the wind coming to the north west, to lay ourselves between Portland and the Caskets, it being not above fifteen leagues from shore to shore.'[38] An observer in the *Waterhound* wrote: 'As we ordered the matter we could hardly have missed them for we stretched the Channel over as far as the Isle of Alderney and were close aboard Cape de Hague.'[39] The idea that the dispositions of the English fleet on the first morning were deliberate is very hard to swallow and the explanations read like a rather lame justification for what had happened, concocted after the event. The true causes were rather different. At night, it calls for great skill to keep a large fleet together. The Dutch captains were the most able in the profession and they were led by the greatest seaman of his age. The English captains were a mixed bunch. Some were very good, but others, though full of potential, had only just achieved their first commands as a result of the extraordinary expansion of the Navy and were very raw. Their commanders were soldiers, learning their craft by trial and error, and they could not get their ships to keep station in the way their Dutch opposite numbers did. Blake made matters worse. He was so determined that the Dutch should not get past him up the Channel, that he stood as near into the wind as he could, all the night of 17/18 February. The natural result was that the more weatherly ships forged ahead of the others. So for a third time, Blake's overeagerness for a fight, come what may, placed the English fleet in a false position.

The English Generals were quick to realise their predicament, but they were determined not to fall back and allow the Dutch to move up the Channel towards safety. The *Triumph* was hauled to the wind and hove to. The movement was imitated by the other ships in the group. They all got as close to their neighbours as they could, so that there were guns facing outwards in all directions. Penn, in the *Speaker*, quickly rallied his squadron. His ships also hauled to the wind but with the different object of going about. The manoeuvre took some time to execute so he could bring no immediate aid to the little group around Blake.

The subsequent manoeuvres are difficult to piece together. For the sake of clarity what follows is given in the form of a continuous narrative. The reader

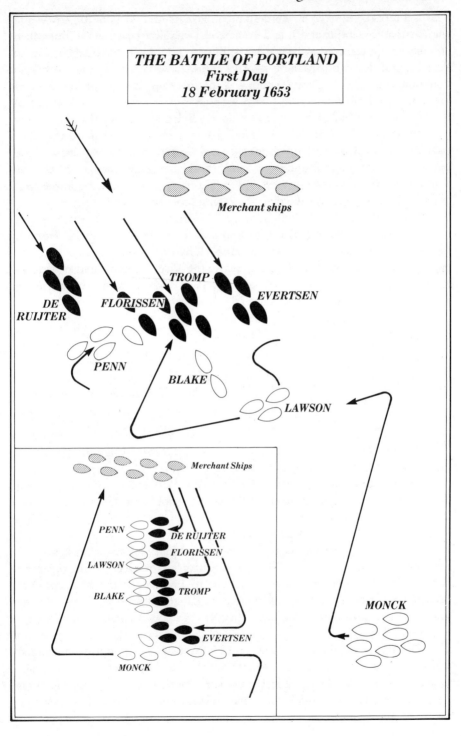

THE BATTLE OF PORTLAND
First Day
18 February 1653

Merchant ships

DE RUIJTER

FLORISSEN

TROMP

EVERTSEN

PENN

BLAKE

LAWSON

Merchant Ships

PENN

DE RUIJTER

FLORISSEN

LAWSON

BLAKE

TROMP

EVERTSEN

MONCK

MONCK

who is interested in alternative interpretations is referred to note 37. Lawson in the *Fairfax*, to windward of the *Triumph*, was in a better position to bring help speedily, by putting his ships on the starboard tack. As he watched the Dutch fleet bearing down on the little knot of ships, Lawson realised that such help could be only of a temporary nature and that his ships, too, could be engulfed and lost. The English plan must be to engage in such a way that only a part of the Dutch fleet could get at them, and that could be done only if the Dutch were put to leeward. With this idea in mind, Lawson tacked his ships so that they passed south of Blake's group. Once they had cleared them to the westward, he planned to bring them round onto the port tack and enter the battle from the south-west. The conception was a very bold one. For the first time in the war, an English flag officer was showing something more than fighting spirit.

Yet Lawson's scheme could have gone horribly wrong. The first result of his move was that Blake and Deane were left to face the full fury of Tromp's assault alone, for almost an hour, because Floriszoon thrust his ships into the gap between Penn and the Generals, before the Vice-Admiral could beat up to their assistance. Floriszoon passed close by Penn's ships, as they were hauling round. 'When we came up with them,' he reported,

> several English frigates that were close together opened a fearful fire on me from their five or six ships all at once. Nevertheless I was not behindhand in answering them, but as I had run to leeward of our fleet and received no assistance from our squadron I suffered heavy damage. The English followed us with their five or six ships, shot our mainyard into two pieces so that it fell on the deck; and our mizen-yard also together with the sails, ropes, courses and brails, so that we had nothing left standing.[40]

Tromp also got a hot reception. This was the sort of fighting that Blake understood. This was Bristol, Lyme Regis and Taunton all over again. The hosts of Midian were encamped around. He would not surrender while a gun could be fired and a man remained to stand shoulder to shoulder with him. Only a few Dutch ships could get close enough to attack and these met with the withering fire of the powerful English guns. Try as he would, Tromp could not isolate a single ship. The English paid a heavy price for their successful resistance. As Evertsen wrote in his log, 'the two squadrons reduced each other to harmlessness'.[41] Evertsen had some leisure to observe what was happening, because he arrived to find that his opponent, Lawson, had disappeared into the smoke billowing out from the battle between Tromp and the group of ships round the *Triumph*.

De Ruijter on the other hand had his hands full. His squadron charged full-tilt into Penn's ships, as they were trying to cross Floriszoon's path and rally to Blake's assistance. At first the Dutch had considerable success. As his ships were in motion, Penn could not imitate Blake's manoeuvre and de Ruijter's squadron was able to get in among them. Despite stubborn resistance, the *Assistance* was boarded, then the *Oak* and the *Prosperous*. The *Assistance*, commanded by John Bourne, the rear-admiral of the Blue, surrendered and an armed merchantman, the *Sampson*, was sunk. When all looked black, Lawson launched his ships into the fray and the English began to reap the benefits of his shrewd appreciation of the position and the coolness of his nerve. The *Oak* and the *Prosperous* were cleared of their Dutch boarders and the *Assistance* was recaptured. Finally, the ring of Dutch ships round the beleaguered *Triumph* was breached. The first phase of the battle was over. The Dutch assault had been repulsed but it had been a near thing.

In the second phase, the rival fleets struggled for the weather gauge. Evertsen, chasing the elusive Lawson round the main action, attempted to outflank him to the south. The manoeuvre failed for two reasons. The ships under the Generals, Penn and Lawson, were withdrawing slowly westwards. The Dutch followed, vainly attempting to grapple. Meanwhile the remainder of the English fleet was beginning to make its presence felt. Since early morning, Monck had been beating up from his leeward position by a series of tacks. Having made up enough ground northwards, Monck directed his ships westwards to frustrate Evertsen's attempt to get round Lawson's southern flank. Soon Monck's heavy ships were closely engaged, but his frigates ignored the main conflict and raced westwards.

For Tromp, the day had been a bitter disappointment. He had failed to breach the cordon round the *Triumph*. All the ships de Ruijter had taken had been lost again. Evertsen had failed to get to grips with Lawson and the English guns were beginning to smash his ships like matchwood. When his lookouts reported what Monck's frigates were doing, he realised that, if he prolonged the struggle any longer, they would be able to tack and get at his convoy, which had been holding away to the northward. With a heavy heart, Tromp gave the order for the fleet to break off the action by tacking northward, in order to get between the frigates and the convoy. The order was easier to issue than to execute. In the confusion, the most badly damaged ships were abandoned and fell into the hands of the English. The victors set off in pursuit but, with darkness beginning to fall, the chase had to be called off.

Evertsen admits to a loss of eight ships. Four of them commanded by Captains Cleydyck, Cornelis Jansen Poort, Isaac Sweers and Abraham Campen had been sunk; the one commanded by Captain Wichelma blew up and the ships of Captains de Munninck, Cruych and Lonque were captured by the English. Commodore Balck and twelve captains were among the dead.[42] The English lost only the *Sampson* but the *Advice, Assistance* and *Oak* were badly damaged and among the dead and wounded were some of the best captains of the fleet. Andrew Ball was killed at Blake's side as was his secretary, Drue Sparrow. John Mildmay, the valiant captain of the *Vanguard* who had behaved so well at Dungeness, and

Anthony Houlding, of the *Ruby*, also died, fighting their ships. Among the wounded were Captains John Day of the *Advice*, John Bourne of the *Assistance*, George Dakins of the *Worcester*, Robert Kirby and Valentine Tatnell. There is no total casualty list but the *Triumph* alone lost 80 killed and wounded, the *Advice*, 35 killed and 40 wounded. Even the *Vanguard*, which came relatively late into the fray, had 30 killed and wounded, in addition to the loss of her captain.[43]

Monck had come through a real baptism of fire unscathed, but Blake had been seriously wounded for the first time in his career. In over ten years of warfare he seems to have had a charmed life but his immunity had now come to an end. A bar of iron had shot away part of Deane's coat and breeches, wounding Blake in the thigh just above the knee.[44] One of the great drawbacks of the heroic style of leadership is that it exposes the revolutionary hero, even more than the men he commands. But there could not be any respite for Blake, because the conflict was not yet over. Though in great pain, he insisted on exercising his command for the rest of the battle, because he believed that he must not show any sign of weakening.

After the final separation of the fleets, Tromp went into conclave with Evertsen and de Ruijter, Floriszoon being too far away to answer the summons. They reluctantly came to the conclusion that they could not afford to expose the convoy again, especially as ammunition was running short. The little which was left in one of the store ships was distributed to those most in need.[45] Next morning, de Ruijter submitted a report on the condition of the fleet to a full council of war on board the *Brederode*. After listening to it, the captains endorsed the decision of the preceding evening. They agreed to Tromp's plan of arranging the men-of-war in a half-moon formation round the merchantmen. Evertsen took the northern cusp and de Ruijter the southern. Tromp posted himself in the centre.[46]

The Dutch tactic of aiming their guns at the sails and rigging of the English had slowed their opponents down sufficiently during the night, to give them time to herd the merchantmen together and establish the defensive ring, before the English got near enough to open fire. The frigates began the engagement about 1 pm, and fighting continued until nightfall. Evertsen admitted to the loss of the men-of-war commanded by Jan le Sage and Bruijn van Seelst, which were cut off and captured.[47] Floriszoon adds the ship commanded by Ghisbert Malcontent. Many of the other Dutch ships ended the day in serious trouble. Floriszoon noted in the log of the *Monnikendam* that 'In the fight my main topmast and mizzen yard were shot down again, after having been previously repaired. We also received several shots under water, so that it was with difficulty we kept afloat.'[48]

De Ruijter lost his main mast and had to be towed out of the action by Captain Jan Duijm[49] and he noted that, despite Tromp's exhortation at the morning council, many captains failed to rally to their flags. Floriszoon commented, 'I also called to Captain Gabriel Theunissen to remain with me in accordance with the written instructions specially given him. In reply I was informed from his ship that he took little account of that. I then called to him that if it pleased God to bring me home again, I would take care to settle with such rascals.'[50] To make matters worse, the merchantmen were beginning to turn recalcitrant. Many of them began the day steering south-west. They were aware that every mile was taking them further away from the friendly French ports, into the Straits of Dover and towards hostile Spanish Netherlands ones. It took repeated instructions and the combined pressure of the men-of-war to force them to steer north-east and make for home.[51] When darkness put an end to the second day of the battle the prospect for the Dutch was very bleak. Their ships were in bad shape and their ammunition almost exhausted; disaffection was rife and the convoy unruly.

Fighting began much earlier on 20 February than on the previous day. The first salvoes were fired around 9 am and the battle raged for the next two hours. As usual, the first shots were fired by the smaller frigates, because it took longer for the heavier ships to get into action. Only one taste of the broadsides of the heavier ships, when they came into play at last, was needed to make the Dutch flee.[52] The rest of the day was spent in a running combat, with a Dutch fleet sadly weakened by desertion and a lack of ammunition. The English frigates ranged ahead, trying to cut off the convoy from the Straits of Dover by getting round to the lee side. A good description of what happened is given by the author of a 'Dutch Account'.

> After this the English got to the leeward of the fleet; seeing this, I tried to get on the lee of the fleet. I got up to them and fired; on this, two more of our ships also bore down upon them, and they moved on with the wind. And the merchantmen advanced with the wind; then I sighted an English man on their lee so I turned and sailed towards them upon which he veered round with the wind and made off. Then I sailed close in among the merchantmen; then hoisted the topsails on the topmasts and tacked again to the rear of them, which I succeeded in doing. Then I did my best again in firing on the enemy whenever I could. The merchantmen closed up, some with the ships of war and some with one another athwart them, so that they all lay together. God knows, if they had only made sail at first, when I told them, there would have been no need for this, but they would not do it at the time.[53]

By this time there were only about thirty-five Dutch men-of-war still fighting and with the English tightening the noose, Tromp was forced to adopt one last desperate resource. Realising that any attempt to run the gauntlet of the Straits would mean another battle, which the Dutch were incapable of sustaining, he bore in, with his fleet and his merchant flock, under Cap Gris Nez.[54] He hoped that the shallow water and the approaching night would deter the English from sailing in for the kill. That Tromp should consider putting his fleet under a lee shore, in winter time, testifies to the dire straits in which the Dutch found themselves.

The last act of the battle is related by Blake and Deane, in deadpan fashion. 'Also as we supposed,' they wrote to the Council of State, 'this night they stole away from us notwithstanding our Pilots and Seamen best acquainted with the Coast said that as the wind was they could not weather the French shore to get home, and for us in the condition we were it was not possible to have done it, or if we had been in a better condition it being night not without extreme hazard to the whole Fleet.'[55] Tromp treated the escape briefly, observing that after darkness fell the whole fleet steered north-north-east and that the lights of the English fleet were not visible after midnight.[56] As if to emphasise the narrow escape that the Dutch had had, a strong wind sprang up and Floriszoon lost his mainmast overboard. If that had happened before Cap Gris Nez had been doubled he would have been on the rocks and he would not have been alone.[57]

The English claimed that the Dutch lost 17 men-of-war and 40 merchant ships. Evertsen only admits to 12 but his figure of only two ships lost, in the confusion of the third day, seems too good to be true.[58] Even if the English figure is the correct one, the Dutch must have counted themselves lucky to have survived at all. For a third time, the English had failed to make the most of their qualitative superiority. At the beginning of the battle, they had been surprised in a divided state, and avoided disaster by a hair's breadth. On the second day, they had failed to close on the Dutch until the afternoon, and by a palpable misjudgement, they had allowed the Dutch to escape at the end. Tromp was astonished when they veered off just as he had given up all hope of survival. Drake would have turned in his grave.

Blake Ashore

*E*VENTS conspired to exclude Blake from the main happenings of the summer at sea. When he re-emerged in September 1654, as the commander of the expedition to the Mediterranean, his whole outlook had undergone a noticeable change. Information about him when he was not at sea is hard to come by, but a number of factors which influenced this change can be isolated.

There was his wound. Initial reactions suggest that it was not considered serious enough to require convalescence ashore. Blake continued to exercise command throughout the battle of Portland, but he caught a cold, which developed into a fever.[1] His signature to the dispatch of 22 February looks very shaky and by the time the fleet anchored off Portsmouth, triumphant but heavily damaged as a result of the fierce battle on the first day, he was clearly unwell.[2]

Blake must have hoped that the respite would be sufficient to allow him a quick recovery. On 27 February it was reported that Blake was 'in hopeful amendment of his fever'.[3] A fortnight later, they were still talking of a slight wound and a bad cold, but the chief surgeon Daniel Whistler was not as optimistic in his report to the Council of State, on 16 March. 'General Blake mends but slowly which detains me here waiting an opportunity of his desired further recovery.'[4] By 21 March Whistler was writing, somewhat apprehensively, to Sir Henry Vane, 'General Blake I hope mends but I am checked from too presumptuous prognostics by that maxim "deseribus non temere sperandum".'[5]

The last act Blake performed was to join with Deane and Monck on 28 March in issuing instructions to Penn.[6] After this date, Blake's name disappears from the letters which are signed by Deane and Monck. On the following day the Vice-Admiral was made a temporary General-at-Sea[7] and, by the end of the first week in April, a Royalist news sheet was confidently predicting that Blake would not go to sea again, 'for one of his hamstrings is broken and he has continual rheum that falls into his eyes, which almost blinds him'.[8]

Then there is silence. Blake appears to have returned to London towards the end of the month, and he was soon well enough to begin galvanising the naval administration into further action to get ships to sea.[9] With Bourne's aid, he assembled a squadron of thirteen ships. On 1 June he ran up his flag in the new frigate *Essex*, and put to sea from Lee Road in search of the fleet. At first he only took his squadron as far as the Gunfleet because he had no up-to-date information about where the two fleets were, and he did not want to run into the Dutch.[10]

The rival fleets had been chasing each other up and down the North Sea, and another battle was imminent. Deane and Monck had received letters informing them of the proximity of Blake's squadron and, once the main fleet was between the Gunfleet and the Dutch, messages were sent urging him to join them as quickly as possible.[11] Even as Blake was beating past Shoeburyness out of the Thames, the same North-East winds which were holding up his progress were conferring the advantage of the weather gauge on his colleagues. The battle began without him. For two days the battle of the Gabbard shoal raged and the Dutch took another pounding. They were already beginning to break, when the sails of Blake's approaching squadron were sighted to the northward. His appearance brought a great cheer from the English seamen. The Dutch just ran for cover as his squadron, led by the *Hampshire* commanded by his nephew, another Robert, charged into them, with all his usual élan and lack of finesse.[12] Only the shoals of the Flemish coast saved the Dutch from total disaster. As Captain Lyons put it, they fled into the shallow water 'like Highlanders among the mountains'.[13]

No English ships were lost. Eleven Dutch men-of-war and 2 hoys were captured, 6 men-of-war sunk, 2 blown up and 1 lost by accident, according to English sources. This total agrees well with Dutch figures. Tromp returned to Texel with 74 men-of-war and he had left with 96. The Dutch lost 1350 men made prisoner and an incalculable number killed and wounded. The English casualties were the lightest of any of the major engagements: 126 killed and 236 wounded. The English did sustain one sad death. Richard Deane was killed by the first broadside of the battle. A colourful report said that a cannonball took off his head as he was standing by Monck's side on the quarterdeck of the *Resolution*. Monck with great coolness dropped his cloak over the body, so that the seamen should not be discouraged by the sight of their dead General.[14] Cromwell was particularly upset at Deane's death. Over a month later he wrote to Penn, 'I often think of our great loss in your General Deane my near friend.'[15] There is no comment from Blake, but Deane's death may well have depressed him as well. It robbed him of an old comrade and left him the only survivor of the triumvirate who had set out to revitalise the fleet four years earlier.

Blake was still very unwell and, soon after the fleet cast anchor in Sole Bay, he went on shore again. On 5 July Monck ended his letter to the Admiralty Commissioners, 'My partner Blake being gone sick ashore could not sign this letter.'[16] The next day he was visited in his quarters at Walberswick by Robert

Blackborne, the secretary to the Admiralty Committee. He described how 'we found him in a very weak condition, full of pain both in his head and left side, which had put him into a fever besides the anguish he endures by the gravel in his kidneys, insomuch that he takes no rest night nor day but continues groaning very sadly.'[17]

Monck confirmed Blackborne's gloomy report on 8 July, writing that 'General Blake is gone sick ashore to Wilderwick near Southwold two days since, being very weak and indisposed of body but sometimes gives hope of amendment though for the most part his condition is very dubious and uncertain.'[18] A week later the newspapers, with their usual exaggeration, were getting ready to write his obituary, reporting that 'Blake is likewise ill on shore that we fear his life; some report him dead and that Colonel Pride must be successor'.[19] They were premature and the General began a slow recovery. On 29 July the 'News from London' reported, 'Blake is still unfit for sea but it's thought he will come to Town within a few days.'[20] There is no mention in these reports of the thigh injury. Fevers often accompanied such wounds and many men who survived the initial hurt, died from them, but Blake's second bout of illness may have had nothing to do with his wound. He could have contracted one of the fevers which, the Generals reported, were sweeping the fleet during the summer.[21]

Blake's second recovery was too late for him to have any part in the last great battle of the war, off Scheveningen. At the Gabbard, the English had the wind. This time they had to beat up from leeward, so the battle was fought more fiercely but the result was the same. The English lost one ship, the *Oak*, which blew up; the Dutch twenty-three by their own admission and probably more. The Dutch at long last were forced to face reality. Their fleet was inferior and there was no immediate prospect of an improvement. The first two of the big new ships *'t Huis te Swieten* and *'t Huis te Kruyningen* were coming off the slipway but there were no big guns with which to equip them. The ships carrying the guns had been captured by Lawson's frigates during the blockade which preceded the battle off Scheveningen.[22]

Scheveningen was a disaster in another way. Tromp was killed early in the fighting. After the battle, violent dissensions rent the fleet about his successor. The republicans would not have such a strong Orange supporter as Jan Evertsen for Lieutenant-Admiral and the captains would not have de With. The result was that the man who was appointed was someone nobody wanted: Jacob Wassenaer, Lord of Opdam. The Dutch made a show of continuing the war throughout the winter, but they could not face the prospect of another summer campaign and peace terms were agreed in March 1654.

Although there were alarums and excursions, Blake himself did not go beyond St Helen's Road in the six months which separated his return to active service, at the beginning of October 1653, and the end of the war. It was perhaps as well. Blake's wound had made him aware of his mortality. His surviving correspondence is notable for its lack of histrionics but, on 29 August 1654, as he was preparing to leave for the Mediterranean, he ended his letter to the Admiralty Commissioners by asking for payment of his salary up to date '. . . it being uncertain whether I may live to see you again. However, my comfort is, and I doubt not but that we shall meet together at the last day in the joyful fruition of that One faith and hope of the common salvation in the Lord, upon whom alone I do wait and to whose free grace and everlasting goodness I do heartily commend you.'[23]

Another element that contributed to the change in Blake's outlook by September 1654 was the way in which the last two battles of the war were fought. After a month spent digesting the lessons of the battle of Portland, a new set of Instructions for the Better Ordering of the Fleet in Sailing were issued on 29 March over the names of all three Generals.[24] The main aim of the Instructions was to improve the discipline of the fleet and make sure that it functioned as a unit. They contain an elaborate series of flag signals and they lay down ground rules for behaviour when keeping together in high winds, stormy weather, and particularly at night.

Instructions were included to try and improve the quality of the scouting but, as Blake was to realise later, they were not really very effective. The Instructions issued before Portland had created a hierarchy of flag officers. The new ones took another step away from revolutionary equality, in the name of good discipline. Instruction Four ordered that in tacking or sailing, the higher ranked officer should go to windward. Where the officers were of equal rank, the senior should take precedence. Violation of this Instruction, in the first instance, was to lead to the loss of three months' pay; in the second, four months'. On the third offence, the officer concerned was to be cashiered.

The most controversial parts of the Instructions were those which related to the arrangement of the fleet in battle. They laid it down that when the General hoisted the red battle flag in his maintop mizzen, 'then each squadron shall take the best advantage they can to engage with the enemy next unto them, and in order hereunto all ships of every squadron shall endeavour to keep in line with their chief.' There are two points to be made about this regulation. The first is that the lines formed were within squadrons, not the whole fleet. The second is that the line was not the line of battle, as it came to be understood in the eighteenth century, but a line of bearing. The fleet to windward would proceed in line ahead until the commander-in-chief gave the signal to engage. All the ships would then turn towards the enemy, so that they were in line abreast. In order to prevent a free-for-all, no ship was allowed to windward of the commander-in-chief until the combat began.

There is no indication that, when they got to close quarters, the ships were to get in line again. Another regulation implies the reverse. If the commander-in-chief is lamed or disabled, 'then every ship of the squadron, shall endeavour to get in a line with the Admiral, or he that commands next in chief to him and nearest the enemy'. If the formation were line ahead the ships would simply close up and the lame one would drop out. No modification would be necessary. What the Instruction is saying, in effect, is that if your leader is disabled in the middle of the action, you must assist him. If he has dropped out of the battle, you must concentrate on the senior officer most hotly engaged. The Generals had in their

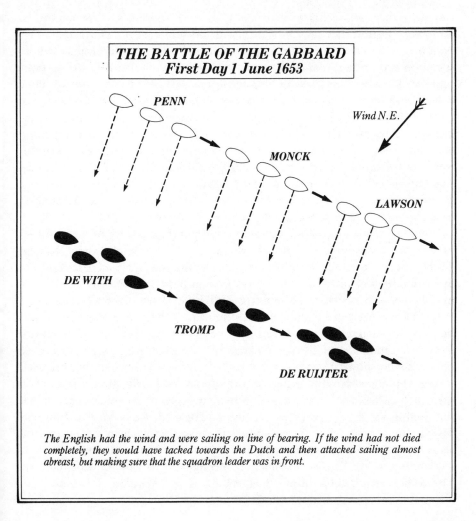

THE BATTLE OF THE GABBARD
First Day 1 June 1653

The English had the wind and were sailing on line of bearing. If the wind had not died completely, they would have tacked towards the Dutch and then attacked sailing almost abreast, but making sure that the squadron leader was in front.

mind's eye the best Dutch practice. Blake would have remembered the way in which the Dutch had been heading westwards, before Kentish Knock, in a rather ragged line and had then tacked, so that they bore down on the English in line abreast. At Dungeness, Tromp had raced him down the Channel in almost line ahead and, when the moment came to strike, the three Dutch squadrons had turned towards him, in line abreast. The same manoeuvre is evident before Portland.

If this is the correct interpretation of the Instructions, then what happened on the first day of the battle of the Gabbard was a total accident. The two fleets approached each other arranged in three squadrons, on line of bearing, the English having what wind there was. The English had just got within gunshot, when the light breeze dropped entirely. In such circumstances, they could not close with their opponents, so there was no point in tacking into the line abreast formation. Instead they stayed in line ahead and subjected the Dutch to a heavy bombardment. The Dutch were in an unenviable position and de Ruijter, whose squadron was leading, did his best to get sufficiently far ahead of his opposite number, Lawson, then tack on him and force the sort of melee, which alone could bring the Dutch victory. For almost two hours, he had no success, the Dutch being subjected to a murderous hail of cannonballs, but then the breeze revived and his plan succeeded. Simultaneously, Tromp spotted a gap appearing between Lawson and Monck, got the ship's boats out and towed the *Brederode* round so that it was pointing into it. His captains quickly followed his example. The remainder of the first day revolved round the attempts of de Ruijter and Tromp to crush Lawson, before Monck could come to his rescue. They failed miserably and the Dutch fleet recoiled in a shattered condition.[25]

Once examination of the captured ships and the evidence of the prisoners of war had been evaluated, Monck who was now in sole command, had no doubts about what needed to be done. For Tromp too, there were lessons, the most important of which was that on no account should the Dutch engage when the English had the wind. The effect was that the battle of the Gabbard cast a long shadow over the battle off Scheveningen. Tromp had the best of the preliminary manoeuvres and gained the weather gauge, but the battle did not follow the earlier set pieces. As the Dutch had the wind, theoretically, they were the ones who should have begun the battle but the English were not prepared to wait. Holding his ships as near to the wind as he could, Monck beat up to the Dutch fleet and began the action. Argument has raged ever since over whether the English fought the battle in line ahead. The evidence is hard to interpret. The famous marine artist, Willem van de Velde the elder, chartered a yacht and actually drew the battle as it took place. Some commentators claim that they can see the head of the English line bursting through the Dutch fleet in his picture. The reader may use his own judgement on that.[26] Witnesses on both sides describe four 'passes' of the English through the Dutch fleet, though whether

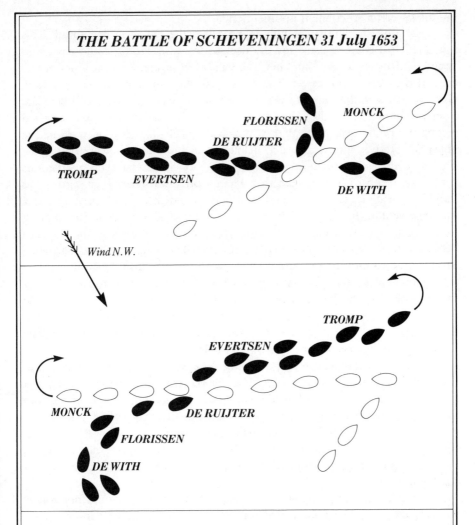

THE BATTLE OF SCHEVENINGEN 31 July 1653

FLORISSEN

MONCK

DE RUIJTER

TROMP

EVERTSEN

DE WITH

Wind N.W.

TROMP

EVERTSEN

MONCK

DE RUIJTER

FLORISSEN

DE WITH

FIRST PASS
The English to leeward begin the battle. Their aim is to break through the Dutch fleet and gain the Windward station. They make contact between de With and de Ruijter, drawing in Florissen's reserve division.

SECOND PASS
Realising what the English are trying to do, the Dutch tack to try and hold the Windward station and this leads to a second clash, only this time the point of impact is between the squadrons of de Ruijter and Evertsen.

THIRD and FOURTH PASSES
Repeat the pattern of Passes One and Two with the English striking the Dutch fleet between Evertsen and Tromp and then achieving their objective. At this point the Dutch disengaged, unwilling to endure a repeat of the battle of the Gabbard, the retreat being covered by de With's squadron which was never able to get into the battle.

the ships were in strict line is not mentioned.[27]

The English, almost certainly, approached the Dutch in line ahead. This formation had become usual for the fleet to leeward. Tromp could have held away but that would have cost him the windward position, so the English line crashed right through his fleet. This happened four times, at different points in his own line, with the ships at the point of impact being subjected to broadsides from one powerful English ship after another. The Dutch fleet was smashed section by section, except de With's squadron, which was left to leeward by the first pass. He was forced to watch helplessly, as his comrades were destroyed. This time the line formation was deliberate, not accidental. The instructions before the Gabbard had decreed that when a prize was taken every endeavour should be made to save the crew but that it should then be burnt.[28] The idea was to prevent the fleet's cohesion being lost by ships taking prizes and attempting to tow them out of the battle. The instruction was not observed at the Gabbard because eleven ships were captured but Captain Lyons does remark that when Tromp tried to lure the 4th rate frigates away from the main body after prizes they refused to be tempted. At Scheveningen it was enforced rigorously. Any captain who left the line endangered the ships next to him. Seven hundred prisoners were taken but every Dutch loss was a ship sunk, blown up or burnt.[29]

At the start of the war, once Blake had understood the advantage the English possessed, he had tried single-mindedly to force a battle, to the extent of rushing off to the Shetlands and leaving poor Sir George Ayscue exposed to the might of the whole Dutch fleet. He believed that all he had to do was set the example and his captains would second him. But fighting the Dutch was not like fighting the Royalists. There was no religious or revolutionary principle to inspire his officers. The Dutch were fellow-Protestants and fellow-Republicans. All the war was about was commercial gain. The captains were willing to fight, but they would count the cost and at Dungeness many believed that the cost was too high.

To Blake this was not good enough. If the captains would not follow willingly they must be bludgeoned into it. So he took the lead in creating a disciplined corps of captains in search of the sort of unity which had characterised the revolutionary years. The introduction of Monck brought the final shift. He was a professional soldier who understood, far better than Blake, the attitudes of professional seamen, anxious to do their best, but unwilling to sacrifice themselves when it appeared totally unnecessary. In Monck's hands, the discipline Blake had imposed was used in the evolution of an effective system of tactics – fighting in line. It is symbolic of the difference in approach that Edmund Chapman and John Taylor, two of the captains dismissed after Dungeness, were given armed merchant ships to command. Both died, bravely fighting their ships, at Scheveningen.[30]

*   *   *

As he pondered the lessons, Blake realised that, whether he liked it or not, the Revolution was over. If he was to inspire the officers and men under his command, he must find some new guiding principle. The upheaval in the political world, during the period of his convalescence, only underlined for him the way in which the old verities were disintegrating. By early 1653 there was growing evidence that the Army and the Parliament were on a collision course. The failure of the Rump to conduct the sort of religious policies that the Army leaders wanted, or to provide for new elections until the eleventh hour, led Cromwell to use force to bring the Long Parliament to an end on 20 April 1653.

Blake's attitude is very hard to define. Biographers have tried to resolve the impasse by one of two responses. The more simplistic sees the Navy as above politics. The task of the fleet was to defend the country against foreign foes. Its admirals would stay out of politics and serve each government, whatever its political complexion. Such an argument may fit twentieth-century ideas, or even the position as it was in the days of Nelson, but it ignores the realities of the English Revolution. In 1642 Blake had taken up arms for a political ideal. In 1649 he had accepted the office of General-at-Sea from a political faction, which represented a small minority of the country. To suggest that he acted without thought for the political consequences, is an insult to his intelligence. Yet he did serve both the Commonwealth and the Protectorate and he did accept orders from governments of differing hues, so some attempt must be made to explain his political shifts.

The other response attempts to cut the knot by making him into a fervent supporter of Oliver Cromwell. There is a good deal of sense in this interpretation but the trouble is that Cromwell was one of the most complex characters in English history. Which Cromwell did Blake support? The religious zealot who in April 1653 seemed about to embrace the ideas of Harrison and his Fifth Monarchists? Or the man who had taken up arms to destroy the tyranny of the Church of England and to protect the rights of the gentry, against the financial and political encroachments of Charles I, through a strengthening of Parliamentary rights?

When Blake arrived in London still sick in body, a week after the Army had forcibly dissolved Parliament, he must have been disturbed in mind as well. The report circulating among the Royalists that he had been 'outed' from his command seems to have been based on a false premise. His failure to sign the declaration of loyalty, circulated by Deane and Monck, was due to his absence from the fleet, not from any opposition to the new regime.[31]

Blake, like Cromwell, would have conceived a 'strange distaste' for the Rump. Like him, he would have become more and more hostile to the 'daily breaking forth into new and violent ... Factions'. On the other hand, under pressure from the Army, the Rump had produced an electoral scheme, which Cromwell, for his own purposes, had then scotched. Blake had collaborated with

Vane, between Dungeness and Portland, when he and the Lord General had worked together against the mercantile hawks in the Rump. Now Vane, the Rump's champion, was Cromwell's 'bête noire'. Blake's past record does not suggest that he had any sympathy at all with Harrison and the Fifth Monarchists, to whose ideas for a Parliament of the Saints Cromwell appeared to be listening. It may have been expressions of hostility from that quarter, which led the Royalist pamphleteer to end Blake's career prematurely. Though Cromwell was lending an ear to Harrison's visionary schemes, he realised that any new dispensation would need the support of moderate opinion, if it was to succeed. A movement among the fanatics for Blake's removal would not have received Cromwell's support. Quite apart from his appreciation of Blake's sterling qualities, he would have been aware that Blake's unpopularity among the sects was as nothing to that of the former Royalist, George Monck.

While Blake was convalescing, representatives from the States of Holland and of West Friesland arrived in London to sound out the possibilities of peace.[32] The indications are that Blake was a member of the 'peace party', but there is no evidence that the Dutchmen met him or that he took any part in the negotiations. He was too much taken up with encouraging an administration sadly shaken up by the turmoil. Blake's absence at sea during June 1653, and his second illness, effectively eliminated him from the political scene. What he thought of Cromwell's renewed offer of political union to the United Provinces, the rock on which full peace negotiations foundered just before the battle off Scheveningen, does not appear in his correspondence and receives no comment from the pamphleteers.

The preoccupation of Blake and Monck with beating the Dutch did not prevent both men from being elected to Barebone's Parliament. This was an assembly of 100 picked men, some of whom were nominated by the dissenting congregations and others by the Army Council. A significant difference between Blake and Monck was that Monck was nominated by the Army Council but Blake sat as a representative of the Somerset congregations, underlining once again his independence of the New Model Army. He was one of the few members of the Rump to obtain a seat.

When Blake returned to duty, after his illness in October 1653, the agitation of the sects was reaching a hysterical climax. The victories of the summer were not enough. The Dutch must be crushed completely. Some of the preachers saw the Dutch merchants as Mammon personified and exulted in their discomfiture. Others saw the Dutch War as part of the wars which would precede the establishment of Christ's Kingdom on Earth. Christopher Feake declaimed from his pulpit, 'Thou gav'st a Cup into the hand of England and we drank of it. Thou carried'st it to Scotland and Ireland and they drank of it. Now thou hast carried it to Holland and they are drinking of it. Lord, carry it also to France, to Spain, to Rome, and let it never be out of some or other of their hands, till they drink and be drunk and spew and fall and never rise any more.'

It is difficult to imagine anything more distasteful to a man such as Blake, all of whose instincts supported good discipline against disorder and revolted from the increasingly anarchical outlook of the sectaries. Cromwell's decision to end the Parliament of the Saints on 4 December 1653 and, by implication, to reject finally the ideas of the Fifth Monarchists, would have been received with great relief by Blake and Penn at Portsmouth, as they kept close watch on the Channel. Both men accepted the establishment of the Protectorate the following February but, in different ways, each man contrived to show that he regarded it as the least of the evils, rather than embracing it with enthusiasm. When Monck's appointment as Commander-in-Chief in Scotland was announced, Penn's appointment as General-at-Sea was made permanent. He was only thirty-three and the first career seaman to be given the command. Cromwell also bestowed on him valuable property in Ireland at the time of his marriage. Yet hardly six months were to elapse before rumours were circulating that Penn had been appointed to command the expedition to the West Indies to get him out of the country, because he was suspected of plotting with the Royalists.

Blake's response was different. He behaved like John Milton who, faced with a similar crisis, retired to his study. There he began dictating to his long-suffering daughters the text of *Paradise Lost*, in which he fought the battles of the Civil Wars over again and tried to explain to himself what had gone wrong. Blake's politics were very different from those of Milton but like him he turned his back on the political scene. This is all the more remarkable in that he could have had a political career if he had wished. From 1645 until his death, Blake was elected to every political assembly that met, often without any campaigning and sometimes in his absence, a great testimony to his popularity in his native Somerset. He had made his military career outside the New Model Army, he had refused the offer of Major-General of Foot in the Irish Army and his election to Barebone's Parliament had been on his own merit. Such a man could have commanded a place on Cromwell's Council of State had he wished it. Absence at sea would have been no bar; the demands of Scotland did not prevent Monck occupying a seat. He had never been an enthusiastic politician but he had always valued a Parliamentary seat for the influence it gave him, so his distancing himself from the new regime betokens not so much opposition to as disillusionment with the whole political process. The picture which emerges is, in many ways, a sad one, of a man racked with bodily pain and trying to hide from himself that all he had fought for was turning to dust and ashes. His reaction to the abrupt change in policy which followed the end of the First Dutch War shows only too clearly his unwillingness to think about the implications of what he was asked to do.

Once the Dutch entanglement was out of the way, Cromwell began to try and implement the policy which he and Vane had advocated, unsuccessfully, at the outbreak of the war in 1652. Cromwell wished to form an Alliance among the Protestant countries of Europe, which would finally break the power of the Roman Catholic Church. But he had to face the reality of the unwillingness of the Protestant countries to act together. The Dutch were unlikely to regard any English initiative with much favour for some time to come. Sweden and Denmark took their Baltic rivalry much more seriously than their common Protestant heritage. Fortunately similar rivalries divided the Roman Catholic powers as well. Spain and France were still at war with each other, so Cromwell could flex the military and naval muscles of England, by supporting one against the other. For Cromwell's Council of State, as it met to plot England's next move, the only question was, which one?

The obvious enemy was France. Over the last decade Cardinal Mazarin had done all he could to embarrass the Parliament and the Republic which followed it. Throughout the Civil Wars and the Commonwealth, France had sheltered Royalist privateers and allowed them to sell their prizes in French ports. In 1645 and 1646 French envoys had encouraged attempts to form a rival army to the New Model Army, based on a combination of Royalists, the Scots and dissident Presbyterians. In 1650 Portugal, which was allied to France, allowed Rupert to use the Tagus as a base and in 1653 he found final refuge at Brest after his epic voyage to the West Indies. Mazarin was motivated not so much by sympathy for Queen Henrietta Maria, the French King's sister, as by the calculation that continued disorder would prevent England interfering in the Thirty Years War. England retaliated where possible. In 1647 an English squadron impounded six Swedish ships which had been sold to France for, allegedly, failing to strike their flags. Retaliatory measures against French trade were one of the major irritants which started the Dutch War. The way in which Blake took time off to destroy Vendome's attempt to relieve Dunkirk in 1652 has already been narrated. Spain on the other hand had gone out of her way to extend the hand of friendship. She had been the first country to recognise the new republic and she had helped destroy Prince Rupert's squadron, by refusing him the protection of Cartagena harbour.

That was not the way the Protector's council saw the position. They believed that a war with Spain in alliance with France would lengthen the Franco-Spanish War, because France was the weaker. The war with Spain could be made to finance itself by seizure of the Plate fleets, and there were West Indian islands, ripe for the plucking.[33] Blake never pronounced directly on the issue. What we know of him suggests that a war with Spain would be more acceptable to him than a war with the United Provinces but there is no evidence that he showed any particular enthusiasm. When, in 1656, some of the captains asked why England should go to war with Spain, a country which had done England no harm, Blake is reputed to have growled, 'It is not for us to mind State Affairs, but to stop the foreigner from fooling us.' What else could he have said? He could not bang the religious drum, as he had done at Lyme Regis and Taunton because he was fighting a war against one Roman Catholic country in alliance with another. Nor could he proclaim the virtues and coming triumph of republicanism, as he had done at Cadiz in 1650, when he was serving a military dictator. The dilemma that faced Blake was one which the Marshals who served Napoleon, or the Generals who fought for Hitler, would have recognised. The advantage of the course he took was that it enabled him to concentrate on perfecting the fleet as an instrument of government policy; the disadvantage, that it turned him into a political eunuch. And the end result was to replace the search for a political or religious utopia, with what could be seen as an unthinking and zenophobic nationalism.

Part IV

The Spanish War

Return to the Mediterranean

C ROMWELL lost little time in implementing his new policy. The Dutch War finished in March 1654, and on 5 June, the Council of State began issuing the orders which would herald the planned change in English foreign policy. Two fleets were to be equipped for sea. The first was to be of fourteen ships, for the 'Western Design', the name given to the plan to conquer the Spanish West Indies. The second was for a fleet of twenty ships to be sent to the Mediterranean. Another resolution provided for four more ships for the Straits of Gibraltar, presumably to free the main fleet from the chore of escorting merchantmen. Complete secrecy was enjoined on all concerned in the plans.[1] The instruction was taken so literally, that the Commissioners of the dockyards were not told and omitted to sheathe the bottoms of some of the ships, because they were unaware that they were bound for the Tropics[2] – the home of the boring ship-worm or teredo navalis.

In spite of these precautions, the preparations could not be concealed and it was not long before an agent in London was reporting to Paris the destinations and objectives of the two fleets. 'It is conceaved,' he wrote, 'all the sheathed ships will attempt the king of Spaine's plate fleete, or the island of Hispaniola in the West Indies, and perhaps both: that a squadron of the other ships will be for the Streights, to annoy you and the Duke of Florence . . .'[3]

The agent was uncomfortably near the truth. Penn was intended for the West Indies. Blake was to command the other fleet bound for the Mediterranean. His instructions have not survived but circumstantial evidence makes it plain that his first task was to thwart French plans in the Mediterranean, in order to pressure them into an alliance with England on Cromwell's terms. Once the alliance was concluded the English fleet was to turn its attention to the Spanish Plate fleet. Should there be any spare time, between the crushing of French ambitions and the beginning of hostilities with Spain, Blake was to devote it to dealing with the depredations of the Barbary pirates of North Africa.

The fleet Blake was given was a powerful one and an interesting reflection of the shipbuilding policy pursued by the Commonwealth and Protectorate governments. The three principal officers were each given a powerful 2nd rate. Blake ran up his flag in the *George* and was given John Stokes as his flag captain. His Vice-Admiral, Richard Badiley, got the *Andrew* and the Rear-Admiral, Joseph Jordan, commanded the *Unicorn*. All three ships dated from before the Civil Wars. The first two were from the building programme of 1619–24. The *Unicorn* was a Ship Money ship launched in 1637. The Interregnum governments had found themselves in the happy position of inheriting a core of capital ships which only needed renovating, so they concentrated their own building on slightly smaller ships. All four of Blake's 3rd rates, the *Langport, Bridgwater, Worcester* and *Plymouth*, had been built since 1649. So had eight of the eleven 4th rates, the *Hampshire, Kent, Foresight, Taunton, Diamond, Ruby, Newcastle* and *Maidstone*. Three of them, the *Langport, Taunton* and *Maidstone* were fresh off the slipway. By contrast the remaining three 4th rates and six out of the nine smaller ships had either been bought or were captured prizes. Only the *Mermaid, Pearl* and *Merlin* galley were built in State yards. None of England's rivals had large frigates which could be commissioned into the fleet, if captured. All of them had privateers, which were suitable for operations in shallow waters, intelligence gathering, as support ships and for carrying dispatches. This was another reason why the Commonwealth and Protectorate governments concentrated on building big weatherly frigates, which could outgun any rivals.[4]

The cruise began in the frustrating fashion which was to be its hallmark throughout. By 19 August the fleet was assembled in the Downs and, directly the wind came round into the right quarter, Blake weighed anchor. The fleet reached Plymouth on 23 August but the victualling ships were not ready and Blake had to wait until 29 September, when they arrived under convoy with the *Maidstone*.[5] Blake wasted no time in getting the fleet to sea but he had hardly cleared the jaws of the Channel before the weather turned nasty. Under the date, 2 October, John Weale, an officer on board the *Amity*, recorded that the 'wind beginneth to frown upon us.' The next day there was 'a very great tempest and some of the fleet spending their masts we are in jeopardy.' Reluctantly Blake turned back but even in Plymouth Sound the fleet was not safe. Weale records how the *Amity* broke loose from her moorings and had to seek shelter in the Catwater. At last, on 8 October, the weather moderated and Blake had the anchors up as soon as signs of the more favourable conditions appeared.

Weale also records how Blake established the discipline he wanted from the beginning. When the fleet left the Downs, the *Amity* sailed without her captain, Henry Pack, who was on shore with his wife. He had to post to Dover to get on board his ship. Similarly, when the fleet finally left Plymouth, the lieutenant of Blake's ship was on board the *Amity*, where he had been marooned by the earlier bad weather. He had to transfer, by boat, when the fleet was out in the Sound.[6] Blake expected his officers to observe the spirit of his instructions. They could read the signs as well as he could and he expected them to be prepared.

There was a good reason for Blake's haste. During the summer, John Thurloe, Cromwell's Secretary of State, had been receiving a stream of letters about French preparations for a Mediterranean offensive against Spain from Charles Longland, the English agent at Leghorn. A fleet and an army were being formed at Toulon. Longland soon convinced Thurloe that the French would probably head for Spanish-controlled Naples and try to help the rebels in Apulia. He reported that the French were expecting ten ships from Portugal to reinforce their fleet at Toulon.[7] Simultaneously the English became aware that the French at Brest were preparing men-of-war for sea. If Blake reached the Straits of Gibraltar quickly he might at least prevent the Portuguese ships and the French Brest squadron from reaching Toulon. The long wait for the victuallers followed by the bad weather destroyed any hope of stopping the Portuguese ships but, with Longland reporting that the French were experiencing difficulties in getting their expedition off and little positive information about the whereabouts of the Brest ships, the English still had a good chance of being able to intervene effectively.

Blake's fleet arrived off Cadiz on 30 October. His reception was a cool one. The King of Spain had agreed to Cromwell's request that the English fleet be allowed to use Spanish harbours, but the preparation of Penn's fleet and its likely destination was known and Blake's own instructions were secret. A talk with the English agent, James Wilson, yielded the information that a squadron of French ships had been reported four days earlier.[8] Blake wasted no time. Instructing Wilson to send on the *Princess Maria*, *Dolphin* victualler, *Maidenhead* galley and *Nonsuch* ketch, which had lost company during the voyage, Blake sailed for the Straits of Gibraltar, hoping that the French had not yet passed into the Mediterranean. The English fleet cast anchor in Gibraltar road on 4 November.[9]

Blake's prompt move was proved right within twenty-four hours of his arrival. The same day that the English fleet reached the Straits of Gibraltar the four missing ships sailed into Cadiz with quite a tale to tell. The previous day they had fallen in with seven French men-of-war under the Duc de Nieuchese. After a brief action the *Princess Maria* captured a French fireship and the French captured the *Dolphin*. Questioning of the *Dolphin*'s crew revealed to the French that Blake was not far away with twenty men-of-war. Nieuchese was so shaken that he released the *Dolphin* with expressions of regret about any damage that might have been done.[10]

The *Princess Maria* remained at Cadiz in order to replace her foremast top which had been lost in the fighting but Wilson ordered the other three to sail to the Straits at once. They reached Blake on 5 November. Blake had already taken the appropriate steps. Six frigates, under the command of Captain Hill of the *Worcester*, were already out scouting to see if they could pick up the French squadron.[11] The *Langport* and the *Pearl* returned to Cadiz to see if there was any more information and to stand by in case the *Princess Maria* needed any assistance in refitting.

Under the date, 7 November, Weale describes an incident that shows how much Blake had learned from the mistakes of the First Dutch War. 'Captain Stayner of the *Plymouth* frigate cometh in and some others,' he wrote. 'The General very angry with them. They immediately go out again to Capt. Hill of the *Worcester* and C in C of the squadron.'[12] The reference to Captain Hill shows that there were two reasons for Blake's anger. The first was that, having made a sweep of the area and found nothing, the captains had believed their job to be done. They had not learned the lessons of Dungeness and Portland. Scouting was not just an occasional activity. If the fleet was to have prompt information about the approach of a possible enemy there must be a constant screen of scouts to give timely warning. The second reason for his anger was that they had left their stations without any reference to Captain Hill, the commander of the squadron. The *Plymouth* was as large a ship as the *Worcester* but Hill was still Stayner's superior and Blake was determined to enforce the hierarchy of officers which had evolved in the Dutch War. The whole incident showed the need for the strict discipline which Blake imposed. If Stayner, one of the most promising of the younger captains, could behave in such an irresponsible way, what would the others do if Blake relaxed his grip?

For a couple of days the fleet was continually on the alert, expecting the French to appear over the horizon at any time. When their tour of duty was completed Hill's squadron of scouts was replaced by another group of five ships, under Captain Curtis of the *Ruby*, which included Weale's own ship, the *Amity*.[13] The *Langport* returned from Cadiz on 8 November, but with little to add to what Blake already knew. However, the same day they hailed a ship passing the Straits who told them that Nieuchese was at Lisbon, cleaning and fitting his ships.[14]

Blake was in a dilemma. He still believed that the best contribution he could make would be to meet and destroy Nieuchese, but how would it look if, while he waited in the Straits, the French overwhelmed the Spaniards in Naples without the help of the Brest squadron! It must have been after much heart searching that he decided to stay put, at least for the moment. A council of war on 14 November, came to no positive decision except to send out six frigates, of which the *Amity* was one, to make yet another search of the sea between Lisbon and the Straits.[15] Blake was not to know Nieuchese was so frightened of him, that he had no intention of stirring from Lisbon while the English fleet was anywhere near.

Another week passed with no sign of the French and, on 21 November, Blake called another council of war. He may have received news from the shore or from passing ships that the French expedition had sailed from Toulon or even of its presence at Naples. Whatever the reason, the return of the *Princess Maria* and the *Pearl* from Cadiz was the signal for the fleet to weigh anchor.[16] The next day the English were off Malaga and on 28 November, the fleet cast anchor at Alicante. Blake remained there two days. He may have been uncertain whether to head for Toulon or for Naples. In the end he decided that the correct course was to make for Cagliari in southern Sardinia. There, if anywhere, he would be able to get up-to-date information. Landfall was made on 5 December and the Spanish governor received them warmly. Here Blake got positive news that the French were before Naples.[17] The fleet left Cagliari early on 10 December and sighted Naples late the following evening. The ships' companies lay mustered all night, expecting action the following day, but when the dawn came it revealed an empty Naples Bay. The English were too late.[18]

The French expedition, 8000 strong and commanded by the Duc de Guise, left the Hyères islands south of Toulon on 26 September, while Blake was still in Plymouth Sound, fretting over his victuallers.[19] Guise's fleet, commanded by the Chevalier Paul, consisted of twenty-two ships, eighteen barques and six galleys. They were seen three days later off the Straits of Bonofacio, which separate Corsica from Sardinia. After that everything went wrong for the French. For sixteen days Guise was buffeted by storms; his fleet was scattered; he completely lost contact with the galleys; and he himself almost drifted under the guns of Cagliari. At last, having gathered his fleet together, he arrived off Malta only to be refused assistance by the Knights of St John. Although Guise managed to capture two small Spanish islands off the west end of Sicily and replenish his supplies, he now made the fatal mistake of abandoning his original plan of landing in Calabria and made for Naples instead. The French landed on 4 November and took Castellamare. Despite going on to take the Annunziato Torre, one of the outworks of the city, it soon became clear that the French had not got the resources to capture Naples; the local population was hostile and provisions were again running short. To make matters worse, renewed bad weather cut Guise off from the fleet for nearly a week. On 7 December, the French re-embarked and returned to Toulon.

When Blake pieced together what had happened he was mortified to realise that the French had landed the very day he cast anchor in Gibraltar road. As Longland wrote to Thurloe on 8 December, when reporting the sighting of seven ships of the French armada off Leghorn making the best of their way back to Toulon, 'This week we hav heard nothing of generall Blake: if he had not stayd at the Streit's-mouth, but com directly for Itally, he had found all the French fleet in a pownd in Naples bay, wher he might hav don what he woud with 'am but al will be for the best.'[20]

Cromwell's reaction to the news was probably quiet satisfaction. Only an estimated 3000 men returned to France. The rest had succumbed to sickness or had been killed in action. Rumour had it that Guise's departure was hastened by news of Blake's approach and Mazarin showed no inclination to listen to the

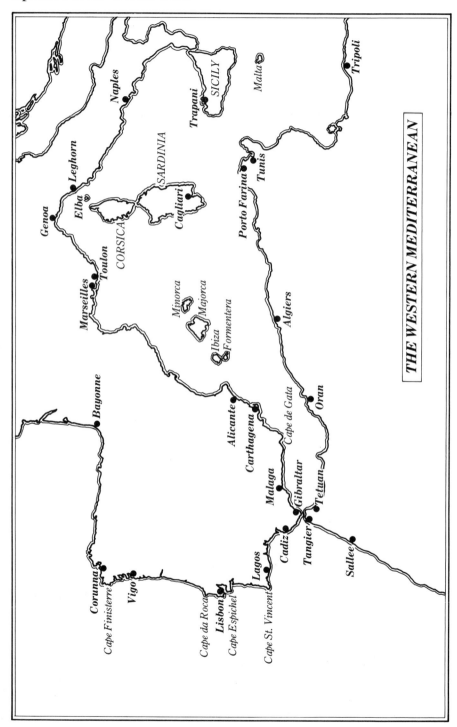

THE WESTERN MEDITERRANEAN

Tripoli

Malta

SICILY

Trapani

Naples

SARDINIA

Cagliari

Porto Farina

Tunis

Leghorn

Elba

CORSICA

Genoa

Toulon

Marseilles

Minorca

Majorca

Ibiza

Formentera

Algiers

Bayonne

Alicante

Carthagena

Cape de Gata

Oran

Malaga

Gibraltar

Tetuan

Corunna

Cape Finisterre

Vigo

Cape da Roca

Lisbon

Cape Espichel

Lagos

Cadiz

Tangier

Sallee

Cape St. Vincent

Duke's importunities for another chance to redeem his reputation while Blake was on the loose.[21] Until the French came to an agreement with Cromwell, Guise could forget his Mediterranean ambitions.

After spending three days at Naples, Blake followed in the tracks of the retreating French, casting anchor by the Malora sandbank off Leghorn, on 21 December.[22] He was received enthusiastically and the Grand Duke of Tuscany eagerly granted him facilities to victual and water his fleet while he ascertained what the next French move would be. Blake was totally unmoved by the attempts of Spanish and Italian notables to court his favour. He does not seem to have landed either at Cadiz or at Alicante. At Cagliari, the Governor and his officials had come on board the *George* to see him because he made no effort to visit them on shore. At Naples, the present which had been prepared for him had to be sent out to the fleet because Blake would not come to receive it. At Leghorn, Blake refused Longland's invitation to dinner, pleading ill health. The English delegation was led by Rear-Admiral Jordan instead. He also presented the captains who accompanied him when they were received in audience by the Grand Duke.[23]

Blake had little taste for the Catholic society of the Mediterranean world. He would have shared Weale's disapproval of the Mass processions he witnessed at Alicante, and of Naples, the largest part of whose revenue, according to Weale, came from its 3000 whores.[24] Justifying his failure to return the courtesies of the Spanish at Cagliari, Blake compared them sourly '... to an ape that hugged so much that she many times killed.' But there must have been more to it than that. Many of Blake's captains were as Puritan as he but they leapt eagerly at any opportunity which varied the monotony of shipboard life and gave them the chance to experience the sights, sounds and smells of a world so different from their own.

For Blake the fleet was now his sole concern. Society and politics alike were for others. How much he had changed was shown by his attitude to the dissolution of the First Protectorate Parliament. When the news arrived he expressed great satisfaction because it had attempted to cut the enormous cost of the Army and the Navy.[25] What price now the opposition to the Ship Money of 1637 and the subsidies for the wars with Scotland, justified because neither had been approved by Parliament?

Blake's bearlike behaviour did have one advantage. It enabled him to mask his intentions more easily. The Venetian envoy at Naples reported that Spanish ministers were beginning 'to feel doubtful over the proceedings of General Blach, whose plans it is not easy to find out.' He was 'a deep, sombre man of few words. Owing to his advanced age [he was 57] he never shows himself even on his own ship except when the sun shines, and although invited, he would never go ashore on a single occasion to see the place and gratify his countrymen.' His colleague at Florence wrote that the Grand Duke of Tuscany at Leghorn 'is trying to keep Blach friendly, the more so because he seems to be a very touchy and particular old man. His Highness has talked to me about the extreme severity with which he treats the captains of his ships.'[26]

The Venetian diplomats would have been both pleased and surprised if they could have divined his intentions. Blake quickly came to the conclusion that the French had no immediate plans for offensive operations, so he turned to the part of his instructions which related to the protection of English trade from the North African pirates. The fleet set sail on 15 January, bound for Trapani in western Sicily, intending to go from there to Tunis and then on to Tripoli. However a close shave off Capri, when the *Worcester* and *Langport* were almost lost, followed by adverse winds and bad weather, forced it to put back to Leghorn.[27] Blake now made straight for Tunis. One reason was that the delay had begun to eat into the victuals he had gathered, but there was another.

Blake was aware that there was a long, wasting war going on between Venice and Turkey. Ten years earlier the Turks had attacked the Venetian island of Crete. They had overrun large parts of it but the Venetian garrison had resisted stoutly and the Turks in their turn had been cut off thanks to the Venetian domination of the sea. The previous year the Turks had prepared a grand fleet to relieve their army but it had been defeated by the Venetians under Mocenigo when it attempted to break his blockade of the Dardanelles. The Turks were now trying to recruit their losses by getting reinforcements from the North African corsair states. Rumour had it that there was to be a grand rendezvous and Blake was determined to do what he could to cross the Sultan's plans, irrespective of the outcome of the negotiations with the Dey of Tunis over his attacks on English shipping.[28]

Landfall was made at Cape Bon on 7 February, and the following day the fleet cast anchor off Goletta. There ensued three days of intensive negotiations. In 1646 Edmund Casson had concluded a treaty with the Dey of Tunis, on behalf of the English government, by which each country pledged itself to respect the shipping of the other and not to make captives of each other's nationals. The English claimed that the Tunisians had broken the agreement and attacked English shipping. Blake demanded the return of a ship called the *Princess*, compensation for other losses and the release of all English captives. The Tunisians refused to consider compensation or to return the *Princess*, claiming with some justice, that the English had broken the treaty first. In 1651, an Englishman named Mitchell had contracted to carry a small contingent of Turkish soldiers to Smyrna. Instead he had sold them to the Knights of St John who had used them as galley crews.[29]

By 11 February the negotiations had reached an impasse and Blake began to cast around for some means of bringing pressure to bear on the recalcitrant Tunisians. Goletta, the port of Tunis, was practically impossible to attack without a force of soldiers and the Tunisians had no commerce worth intercepting, but information reached him that there were some ships at the harbour of Porto

Farina, some distance to the northward. Captain Hill in the *Worcester* was sent to investigate, together with the *Amity*, *Newcastle*, and *Maidstone*. When the squadron arrived off Porto Farina the castle saluted it with three guns but when Hill got his boats out and began to sound the bay, the garrison's attitude changed and they fired on the English in an attempt to prevent them completing their task. Hill refused to be deflected from his purpose so the Tunisians began to make preparations for the expected assault.[30]

On 22 February the rest of the fleet appeared at the same time as a Tunisian army led by the Dey himself.[31] All appeared to be in readiness for a clash but the council of war on board the *George* decided against an immediate attack. Hill reported that there were nine ships there, eight Turkish men-of-war and the *Princess* which was one of the objects of the dispute. His investigations had shown that there was sufficient depth of water, but some of the captains were worried that there was not enough room for the ships to turn. Doubts were expressed about whether Blake had authority to attack Turkish ships, especially as the Sultan's representatives had done what they could to persuade the Dey to come to terms.[32] But what swayed Blake most was the shortage of bread and water caused by the fortnight's delay. When the main body of the fleet set course for Cagliari, Weale for one was quite certain that Blake intended 'to give them a more sudden and hotter visit'.[33] His opinion was confirmed by the decision to leave a squadron under Captain Stayner consisting of his own ship the *Plymouth* together with the *Kent*, *Foresight*, *Newcastle*, *Taunton* and *Mermaid* to make sure that the birds could not fly away.[34]

The fleet reached Cagliari after a passage of four days where they were joined by the *Langport*, *Diamond*, *Ruby*, and *Pearl*. They had been sent to try and locate French privateers which had been attacking English commerce around the Balearic Islands. Captain Cuttance was able to show one of the Frenchmen, which he had taken prize, and report that two more had been driven ashore on Majorca and sold to the Spanish governor.[35] He was not allowed to remain long. Blake soon realised that Cagliari could not supply all his wants. The *Langport*, *Guinea* and *Diamond* were dispatched to the Balearic Islands and eastern Spain for bread and the *Maidstone* and *Hampshire* to see what they could pick up at Genoa and Leghorn. The *Hope* flyboat was left to bake bread at the bakehouse in Cagliari and on 15 March the rest of the fleet started back to North Africa.[36] Five days later it was off Tunis once more.

Blake's attempts to re-open negotiations met with no success. In his letter to Thurloe he characterised the Dey's attitude as insolent.[37] The Tunisians had concluded that there was nothing Blake could do. At a council of war the decision was taken to attack Porto Farina but, in order to lull the Tunisians into a false sense of security, course was set for Trapani where the fleet would wait for the right weather conditions. It was 31 March[38] before Blake could give the signal for the third visit of the English fleet to the North African coast. Land was in sight the next day but the wind was blowing right in the teeth of Blake's ships. A council of war on 2 April took the decision to attack at the first suitable opportunity but the fleet was not in position off Porto Farina until 4 pm the following day.[39] There was then a further delay because Blake's plan called for an attack at first light.

At about 4 am, taking advantage of the sea breeze and led by the *Newcastle* commanded by Nathaniel Cobham, the ships of the 4th rate and below filed into the harbour through the El Bahira entrance and drew up opposite the Turkish men-of-war. An anonymous account lists them as the *Newcastle, Kent, Foresight, Amity, Princess Maria, Pearl, Mermaid* and *Merlin*.[40] Weale adds the *Ruby* and *Diamond*.[41] The larger ships, the *Andrew* leading, followed by the *Plymouth, George, Worcester, Unicorn* and *Bridgwater* were to take on the castle and the fortifications. They coolly anchored within musket shot of their targets. The first broadsides from the English ships were devastating. The Tunisian guns, which had never been particularly powerful or well disciplined, were quickly silenced and many of the gunners abandoned the batteries. The Turkish sailors only waited until the picked boarding crews under the direction of Captain Stokes began leaving the English frigates in their ships' boats, before fleeing ashore. Many jumped overboard in panic and swam to the land. Others started destroying part of the fortifications before taking refuge in the castle.[42]

By now the sea breeze was sweeping the clouds of smoke from the broadsides over the coast, so that even those Tunisians who were still firing could not see their targets. No attempt was made to make any of the ships prize. All of them were set on fire, including the *Princess*, by the boarding parties who then returned to their ships. There was going to be quite enough to do to get their own ships out against the wind without being burdened by prizes.[43] Blake and his council had thought hard about this crucial difficulty and they had come to the conclusion that the solution was 'warping out'. Each ship, before it went in close, dropped its anchors and then sailed on, paying out its anchor cable. When the time came to retreat each ship hauled itself back along its anchor cable to its anchor.[44] The exercise was a slow and tricky one. The bigger ships provided cover for Cobham's division as it disengaged, once Stokes was convinced that the fires could not be put out. They then left the harbour in turn, Badiley in the *Andrew* being the last out. The attack began around 4 am, all the Turkish ships were on fire by 8 am and by 11 am the last English ship had warped out of Porto Farina. The English lost twenty-five killed and eighty wounded, most of them in the boarding parties.[45]

The very ease of the victory tends, in hindsight, to diminish Blake's achievement but to attribute the English success to the poor standard of Tunisian gunnery would be to miss the point. By raking through the annals of Tudor and early Stuart naval history Sir Julian Corbett manages to come up with three examples of ships taking on shore batteries with success,[46] but he has to confess that none of them comes up to what happened at Porto Farina.[47] The victory marks the emergence of Blake as a mature fleet commander. The passage at Porto Farina was as narrow in April as it was in February when the council of war had decided not to attack, and Cromwell's instructions were no less ambiguous. We must conclude therefore that Blake persuaded some of his captains to change their minds or defied a majority of his council. The mature Blake was well aware of how powerful his armament was if he could get to close quarters, but he did not make the mistake of thinking that all he had to do was rush the harbour, as the Blake of the Dutch war would have done. That might also have succeeded, but at a heavy cost. The operation was carefully planned. He knew that the sea breeze would carry the ships in; his battle experience would have told him that smoke from the guns of ships to windward would blow over their opponents. The germ of the warping-out idea was already present in the Jersey operation though there the Parliamentarians had hauled on their anchor cables to get themselves inshore. Most important of all, he had learned from Monck that taking prizes must be subordinated to the tactical battle plan. To have taken prizes at Porto Farina would have endangered the whole operation so all nine ships were burnt until they were no more than blackened timbers.

According to Robert Southey, Little Peterkin asked old Caspar about the battle of Blenheim. ' "But what good came of it at last?" "Why that I cannot tell," said he, "but 'twas a famous victory" '. Southey would have had more cause to pin the epitaph on Porto Farina. The shattering of the ships shook the Dey of Tunis but it did not move him. He was just as adamant in his refusal to negotiate after the battle as before. As he pointed out to Blake, they were the Sultan's ships not his. A week after the battle news came that Algiers was ready to conclude a Treaty with England but the friendly attitude of the Algiers men-of-war which the English met in the Straits of Gibraltar the previous November suggests that the Algerines did not need a Porto Farina to convince them that Cromwell and Blake were not men to be trifled with. Nor sadly did the destruction of the Turkish ships do more than delay the fate of Venetian Crete.

On 16 April the English cast anchor in Cagliari harbour. They did not remain there long. After writing a letter to Sir Thomas Bendish, the English representative in Constantinople, to warn him of the possible consequences for English trade of the action at Porto Farina, Blake issued orders for the fleet to sail for Algiers. He was needed there to ratify the treaty which had been concluded and besides, Algiers was the only remaining port that was both willing and had the resources to victual the English fleet. So bad had the situation become that when the *Amity* made landfall to leeward of the port the crew feared that food would run out before the ship could beat back.[48]

The welcome at Algiers was a very friendly one. There was only one slight hitch. The treaty provided for the release of all English and Irish slaves but there were some Dutch slaves working on the quay. They managed to escape from their taskmasters, jump into the harbour and swim to the English ships. They were not covered by the treaty but Blake knew that it would damage his standing if he insisted that they were returned. In the end the Dey agreed to release them if the English would buy them from him. The seamen then offered to sacrifice pay to keep their new comrades, an offer Blake accepted.[49]

On 10 May the English fleet left Algiers bound for the Balearic Islands and reached Formentera four days later. One of the reasons was to get firewood but Blake had also appointed the archipelago as a place where any ships from Leghorn or Genoa carrying dispatches could find him. He was not disappointed. The *Warwick* pink came in soon after his arrival.[50] When he had read the dispatches he summoned the captains of the *Amity* and the *Hector* on board. They were to take Consul Browne to Alicante where he was to claim the guns from the Royalist ships which were still there. They were to take them on board and bring them to the fleet at Gibraltar if it was there, or go and cruise in Rota road if it was not.[51] Events were now proceeding inexorably towards a break with Spain and Blake knew that it was the last chance he would get.

The first sign of a change in the wind had come during Blake's second visit to Tunis. When he dropped anchor there was a French vessel in the road. At first she took great care to remain well clear of the fleet but after the arrival of dispatches whose contents are unknown to us, she sailed in among the English ships.[52] Another indication came at Algiers. The ships which had been detached to guard English shipping in the Gulf of Lyons came in and they were not replaced.[53]

On 24 May Blake received the news that he was waiting for. For some time he had been importuning the Navy and Admiralty Commissioners to send out victualling ships because the Mediterranean states either could not or would not provide adequate food for his hungry seamen. He now learned that they were in Gibraltar Bay.[54] Blake immediately weighed anchor and shaped course for the Straits where the *Amity* and the *Hector* rejoined the fleet with the guns safely in their holds.[55] Then much to his relief the victuallers, escorted by the *Centurion* and the *Dragon*, appeared just as the fleet was taking station off Cadiz.[56]

Food and drink were not the only problems Blake faced. Many of his ships were in a bad state and the larger pre-Civil War 2nd rates were in no condition to face an Atlantic winter. He wrote home, proposing that they be replaced by frigates. Until a decision was reached he intended to send a ship home with each set of dispatches and he suggested that a fresh one should be sent with each reply.[57] The first ship selected was the *Amity* but fortunately for us, our diarist John Weale decided to transfer to the *Maidstone* rather than go home early.[58]

Another problem was that Blake was far from certain what Cromwell wanted him to do. A rupture with Spain was clearly not far away. Wild rumours were circulating about what Penn was doing in the West Indies so when the Governor of Cadiz made an offer to allow Blake to water his ships ten at a time he did not take it up. A further indication of the way things were shaping was the improvement in relations with Portugal. Negotiations for a treaty had begun when Thomas Maynard arrived in Lisbon in the *Assurance*. They were to break down over the question of compensation for the damage done by Rupert, but the King was already sending Blake presents and instructing the Governor of Lagos to allow English ships to take on water there, on the basis that anyone who embarrassed Spain was worth encouraging.[59]

Despite all this there had been no declaration of war. Most of the letters from Cromwell and Thurloe have not survived and Blake's exact instructions are unknown. In his letter of 12 June Blake refers to secret instructions about the silver fleet.[60] Presumably they ordered him to waylay it. Later events indicate that when he arrived off Cadiz his orders were that he was to defend himself if attacked but he was not to start hostilities. They were soon modified. Cromwell was becoming apprehensive that the Spaniards would send a fleet to the West Indies to fight Penn so on 13 June he authorised an alteration to the instructions which allowed Blake to attack any Spanish fleet bound for the West Indies.[61] This modification, which Blake acknowledged on 4 July, only created confusion. If a Spanish fleet put to sea how would the English know where it was going?

The following month Blake was faced with this very dilemma. Intelligence reached the English fleet that the Spaniards were preparing a fleet of over thirty ships for sea.[62] According to the informant Eustace Smyth, captain of the merchant ship *Anne and Martha*, the fleet was intended for the West Indies. In order to put Blake off the scent and to allow the crews to get over seasickness, the commander had orders to shape course for North Africa but he was to go from there via the Canaries to the West Indies.[63] Acting on this intelligence Blake took the fleet to the North Africa coast at Mammora but found nothing. While he was there he received a message from the frigates he had left on watch off Cape St Vincent. On 12 August the *Nantwich* had captured a Spanish man-of-war which had lost its main top and was returning to Cadiz for repairs. The crew declared that the whole Spanish fleet was out.

Blake hastened back and sure enough, on 15 August the English fleet came in sight of the Spaniards. Weale tells us what happened. First some straggling ships were sighted then the whole Spanish fleet came in view. They were close under the shore near Lagos and made no effort to engage; only the leading English frigate, the *Nantwich*, came close enough to exchange verbal defiances with the Spanish Vice-Admiral who was protecting the rear. The next day was different, and the English managed to draw abreast of their opponents.[64] Blake seems to have been determined to fight and was about to fly the signal to engage when he was informed that the swell was too great for the lower tier of guns to be run out. After checking the truth of the report by going onto the *George*'s gundeck to see for himself, he reluctantly ordered the fleet to tack away from the Spaniards. The wind then fell and there was no further opportunity to engage that day.[65]

In the evening Blake called a council of war. Weale was convinced that it 'resolved to fight them if we have the like opportunity.'[66] He was wrong. After giving an account to Cromwell very similar to Weale's Blake excused his failure to fight on 17 and 18 August by saying that his instructions did not allow him to begin hostilities.[67] Just how he concluded that the fleet was not bound for the West Indies is not clear. Weale says that the captured Spaniards told the English the name of their commander, Don Juan Custando, and something about his background. Though he does not record it, they may also have provided the information that their task was not to go to the West Indies but to await the coming of the Plate fleet and escort it into Cadiz. The council of war would have been inclined to believe the information because Smyth had said the fleet for the West Indies was to sail south to North Africa and this fleet was in Lagos bay which was north of Cadiz. They were right. The Spanish fleet was stationed to watch for the Plate fleet and it did not go to the West Indies.

Blake's behaviour again underlines the change in his attitude. The Blake of the Dutch War would have engaged on 16 August, whether he could have run out his guns or not. The new Blake was determined to wait for the right operational conditions so that he could crush his enemy with the least loss to his own fleet. His lack of interest in which Continental rival the Protectorate fought is emphasised by the difference between his behaviour at Tunis and off Cadiz. In both cases he was plagued by ambiguous instructions. From the beginning he intended to attack the Turkish ships and it was the tactical conditions which caused the delay. For Blake, destroying the fleet at Porto Farina was striking a blow for Christendom against the infidel and he was willing to risk Cromwell's displeasure. By contrast he regarded the choice between France and Spain much as the Irish airman of Yeats's poem looked on the English and the Germans: 'Those that I fight I do not hate, those that I guard I do not love.' So he suppressed his first instinct to engage and read the 'fine print' of his instructions instead.

As Cromwell made clear in his letter of 13 September, Blake had misinterpreted his wishes.[68] The Protector realised that a golden opportunity had been missed. Blake would never get another chance to engage the Spanish battle fleet in the open sea. On 24 August Blake compounded his error by abandoning his vigil off Cape St Vincent and bringing the fleet into Cascais road.[69] He had good reason to do so. Instead of acceding to Blake's wish that the fleet should be replaced gradually by new vessels, Cromwell had ordered him to keep the whole fleet out, the *Amity* being replaced by the *Nantwich*. Many of the ships were now in a very bad state indeed and he was almost out of carpenter's stores. Victuals were beginning to run short again and some ships had almost exhausted their beverage wine. He had written at the beginning of July about the necessity of three months' extra supply being sent if the fleet was to remain out but he had heard nothing.[70] The men were becoming very discontented because of the long time they had spent away from home and the way the vigil off Cadiz had confined them on shipboard.[71]

Blake concluded his letter of 30 August by a reference to his personal problems. He would not trouble Cromwell 'with any complaints of myself, of the indisposition of my body, or troubles of mind, but rather of the firm purpose of my heart, with all faithfulness and sincerity to discharge the trust, while reposed in me.'[72] While one must admire his fortitude and sympathise with his ill health, he increased his problems by rarely leaving his cabin and never going on shore; a practice which must have contributed to his belief that everybody had forgotten him.

On 1 September the *Hampshire* went home with Thomas Maynard on board to report the failure of the Portuguese negotiations. Jordan was allowed to go home on personal business in her and Stokes was promoted to Rear-Admiral.[73] When another week went by without any information about the victualling ships the council of war felt there was no option but to go home, and the *Nantwich* was ordered out on patrol to turn back the victuallers if they should have started.[74] Orders were issued for the voyage home on 7 September, though exactly when Blake left Lisbon is not clear. It may have been shortly afterwards. He had certainly left by 22 September because there is an order to Captain Cobham of the *Newcastle*, from Blake on board the *George* at sea, of that date, instructing him to make all speed to England in company with the *Langport*, *Centurion*, *Dragon*, *Kent* and *Foresight*.[75] There is a like order to the Captain of the *Taunton*, who was given a packet of letters for the Admiralty Commissioners. Weale adds the *Little Betty* and the *Assurance* to the group.[76] Blake cannot have been far behind them because he reached the Downs on 6 October.[77]

Blake's return was the culmination of an infuriating autumn. Penn had reached Portsmouth from the West Indies on 31 August, to be followed scarcely a week later by General Venables, each with their tale of woe, each blaming the other and with only Jamaica to show for the money spent on the expedition. Neither had received permission to come home and both found themselves lodged in the Tower. Now Blake had returned too. True, Blake had been given permission to use his own judgment but the letter allowing him that latitude had only reached him when he was well on his way home.[78] In a way Blake's voyage had been as barren as Penn's. Blake had played little part in Guise's defeat; he had got no change out of the Dey of Tunis; he had failed to engage the Spanish fleet and by returning home he had left the way clear for the Plate fleet.

But Cromwell understood the value of seapower and its practicalities better than any other seventeenth-century ruler. Just as he rapidly grasped the strategic value of despised Jamaica, he was quick to appreciate the difference between the performances of the two men. Penn had been away only seven months; Blake had endured a whole year and had a genuine reason for needing to return. Cromwell was forced to concede that though the victuallers had set sail on 13 September, storms had forced them into Plymouth and they did not reach Cascais Road until 30 September.[79] They would not have been in time. Above all there was the different impression that the two expeditions created. The West Indian expedition was a disastrous failure by any measure. The voyage to the Mediterranean showed every State in Europe how long England's arm was and did more to raise the reputation of the Protectorate in Europe than anything the New Model Army had done. What happened was far less important than what might have happened, as the French were quick to see. Blake's exploits were the main factor which forced Mazarin to the negotiating table and which compelled him to pay Cromwell's price for an English alliance. With great reluctance the French were forced to agree that the first campaign should be against Dunkirk and that, when the port was captured, it should be ceded to England.

The Spanish Blockade

B *LAKE* returned to an unhappy and divided England. As his ships lost sight of Land's End in October 1654 on their way to the Mediterranean, the first Protectorate Parliament was assembling. By the end of the mandatory five months, Cromwell and the majority of the M.P.s were at loggerheads over finance. They wished to cut the Army and Navy establishment drastically so that the monthly assessment tax could be abolished, a course of action the Generals would not allow. The end was precipitated by a small number of Republicans, who exploited the situation for their own ends. As soon as the Parliamentary session ended, Cromwell moved against the republicans and their allies in the Army, who were led by Major-General Overton, the Governor of Hull. The summer brought a Royalist plot, known as Penruddock's Rebellion.

Cromwell's disillusionment was such that for the moment he abandoned all pretence of constitutional rule and resorted to outright military dictatorship. The country was divided into eleven military districts each ruled by a Major-General who was directly responsible to him. The country gentry, who had previously controlled politics at county level, adopted an attitude of sullen hostility. By the time Blake reached England once more, the system had been in operation for six months. Passive resistance was widespread and making tax collection difficult, while Thurloe's agents were continually exposing attempts by Royalists and Republicans to take advantage of the discontent.

Nor was the Navy immune from the problems on shore. By the end of the First Dutch War, wages were in arrears and many of the captains complained that they had not received the prize money due to them.[1] The discontent was used by the radicals, led by Vice-Admiral Lawson, to fan the flames of mutiny. Under his guidance, the Channel fleet submitted a petition to the Protector, asking that the arrears be paid, that impressment be abolished and that seamen should be allowed to choose whether to go on expeditions outside home waters or not.[2] Cromwell recognised the danger signals. Discipline would be irretrievably damaged if the seamen were allowed to choose when and where to serve, and the fleet could not be manned without impressment, but he did raise a loan of

£16,000 from the merchant, Martin Noel, with which to pay the outstanding arrears.[3]

The money headed off the potential rebellion, at the cost of making Lawson the most popular man in the fleet. Lawson had no liking for the Protectorate. He was a Baptist and was among those recorded as being at a Leveller meeting along with the notorious Army malcontents, Okey, Alured, Saunders, Hacker and Wildman at the beginning of September 1654.[4] When Cromwell moved against Overton the Army officers were arrested, with the exception of Wildman who went underground. No action was taken against Lawson and he was left in command of the Channel fleet for over a year, though the agents of Cromwell's Secretary of State, John Thurloe, were aware of his contacts with Edward Sexby. Sexby was a Leveller who fled abroad to Bordeaux after the arrest of Overton and was busy trying to get the Royalists and Levellers to unite. A key element in the scheme was the instigation of a revolt in the Channel fleet.[5]

The position was fraught with danger and, when Blake returned, Cromwell seized the opportunity to reduce Lawson's influence. He began to equip a new fleet, which was to return to the coast of Spain as quickly as possible. Blake was appointed to command the fleet, with Lawson as Vice-Admiral.[6] This was a very neat solution. Blake was the one man who could outrank Lawson and whose influence in the fleet was greater. The appointment could not be regarded as a demotion but it would remove Lawson from the Channel fleet and leave him tossing impotently on the Atlantic swell off Cadiz. To make doubly sure, on 2 January 1656, Cromwell appointed a new General-at-Sea to share the command with Blake. His name was Edward Mountagu.[7] Mountagu had played no part in affairs between 1645 and 1654, and owed his entire political rehabilitation to Cromwell so he could be relied on to support the Protectorate loyally. He was the seventh, and last, General-at-Sea to be appointed.

Lawson watched the construction of the cage around him with alarm. He knew that once the fleet sailed, his wings would be effectually clipped and he had come to the conclusion that, without some provocation from the Protectorate government, a fleet mutiny was unlikely. He had been dismayed by the interception by Thurloe's agents of money being sent to him from the Continent, and he reasoned that he would be more use to his associates in England than off the coast of Spain, so he resigned. Lawson's action seems to have been taken without consultation with his confederates, because it caught everyone by surprise. He gave as his reason, unwillingness to go on an expedition governed by sealed orders of which he had no knowledge.[8]

The Vice-Admiral's resignation caused little trouble among the seamen but the captains were more disturbed and three of them also resigned.[9] Captain Hill said flatly that he would only fight the Spaniards in the Channel. Captain Lyons began by expressing dissatisfaction with the way in which the seamen had been treated but ended by admitting that he too had no quarrel with Spain. Captain

Ableson maintained that separation from his family was his only motivation in refusing to go. How far the reasons were genuine is difficult to determine. Lyons admitted that he had given the ill treatment of the seamen as his first reason, at the suggestion of Lawson, and Ableson was related to the Vice-Admiral by marriage, so there was the suspicion that all three were more concerned with what was going on in England, than with any supposed wrongs which were being done to Spain.

And what of Blake? Was Mountagu appointed to make sure that he did not stray from the straight and narrow? There were elements in the situation which suggest that this was indeed the case. Cromwell spied on everybody and trusted nobody entirely who did not owe his preferment to himself. Blake had risen on his own merits and, with his immense reputation in the Navy, he was in a better position to lead a revolt than any other man in the country. Cromwell had been forced to accept that Blake's unlooked-for return to England in October was the result of yet another victualling failure but, coming after Penn's unscheduled reappearance from the West Indies on 3 September, and that of Venables six days later, questions were bound to rise in the Protector's mind, especially in view of Blake's failure to attack the Spanish fleet. Sources hostile to the Protectorate were quick to assume that Cromwell was not satisfied about Blake's loyalty and to cast Mountagu in the role of a watchdog.

Rumours which were put about that Blake was upset and annoyed that he had not been left in sole command seem to have been misplaced. On the contrary, the appointment of another General appears to have been at his request.[10] The position resembled the one after Dungeness. Blake was determined that if there were any further miscarriages or disputes over the interpretation of instructions, he was not going to carry the blame alone. The appointment of another General was overdue. At the end of the First Dutch War there were four: Blake, Monck, Penn and Disbrowe. Monck was not available, being Commander-in-Chief in Scotland, Penn had been dismissed and Disbrowe's responsibility was administrative. There was never any intention that he should go to sea, so there was a vacancy. The man selected may have been a surprise but, like Blake, he had an excellent military reputation. The Dutch ambassador Nieuport reported, 'I hear he was never much at sea but he is counted by everyone for a man of conduct and courage.'[11] Of course, he had to be. Cromwell did not want to antagonise Blake, by giving him a colleague he could not respect.

Blake's discomfort stemmed from other considerations. Mountagu had been inactive between 1645 and 1654, not through incapacity, but because he disapproved of the course of English politics. He detested the Commonwealth and all its works. Later, he was to encourage Cromwell to reach for the crown and, when the Protectorate proved a broken reed, he supported the Restoration. Hardly a congenial companion for an old republican like Blake. Another cause of friction may well have been what Blake regarded as his younger colleague's idleness. While Blake worked hard to get the fleet ready. Mountagu remained on his estate at Hinchingbrooke. On 7 January his father-in-law, John Crewe, counselled him, 'Your reasons for coming up [to London] are good but deferre it as long as you can, it be for your health, to take good store of the January ayre in the country.' Mountagu seems to have taken the advice because a month later, Nieuport was informing the States General that 'Blake went yesterday to the fleet but Mountagu is still on his estate in Huntingdon.'[12] There was a good case for suggesting that Blake, who had returned from the Mediterranean, tired and ill, should have been resting in the country, and Mountagu should have been pushing on the preparations.

Finally, there was Blake's initial reluctance to work with someone whom he did not know. In 1649, when he found himself obliged to work with Richard Deane whom he knew only slightly, he had persuaded the Commonwealth to add Edward Popham to the command. He quickly grew to like Deane. In 1653 the pattern repeated itself: Blake and Deane commanded the Red squadron together and Monck was exiled to the outer darkness of the White squadron. This lukewarm start was similarly attributed to politics but did not seem to hamper cooperation between Blake and Monck, in the later stages of the war. Now, wracked with the pain of his old wound, Blake was turning in on himself more and more and resented the necessity of building a working relationship with yet another new partner.

Fortunately for Blake's peace of mind, Mountagu proved the ideal colleague. Pepys was later to describe his patron as the perfect courtier. No one knew better, how to humour those around him and it was not long before Mountagu divined the way to soothe Blake's savage breast. The first thing was to be a good pupil and study the trade of a General-at-Sea properly. From the beginning, Mountagu proved genuinely anxious to learn. Of all the soldiers appointed to command at sea during the Interregnum, Mountagu was the one most deeply interested in the technicalities of his new profession, as his Journal of the expedition to the Sound in 1659 shows. Once the initial tension relaxed, Mountagu's tact, combined with his genuine desire for information, broke down the barriers which separated the two men.

The improving relationship was assisted by Blake's realisation that Mountagu's presence removed one of his worst burdens. Here was a man who was identified with the Protector. He could take the political decisions and absolve Blake from any responsibility for the results. If Cromwell wanted to drive a hard bargain with the Portuguese, then Mountagu would do the driving not Blake. If there were any ambiguities in the instructions this time, then Mountagu could resolve them. If there were any political troubles in the fleet, Mountagu could be seen as the villain. Blake was personally loyal to the Protector, not because he liked what he saw, but because he regarded the alternatives as worse. The path which men like Penn were treading led to the Hell of a Restoration; the path

Lawson would have him follow could only result in a Miltonian chaos of conflicting sects, with no respect for authority in Church or State. He preferred to restrict his mind to the immediate problems of his fleet and to fulminate to Thurloe against the 1654 Parliament for its refusal to vote enough money for the Navy, while ignoring the matters of political principle which actuated that assembly.[13]

By the end of the first week of March 1656, the fleet was almost ready and Blake was fretting to be away, writing to the Navy Commissioners from the Downs that he was still waiting for the fire ships and some last-minute provisions but that, if the wind was right in the morning, he would sail without them.[14] There was one final crisis when Richard Badiley, who had been appointed Vice Admiral in Lawson's place, was arrested for debt at the instigation of the plotters surrounding Lawson, but he was released in time to join his ship.[15] His arrival, on board the *Resolution*, coincided with the departure of its lieutenant, who had been implicated in Lawson's schemes. Next day the fleet sailed down the Channel, reaching Plymouth on 17 March.[16]

The fleet which Blake and Mountagu commanded was a truly formidable armament. It was divided into three squadrons,[17] but their exact composition is difficult to determine because during the cruise many of the ships were replaced, and others carrying dispatches were continually passing between the Generals and the home government. In the original fleet there were thirty-seven capital ships. Each squadron had two powerful great ships, the remainder being the pick of the frigates built since 1649, commanded by the best captains available. Blake and Mountagu commanded the first squadron from the newly launched 1st rate, *Naseby*. The Vice-Admiral, Richard Badiley, commanded the second, from the *Resolution*. John Bourne was appointed Rear-Admiral and put in charge of the third, with his flag in the *Swiftsure*.

The fleet sailed from Plymouth on 18 March but contrary winds held it in Torbay until the end of the month.[18] The fleet then made a quick passage and the Burlings were sighted on 6 April.[19] After a brief look into the Tagus, Blake sailed on to Cadiz. On 11 April, the *Amity* and the *Foresight* were dispatched to reconnoitre Cadiz and collect information. The news they brought back was rather dampening. While preparations for the expedition had been going forward in England, the Plate fleet for which Blake had waited so long had finally arrived. It was some consolation that only two galleons and four smaller vessels had reached Spain, the remainder being wrecked in the West Indies. The frigate captains also reported that not more than a week before thirty ships had left to reinforce the Spanish West Indies but they were not intended for an attack on Jamaica. Twenty more galleons were at anchor in Cadiz harbour, but they were immobilised for want of rigging. The necessary stores were reported to have been bought in the Baltic, and to be on their way in Flemish merchant ships.[20]

After posting frigates to intercept the Flemish ships, Blake and Mountagu called a Council of War, which debated what should be done next. Much to Mountagu's annoyance, the captains would not consider a voyage to the West Indies because of the mortality rate and the distance from home. Nor was there anything in the instructions, which would justify the Generals in overriding their opposition.[21] A second possible course of action was an attack on Cadiz itself. Cromwell was known to want some dramatic exploit but the idea was given up after information was obtained from some Dutch ships, about the preparations the Spaniards were making. Earthworks and batteries were being hastily erected and garrisoned with troops. This in itself might not have deterred the English from an assault across the narrow promontory which linked Cadiz with the mainland. Unfortunately, the Spaniards had taken the added precaution of moving the ships into the inner harbour and guarding the narrow Carraca channel, which gave access to it, with two 60-gun galleons. Worse, two miles further up was a chain and a raft of masts with two old ships, which would be sunk in the fairway if an attack was made. The declaration that they would have made the attempt if a pilot could have been found to guide the ships in was, almost certainly, an excuse to justify their conviction that to force their way in was impracticable.[22] Cadiz was not Porto Farina or Teneriffe. Without an army, even a fleet as powerful as the one commanded by Blake and Mountagu, could do little.

As they considered the options, the Council of War realised with sinking hearts that, with the next Plate fleet not due for some time and Cadiz impregnable, they faced a long and wearisome blockade. Already a familiar problem was looming: lack of fresh water. By a mistake, the ships fitted out at Portsmouth had not been given their proper proportion of casks by the victuallers, so they were running short.[23] On 7 May, the fleet divided. Bourne was left off Cadiz with fourteen frigates. The remainder sailed for Tangier to fill their casks.[24] The problems of supplying a fleet, which was far from home, had been highlighted by Blake's Mediterranean cruise of the previous year. Charles Longland, the English agent at Leghorn, believed that there was only one solution. The English must secure a permanent supply base. Cromwell had been receiving the same advice from his victualling contractors, who claimed that one of the reasons for the bad victuals was the use of victualling ships, which led to the food being long at sea before reaching the men for whom it was intended. It was more expensive too, because proper accounting became very difficult.[25]

Such arguments strengthened the Protector's belief that the right way to increase English power and influence in the World would be to create a string of bases at strategic points, supported by a large fleet. This was the aim behind the demand for Dunkirk from the French and the tenacious way he held onto Jamaica. The same purpose informed the abortive schemes to secure Emden and Elsinore.[26] This profound strategic concept which foreshadowed the policies of the eighteenth and nineteenth centuries should be borne in mind when considering the clauses in the instructions to Blake and Mountagu about a possible seizure of the Rock of Gibraltar. Permanent control of the Straits of Gibraltar was the key to establishing English dominance in the Western Mediterranean.

The possibility of an operation against Gibraltar was considered at the same council of war which came down against an assault on Cadiz. Mountagu reported to Thurloe, 'We had then some debate of Gibraltar and there appeared no great mind to it in regard of hardness and as also want of landmen formed and officers and numbers of men to all which are real obstacles as you may judge upon the description of the place, the numbers and quality of our men.'[27] What Mountagu was trying to say was that there were quite a large number of soldiers with the fleet, but they were not in regiments and they had no officers. A possible alternative was using seamen, but the achievements during Penn's West Indian expedition, of Goodson's sea regiment at Santo Domingo on Hispaniola in saving Venables' army from a rout notwithstanding, Mountagu was very disparaging about their military qualities. 'And to say truth,' he wrote dismissively, 'the seamen are not for land service unless it be for sudden plunder; they are then valiant much but not ruled and kept in government on shore nor have your officers much stomach to fight on shore.'

No one knew better than Mountagu the way in which Cromwell thought about the connection between foreign policy and seapower. He realised that the Protector would be very disappointed and he promised that he would examine the Rock for himself at the first opportunity, so that he could send more detailed findings. While the fleet was watering and taking on ballast at Tangier, Mountagu fulfilled his promise. Taking two frigates, he crossed the Straits and examined the Rock closely. His report only dotted the Is and crossed the Ts of the council's conclusions. He conceded that a surprise attack on the neck of land which joined the Rock to the mainland might do the trick because the Spaniards rarely provided the garrison with more than one month's supply of victuals. The problem was holding Gibraltar once it had been captured. Mountagu estimated that 4–5000 men, properly formed into regiments, would be required. What Blake thought is not recorded. He would have expressed an opinion only if Mountagu had come out in favour. Then he would have made his views on the likely success of the attack very clear.[28]

When Cromwell received Mountagu's second report he reluctantly gave up the Gibraltar scheme, at least for the present, but neither he nor Mountagu forgot the main objective of controlling the Straits of Gibraltar. The Rock may have been a disappointment but the English were most impressed with Tangier, which lay on the other side of the Straits. Mountagu retained his first favourable impressions and was to play an important role in the negotiations which secured the port for England as part of the dowry of Catherine of Braganza in 1661. Curiously an unfortunate episode, when the captain and three of the crew of the

Old Warwick were killed by Moors while trying to collect firewood, did not alert him to the possibility that Tangier might need a far bigger garrison than Gibraltar.[29]

The immediate supply problem was relieved by the conclusion of an alliance with Portugal, which opened Lisbon to the English fleet. The alliance was one of convenience not of love, so the negotiations were protracted and rather acrimonious. The Protector drove a hard bargain. He insisted on the English being admitted to the Brazil trade on favourable terms, he demanded £50,000 as compensation for the damage done by Royalist privateers based on Lisbon, and he required that English families living in Portugal be allowed to worship freely in their own houses. If these conditions were satisfied, he was prepared to conclude an alliance with Portugal against Spain.[30] One result of a successful outcome would be that Portuguese ports would become available to the English fleet.

King John knew that hostile action by the English fleet would be fatal to Portuguese independence, maintained on a precarious footing since the revolt against Spanish control in 1640, but he tried every delaying tactic he could to get better terms. As in 1650, the main way in which the English could bring pressure to bear was by threatening the Brazil fleet. At one point he managed to persuade the English envoy Philip Meadowe, to bind Blake and Mountagu not to resort to hostilities, until disagreements between the two governments had been referred to Cromwell. He may well have hoped that during the delay the fleet would arrive and he could continue fencing for another year. If that was his scheme it failed. New instructions arrived from Cromwell and an unsuccessful attempt on Meadowe's life justified him in retracting his earlier offer. The King's embarrassment was completed by the appearance of the English fleet in Cascais road. The Brazil trade was conceded, the compensation money was loaded, the English in Lisbon were allowed freedom of worship, and the alliance was concluded.[31]

The tortuous course of the negotiations highlighted a difference in approach between Blake and Mountagu. Meadowe informed Thurloe on 16 June, 'Being aboard the generals, I found general Blake satisfied with the peace, but general Mountague somwhat scrupulous, nay, which is more, he told me, that I should have had more thank at Whitehal, if I had not concluded it.'[32] Mountagu was incensed at the attempt on Meadowe's life and he thought that he should have stuck to the letter of his instructions, which ordered him to come away if the treaty had not been signed after the twenty days originally allowed for. Mountagu had no faith in a 'delusive agreement' and he was convinced that a great opportunity was being lost. 'You have at this time the Portugal upon his knees, and if we had authority to make further demands, we might ask what we would (almost) and he durst not but perform it or his country would all be in rebellion.'[33] Mountagu may have been influenced in his attitude by a fiery letter from Thurloe in response to his earlier criticisms of King John's behaviour, in which the Secretary of State had suggested that teaching the Portuguese a severe lesson could be done without prejudice to Spanish affairs provided 'wee strike to the heart'.[34]

Blake almost certainly agreed with Mountagu that Meadowe had been wrong to bind the hands of the English fleet. He may well have shared Mountagu's belief about Portuguese dissimulation. But he supported the conclusion of the treaty. Where the two men differed was over the practicalities of the situation. Meadowe wrote 'But then consider, if the Brazil fleet had got home, and the treaty not ratified, in what condition had his highness affairs been in? and it may well be considered, for 'tis three to one, as general Blake himself affirms, that our fleet meet not the Brasil fleet, tho' they make it their sole worke.' There was also the possibility of reprisals against English merchants in Lisbon and Blake did not agree with Mountagu that they would be protected most effectively by drastic action. Blake knew better. He remembered the events of 1650. Then he had tried to act as Mountagu wanted to do now. The result had been the abortive attempt to force the Tagus and the fruitless summer cruise, when even the seizure of half the Brazil fleet had failed to move King John one inch. Blake had learned the limitations of seapower the hard way.

When the Protector learned of what had happened he endorsed Meadowe's view. The treaty gave the English as much of what they had originally demanded as could reasonably be expected. The object of the exercise was to fight Spain. England and Portugal did not see eye to eye on many matters but they did have a common enemy. What good would it do if, as the result of the further demands Mountagu wanted to make, Portugal 'would all be in rebellion'? How would the blockade of the Spanish coast be maintained if access to Portuguese ports were denied to the English fleet?

Blake and Mountagu had poured cold water on both Cromwell's schemes for striking a great blow against Spain, when they rejected his suggestions for attacks on Cadiz and Gibraltar. The Protector still cherished the idea that something noteworthy might be achieved,[35] but it seemed that even the most limited of initiatives were doomed to failure. He soon learned that the frigate *Cullen*, and the merchant ship *Industry*, loaded with ammunition and entrenching tools, had been captured by Spanish privateers and carried into Bayonne.[36]

The war was not going to be easy and cheap; it was going to be long and costly. One commentator complained that the Dutch were always prepared to come out and fight but the Spaniards skulked in their ports, avoided the English fleet and attacked English trade. The reason was not that the Dutch were braver than the Spaniards. The former had to fight to defend their trade. Contrary to the illusions harboured in England, Spain had little seaborne commerce to defend but she was strategically placed to attack that of England. Swarms of privateers from Dunkirk and Ostend attacked English trade in the Channel and the North

Sea, while ships equipped in Spain's Atlantic ports preyed on English ships bound to the Mediterranean and the Indies.[37]

In the north Cromwell looked to a Flanders campaign, in alliance with France, against the privateer strongholds. In the south, the one point of leverage was the annual Plate fleet. Both seemed distant prospects, so for the moment trade protection was paramount. The Protector wrote to Blake and Mountagu with a note of resignation, to remind them of their instructions about the Barbary states. They were to cement the understanding with Algiers, to try and negotiate a treaty with Sallee and, if they thought it practicable, to send a squadron to Tripoli. Should they think that there was nothing of great moment that they could do, they should send some of the ships home. He preferred 4th rate frigates because they would be useful in the blockade of Ostend and Dunkirk.[38] Blake and Mountagu did as they were bidden. On 30 June, a council of war was called, off Cadiz. Eleven ships were selected to go home. Except for the *Unicorn* they were all 4th rate frigates, as Cromwell requested. The Generals explained that the *Unicorn* had been included because her commander Robert Clarke was a reliable and experienced officer.[39]

The departure was not destined to be an orderly one. Even as the captains were coming on board the flagship, the wind was rising and by the time the council broke up, conditions were so bad that many of them were unable to return to their ships. Weale, from his vantage point as lieutenant of the *Jersey*, recorded the night's events without much emotion. 'At an anchor before Cadiz and the wind bloweth very hard. This day we took up a small vessel that was forced from her anchor, the *Bridgwater*'s boat coming after her with our anchor lay at our stern some part of the night but it being extraordinary ill weather was in the night sunk. A great tempest.'[40]

Mountagu was a great deal more excited, perhaps because it was his first experience of really bad Atlantic weather. He told Thurloe that the storm was reputed the worst for seven years. Much tackle was lost but fortunately no ship. The *Naseby* had a narrow escape: 'the *Taunton* driving upon us in the dead of night, it being very dark and so right with us, that our officers concluded it impossible to escape her.' Preparations were made to cut the *Naseby*'s cable, 'but it pleased God that the *Taunton* got up her foresail and let slip her cable, and missed her not a ship's length when the sea ran mountainous high.' If that was what could happen in July, 'Judge you what this sea is to ride in the winter time.'[41]

The fleet took some time to sort itself out, so when the *Unicorn* left on 4 July, she was only accompanied by the *Jersey*, *Dragon* and *Little President*.[42] The *Bristol*, *Kentish* and *Mermaid* followed on 8 July, and the *Taunton* and *Guinea* the next day.[43] The last ship, the *Assurance*, did not leave until 31 July. She was absent at the time of the storm, taking a prize into Lisbon.[44] Another result of the storm was that Blake and Mountagu scaled down their plans. The council had decided to divide the fleet in three, one part to go home, a second consisting of the great ships to remain off Cadiz, and a third composed of the remaining frigates to visit Tripoli and Sallee to try and stop the attacks on English shipping. So many ships sustained damage that the voyage to Tripoli was abandoned. No English squadron went there until 1659.[45]

The opening of Lisbon as a secure base, from which the fleet could operate, which provided shelter and water, and which acted as a listening post, terminated the first phase of the cruise. The next was the establishment of the blockade. The early months were lively. On 12 June Captain Edward Blagg was sent with his own ship the *Fairfax*, *Tredagh*, *Bristol*, *Newcastle*, *Centurion*, *Assurance*, *Guinea*, *Fox* and *Beaver* to shoot up the Galician and Biscayan ports.[46] The *Bristol* was sent to Pontevedra but found nothing worth attacking. The *Tredagh*, *Newcastle*, *Guinea* and *Fox* likewise came back empty handed from Bayonne. They had hoped to recapture the *Cullen* and *Industry* but found them drawn up under the castle.

Blagg himself was more fortunate. A reconnaissance on the evening of 24 June, produced no information about the situation at Vigo. Despite this Blagg decided to attack, relying on earlier reports of seven sail being in the harbour. In the early morning the *Fairfax*, *Centurion*, *Assurance* and *Beaver* stole quietly through the isles which lie off the port. As there was a flat calm the ships had to be towed by the boats, but the hard work was worthwhile. The lack of a breeze until 9 am lulled the Spaniards into a false sense of security, so that the attack came as a complete surprise. Two Ostend privateers and one of their prizes were in the harbour. They got sail on, as quickly as possible, and fled up the river towards Rondella, in a desperate effort to reach water which was too shallow for the larger English frigates to navigate. They were not quick enough. All three went aground in their hurry. A lucky shot found the magazine of the *Sta. Theresa* and she blew up. The murderous English gunnery soon set the *St Peter* on fire and she blew up too. The prize was captured but it proved impossible to refloat her so she was burnt. There were two more prizes at Rondella, one French and one Portuguese. As they were empty, Blagg tried to get at them to burn them. He reported that the *Fairfax*'s boat got within a ship's length of the Portuguese prize, 'but the enemy lined both sides of the creek with small shot and manned vessels so that she put them off.'

When Blagg returned, a second foray was organised in the opposite direction, under Captain Eustace Smith, of the *Lyme*.[47] He had with him his own ship, the *Newbury*, *Maidstone*, *Nantwich*, *Ruby* and *Fox* fireship. They sailed through the Straits of Gibraltar and attacked the shipping in Malaga road. While the frigates swept the town with a hail of shot, Captain Pickering of the *Fox* manoeuvred his ship into position and set her on fire. Altogether five ships were burnt, either by the *Fox* or by boarding parties from the frigates. So complete was the English ascendancy that when he had fired his ship, Pickering was able to land and spike the guns in one of the forts, all of whose garrison had fled to avoid the English bombardment. The report went on to say that the *Lyme* and two other frigates pursued a rich merchant ship towards Alicante but as there are no subsequent references to her, she must have escaped.

Such activity soon ceased for lack of suitable targets. Merchant shipping began to avoid the area of conflict and the Spaniards, learning from their losses, drew their ships up out of harm's way. The fleet found itself confined to searching neutral merchantmen going in and out of Cadiz. Blake must have recalled only too well the seemingly endless dreary months off Kinsale in 1649 and Lisbon in 1650, and wondered whether he was in for as long a wait. This time the first reward for his vigilance came more quickly. The curious progression, noticeable from one blockade to another, induces the thought that it may not have been as fortuitous as it appeared on the surface. In 1649 Blake had cruised off Kinsale the whole of the summer, only to lose the fruits of his vigil when an October gale blew him off station and let Rupert out. In 1650 a powerful Commonwealth fleet spent the entire summer off the Tagus with little result. Not until the majority of the fleet had gone home did Rupert emerge and provide Blake with the opportunity to chase and destroy most of his ships. Even more significantly in 1655 while Blake was chasing a phantom Plate fleet off the North African coast, the main Spanish fleet had put to sea. If Blake had learned anything from these events, it was that circumstances had to be created which would tempt the Spanish into some rash exploit that he could turn to his advantage.

At the beginning of August Blake, either deliberately or accidentally, created just such a situation. The Spanish in Cadiz remaining completely inert, Blake divided the fleet in three.[48] Mountagu took one squadron and sailed to Sallee, to carry out Cromwell's instructions and negotiate a treaty. Blake cruised off Cape St Vincent with the second. The third, consisting of eight of the fittest frigates, was to remain in Cadiz Bay under the command of Captain Richard Stayner in the *Speaker*. Stayner was instructed to keep well out to sea. There were two quite practical reasons for the order. Weale's journal shows that there was quite a number of galleys in Cadiz harbour.[49] In normal conditions, galleys were no threat to large sailing vessels, but they could become a serious menace if one of Stayner's squadron was separated from its consorts in a flat calm. The second reason was the danger of being caught on a lee shore. No ship was lost in the gale of the previous month because the wind was off-shore, but the position might have been very different if it had been blowing towards the Spanish coast.

The system of a small inshore squadron, backed up by a much larger one out at sea, was to become standard practice in the English navy but in the circumstances of 1656 it was tailor-made for deception. Blake's squadron was plainly visible from the Portuguese coast, cruising backwards and forwards, but the whereabouts of Mountagu and even the existence of Stayner's ships may well have been unknown. Consequently when Blake too vanished and failed to reappear, either off Cadiz or in the Tagus, the rumour swept Lisbon that the English had gone home. Blake had done nothing of the sort of course. Letters had arrived from Mountagu informing him that negotiations at Sallee had stalled, so Blake had gone to join him. With Porto Farina still fresh in everyone's memory, Mountagu was hoping that Blake's presence would remind the pirates of what could happen if they were obstinate. He was to be disappointed. Negotiations dragged on for nearly another month and eventually broke down over the fate of two children.[50]

Meanwhile the 1656 Plate Fleet was approaching the Spanish coast. While its commander was wondering what to do, one of the escorting men-of-war chased and captured a Portuguese prize. Close questioning of the crew revealed the belief of most people in Lisbon, that the English had gone home.[51] The news should have been treated with great suspicion, because the usual difficulties of assessing the truth of the reports were compounded by the possibility of deliberate misinformation. In the run-up to the battle of Dungeness in 1652, Blake had made the mistake of basing his course of action on intelligence culled from an enemy merchantman, unsupported by confirming evidence from other sources, with almost fatal results. The Spanish admiral made the same mistake and decided to make a dash for Cadiz and safety.

Stayner described what happened. On 8 September, the wind came up westerly so, mindful of his instructions to keep well away from the coast when the wind was in that quarter, he had his squadron beat out of the bay. The next day the wind shifted around to the North-East and in the evening the Plate Fleet was spotted some five or six leagues west of Cadiz. Stayner seems to have strung his frigates out to make sure that nothing slipped past, because only the *Bridgwater*, the *Plymouth* and the *Speaker* were initially involved. Each of them chased and engaged a Spaniard.[52] Stayner who led the chase, overhauled the Admiral and Vice-Admiral without recognising them. He gave each a withering broadside, before concentrating on what appeared to be the most powerful ship. After a sharp struggle, the *Speaker*'s crew boarded and captured it. The real Admiral was a small ship and was similarly ignored by the *Bridgwater* and *Plymouth*, which took on two of the other ships that Stayner had passed. The Spanish crew of one of them quickly realised that the conflict was hopeless and fired their ship, so that the English would not secure its plate. The struggle over the Vice-Admiral was long and fierce, but when it appeared that the ship must fall, the Spaniards set it on fire as well. The *Bridgwater*, which had grappled with it, had great difficulty in getting its men off and was fortunate to avoid being burnt in the conflagration. Meanwhile the remaining ships of the squadron were trying to get into action. The nearest was the *Tredagh*, which managed to cut off a fourth Spanish ship as it made for home. When he wrote his dispatch Stayner believed that the two remaining ships, the Admiral and the Portuguese prize, had escaped but later information showed that both had been forced on shore.

There was great jubilation in the English ranks. This was the first time that the Spanish Plate Fleet had been destroyed since 1591 and it struck a great blow at the Spanish war effort. Reports from Cadiz said that plate worth nine million pieces of eight had been lost.[53] When Captain Robert Storey of the *Hampshire* reached England with the dispatch, his news was like manna in the wilderness to Cromwell. The experiment with the Major-Generals had failed and Cromwell had called Parliament once more. The good news was enough to persuade the Commons to endorse the war with Spain, on 1 October 1656. In another way it was a great disappointment. When the money that had been captured was all counted, it came to about £200,000.[54] That was quite a tidy sum but it was not going to pay for the Navy, never mind the Army which would soon be needed in Flanders. The relatively small sum was the result of two miscalculations. Only the prize captured by Stayner had any considerable amount of plate on board; the *Tredagh*'s prize contained mostly hides. A lot had been lost when the Vice-Admiral sank and the richest ship had eluded them because Stayner was ignorant of the Spanish habit of putting most money on the fastest and not the strongest ship. In fact, the extent of Spanish wealth was always miscalculated. Even if the Plate Fleet were captured every year, it was not going to pay for the war.

Teneriffe

*T*HE capture of the Plate Fleet brought to an end the third phase of the blockade. Blake and Mountagu had been saying for some time that keeping the great ships out during the winter would not be advisable. Before news of the victory arrived, Cromwell had sent instructions for Blake to stay out and for Mountagu to come home with the larger ships. Mountagu took charge of the treasure and at the end of September left for England with the *Naseby, Resolution, Andrew* and *Rainbow*.[1] With him went the Vice-Admiral, Richard Badiley. He had been a last-minute replacement for Lawson and he wished to return to England. Blake shifted his flag to the *Swiftsure*, John Bourne was promoted Vice-Admiral and Richard Stayner took Bourne's place as Rear-Admiral.

The fleet which Stayner had intercepted was smaller than usual. Prisoners travelling from Peru gave graphic descriptions to their English captors of a terrible earthquake, which had claimed thousands of lives in Peru. The workings in the silver mines collapsed, reducing the amount of specie to a thin trickle. A recovery had since taken place and there was a large amount of gold and silver from Mexico awaiting shipping. They anticipated that another larger and richer fleet would be dispatched in the New Year.[2] When Mountagu communicated their depositions to the Protector, he decided to reinforce Blake with the 2nd rate *George*, and to send back the *Unicorn* and the 4th rates *Bristol, Taunton, Phoenix* and *Jersey*.[3]

Sending ships was one thing, ensuring a regular supply of victuals was another. Mountagu was very angry when he arrived at Portsmouth[4] to find that the supplies for Blake's fleet were not ready. He did all he could to galvanise the victualling agents into action. Without the spur that he provided, there would have been a similar failure to that of the previous year. The victualling office seems to have been in chaos. Colonel Pride and his syndicate had given up the concession and had been replaced by Captain Thomas Alderne. Alderne tried his best but he was battling against a government reluctant to give him a regular supply of money which was sufficient to satisfy the contractors, and he was overwhelmed by the sheer scale of the business. In the end, he fell ill and died the following year. Disbrowe, the General charged with responsibility for the administration, seems to have been powerless to do anything about it. Mountagu was also instrumental in getting the Council of State to consider the next supply, which would be due the following February. He played a great part in securing the much prompter attention to the needs of the distant fleet, which was vital to its success.[5]

Blake must have realised at an early stage that the Plate Fleet was not going to make the same mistake twice. Brooding in his cabin, he cannot have taken long to come to the conclusion that this time the Fleet would come to some convenient staging point and there wait, until it was sure the coast was clear. An examination of the Atlantic charts would have shown that the obvious course of action for the Spanish admiral was to make for the Canary Islands. They were near enough to pick up information but far enough away to make it necessary for the English fleet to leave the Spanish coast unguarded, if it went in search of him. The island of Teneriffe, which boasted one of the best harbours in the whole of the Atlantic, was well able to accommodate the largest Plate Fleet.[6] At some point Blake was going to have to make a difficult decision. If the Plate Fleet would not come to him, he must go to it. The conditions would have to be just right and he could afford little delay in the execution of the design. Otherwise the position achieved by the blockade would be destroyed as the Spanish admiral intended, the Spanish fleet would get to sea, Jamaica would be imperilled, and English trade in the western Atlantic seriously damaged.

In October 1656 all that was in the future and the immediate prospect was of a long wait, during which much could happen. In the event nothing did. Blake wrote stoically that his health was sufficient to see him through to the following summer. In other words his thigh wound was hurting, the gravel in his kidneys was very painful and he was suffering from dropsy, but he did not think he was dying yet. Stayner wrote later that he was living on broths and jellies.[7] Apart from that and the winter weather, another imponderable was the Spanish fleet. There were repeated rumours of great preparations in Cadiz against the spring. Long experience was to teach that, even if the Spaniards had managed to get a fleet ready and it had got to sea, the chances of it taking on Blake's fleet successfully were very small. Blake's ships may have suffered through long cruising in the open sea, but his men were battle-hardened and he had had the chance to weld them into an efficient fighting force. The Spanish admiral, confined to port for many months with his crews rusting in the quayside taverns, would be at a serious disadvantage.

The real threat was rather different. The United Provinces had found the 1654 treaty very hard to swallow. When Penn and Venables arrived at Barbados in 1655, they found Georgetown Harbour crammed with Dutch merchantmen, trading in contravention of the Navigation Act. Even as Mountagu was coming home in triumph with Spanish silver in his holds, a serious incident was taking place in Torbay, in which Dutch ships refused to strike their flags and attempted to stop English men-of-war searching them for contraband.[8] So when it was known that the Dutch were setting out a fleet under the formidable de Ruijter, to go to the Mediterranean, the diplomatic dovecotes were set fluttering all over Western Europe.

According to one rumour, de Ruijter was bound for Cadiz where he would reinforce the Spanish fleet or at least cover its departure from Cadiz. Another had it that he was ordered to the Canaries to escort in the Plate Fleet, because the money would be used to repay loans from Dutch financiers. A third made the Portuguese Brazil fleet his target. This was a more sensible speculation as the colonial rivalry 'beyond the line' was as hot as ever, with ships from the East describing graphically the struggle between the two nations for Colombo in Ceylon.

During October and November Blake was content to cruise off Cape St Vincent and maintain an inshore squadron in Cadiz Bay. By the beginning of December shortage of victuals compelled the main fleet to return to Oeiras Bay. The prospect of a forced return to England loomed once more, especially as reports were circulating that their supplies had been diverted to Jamaica. Fortunately the victualling ships arrived in the nick of time, thanks to Mountagu's importunities. When the fleet got to sea once more it took station inside the Straits of Gibraltar. One reason was to keep an eye on the activities of the Barbary states in general, and to persuade the Dey of Algiers to be constant to his treaty in particular. Blake also visited Tetuan, in order to explore the possibility of using it as a victualling station.

Another reason for the change in station was the presence of de Ruijter. His fleet proved to consist of just nine ships. True they were the latest and biggest the Dutch possessed but they were never going to take on Blake's twenty.[9] De Ruijter called at Cadiz in January 1657. The Spanish commander, the Duke of Medina Celi, tried to convince de Ruijter that an alliance had been concluded between their two countries, and that he was to give Spain any assistance in his power. The Dutchman listened impassively, and then told the Duke that there was nothing in his instructions to justify him interfering in any way in the quarrel between England and Spain.[10]

The Dutch visit passed without incident and they sailed into the Mediterranean soon afterwards. There de Ruijter carried out his mission which was to safeguard Dutch shipping, by negotiating agreements with the Barbary States and by trying to do something to stop the attacks of French privateers based on ports in Provence. Blake did not possess the historian's advantage of hindsight. The Spanish thought it worthwhile to canvass the possibility of gaining Dutch support and even Thurloe, the best informed man in Europe, believed that de Ruijter intended to escort the Plate Fleet home. So it cannot be wondered at that Blake posted his fleet in the best position to keep an eye on the Dutchman's movements. The shift to a vantage point far from his base at Lisbon, brought the usual penalty. The fleet was engulfed in a storm and blown back through the Straits of Gibraltar. The damage to the fleet was serious. All thoughts of policing the Mediterranean were shelved and Blake wrote that another such experience would force him to abandon the blockade.[11]

The fleet had hardly returned to its more usual station off Cape St Vincent, when Blake got his first hard news of the progress of the 1657 Plate Fleet. An English merchant ship, the *Catherine* commanded by David Young, returning from a trading voyage to Brazil, had seen it west of the Canary Islands. He had been lieutenant of the *Amity* before leaving the service, so his first thought was to find Blake and tell him what he had seen. He reported counting twelve galleons.[12] There was great excitement in the English fleet when the news spread. Blake called a council of war to debate what should be done. The captains, led by Stayner and Bourne, suggested that a squadron of eight of the fittest frigates should be given six months' victuals and sent in search of the Spanish fleet. Much to their disappointment, Blake refused to entertain the idea at all. The most he would consent to, was a southward sweep to the North African coast in the hope that, if the Spanish tried to come directly for Cadiz, they would fall into the hands of either the fleet or the inshore squadron, patiently patrolling the waters of Cadiz Bay. When the move produced no result, the fleet returned to Cape St Vincent.

Blake's veto on the plan put forward by his subordinates was only sensible. If the Plate Fleet were still at sea, the chances of the English squadron finding it were very small. If it were in Teneriffe Harbour, the squadron would be insufficient. There was also a logistical problem. If some of the ships were to be given six months' victuals, then those available to the others would be proportionately reduced. The fleet had already consumed getting on for half of what had reached them the previous December. Should the victuallers run it as fine as they had last time, some of those ships which had been robbed to make up the supplies of the squadron could be forced to return to England, giving the Spanish in Cadiz an opportunity to get to sea. An added consideration was the serious damage which had been done by the storm. If the blockade was to be abandoned for any length of time, Blake wanted to be quite sure of achieving his objective. The captains had seen the riches which could be theirs from Stayner's exploit, but Blake was not prepared to imperil the position he had built up, just to satisfy their lust for prize money.

Glumly the captains returned to their dismal vigil off Cadiz and for eight more weeks the English fleet ploughed its weary furrow between Cape St Vincent and the Straits of Gibraltar. But the crisis was approaching and Blake knew that a decision must be made soon. The catalyst was tidings brought by an English privateer commanded by William Saddleton or Sadlington, which visited the fleet off Cadiz on 12 April.[13] Its master confirmed what Blake already suspected, that the Plate Fleet was at anchor at Teneriffe in Santa Cruz Harbour. The Spaniards had no intention of coming any further, unless there was firm news that the English had gone home or the fleet at Cadiz managed to run the blockade and reach the Canary Islands. Blake called another council of war. Again the captains urged him to send a powerful squadron to the Canaries. They now knew where the fleet was, the storm damage had been repaired and they had just received a fresh supply of victuals. For a second time Blake turned down the idea.[14] A voyage foraging for prizes was not good enough for Blake. His own wants were simple and he had neither wife, family nor home on which to spend prize money, even if he got it, but it was not that which motivated his action. The captains' plan would have secured only partial victory at best and probably not even that. The whole history of the past half century of naval warfare taught that the quest for prizes was inimical to proper strategic planning.

There was another reason for rejecting the idea. De Ruijter was once more at Cadiz and the latest information was that he had been reinforced and now had eighteen ships under his command.[15] Blake was not to know that de Ruijter's strength was grossly exaggerated and while such a potentially dangerous opponent was around he could not afford to divide his fleet. Yet if he did nothing the prize might slip from his grasp. Might not de Ruijter succumb to Spanish blandishments and sail to Teneriffe himself? Blake could not afford to ignore the possibility. After a last look into Cadiz convinced him that the Spanish would not be ready for sea for a long time, he made the momentous decision to take the whole fleet to the Canary Islands. The only exception he made was that he did not recall the *Rainbow, James* and the *Providence*, posted off Cape Finisterre to keep the Biscay ports under surveillance. A ketch was to be left to watch Cadiz.[16]

The English fleet started on its momentous voyage on 14 April. Teneriffe was sighted late on 18 April, but the attack was delayed until 20 April. Landfall was made on Saturday evening. Stayner wrote later that Blake was reluctant to fight on a Sunday. The main narrative of the battle published by order of Parliament, makes no mention of any such scruples. Navigation was far from an exact science in the mid-seventeenth century. The weather on the Saturday was foggy and Blake was not certain that the landfall he had made was the island of Teneriffe.

Once again Blake summoned a council of war on board the *George*, to which he had shifted his flag when it arrived back in the fleet. For a third time Stayner proposed the selection of a squadron of frigates to make an immediate attack before the Spaniards were aware of the presence of the English fleet. Blake seems to have lost his temper and gave the captains such a dressing down, that no one would venture to offer any further suggestions.[17] By the time that the weather relented and the English lookouts confirmed that the land was indeed Teneriffe, it was the middle of Sunday. Blake's own scheme was to repeat the

Porto Farina operation on a larger scale. For that he needed the advantage of the sea breeze, so the attack was postponed until the following morning.

In the early hours of Monday morning, Blake summoned a last council and outlined his plan. When Blake asked for comments he was met with a stony silence, which was only broken by one of the captains asking him to name the attacking force. They were not prepared to invite another scene like that of the preceding Saturday. Blake selected twelve frigates, four from his own division, four from the division of Vice-Admiral Bourne and four from the division of Rear-Admiral Stayner. They were the *Speaker*, *Lyme*, *Langport*, *Newbury*, *Bridgwater*, *Plymouth*, *Worcester*, *Centurion*, *Winceby*, *Newcastle*, *Foresight* and *Maidstone*. Blake then asked them whom they wanted to command the attack, and they unanimously asked for Stayner.[18]

The task which faced the English fleet was a formidable one. The main roadstead lay in front of the town of Santa Cruz. In mild weather goods were landed from merchantmen at a creek near the custom house but, to facilitate transhipment in all weathers, a large mole had been constructed. This was built at a northerly angle, enclosing the main harbour. Ships could anchor anything from a cable length to half a mile from the shore in complete safety. Even before the English could come to grips with the man-made defences, they had to encounter a natural hazard. The coastline was scored by three deep valleys which could produce quite unpredictable squalls, a justification in itself for Blake's caution in rejecting an attack on the Saturday, before inspecting the position.

The bay was a shallow semi-circle with the town roughly in the middle. A mile to the northward of the mole was the large square fort of St Philip, equipped with over forty powerful guns. There were more forts and batteries beyond it, the most important of which was known as Passo Alto. There were batteries to the south of the town too, terminating in the fort of San Juan. Beyond them the shore was so rocky, that a landing was out of the question. The possibility of an English attack had been in the mind of the Spanish authorities for some time. The forts opposite the harbour had been joined by a triple row of breastworks manned by musketeers. English accounts agree that there were sixteen ships in the harbour. Seven were great galleons of 1000 to 1200 tons. The remaining nine averaged 300 tons. Spanish sources give the Plate Fleet a total of eleven ships, two men-of-war and nine armed merchantmen, so there must have been five other ships outward bound to complete the total.[19] The ships had all been unladed and the gold and silver taken inland for safety. The smaller ships lay close to the shore, the greater galleons further out, their broadsides facing towards the sea.

As soon as the sea breeze began to blow, the English launched their attack. Stayner led the way in the *Speaker*. He was followed by the other eleven ships in the order laid down by Blake. 'I stood,' Stayner says, 'upon the forecastle of our ship to seek a good berth for the better doing our work ... We went as near as we could with safety and were within pistol shot of the admiral and vice admiral and little more of the rear; they were all great ships which rode near the castle, 1000 and 1200 tons a piece.'[20] This seems to suggest that he manoeuvred the *Speaker* between the galleons and the smaller ships. Stayner's orders to the other captains were to follow him but to anchor three or four cables' length from the shore, so that they might have room to swing their ships round during the fight. The space would also allow them to warp out at the end, as they had done at Porto Farina. They were instructed not to fire until they were at anchor, which shows that the English appreciated the importance of the first broadside. A little disorder was caused by the *Plymouth* and the *Nantwich*, which returned late to the fleet and missed the council. The *Plymouth's* captain appears to have been unaware of the order not to fire and accounts say the ship fired twice before he grasped what Stayner wanted. The *Nantwich* was not in the original twelve and when it joined the line, there was a certain amount of jockeying for position.[21]

The English must have expected to take considerable punishment from the batteries on shore before they could get at the Spanish ships, in the same way that an army which attacks the entrenched position of an opponent expects to meet a withering fire before it can come to close quarters. They were spared the anticipated hot reception by bad Spanish dispositions. The ships in the roadstead masked the batteries, which could only fire at the English over or through them. The attack began at 8 am. By 9 am the thirteen frigates were in position. The superior English gunnery once more quickly did its work. By 11 am, most of the smaller ships had either struck their colours or were on fire. The *Lyme* commanded by Captain Eustace Smith, did particularly good work.

The greater galleons were a tougher proposition and took longer to subdue. Their fate was sealed by the entry of the larger ships into the bay, which seems to have been about midday. The English guns were so powerful, that they silenced the St Philip fort, those of its garrison who were not killed abandoning their batteries in panic. Soon afterwards the Spanish Admiral and Vice-Admiral were seen to blow up in quick succession, the coup de grace, apparently, being administered by the *Bristol*, around 2 pm.

The next phase of the battle was the systematic destruction of the Spanish ships which were still afloat. A vivid description of it was published later by the boatswain of the *Bristol*, Thomas Lurting. The first galleon the *Bristol* attacked fired at the ship's boats but all the shot passed over their heads, and the crew deserted when the English boarding party swarmed up the side. The next ships they turned their attention to were still occupied but had suffered appalling damage from the English bombardment. They were 'ashore all on board one another; one of them along the shore and one across her hawse, and one across her stern about a musket shot from our ship. There was a castle on one side of

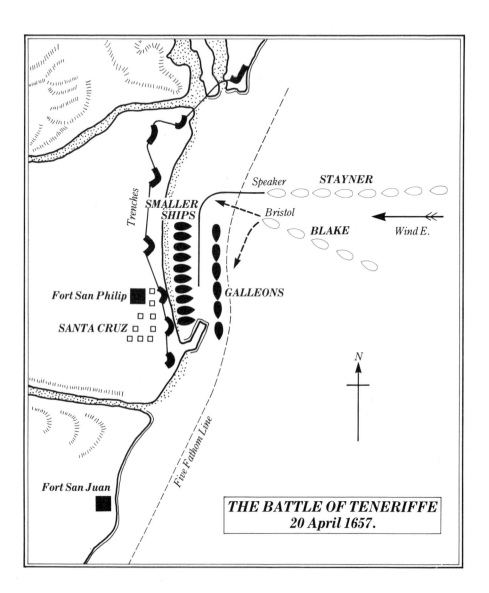

THE BATTLE OF TENERIFFE
20 April 1657.

them and a breastwork on the other with about 50 or 60 men in it, as was supposed. The galleons lay about a cable's length from the castle.'[22] Lurting's account underlines the value of the trial run at Porto Farina. The captains of the frigates had all been instructed to fire their guns before attempting to board, so that the smoke blew over the ships and the shore batteries, making it difficult for them to see what they were firing at. He describes how his captain remembered his instructions at the beginning but forgot, after the boarding party had fired two of the ships. This gave the soldiers on shore their first real sight of his men with nearly disastrous results. He reckoned himself lucky to have got off with only two men killed.

As far as the Spanish fleet was concerned, the battle was over. Every ship had been either captured or destroyed. The only question left was how heavily the English would be made to pay for their victory. Every time a Spanish ship was sunk a gap opened, through which the shore defences could fire at the English ships. Now was the time when the English discipline would be tested to its fullest.

It was at this point that an old canker began to show itself. Contrary to orders the four ships in Stayner's division, the *Speaker, Plymouth, Worcester* and *Maidstone*, all had secured a prize. In addition the *Swiftsure* was trying to bring off a ship which had been left, correctly, by the *Bridgwater*.[23] The behaviour of the five captains, among them the Vice-Admiral, the Rear-Admiral and Thomas Adams, who had been with Blake since Civil War days, was totally irresponsible. There are indications in the accounts, that Stayner's lust for more prize money may have been one of the factors in the earlier prolonged resistance of the Spanish Admiral and Vice-Admiral.[24] Now the attempt to bring out prizes threatened to slow down the already difficult task of warping out of the bay under fire against the wind, with the risk of greater casualties and loss of ships. Blake would have none of it. Peremptory orders were sent to fire the ships. That Blake had to repeat the orders three times before the captains obeyed, shows what might have happened under less strict leadership.

By 3 pm the destruction was complete and the difficult withdrawal began. The official narrative related:

> It remained to complete this Mercy, that our own Ships should come off well, wherein the greatest hazard and difficulty lay; for some riding near into the Shore, and being sorely maimed did require to be warped off, others when we came to weigh, drove with the wind, [which was] all the while blowing right into the Bay, and one of our best Frigates struck: The Enemy in the meantime supplied fresh men into his Forts for those we had killed and beaten out, in the heat of the Action, and from them and the Castle continued plying upon us, till about seven of the clock at night every Ship and Vessel belonging to the Fleet, were by the good hand of God got safely out of command.[25]

The last ship to leave was the *Speaker*. She was so badly damaged, that she was barely seaworthy. The crew warped her off for a full half mile but it was as much as they could do to keep her afloat. 'We had now no shift to keep her from sinking,' related Stayner, 'but by nailing hides over the holes and nail butt staves along the sides of the hides, for we had 8 or 9 foot water in the ship.' The rigging had been so severely damaged that Stayner reported, 'We had not one whole rope overhead'. This made it almost impossible to get any sail on her but the spritsail and sprit top sail, which were usually set simply to help the steering. The lack of ropes made it difficult to keep the masts upright and Stayner's problems were made worse by the shooting away of the mainyard and the foreyard, during the battle.[26]

Blake was alert to Stayner's troubles and sent Vice-Admiral Bourne, in the *Swiftsure*, to tow him off. This led to the one serious breach of discipline in the whole battle. For some reason which has never been explained, Bourne cast off the tow rope while the *Speaker* was still within range. 'They paid us extremely,' wrote Stayner. 'So we rid till the sun went down; then the wind came off shore, and we set those pieces of sail we had, and cut away her anchor.' At last, still firing her guns defiantly, the *Speaker* crept out of the harbour. She was hardly in the open sea before her foremast fell overboard. Fortunately, the *Plymouth* came to her rescue and towed her into the fleet, where boats brought carpenters and seamen to repair the worst of the damage.

The battle of Teneriffe was one of the most complete victories ever gained by an English fleet. All sixteen ships in the harbour were destroyed. Even the Royalists in exile were forced to concede the magnitude of Blake's achievement. 'The whole action was so miraculous,' wrote Clarendon, 'that all men who knew the place concluded that no sober men, with what courage soever endued, would ever undertake it; and they could hardly persuade themselves to believe what they had done; whilst the Spaniards comforted themselves with the belief that they were devils, and not men, which had destroyed them in such a manner.'[27] Only Nelson's great victory at Trafalgar outranks it. Indeed Nelson himself would have been very well aware of Blake's extraordinary achievement. He had unpleasant recollections of Teneriffe from 1796. 'Of all the places which ever came under our inspection,' wrote one of Nelson's officers, 'none we conceive is more invulnerable to attack or more easily defended.'[28]

The most remarkable feature was the completeness of the victory. Though many of the ships were badly damaged, not a single one was lost. The English sustained 200 casualties, of which sixty were killed. The worst hit ship was the *Speaker*, with fifteen killed and thirty wounded. Whether we compare these figures with losses in the pitched battles of the Dutch Wars or try to estimate what could have happened to a fleet engaging the defences of one of the best protected harbours in Western Europe, the total is incredibly small. The sheer efficiency of the operation was a measure of how sure Blake's touch had become.

The key from first to last was discipline: Blake's insistence beforehand, that this would be a properly planned attack, not a prize raid; the silent way the frigates had filed into the bay, with hardly a shot being fired until they were in position; the reiterated commands to burn the prizes – only Blake could have made such orders stick. They ensured victory and they saved lives.

Even more remarkable was the way in which the opportunity had been created. The victory at Teneriffe cannot be isolated from the blockade which had preceded it. The first part of the blockade had led to the attempt of the Spanish to run the Plate Fleet into Cadiz. English vigilance had thwarted that. Against all precedent the blockade had gone on and on, forcing the Spaniards to choose a staging post, where the Plate Fleet could wait until the English patience was finally exhausted. The remorseless pressure which created the opening was all Blake's doing. No one else had the tenacity for such an operation.

The consequences of the battle of Teneriffe were to be far reaching. It made an enormous contribution to the final collapse of Spain as a major power. The bullion had been preserved but it was locked up in the Canary Islands. For two years in succession the Spanish treasury had not received the money from the New World which it needed to pay its armies. The Spanish defeat in 1658 outside Dunkirk, at the Battle of the Dunes, by an Anglo-French army was at least partly due to the English blockade which made it impossible for them to pay their soldiers. It certainly was a major factor leading to the Treaty of the Pyrenees which ended the war between France and Spain in 1659. For a long time Spain obstinately refused to accept the reality of Portuguese independence. After the Restoration Charles II married the Portuguese princess, Catherine of Braganza and she brought with her as dowry Tangier and Bombay. The negotiations were conducted by Edward Mountagu, now Earl of Sandwich. In return England sent an expeditionary force to help the Portuguese which was carried by a fleet commanded by Sir Richard Stayner. This finally forced the Spanish to the negotiating table and Portuguese independence was conceded in 1664. Sadly Stayner did not live to see it. He died of a fever on his ship in the Tagus in 1663.

After spending five days off Teneriffe repairing the worst of the damage, the English took advantage of a change in the wind on 25 April to begin the return journey to the Spanish coast. The voyage was uneventful and landfall was made on 5 May.[29] When news spread of what Blake had done to the Plate Fleet, there was even less inclination among the captains in Cadiz to put to sea and try conclusions with him than there had been before, so there was even less to do.

Blake wrote home, detailing the defects of the fleet and repeating his earlier opinion, that the great ships could not stand another winter off the coast of Spain. Cromwell agreed. He sent a letter congratulating Blake on his victory and enclosing a small jewel as a token of his affection. With it came instructions for the disposal of the fleet. A squadron of fourteen frigates was to be left to block up Cadiz and five ships allotted to commerce protection around the Straits of Gibraltar. The rest were to come home at the time Blake judged the fittest. Cromwell left it to Blake to select the captains and ships to stay out. 'For commodore of the 14 ships, we here have thought of captain Stoakes, but do refer it to you to do therein as you shall judge most convenient.'[30]

While the instructions were on the way, Blake had the satisfaction of tidying up a piece of unfinished business. Leaving a small blockading force at Cadiz, he carried the fleet to Sallee. This time his reception was very different. News of his great victory had preceded him and a treaty of friendship between the Dey and England was quickly signed. All English slaves were to be released and immunity from attack granted to English shipping.[31] Blake was back off Cadiz by 26 June, to find that an attempt had been made to get some of the silver to Spain. The four frigates left on guard, the *Providence, Foresight, Centurion* and *Nantwich* had chased on shore the *Flying Fame* of Amsterdam, bound for San Lucar. According to the Venetian Ambassador, it had 600,000 pieces of eight on board. The crew managed to land most of the silver in boats before the English could board.[32] Three days after the return from Sallee, Cromwell's instructions arrived. Blake concurred in the appointment of Stokes. He was a capable officer, he had had a spell in England and he had not been to the Canary Islands, so he was relatively fresh. During the next week the fleet was separated into two halves and on 9 July, Blake set out for England with the *George, Swiftsure, Newbury, Worcester, Bridgwater, Newcastle, Foresight, Maidstone, Colchester* and *Nonsuch*, ketch.[33]

By the time the homeward voyage began, it must have been clear to those around him that Blake was dying. He had known that his days were numbered for some time, as his cryptic remark in his letter to Mountagu of 9 February, about his health being good enough to last the summer, testifies.[34] A month later he was writing that his body was growing weaker and weaker but that he hoped the Lord would support him till 'the appointed time'.[35] Once the Plate Fleet was smashed and Blake knew that his task was accomplished, a steady decline set in. Thomas Maynard, the Protectorate agent at Lisbon, noted with concern on 11 July, 'The General is very weake; I beseech God to strengthen him.'[36]

Blake wanted to set foot for one last time on English soil before he died and the *George* was diverted to Plymouth, so that his wish should be granted. Appropriately the flagship was accompanied by the *Newbury* and the *Colchester*, commanded by his nephews, Robert and Samuel. The remainder of the fleet sailed up the Channel for Portsmouth and the Thames.[37] The voyage was a long one and Blake did not get his wish. He breathed his last as the *George* entered Plymouth Sound at 10 am on 7 August 1657. Blake's dying plea was entirely typical of the man. Reporting his death, Captain Clarke wrote to the Admiralty

Commissioners, 'May it please your Honours, it was the General's charge yesterday to humbly to offer unto you the remembrance and sad condition of the fleet we left behind under the command of Captain Stokes, Mr Creed being able to give your Honours a just and true account.'[38] Captain Henry Hatsell, the Plymouth Navy agent, put it simply. 'As he lived so he continued to the death, faithful. The Lord grant that a supply of his great loss may be made up for the good of his poor people.'[39] His sentiments were echoed by Secretary Thurloe who wrote, 'a very worthy and brave man is gone and a faithful servant of his Highness.'[40]

Blake had made his will on 13 March 1656 just before leaving for the Spanish coast. It was a simple affair.[41] After giving £100 for the poor of each of the two towns of Bridgwater and Taunton, there followed a series of bequests to his numerous relatives. They show that his possessions in property were modest. The manor of Puriton, which he gave to his brother Humphrey, and the dwelling house in Bridgwater, which went to Benjamin, were both inherited from his parents. His only addition to them was the house which he had bought from widow Coxe. He had capital of over £3000, a lot of money for the mid-seventeenth century, and all his relatives benefited. His mode of life suggests that he did not spend much, not even investing in a London town house, an extraordinary omission for a man who was a Member of Parliament.

Blake's body was taken ashore and embalmed by Matthew Lynde, his old surgeon and comrade, who received a fee of £30. The bowels and other parts, which were extracted during the process, were buried before the Chancel of St Andrew's Church.[42] The embalmed body was then embarked on the *Colchester*, which was commanded by Blake's nephew Samuel, to be taken to Greenwich, where it lay in State.[43] The funeral took place in great pomp on 4 September and his remains were buried in the King Henry VII chapel in Westminster Abbey.[44]

Clarendon has a particularly biting description of the obsequies: 'But he [Blake] wanted no pomp when he was dead, Cromwell causing him to be brought up in all state that could be; and then, according to the method of that time, to encourage his officers to be killed that they might be pompously buried, he was with all solemnity possible, and at the charge of the public, interred in Harry the Seventh's chapel, in the monument of the kings.'[45] Clarendon undoubtedly reflected Blake's own views. What could be more incongruous than an old republican laid to rest among monarchs? What place was there for Blake in the new court of King Nol? The political expediency, which required the Protector to do such violence to the dead man's wishes, is a mark of how the Revolution, which both desired, had failed. It was full time that Robert Blake, the greatest of the Generals-at-Sea, should be gathered to his fathers.

*   *   *

The Puritan Revolution may have failed but Blake has a secure place in our naval history. Some of the reasons for his success were due to the times in which he lived. There never has been another period in which the power of naval guns so nearly approached that of land-based artillery. Fifty years later, Teneriffe would have been impossible. This technical advantage possessed by the English fleet was the work of the Tudor Navy. Blake cannot be credited with either the introduction of broadsides or the line formation. Broadsides, whether Tudor or Stuart in origin, were being fired long before he appeared. The line formation evolved after he retired, hors de combat, at the end of the battle of Portland. Some would claim that genuine fighting in line did not appear until later in the seventeenth century. Fleets of anything up to a hundred, of different sizes and sailing capacities, could not be arranged in proper lines. Once other nations equipped their ships with big iron guns, it became clear that vessels under a certain size were a liability and they ceased to take part in fleet actions. The resulting homogeneity and smaller size of the fleets made the manoeuvring of ships in line simpler.

But in other ways Blake's influence was felt throughout the subsequent great age of sail. Most of Britain's sea wars were to be more like the war with Spain than the war with the United Provinces. They were wars of blockade more than wars of fleet actions. The methods Blake evolved through painful experience, were to remain standard practice until steam supplanted sail. The cruise of 1656–7 is a text-book example of how such a war should be fought. In order to achieve that perfection, Blake had to impose a discipline on his captains, which was irksome in the extreme, but which paid handsome dividends. There was a danger that what he had done would be undone by the follies of the Restoration. Thanks to the dedication of Samuel Pepys in creating a body of professional captains who perpetuated the values Blake had taken such trouble to instil in his subordinates, his work was preserved. What was to distinguish the British Navy from its rivals was not its great admirals, but the high quality of its captains and for that Blake must take a large part of the credit.

There were two Blakes. To the ordinary soldier and seaman, he was the man who challenged the Royalists to a twelve-a-side combat at Lyme, who vowed he would eat his boots before he considered surrendering at Taunton, who when challenged by Rupert in 1650, said to Captain Arkinstall, 'Can you stem him?' He was the man who drank a glass of Malaga with the new recruits in May 1652, and swapped stories about Schiedam with captured Dutch fishermen in June of the same year. The seamen cheered him to the echo when his squadron came crashing through at the battle of the Gabbard, even though the hard work had already been done by Monck. But there was a different Blake who was a holy terror to the captains working under him. In 1652, Captain Myngs was reproved for risking his ship when he brought in three prizes, and Captain Taylor was censured for only running his opponent on shore. The fleet held its breath when the captains 'lay by', before dealing with the ships guarding the Dutch herring fishery off the north of Scotland. At Dungeness six captains were dismissed in what appears in retrospect, in five of the cases, to have been a miscarriage of justice, yet the confidence of his subordinates was unimpaired. Three times in the run-up to Teneriffe Blake slapped his captains down, on the last occasion reducing them to sullen silence. Yet they fought like madmen for him, because he made them share his vision of the Navy, and because of the passionate conviction he brought to everything he did. They would curse him but they would do what he demanded.

Not all men who fail to marry are lacking in passion. Some turn the emotions that most men direct at women, in other directions. Blake spent his life searching for some cause on which to fix the ambitions which are usually absorbed by family life. He tried academic life and it failed him. He devoted his energies to business without success. He turned to politics, but was disgusted at its inevitable compromises. Only when he joined the Parliamentary Army did he begin to glimpse his role in life. Only when he went to sea did he know true fulfilment. The fleet was his family. He had no other. His captains were not a band of brothers, they were unruly children who needed chastisement, but he loved them all the same. His last thoughts were for Captain Stokes and the ships left behind off the coast of Spain.

Bibliography

ORIGINAL SOURCES

Bodleian Library, Oxford
Rawlinson Collection
A224, Committee Book of the Committee of the Navy, 1649
A225 and 226, Committee Book of the Committee of Admiralty, October 1650–November 1652
A227, Committee of Admiralty Letter Book 1653
Tanner Collection, volume 56
Carte Papers, volume 73

British Library, London
Add.Mss. 9300, 9304, 18,982, 18,986

Dorset Record Office, Dorchester
B2/12/1 and B2/13/1, Records of the Company of Freemen

Public Record Office, London
C66 Patent Rolls
1080/2289, Grant of the Rectory of Bridgwater
2860/4, Pardon for breach of the Statute of Mortmain
C142, Inquisitiones Post Mortem
Vol. 422 No, 18, Mrs Blake's Marriage Trust
C181, Commissions of Sewers and Charitable Uses for Somerset
E174/121, 1628 Subsidy List for Somerset
E190, Port Books for Bridgwater, Lyme Regis and Minehead
E407, Somerset Knighthood Fines
SP 28, Commonwealth Exchequer Papers, particularly 253A and 300
WO 47/2, Gunnery establishment of the *Foresight*
S. P. Domestic Series, volume 46

Somerset Record Office, Taunton
D/B/Bw, Records of the Borough of Bridgwater
1615, Accounts of Humphrey Blake, Receiver for 1639–40
1745 and 2412, Earl of Suffolk and the Rectory, 1634
1833, 1647 Petition which has selected incomes for several rectories and vicarages attached
including Bridgwater itself
2418, Change of Rectory Trustees in 1628
2427, Establishment of the Trust for the Rectory in 1614
D/D/Ca 309 and 313, Prosecution of the Bridgwater Churchwardens
D/D/Cd/71, Case of Bale als Culliford v Garvin which shows seating arrangements in Bridgwater
church

D/P/Bwm/2/1/1, Bridgwater Parish Registers
Transcript of 1642 Protestation

PRINTED SOURCES

Abbott W. C. *Letters and Speeches of Oliver Cromwell* 4 vols., Harvard 1937–47

Aitzema L. *Saken van Staet in Oorlogh*'s Gravenhage 1670

Bettey J. H. (ed) *Calendar of the Correspondence of the Smyth Family of Ashton Court*, Bristol Record Society vol. 35, 1982

Birch, T. (ed) *Letters and Papers of John Thurloe* 7 vols., London 1742

Carr, C. T. (ed) *Select Charters of Trading Companies* 1530–1707, Selden Society vol. 28, 1913

Coates W. H., Snow V. F. and Young, Anne S. *Private Journals of the Long Parliament* 2 vols., London 1984 and 1987

Firth, Sir C. H. (ed) 'Richard Stayner's Account of the Battle of Teneriffe', *Naval Miscellany* vol. ii, pp123–36, Navy Records Society vol. 40, 1910

Firth, Sir C. H. (ed) *The Clarke Papers* Camden Society, New Series vols 49 and 54, 1891–1901

Firth, Sir C. H. and Rait R. S. (eds) *Acts and Ordinances of the Interregnum* 3 vols., London 1911

Foster, Joseph (ed) *Records of the Honourable Society of Lincoln's Inn* 2 vols., London 1896

Foster, Joseph (ed) *Alumni Oxoniensis, 1500–1714* 4 vols., Oxford 1891

Foster, Sir W. (ed) *English Factories in India 1618–69* 13 vols, London 1906–27

Gardiner, S. R. and Atkinson, C. T. (eds) *Letters and Papers relating to the First Dutch War 1652–54* 6 vols. Navy Records Society vols. 13, 17, 30, 37, 41 and 66, 1899–1930

Gardiner, S. R. (ed) 'Prince Rupert at Lisbon', *Camden Miscellany* Camden Society, 3rd Series, vol. x, 1902

Gomme, Bernard de 'Diary of the Siege of Bristol', *Army History Review* vol. 4, December 1925

Green, M. A. E. (ed) *Calendar of State Papers, Domestic, Commonwealth Series* 13 vols., Public Record Office 1867–86

Green, M. A. E. (ed) *Calendar of the Proceedings of the Committee for the Advance of Money* 3 vols., Public Record Office, 1888

Hinds, Allen B. (ed) *Calendar of State Papers, Venetian* vols. 28 and 29

Historical Manuscripts Commission:
> *4th Report* – House of Lords Mss
> *7th Report* – Sir H. Verney Mss
> *8th Report* – Earl of Jersey Mss
> *Egmont*
> *Leyborne Popham*
> *Portland* vols. i and iii
> *Salisbury* vol. v
> *Wells*

Journals of the House of Commons vols. ii to vii

Journals of the House of Lords vols. iv to x

Lurting, Thomas *The Fighting Seaman turned Peaceable Christian* Gloucester n.d.

Macray, W. D. (ed) *Calendar of Clarendon State Papers* vols. i and ii, Oxford 1872

McGowan, A. P. (ed) *The Jacobean Commissions of Inquiry 1608 and 1618* Navy Records Society, vol. 116, 1971

Mayo, C. (ed) *Municipal Records of the Borough of Dorchester* Dorchester 1908

Powell, Rev. J. R. (ed) *Letters of Robert Blake* Navy Records Society, vol. 76, 1937

Powell, Rev. J. R. (ed) 'Journal of John Weale' in *Naval Miscellany* vol. iv, pp85–162, Navy Records Society, vol. 92, 1952

Return of Members of Parliament Part I House of Commons 1878

Shilton, Dorothy and Holworthy, Richard *High Court of Admiralty Examinations 1637–8* London 1932

St George, Sir R. and Lennard, S. *Visitation of Somerset, 1623* Harleian Society vol. 11. There are additions made in 1838 by R. Mundy in the Sir Thomas Phillips Tracts in the British Library

Sturgess, H. A. C. (ed) *Register of Admissions to the Middle Temple* 2 vols., London 1949

Tanner, J. R. (ed) *The Two Discourses of John Hollond, 1638 and 1659* Navy Records Society vol. 7, 1896

Tanner, J. R. (ed) *The Tracts of Sir William Monson* vol. iv, Navy Records Society, vol. 45, 1913

Thomason, George *Tracts as listed in the Catalogue of Books and Pamphlets etc. relating to the Civil War, Commonwealth and Restoration collected by G. Thomason 1640–1661* British Library, 1908

Warner, Sir George F. (ed) *The Nicholas Papers* 4 vols., Camden Society, New Series 40, 50, 57 and 3rd Series, 31

SECONDARY SOURCES

Adair, John *Roundhead General* A Military Biography of Sir William Waller, London 1969

Anderson, R. C. 'The Royalists at Sea 1649', *Mariner's Mirror* vol. xiv, 1928, pp320–8

Anderson, R. C. (ed) 'The Royalists at Sea 1650', *Mariner's Mirror* 1931, pp135–68

Ballhausen, C. *Die Erste Englische-Hollandische Seekrieg* 's Gravenhage, 1923

Baumber, M. L. 'The Navy during the Civil War and the Commonwealth, 1642–51', MA thesis, University of Manchester, 1967

Bayley, A. R. *The Great Civil War in Dorset* Taunton 1910

Beadon, Robert *Robert Blake, Sometime Commanding all the Fleets and Naval Forces of England* London 1935

Binding H. and Stevens D. *Minehead, A New History* Minehead 1977

Burne, Col. A. H. and Young, Brigadier P. *The Great Civil War* London 1959

Chapman, G. *The Siege of Lyme Regis* Lyme 1982

Clarendon, Edward Hyde, Earl of *History of the Great Rebellion and Civil Wars in England* (ed. W. D. Macray) 6 vols. Oxford 1888

Colliber, S. *Columna Rostrata* London 1727

Corbett, Sir J. S. *England in the Mediterranean* 2 vols. London 1904

Curtis, C. D. *Robert Blake, General at Sea* Taunton 1934

Dixon, W. H. *Robert Blake, Admiral and General-at-Sea* London 1856

Edgar, F. T. *Sir Ralph Hopton, The King's Man in the West* Oxford 1968

Elias J. E. *Vlootbouw in Nederlands in de Eerste Helft der 17e Eeuw 1595–1655* Amsterdam 1953

Ellis, M. F. H. 'The Channel Islands and the Great Rebellion', *Bulletin of the Societé Jersaise* vol. xiii, 1937, pp191–216

Firth, Sir C. H. *The Last Years of the Protectorate* 2 vols. London 1909

Firth, Sir C. H. (ed) *Memoirs of Edmund Ludlow* 3 vols., London 1894, originally published Vevey 1693

Fletcher, A. *The Outbreak of the English Civil War* London 1981

Gardiner, S. R. *The History of the Great Civil War* 4 vols. 1893 edition reprinted London 1987

Gardiner, S. R. *History of the Commonwealth and Protectorate* 3 vols. London 1894–1903

(Gentleman) *History and Life of Robert Blake esq. of Bridgwater, General and Admiral of the Fleets and Naval Forces of England by a gentleman brought up in his family* London n.d.

Green, Emmanuel 'Siege and Defence of Taunton', *Somerset Archaeological and Natural History Society Proceedings* vol. 25, 1879, pp33–48

Hannay, David *Admiral Blake* London 1886

Hasler, P. W. (ed) *The House of Commons, 1558–1603, Introductory Survey.* Volume in the History of Parliament series, London 1982

Hill, C. *God's Englishman* London 1970

Hogue, Arthur *Origins of the Common Law* London 1966

Hollond, John *The Discourses of John Hollond* edited by J. R. Tanner, Navy Records Society, vol. 7, 1896

Howarth, David *The Men-of-War* Amsterdam 1978

Israel, Jonathan 'Competing Cousins. Anglo-Dutch Trade Rivalry', *History Today* July 1988, pp17–22

Keegan, John *The Mask of Command* London 1987

Keeler, Mary Frear *Members of the Long Parliament* Philadelphia 1954

Laughton, L. G. Carr 'Gunnery, Frigates and Line of Battle', *Mariner's Mirror* vol. xiv, 1928, pp339–64

Ludlow, *see* Firth

Oldmixon, John *History and Life of Robert Blake* London 1740

Oppenheim, Michael *A History of the Administration of the Royal Navy and of Merchant Shipping relative to the Royal Navy* London 1896

Parker, G. *The Military Revolution* Cambridge 1988

Parker, G. 'Why the Armada Failed', *History Today* May 1988, pp26–33

Penn, Granville *Memorial of the Professional Life and Times of Sir William Penn* 2 vols., London 1830

Powell, Rev. J. R. 'Blake's reduction of the Scilly Islands', *Mariner's Mirror* vol. xvii, 1931, pp205–20

Powell, Rev. J. R. 'The Siege of Lyme Regis', *Mariner's Mirror* vol. xx, 1934, pp448–74

Powell, Rev. J. R. *Robert Blake, General-at-Sea* London 1972

Reid, William, FSA 'Commonwealth Supply Departments within the Tower and the Committee of London Merchants', *Guildhall Miscellany* vol. 2, 1966

Roncière, Charles de la *Histoire de la Marine Francaise* vol. v, Paris 1919

Spalding, T. E. *Life of Richard Badiley* London 1896

Stevens, D. *War and Peace in West Somerset, 1620–70* Minehead n.d.

Stieg, Margaret *Laud's Laboratory: The Diocese of Bath and Wells in the early Seventeenth Century* Bucknell USA, 1983

Underdown, David *Pride's Purge* Oxford 1971

Underdown, David *Somerset in the Civil War and Interregnum* Newton Abbot 1973

Underdown, David *Revel, Riot and Rebellion* London 1987

Warburton, B. E. G. *The Memoirs of Prince Rupert and the Cavaliers* 3 vols. London 1849

Waters, Lieut-Commander D. W. 'The Elizabethan Navy and the Armada Campaign', *Mariner's Mirror* vol. xxxv, 1949, pp90–135

Wells, J. *Wadham College* London 1898

Wilson, J. *Fairfax* London 1986

Woolrych, A. *From Commonwealth to Protectorate* Oxford 1982

Worden, B. *The Rump Parliament* Cambridge 1974

Wroughton, John *The Civil War in Bath and North Somerset* Bath 1973

Wyndham, H. A. *The Wyndhams of Norfolk and Somerset, 1410–1688* Oxford 1939

Wood, Anthony *Athenae Oxoniensis, to which are added the Fasti* 4 vols, London 1813–20

Notes and Sources

ABBREVIATIONS

C.J.	*Journals of the House of Commons*
L.J.	*Journals of the House of Lords*
F.D.W.	*Letters and Papers relating to the First Dutch War 1652–4*, S.R. Gardiner and C.T. Atkinson (Editors)
M.M.	*Mariners Mirror*
T.T.	Thomason Tracts
Letters	*Letters of Robert Blake*, the Rev. J.R. Powell (Editor)

CHAPTER 1   BEFORE THE CIVIL WARS   1598–1640   pp 3 to 14

1. Bridgwater Parish Registers – Somerset Record Office (SRO) D/P/Bwm/2/1/1
2. Official Guide to the Blake Museum
3. See note 1
4. Humphrey Blake's will, proved 11 May 1559, Archdeaconry of Taunton, and Robert Blake's will, proved 16 October 1592, 76 Harrington, both quoted in Curtis, C.D. *Robert Blake, General-at-Sea* p175.
5. Powell, Rev J.R. *General-at-Sea* p12
6. ibid. quoting Curtis p1
7. They are mentioned in the accounts of the water bailiff but not described, e.g. that of 1640–1 SRO D/B/Bw/1515
8. *Fasti* 2, 329
9. H.M.C. Wells p246 mentions Attwood's appointment
10. *Alumni Oxoniensis* vol. i, p290
11. Dixon, W. Hepworth *Robert Blake, Admiral and General-at-Sea* p14
12. *Alumni* vol. ii, p347
13. ibid. vol. iii, p391
14. Wells, J. *Wadham College* pp22–7
15. Dixon, p14
16. Oldmixon J. *History and Life of Robert Blake* 1740, p5
17. Curtis C.D. and Beadon R. *Robert Blake* take this line. Powell, p15, records the Durham case but prefers not to speculate about whether it had an influence on the Merton election.
18. Clarendon, Edward Hyde, Earl of *History of the Rebellion and Civil Wars in England* vol. vi, p37
19. Wells, p41

244

20. details from *Alumni*
21. Oldmixon quoted by Powell, p15
22. ibid.
23. SRO D/D/Cd 71 The case of Bale als Culliford against Garvin shows that the women had separate pews in 1634 and the preacher, John Devenish, deposed that the separation had already taken place when he was appointed in 1605
24. *Alumni* vol. ii, p309 and vol. iii, p315
25. Sturgess H.A.C. (ed) *Register of Admissions to the Middle Temple* vol. iv, p109
26. *Return of Members of Parliament* pp465, 471 and 478
27. *Alumni* vol. ii, p1693
28. Foster, Joseph (ed) *The Records of the Honourable Society of Lincoln's Inn* vol. i, p185
29. *Return* and *Alumni* vol. ii, p1693
30. Wyndham, H.A. *The Wyndhams of Norfolk and Somerset 1410–1688* p175
31. Bridgwater Parish Registers
32. Will of Robert Blake, senior, infra
33. Inquisitiones Post Mortem C142, vol. 422 no. 18
34. Bridgwater Parish registers
35. He refers to his (step) brother Smithes, a goldsmith of Cheapside
36. *HMC Salisbury* p393 gives a total of customs collections for each Port. Bridgwater and Minehead totalled £8–16–11 the lowest on the list. By comparison Cardiff was £38, Milford £75, Bristol £1533 and Plymouth £1605.
37. ibid. vol. iv, p121
38. See Bridgwater Port books PRO E190
39. *Visitation of Somerset* – copy in the Sir Thomas Phillips Tracts with additions by R. Mundy 1828
40. *Select Charters of Trading Companies, 1530–1707* pp62–78
41. See section about the Rectory of Bridgwater in Chapter 2
42. PRO C181/3/186–7
43. Will of Humphrey Blake, 35 Hele
44. PRO E174/172/390
45. Bridgwater Parish Registers. William Ceely is often mentioned in the Bridgwater records at the SRO.
46. The marriage is mentioned in nineteenth-century editions of the Visitation of 1623
47. Repeated most recently by Powell, pp15–6
48. Binding H. and Stevens D. *Minehead, A New History* 1977, p60
49. See the Minehead Customs books in PRO E190
50. I used the transcript in the SRO
51. PRO E407/35
52. I have nothing to add to Powell's dismissal of the Moroccan Blake, p19. As I shall show the question of whether Blake had been to sea before 1649 had little or nothing to do with his appointment as General-at-Sea.
53. DRO B2/13/1 Day Book of the Company of Freemen
54. ibid.
55. Curtis, pp13–14
56. B2/12/1 also contains a copy of the 1621 Charter with the signatures of all the seventeenth-century freemen. Many are very difficult to read but regrettably Blake's does not seem to be among them.
57. Gardiner, S.R. (ed) *Documents relating to the First Dutch War* vol. i, p402
58. Shilton, Dorothy and Holworthy, Richard *High Court of Admiralty Examinations 1637—8* p223
59. Curtis records, p12, that he had a search made but with no result

CHAPTER 2   THE NATION DIVIDES   1640–1642   pp 15 to 25

1. Return of Members of the House of Commons, 1878
2. Hasler, P.W. (ed) *The House of Commons, 1558–1603* vol. i, Introductory Survey, p235
3. J.H. Bettey (ed) *Calendar of the Correspondence of the Smyth Family of Ashton Court* p85–6
4. The Return for Minehead mentions that Wroth was the Returning Officer, see Return, p483
5. Underdown, D. *Revel, Riot and Rebellion* p135
6. Wyndham, pp177–9, and Keeler, Mary Freer *Members of the Long Parliament* pp395–6
7. The Proceedings can be found at the Somerset Record Office D/D/Ca/309 Bridgwater 1636 and 313, 31 October 1636, 15 November 1636. The case is discussed in Stieg, Margaret *Laud's Laboratory: the Diocese of Bath and Wells in the Early Seventeenth Century* p295, p303
8. SRO D/D/Ca 313, 27 March and *Laud's Laboratory*, p303
9. Hasler, op. cit.
10. ibid.
11. Keeler, p401–2
12. *Calendar of Patent Rolls 1569–72* p307
13. SROD/B/Bw/1833. The exact position is difficult to disentangle. The original agreement seems to have been about only a parcel of the tithes but at some point the whole of the rectory became appropriated.
14. SRO D/B/Bw/2427
15. ibid. 2418. The next transfer took place on 21 April 1661.
16. SRO D/B/Bw/1745 and 2412
17. Wyndham, op. cit., and Keeler, op. cit.
18. I have inferred the course of events from the payments recorded in Humphrey Blake's accounts. SRO D/B/Bw/1615
19. Patent Rolls PRO C66/2860/4
20. C.J. vol. ii, p71a
21. *Calendar of the Correspondence of the Smyth Family* p200
22. ibid. p168
23. Fletcher, A. *The Outbreak of the English Civil War* p97 puts the Bridgwater campaign in the context of the campaign against the bishops but he does not really explain how electing Smyth rather than Wroth would help. Pyne's motivation was probably tactical. Smyth could call on a wider spectrum of support. Such an explanation suggests that his original preference for an anti-Arminian campaign sprang from the same roots and that he may have been in favour of 'Root and Branch' long before the London Petition.
24. ibid. p128
25. *HMC 4th Report*, House of Lords Mss, 10 December 1641
26. BL Thomason Tracts (T.T.) 669 f3 No. 44 and *Private Journals of the Long Parliament* vol. ii p465
27. T.T. E200 No. 33
28. *Private Journals* vol. i
29. T.T. E200 No. 33
30. *Private Journals* vol. ii p280
31. T.T. E202 No. 10 and No. 11
32. T.T. E202 No. 31
33. Like many of these stories, this one has to be treated with care. Even if it is true, the dating may be wrong. David Hannay, in his life of the Admiral, repeats the very circumstantial story of the death of Blake's brother, Samuel, at the beginning of the war (pp14–5). Beadon (pp27–8) has since drawn attention to the letter of December 1644, that I quote later, which has Samuel's signature attached to it.
34. L.J. vol. v, p222b
35. Dixon, p27. Ashe's letter is in L.J. vol. v, pp278–9.

36. Dixon, p27
37. SP 28/253A and 300, particularly Part vii

CHAPTER 3   BRISTOL AND LYME   MARCH 1643–JULY 1644   pp 26 to 39

1. Thomason Tracts. E83 No. 13 and Robinson R. *The Sieges of Bristol* p11

2. According to John Adair in his *Roundhead General – A Military Biography* Sir William *Waller* p58, Fiennes had the foot regiments of Essex and Popham, each with 600 men, his own cavalry and three other troops of horse

3. T.T. E104 No. 4. The spelling 'Blaugh' appears in the list of the Committee for Sequestrations of March 1643 and the Committee for the Weekly Assessment of August.

4. T.T. E256 No. 2. I have taken the words 'even now' to mean that the cavalry troop had been with Waller for a considerable time, but it is quite possible to argue, as Powell does, that the men were raised at the same time as the foot regiment for Essex and joined Waller in September 1644 at the rendezvous between Bridgwater and Taunton.

5. Wroughton, John *The Civil War in Bath and North Somerset* pp67–8 and Adair, p71

6. Robinson, pp18–24 contains a detailed account of the efforts Fiennes made to improve the defences. Fiennes' Relation, T. T. E64 No. 12.

7. The main source is a Royalist one, 'the diary of Bernard de Gomme' printed in the *Army History Review* vol. iv, December 1925, pp183–97. There is a brief account by a soldier, Thomas Taylor in T.T. E255 No. 16.

8. T.T. E67 No. 36 – An Answer to Colonel Nathaniel Fiennes' Relation, mentions these men

9. T.T. 255 No. 16. The Trial of Nathaniel Fiennes, 12th Charge and the evidence of Richard Winston a member of the garrison of Brandon Hill Fort. Fiennes seems to have made no answer at all to this charge.

10. This is at best a guess. When Blake arrived is obscure. In his Apology (T.T. E21 No. 34), John Were wrote 'I desire all Devonshire men to consider whether I had not become master of the field as far as Exon., this was done before Lieutenant-Colonel Blake's coming down.' On the other hand, the 300 who came from Waller later, did not land until 11 May, and Blake was certainly there earlier on e.g. the Blewitt incident. The 120 are mentioned in the Proceedings of the Committee of Both Kingdoms for 7 May, *CSPD 1644*, p150 but it is not at all clear whether they were sent or formed part of the later 300. Nor is there any indication of the regiments from which they were drawn. They could have formed part of Alexander Popham's regiment, which was with Waller (see Essex's letter mentioned in Chapter Four).

11. Chapman, Geoffrey *The Siege of Lyme Regis* p11–12

12. How many men there were in Lyme is difficult to work out. A full regiment is 1000 men. If we add Were's 200, Blake's 120, the 300 soldiers landed on the 11 May and the 300 seamen landed by Warwick, we get 1920. But Warwick declared that, even at the height of the siege, the garrison did not exceed 1500 including seamen. The explanation must be that Ceely did not have a full regiment. At Bristol, the regiments of Popham and Thomas Essex numbered no more than 600 each.

13. With the siege of Lyme Regis, Blake's career emerges into the light of day. There is little dispute about his general role but few direct references. The classic account of the siege, based on Edward Drake's diary, can be found in A.R. Bayley's *The Great Civil War in Dorset*. New material has been added in the Rev. J.R. Powell's article, on the siege, in the *Mariner's Mirror* for October 1934 and, more recently, in Geoffrey Chapman's little book, op. cit. note 11. I have preferred Chapman's disposition of the Royalist forces to that of Powell. Otherwise, any differences I have with these accounts are matters of interpretation, not of fact.

14. Chapman, p41

15. The *Mayflower* was one of the most powerful armed merchantmen in the Parliamentary Navy but it is unlikely that she had a demi-cannon as part of her regular equipment so the gun may have been sent by either the Mayor of Poole or the Governor of Portsmouth

CHAPTER 4   TAUNTON   JULY 1644–JULY 1645   pp 40 to 53

1. Burne, A.H. & Young, P. *The Great Civil War* p148

2. Warwick–Committee of Both Kingdoms, on board the *James*, Lyme Road, 1 June; *CSPD 1644* p190. For the extraordinary way in which Essex rationalised his behaviour see Essex–Speaker of the Lords, LJ vol. vi, p602–3.

3. All of this follows the letter of the Earl of Essex to the Committee of Both Kingdoms, dated Tiverton, 10 July 1644, *CSPD 1644* pp335–6. I have preferred his version to that of the Pamphleteers who give all the credit to Blake and do not so much as mention Pye. It does need to be said, however, that the hostility of Essex to anyone having anything to do with Waller was so great that he could have just left out Blake's part.

4. Clarendon, vol. iii, p426

5. Essex's letter, infra, shows what Blake was doing. Logically men raised in Wellington would have responded best to being commanded by Edward Popham, but he was not made a full colonel until the spring of 1645. Most accounts make Blake lieutenant-colonel of Alexander Popham's regiment at the time of his arrival at Lyme Regis, though most of the men from Waller's army appear to have been from Sir Arthur Haslerigg's regiment. (T.T. E312 No. 3).

6. T. T. E256 No.22

7. Clarendon, vol. iii, p426

8. Sir Anthony Ashley Cooper's letter, quoted supra, mentions no defensive works, so I have assumed that the ones mentioned in the dramatic events of May were constructed later than December 1644

9. T.T. E256 No. 22 and E256 No. 39

10. Stevens, D. *War and Peace in West Somerset* 1620–70, p36

11. Green, E. 'Siege and Defence of Taunton', *Somerset Archaeological and Natural History Society* pp36–8

12. e.g. Diary or Exact Journal, T.T. 254 No. 3 only names Blake. Perfect Occurrences T.T. E252 No. 51 does not name any officer. Pye was not mentioned until Vicars wrote his chronicle some months later. T. T. E312 No. 3.

13. Perfect Occurrences T.T. E256 No. 22

14. *CSPD 1644–5* p124

15. *CSPD 1644–5* p102 and pp114–15

16. ibid. p124; Waller–Committee of Both Kingdoms, 14 November

17. Diary or Exact Journal, T.T. E21 No. 1

18. Ludlow, E. *Memoirs* vol. i, p135; Scottish Dove, T.T. E21 No. 17 and Mercurius Britannicus, T.T. E21 No. 8

19. Perfect Passages, T.T. E21 No. 26

20. Sir Anthony Ashley Cooper, Earl of Essex *HMC Portland* vol. i, p197

21. Wyndham–Prince Rupert, 6 January 1645, Chard; B.M.Add.Mss. 18, 982 f3b

22. ibid.

23. T.T. E24 No. 10

24. Perfect Passages T.T. E25 No. 17

25. Mercurius Civicus T.T. E26 No. 13

26. Scottish Dove T.T. E26 No. 2

27. London Post T.T. E25 No. 13

28. T.T. E269 No. 3

29. T.T. E269 No. 14

30. T.T. E270 No. 29

31. Cooper–Essex, *HMC Portland* vol. i, p197

32. Committee of Both Kingdoms–Manchester, 14 November 1644; *CSPD 1644–5*, p124

33. Weekly Account, 1–8 January 1645, T.T. E24 No. 7. Committee of Both Kingdoms–Colonel Weldon, 8 January 1645, *CSPD 1644–5* p239.

34. Adair, 182; C.J. vol. iv, p67b for 4 March. 'They are commanded into the West all excuses set aside.'
35. Numbers vary. One account puts the Royalists at 8000, another at as little as 4–5000. But most estimate in region of 6000, e.g. Clarendon vol. iv, pp14–5; Sir John Culpepper–King, 11 May 1645 *CSPD 1644–5* p478; Weekly Account T.T. E288 No. 2.
36. Mercurius Aulicus, 23–30 March 1645. T.T. E278 No. 2.
37. Grenville's wounding, The Weekly Account T.T. E278 No. 23 and The Scottish Dove, T.T. E278 No. 31. The taking–Moderate Intelligencer T.T. E281 No. 5; Scottish Dove T.T. E281 No. 10 and Kingdom's Weekly Intelligencer, T.T. E279 No. 11
38. Weekly Account T.T. E278 No. 12; A Diary or Exact Journal, T.T. E278 No. 29; The Scottish Dove, T.T. E278 No. 31
39. Weldon–Fairfax, 11 May 1645, LJ vol. vii, p374a–b; Kingdom's Weekly Intelligencer T.T. E282 No. 2 gives the number of people in Taunton; Sir John Culpepper-King, 11 May, *CSPD 1644–5* p478–80; Letter from Weldon's Quarters at Pitminster to Fairfax, 12 May, T.T. E284 No. 11; E. Green, pp41–4. There is some disagreement about the food situation. One source says there was a general shortage, another that only horse meat was in short supply. It seems that the castle had plenty but the town did not.
40. T.T. E284 No. 11; Scottish Dove, T.T. E285 No. 9
41. Gardiner, S.R. *History of the Great Civil War* vol. ii, pp206–7
42. A Brief narrative of the Relief of Taunton, T.T. E285 No. 10
43. Sir E. Nicholas–George, Lord Digby, 12 May, *CSPD 1644–5* p483
44. Scottish Dove T.T. E285 No. 9
45. T.T. E284 No. 11; Culpepper–(Digby), Bristol, 16 May, *CSPD 1644–5* p493
46. *CSPD 1644–5* pp525–6
47. Parliament's Post 13–30 May 1645, T.T. E284 No. 22 reports Massey's appointment. The Ordinance was passed 24 May, L.J. vol. vii, p393a–b. Lloyd is described as Governor of Gloucester in a letter dated 26 May, op. cit. note 47. *CSPD 1644–5* p595; Moderate Intelligencer, 19–26 June 1645, T.T. E289 No. 17.
48. T.T. E285 No. 3
49. Clarendon vol. iii, p49. Parliamentary accounts try to pass the matter off as a skirmish but it is clear that Weldon had a narrow escape.
50. ibid. p50
51. Letter from Bridgwater to the King, *CSPD 1644–5* p581
52. For Fairfax's movements see Burne, A.H. & Young, P. *The Great Civil War* p210 and Wilson, J. *Fairfax*, pp76–8

CHAPTER 5   THE VICTORS QUARREL   JULY 1645–DECEMBER 1648   pp 54 to 63

1. True Informer, T.T. E293 No. 12 carries the Christabella Wyndham incident. Other accounts can be found in Mercurius Civicus, ibid. No. 24; L.J. vol. vii, p511b; *HMC Portland* vol. iii, p138; *HMC 7th Report* p451b Sir H. Verney Mss.
2. Hannay, pp14–15
3. *Somerset Archaeological and Natural History Society Proceedings* vol. v, 1854, p12
4. Massey's movements, August–September 1645, can be traced through the newspapers in T.T. E295–301
5. T.T. E304, Nos. 8, 9, 11 and 18
6. True Informer T.T. E309 No. 17
7. Perfect Passages, T.T. E314, No. 20; Weekly Account, ibid. No. 28; Scottish Dove, T.T. E316 No. 2.; Mercurius Civicus, ibid. No. 9
8. Gardiner vol. iii, pp59–60
9. Stevens, p58. Perfect Passages, T.T. E323 No. 15; A Diary or Exact Journal, ibid. No. 18; Mercurius Civicus, ibid. No. 20; Perfect Occurrences, No. 22.
10. Gardiner, vol. iii, pp65–9

11. Copy of a Letter from Sir Thomas Fairfax's Quarters, 30 March 1646, T.T. E330 No. 20

12. T.T. E333 No. 2

13. ibid. No. 13

14. ibid. No. 23

15. Four Strong Castles taken, T.T. E334 No. 8; Stevens, p61

16. *Calendar of ... the Committee for the Advance of Money* vol. ii, p815

17. Firth, Sir C.H. & Rait, R.S. *Acts and Ordinances of the Interregnum* vol. i, p116

18. ibid. p235

19. ibid. p460

20. Underdown, D. *Pride's Purge* Appendix, p368. Account of Edward Ceely for 1646 in SRO D/Bw is countersigned by Humphrey Blake as Mayor.

21. CJ vol. iv, p286b

22. Problems propounded to the Cavaliers T.T. E343 No. 6

23. Underdown, D. *Somerset in the Civil War and Interregnum* p146

24. Clarendon vol. vi, p37

25. T.T. E285 No. 10. See also E284 No. 7; E282 No. 2; E285 No. 10.

26. *HMC Egmont* vol. i, p297–300

27. LJ vol. ix, p172a–b

28. CJ vol. iv, p28b 25 December 1646

29. Introduced 14 January 1647, ibid.

30. Text SRO D/B/Bw/1833

31. CJ vol. iv, p103a, 2 March 1647 and ibid. p115b, 17 March 1647

32. Willis's connection with the Clubmen is made clear by the later documents

33. T.T. E300 No. 13

34. Willis's attack on the County Committee is dated 14 July 1646 and is in T.T. E345 No. 3. The Scottish Dove for the 22–31 July 1646 also carries an account of discontents in Somerset which coincides with the presence of Jephson's regiment. Willis was also the author of Time's Whirligig of 9 February 1646/7 in T.T. E374 No. 10. For the whole controversy see Underdown *Somerset in the Civil War and Interregnum* pp138–43.

35. T.T. E430 No. 16

36. *HMC 8th Report* Earl of Jersey Mss contains the accounts for September 1656–September 1657. One item runs '£3815–16s–0d to Collonel Robert Blake for his personal pay for his land service in England.'

37. C.J. vol. v, p485a

38. C.J. vol. iv, p217b, 19 June 1647; List of Officers with the Lines of Communications

39. ibid. p278a

40. 9 February 1648; T.T. E430 No. 16

41. A criticism of Popham's behaviour along these lines can be found in T.T. E457 No. 19; see also ibid. No. 21

42. C.J. vol. v, p569b

43. ibid. p593a

44. The date of his reappointment is not recorded but he was in charge again by 19 August 1648 because a pamphlet of that date includes him in a list of M.P.s who also held military commands. T.T. E458 No. 12. A rebuttal contained in T.T. E462 No. 1 confirms that Blake was not claiming his pay.

45. C.J. vol. vi, p34

46. ibid. p67a

CHAPTER 6   IRELAND   1649   pp 67 to 80

1. For more details see Baumber, M.L. 'The Navy during the Civil Wars and the Commonwealth', M.A. thesis, University of Manchester, 1967, pp217–47

2. This is the committee described by William Reid FSA, in his article, 'Commonwealth Supply

Departments within the Tower and the Committee of London Merchants', *Guildhall Miscellany* vol. ii, pp319–52. He does not recognise that the Richard Hutchinson, at whose house most of the meetings were held, was Vane's deputy as Treasurer of Navy and succeeded him in 1650, nor that the non-voting members were the other Navy Commissioners. He provides much fascinating information but I cannot agree with his praise of the committee's activities.

3. Walton reported the appointment of the three Generals-at-Sea on 12 February 1649, C.J. vol. vi, p138. The regularity of his attendance is shown by the committee book, Bodleian, Rawlinson A224.

4. For those interested in the semantics, Walton's report gives the order Richard Deane, Robert Blake and Edward Popham. The Act appointing them adopts the sequence Robert Blake, Edward Popham and Richard Deane (*CSPD 1649–50*, p17) but on 26 February, the Council of State, issuing their Commission, laid down the seniority as Edward Popham, Robert Blake and Richard Deane (ibid. pp19–20). None of the documents puts Blake in the traditional third place.

5. *Pride's Purge* p368 for Blake and p383 for the Pophams
6. L.J. vol. x, p116. He was down for the *Swallow*.
7. *CSPD 1648–9*, p195 and p201
8. *HMC Leyborne–Popham* p38
9. Shilton, Dorothy and Holworthy, Richard *High Court of Admiralty Examinations* 1637–8, p545. The Plymouth Customs book for 1631–3, under the date 24 November 1633, describes a cargo of deals, iron work and beams belonging to him, on the *Matthew of Plymouth* from Gothenburg. PRO E190/1033/26.
10. *CSPD 1649–50* p48 and Deane & Blake – Council of State; *Letters* p20
11. Rawlinson A224 f26, 24 February 1649
12. *CSPD 1649–50* p34
13. *The Discourses of John Hollond* pp126–7
14. *CSPD 1649–50* p42
15. ibid. p40
16. ibid. p27 and T.T. E527 No. 104 and E529 No. 21; also *Letters* p39
17. Firth Sir C.H. & Rait R.S. *Acts and Ordinances of the Interregnum* vol. ii, p66
18. *CSPD 1649–50* p61
19. ibid. p35 and pp39–40
20. ibid. p134
21. *Letters* pp29–30; Act reported 14 April, see C.J. vol. vi, p186b
22. *HMC Leyborne–Popham* p11
23. *CSPD 1649–50* pp119–20; Popham's letter in Tanner vol. 56 No. 9, f16
24. *Letters* p37
25. ibid. pp72–3
26. *Letters* p44
27. ibid. p72
28. *HMC Leyborne–Popham* p17 and *CSPD 1649–50*, p193
29. ibid. p18 and *Letters* pp71–2
30. ibid. pp21–2 and *Letters* pp73–4
31. ibid. p42
32. ibid. pp25–6
33. ibid. pp34–5
34. ibid.
35. ibid. p38
36. *CSPD 1649–50* p326
37. *Letters* p46. The ships are worked out by elimination.
38. ibid. p47; *HMC Leyborne–Popham* p43
39. Cary, H. *Memorials of the Civil Wars* pp189–97
40. Tanner vol. 56 No. 68, f137
41. *CSPD 1649–50* p425

CHAPTER 7   PORTUGAL   1650   PP 81 TO 93

1. *CSPV* vol. xxviii, p35. Morosini–Doge & Senate, 8 Jan 1650

2. *CSPD 1649–50* pp483–5 Additional Instructions for the Generals of the Fleet for the Southern Expedition are dated 17 Jan 1650

3. *Constant Reformation, Swallow* and *Convertine*

4. *HMC Leyborne–Popham* p42

5. *Letters of Blake* pp78–80; John Hastock–Capt. T. Harrison, from aboard the *Bonadventure*, Lisbon river, 28 March 1650

6. ibid. pp78–80 (see note 5); pp54–5 Blake–King of Portugal, 10 March 1650; pp56–8, Blake–Generals of the Fleet, 30 March 1650; pp81–5, Letter from Captain Thorowgood

7. *CSPD 1650* p7; Jane Short–Thomas Short (at La Rochelle) 20 February 1650

8. See note 6

9. Camden Society 3rd Series vol. x, Prince Rupert at Lisbon, appendices B, C and D, pp12–17

10. *Letters* Blake–Generals of the Fleet, 30 March 1650

11. Camden Society 3rd series vol. x, Prince Rupert at Lisbon, Appendix E, pp17–20; and *CSPD 1650*, pp115–6

12. *Letters* pp74–6

13. ibid. pp76–8; Agreement between Charles Vane and Lord John Mendes de Vasconcellas

14. ibid. Blake–Generals of the Fleet, 30 March 1650

15. ibid. Hastock–Harrison, 28 March 1650

16. ibid. pp85–6

17. ibid. pp55–6; Blake–Charles Vane, 29 March 1650

18. Dating of the event differs. *Letters* say 6 or 7 June; Corbett, Sir J.S. *England in the Mediterranean* vol. i, p181 gives 16 May. R.C. Anderson in his article in M.M. 1931, p143 makes it 21 May. I have taken the view that it was before the arrival of Popham on 26 May. Otherwise he would have seized the entire fleet.

19. *HMC Leyborne–Popham* p64; *CSPD 1650* pp99–100 has the *Crescent* for the *Great Lewis*. The *Crescent* was lost off Guernsey during April. Captains are from the Fleet list in C.J. vol. vi, p325.

20. *HMC Leyborne–Popham* p65

21. *CSPD 1650* pp102–4

22. See note 20

23. *HMS Leyborne–Popham* p74; Popham–his wife, 27 May 1650

24. *CSPD 1650* p200; Popham–Sir Henry Vane, junior, 12 June 1650

25. *HMC Leyborne–Popham* p67; Popham's Journal

26. ibid. p68

27. *Letters*, letter from Captain Thorowgood

28. Arrived at after subtracting ships known to be absent

29. M.M. 1931, p148

30. Warburton, C. *Prince Rupert and the Cavaliers* vol. ii, p309. Pilchar is Cape Espichel

31. M.M. 1934, p109; Popham–Sir Henry Vane, junior, 14 August 1650

32. *Letters* pp60–3 and pp87–9

33. See note 31

34. *Letters* p62

35. ibid. and M.M. 1931, p149

36. ibid. pp63–5; Blake–Council of State, 14 October 1650

37. Gardiner S.R. (ed) *Letters and Papers relating to the First Dutch War* vol. i, p134

38. See note 36

39. Blake–Council of State, *Letters* p65

40. *Letters* pp63–9

41. Reminiscences of Richard Gibson, F.D.W. vol i, pp7–8

42. *Letters* pp69–70, Blake–Council of State, 5 December 1650; ibid. p90, Saltonstall–Coytmor, 22 November 1650; *Calendar of Clarendon State Papers* vol. ii, p86, Goulding–Cottington & Hyde. Saltonstall names the ship captured as the *Roebuck*. Other accounts show that this is a mistake. The *Roebuck* was captured by the *Tiger* presumably somewhere in the Channel and was at Plymouth on 30 October 1650.

43. Blake–King of Spain, 7 November 1650, *Letters* pp67–8

44. Officers at Cartagena–Cottington and Hyde *Calendar of Clarendon State Papers* vol. ii, p86

45. See Blake–Council of State, 5 December 1650 *Letters* pp69–70

46. Corbett, Op. Cit.

47. C.J. vol. vi, p534a

CHAPTER 8   THE SCILLIES AND JERSEY   1651   pp 94 to 105

1. *HMC Leyborne–Popham* p83, Popham's Journal, 10 April 1651; *CSPD 1651* p134, Council of State–Capt. Lionel Lane (of the *Victory*), 7 April 1651; ibid. pp140–1, Council of State, Days Proceedings, 10 April 1651

2. Rawlinson A225, p99 Committee of Admiralty, 24 April 1651 gives the list; ibid. p49 for the statement under 14 Jan. 1651

3. Rawlinson A225, p78; 15 March 1651; ibid. p80; 20 March 1651

4. T.T. E384. No. 4.

5. The account of the preliminaries to the Scilly operation is drawn from the article in M.M. vol. xx, 1934, p50ff

6. Rawlinson A225, p92, has an instruction directed initially to Popham to arrange their exchange

7. *CSPD 1651* pp123–4

8. *CSPD 1651* p86 and p108

9. Rawlinson A225 pp88–9, 2 April 1651

10. The list in CJ vol. vi, p526, 25 February, lists Ayscue's ships but A225, p49 shows that the *James* had been replaced by the *Malaga* merchant on 14 Jan.

11. T.T. E384, No. 34

12. M.M. vol. xx, 1934, pp62–3; *Letters* pp112–5

13. T.T. E385 No.12

14. CJ vol. vi, p526

15. T.T. E875 No. 24

16. *Nicholas Papers* vol. i, p251; Down–Nicholas, 13 May 1651

17. Account of Joseph Lereck; *Letters* p120

18. ibid.

19. See rival accounts of Joseph Lereck and a Private hand in *Letters* p120 and p130

20. ibid. p123

21. ibid.

22. Tromp's Journal in M.M. vol. xx, 1934

23. *Letters* pp99–104

24. *Nicholas Papers* vol. i, p251

25. *CSPD 1651* p312; 10 August 1651

26. *Letters* pp105–6

27. ibid. *CSPD 1651* p357

28. ibid. p379

29. ibid. pp396–7

30. This combines the list of the winter guard CJ vol. vii, pp32–3 with the list given in Add.Mss. 22, 546 f43. The Captain of the *Tresco* is called George Blake in CJ and Captain Blake in Add. Mss. There are two Georges: one Blake's brother, a merchant in Plymouth, who survived the Restoration and the other, his nephew, son of Samuel. However Blake's will contains a bequest to a Thomas Blake, son of his cousin William Blake, once commander of the *Tresco* frigate, deceased.

31. *Letters* p111
32. ibid. p136; Hilliard–Clarke
33. ibid.
34. Ellis, M.F. *The Channel Islands and the Great Rebellion* p228
35. *Calendar of Clarendon State Papers* vol. ii, p1
36. ibid. pp228–9
37. *Letters* p136
38. Ellis, p230
39. There are accounts of the landing in Ellis, pp230–1 and in the *Letters* from Blake himself (pp111–2), Hilliard (pp136–40) and two anonymous hands (pp140–2). Also pp113–29
40. Ellis, p232

CHAPTER 9   REPUTATION AND REALITY   1652   pp 109 to 120

1. The figures are taken from Oppenheim, M *The Administration of the Royal Navy 1558–1600*. He estimates the English total at the beginning of 1652 as 80 (p306) and six more were added before the outbreak of war. He lists all acquisitions between 1649 and 1660 on p330ff.

2. Parker, G. 'Why the Armada Failed' *History Today* May 1988, pp26–33. Later references to 'recent research' are drawn from this article.

3. Elias, J.E. *Vlootbouw in Nederlands, 1595–1655*. All the Dutch details come from his book, particularly pp40–97 unless otherwise stated.

4. Gardiner, S.R. (ed) *Letters and Papers relating to the First Dutch War*, vol. i, pp260–6

5. ibid. vol. ii, pp146–7

6. See the reproduction of van de Velde's drawing

7. C.J. vol. vii, p69

8. Oppenheim, p341

9. PRO WO 47/2 9 March 1652. Gunnery establishment for the Foresight.

10. Tanner, J.R. (ed) *Tracts of Sir William Monson* vol. iv, p37

11. Elias, p157

12. Geoffrey Parker's contention that the galeasses were only intended to fire one round, at close quarters, is confirmed by the Instructions quoted later. It is difficult therefore to understand why the ships had so much shot on board when they were wrecked or reached home. See *The Military Revolution* Cambridge, 1988, p94.

13. McGowan, A.P. (ed) *The Jacobean Commissions of Inquiry 1608 and 1618*. NRS vol. 116, p289

14. Waters, Lieut. Commander D.W. 'The Elizabethan Navy and the Armada Campaign', M.M. vol. xxxv, 1949, pp90–135

15. Foster Sir W. (ed) *English Factories in India 1624–9* p49. Broadside firing is noted earlier. It is mentioned within the Spanish instructions for the Armada but it is made clear that only one was to be fired at the beginning of the battle, presumably because the guns would be difficult to reload once the fighting had begun. Broadside firing in this sense is clearly older than the Armada. Parker produces a number of examples from fighting in the East but does not make it clear whether brass or iron guns were being used. Or did da Gama have truck carriages in 1502? *The Military Revolution*, pp93–4

16. Monson, vol. iv, pp93–5

17. F.D.W. vol. i, pp19–20 and Spalding, T.E. *Life of Richard Badiley* pp140–3

18. T.T. E325 No. 7

19. T.T. E340 No. 31

20. The Downs victory took place in 1639 but I have assumed that this was the battle intended and that the date 1640 is a slip

21. F.D.W. vol. i, pp7–8

22. ibid. pp12–13. Gibson says quite clearly that incident took place just before the war started.

Contrast this with the strictures on Taylor for not risking his ship in the shoal-infested waters of Flanders, p131.

CHAPTER 10   THE SKIRMISH OFF DOVER AND THE SHETLAND
EXPEDITION   MAY–JULY 1652   pp 121 to 134

1. CJ vol. vii, p69
2. This analysis is based on an article by Jonathan Israel in *History Today* July 1988, pp17–22. The book for which the article is a trailer, has not yet been published.
3. Gardiner, S.R. *History of the Commonwealth and Protectorate* vol. i, pp97–8 and p114
4. Board of Admiralty of Zeeland–States General, 4 February 1652 F.D.W. vol i, pp75–9; Dutch Ambassadors–State General, 5 February 1652, ibid. pp79–80
5. Extract from a Resolution of the States General, 22 February 1652, ibid. p85
6. First mentioned 23 January 1652, ibid. pp72–3
7. Instructions to Lieutenant-Admiral Tromp, 30 April, ibid. pp155–9
8. Tromp–States General, 20 May, ibid. pp196–9; Rear-Admiral Bourne's Relation, 29 May; ibid. pp250–6
9. See note 8
10. Letter from Dover, F.D.W. vol. i, pp192–4
11. Examinations before the Lord General and Denis Bond, ibid. pp209–14
12. See note 11
13. Tromp–States General, 20 May 1652, F.D.W. vol i, pp196–9
14. Young–Speaker of the Commons, Plymouth Sound, 14 May 1652, ibid. pp178–81
15. See notes 14 and 15
16. Experiences of Richard Gibson. F.D.W. vol. i, pp8–9
17. Instructions to Lieutenant-Admiral Tromp, see notes 7 and 8
18. Gibson, F.D.W. vol. i, pp9–11. Blake–Speaker, 20 May, *Letters* pp158–9
19. Accounts of Blake, see note 18. Bourne, see note 8, and the two captured Dutch captains examined by the Lord General and Bond, see note 11
20. Gibson, op. cit.
21. Blake–Speaker, see note 18
22. Bourne, see note 8
23. Examinations, see note 11, Tromp–States General see note 8
24. Bourne, see note 8
25. Gibson, see note 18
26. Blake–Coytmor, 29 May, *Letters*, p160
27. Tromp–States General, 20 May, F.D.W. vol. i, pp196–9; Statement by 40 Dutch captains, 23 May, ibid. pp218–21; Declaration by 14 Officers of the *Brederode*, 4 June, ibid. p276–8; Tromp–Dutch Ambassadors in London, 6 June, ibid. p281–5
28. Report by Tromp–States General, 3 May 1652, F.D.W. vol. i, p159–60
29. Gardiner *Commonwealth and Protectorate* vol. ii, p119
30. Orders of the Council of State, 7 June, F.D.W. vol. i, p286–8
31. Further Instructions from the Council of State–General Blake, 10 June, F.D.W. vol. i, p301–2
32. Tromp–States General, 2 July, F.D.W. vol. i, p338–9
33. Navy Commissioners–Blake, 1 June, F.D.W. vol. i, pp267–8 shows that Ayscue had reached Plymouth by that date
34. Penn, Granville *Memorials of Sir William Penn* vol. i, p152. List included *Resolution* and *James* but the former went with Blake and the latter was under repair.
35. Ayscue–Earl of Pembroke and Montgomery, 3 July, F.D.W. vol. i, p341–3 Orders of the Council of State, ibid. p344
36. A Journal of the Movements of the Fleets in the Downs, 13 July, F.D.W. vol. i, p369–71 gives Tromp's numbers as 102 plus 10 fire ships. Tromp gives them as 96, 3 galliots and 10 fireships.

37. Orders of the Council of State, 7 July, F.D.W. vol. i, p352
38. Tromp–States General, 6 July, F.D.W. vol. i, pp365–8
39. Tromp–States General, 12 July, F.D.W. vol. i, p369–71; Journal of Movements, see note 36
40. States General–Tromp, 4 July, F.D.W. vol. i, p345
41. Gibson's account, F.D.W. vol. i, p17–18, List of Dutch ships taken off Shetland, ibid. p383; Letter from General Blake's fleet, 26 July, ibid. pp385–6
42. As note 41
43. Council of State–Blake, 10 June, F.D.W. vol. i, p292–3
44. Gibson see note 41
45. Chief Officers–States General, F.D.W. vol. i, p395–9
46. Resolutions of the Officers of Lieutenant Admiral Tromp's fleet, 27 July, F.D.W. vol. i, pp391–3 and see note 45
47. See note 45
48. Curtis C.D. *Blake, General and Admiral at Sea*, p104–7, F.D.W. vol. i, p404
49. Copy of the Resolution of the Chief Officers of Tromp's fleet, 26 July, F.D.W. vol. i, p389–91 and note 45
50. ibid.
51. Account of Lieutenant Admiral Tromp's Voyage, F.D.W. vol. i, p400–6
52. News from Westminster, 16 August, ibid. p410–11, says the Orkneys but this is clearly a mistake
53. See note 38
54. See notes 49 and 51
55. See note 51
56. See note 51

CHAPTER 11   DE RUIJTER IN THE CHANNEL AND KENTISH KNOCK
AUGUST–SEPTEMBER 1652   pp 135 to 150

1. Orders of the Council of State, 19 July 1652, F.D.W. vol. ii, p19–20
2. Letter from Portsmouth, 21 July, ibid. p34–5
3. de Ruijter's Log, 2 August, ibid. p.189 says 42; same–Zeeland Admiralty, 4 August, ibid. p68–9, says 45
4. Another Letter from Plymouth, 17 August, ibid., p107–8. Orders of the Council of State, 16 July, ibid. p16–17.
5. A Letter from Sir George Ayscue's fleet, 30 July, ibid. p55. Sir George Ayscue–Speaker, 31 July, ibid. p56. A Letter from Sir George Ayscue's Fleet, 4 August, ibid. p76–7.
6. Deputies of the Boards of the Admiralty–States General, 5 August, ibid. p71–2. Resolutions of the States General, 6 August, ibid. p77.
7. Log of Commodore de Ruijter, 31 July, ibid. p188
8. Board of Admiralty of Zeeland–States General, 6 August; ibid. p78. Same–same, 8 August, ibid. pp81–6
9. Commodore de Ruijter–States General, 11 August, ibid. p93–4
10. Letter from Plymouth, 17 August, ibid. p105–6
11. Anon–Council of State, 22 August, ibid. p120–2
12. See n. 10 and List of Commodore de Ruijter's fleet, ibid. pp146–7
13. De Ruijter, writing to the Zeeland Admiralty, says that Verhaeff was under his lee. 29 August, ibid. p142–6
14. Account of the Seafight between Ayscue and de Ruijter, ibid. pp147–53
15. See n. 11
16. A Letter from Plymouth, 20 August, F.D.W. vol. ii, pp116–17
17. See n. 14
18. C.J. vol. vii, p69. This *Bonadventure* was an armed merchant man. The State man-of-war of

the same name was serving with Badiley in the Mediterranean. Curiously, the captains of both ships were named Witheridge, one John the other Edward.

19. See n. 11
20. See n. 13
21. ibid.
22. See n. 10, see n. 4, A Letter from Plymouth, 31 August, F.D.W. vol. ii, p158–9, Orders of the Council of State, 14 September, ibid. p173–4
23. See n. 10
24. See n. 13
25. Proceedings of the Council of War of de Ruijter and his officers, 18 August, F.D.W. vol. ii, p111–12. De Ruijter's Log, 19 August, ibid. p197.
26. See n. 16
27. A Letter from Newcastle, 5 August, F.D.W. vol. i, p407. Letter from General Blake's Fleet near Southwold, 12 August, ibid. p96.
28. Council of State–General Blake, 15 August, ibid. p100. Same–same, 18 August, ibid. p110.
29. Letter from General Blake's Fleet, see n. 27. News from London, 19 August, F.D.W. vol. ii, pp113.
30. Blake–Council of State, ibid. p134
31. Blake–Council of State, 26 August, *Letters* pp172–3
32. Council of State–Navy Commissioners, 20 August, F.D.W. vol. ii, p115–16
33. Council of State–Navy Commissioners, 27 August, ibid. pp138–9
34. Same–same, 6 August, ibid. p74–5; Same–Victuallers, 15 August, ibid. p132
35. M.M. vol. xxi, 1935, pp56–60
36. ibid. and News from Dover, 5 September, F.D.W. vol. ii, p166; Roncière C. *Histoire de la Marine Francaise* vol. v, pp190–5
37. Ballhausen C.P. *Die Erste Englische–Hollandische Seekrieg* p346–7
38. Board of Admiralty at Amsterdam–Commodore Verburch, 31 July, F.D.W. vol. ii, p56
39. Resolutions of Commodore de Ruijter and his Council of War, 2 September, ibid. p163
40. Penn, G. *Memorials of Sir William Penn* vol. i, p440
41. ibid.
42. Resolutions of Commodore de Ruijter and his Council of War, 17 September, F.D.W. vol. ii, p181–3
43. See n. 40
44. See n. 42
45. Log of Vice Admiral de With, 22 September, F.D.W. vol. ii, p352
46. Log of Commodore de Ruijter, 26 September, ibid. p293–4
47. Tromp–States General, 6 August, F.D.W. vol. i, p407–8
48. News from Westminster, 16 August, F.D.W. vol. i, p410–11, Same, 18 August, ibid. p411–12
49. A Letter from Yarmouth, 19 August, ibid. p413–5; Letter from Rotterdam, 27 August, F.D.W. vol. ii, p223–4
50. Log of Vice Admiral de With, 2 September, ibid. p340; de With–States General, 3 September, ibid. p231–2
51. De With–States General, 23 September, F.D.W. vol. ii, p252–5 says nine. De Ruijter–same, ibid. p185–7 says ten
52. Log of de Ruijter, 28 September, ibid. p294–5
53. Extract from the Resolutions, 22 February, F.D.W. vol. i, pp85–6; Same, 27 February, ibid. p89–96
54. De Ruijter–Comte de Glarsyes, Calais, 2 August, F.D.W. vol. ii, pp61–2. De With–States General, 25 August, ibid. p220–2.
55. De With–States General, see note 54
56. A Letter from the Hague, 10 September, F.D.W. vol. ii, p235–6

57. For examples of problems with captains see De With–States General, 23 September, ibid. pp252–5. Log of Vice Admiral de With, ibid. p352–5
58. De With–States General, 3 September, ibid, p231–2
59. Log of Commodore de Ruijter, 26 September, ibid. p293–4
60. A Letter from General Blake's Fleet in the Downs, 26 September, ibid. p263–4
61. Blake–Council of State, 2 October, *Letters* pp176–9
62. ibid. and F.D.W. vol. ii, p305–9
63. Captain John Mildmay's Account, 1 October, F.D.W. vol. ii, pp268–72
64. De With simply says he 'made towards the enemy'. Penn says the Dutch were standing to the southward, ibid. pp276–80.
65. 3 October, ibid. pp282–4
66. Log of Vice Admiral de With, 28 September, ibid. p356–8
67. ibid.
68. 2 October, ibid. pp276–80
69. Letter from General Blake's Fleet, 3 October, ibid. p282–4
70. Ballhausen, p376–9
71. See n. 63
72. De Ruijter's Log, ibid. p295–6
73. ibid. and Log of de With, pp356–60
74. Aitzema, L. *Saken van Staet in Oorlogh*, vol. iii, 747, 749, 750 quoted in F.D.W. vol. ii, p302–4; Curtis, C.D. p109–13
75. De With–States General, 13 October, F.D.W. vol. ii, pp329–30
76. See n. 61 and n. 64

CHAPTER 12   DUNGENESS   OCTOBER–DECEMBER 1652   pp 151 to 163

1. See previous chapter
2. Letter from the Hague, 8 October 1652, F.D.W. vol. ii, p311–13. De With–States General, 10 November, F.D.W. vol iii, p53–6; Letter from Amsterdam, 15 October, F.D.W. vol. ii, p367–8
3. Elias, J.E. *Vlootbouw in Nederland in de Eerste Helft der 17e Eeuw 1596–1655* p99
4. ibid. p103. The reader is referred to the discussion in Chapter Nine.
5. Board of Admiralty at Rotterdam–States General, 10 December, F.D.W. vol. iii, p152–4
6. Vlootbouw, p109
7. ibid. p114 et seq
8. C.J. vol. vii, p209b
9. Orders of the Council of State, 6 November and 15 November, F.D.W. vol. iii, p45 and p63–4
10. Letter from the Hague, 8 October, F.D.W. vol. ii, p311–13. Letter from Amsterdam, 8 October, ibid. p313–16, John Bowker–Navy Commissioners, 15 October ibid. p364–5. News from Copenhagen, 20 October, ibid. p384–5. Captain Ball's Voyage, F.D.W. vol. iii, p12–13.
11. Orders of the Council of State, 12 November and 17 November, ibid. p58–9 and p67
12. Worden, B. *The Rump Parliament* pp313–14
13. Bodleian Rawlinson A225, Committee of Admiralty book; author's own analysis
14. Orders of the Council of State, 5 and 6 October, F.D.W. vol. ii, p287–8 and p292–3
15. Orders of the Council of State, 7 October, ibid. p293
16. Orders of the Council of State, 30 October and 6 November, F.D.W. vol. iii, p28–30 and p45
17. Capt. Francis Willoughby–Navy Commissioners, 30 October, ibid. p30
18. Navy Commissioners–Council of State, 24 November, ibid. p73–4
19. ibid.
20. News from Antwerp, 5 November, ibid. p42–4, comments on the folly of the English in putting their fleet into winter quarters

21. Letter from the Hague, 15 October, F.D.W. vol. ii, p365–6
22. Blake–Council of State, Downs, 24 November *Letters* p182–3
23. Blake–Council of State, Downs, 24 November *Letters* p183
24. Tromp–States General, 26 November, F.D.W. vol iii, p78–81
25. 25 November, ibid. p250
26. Florissen's Journal, ibid. p203
27. Order by Tromp, 26 November, ibid. p77
28. Letter from the Fleet, 1 December, ibid. p93–5. A little inflated: Dutch put their strength at 88.
29. Blake–Admiralty Commissioners, 1 December, *Letters* p184–6
30. 30 November, F.D.W. vol. iii, p251–2 and Tromp–States General, 4 December, ibid. p116–20
31. News from the Fleet, ibid. p100–2
32. See note 29
33. Tromp–States General, F.D.W. vol. iii, p116–20
34. ibid.
35. ibid. and see note 29
36. This is my reconstruction of what happened from the material available. See map and note 29.
37. Letter from the Fleet, 1 December, F.D.W. vol iii, pp93–5
38. See note 33
39. News from Dover, 4 December, F.D.W. vol. iii, pp115–6
40. News from the Fleet, 4 December, ibid. pp108–9, and see note 33
41. Blake–Council of State, 4 December *Letters* pp187–8
42. Resolution of Tromp's Council of War, F.D.W. vol. iii, pp154–7
43. De Ruijter's Journal, ibid. p258, shows that he left Dover road on the 19 December
44. Tromp–States General, 26 November, ibid. p78–81
45. See note 33
46. See note 29
47. Deputed Commissioners–Council of State, 9 December, F.D.W. vol. iii, pp147–8 infers that they had been hard at work at least by the previous day
48. Orders of the Council of State, 6 December, ibid. pp125–8
49. Orders of the Council of State, 3 January 1653, ibid. pp337–8
50. Orders of the Council of State, 13 December for examination and 16 December for commitment to the Tower, ibid. pp162–4 and pp173–6. Ordnance return, 27 December, pp315–6. I have followed other writers in regarding Captain Chapman and Captain Chaplin as the same man.
51. Orders of the Council of State, 13 December, see note 50
52. *CSPD 1649–50* p260 and p367. See also Spalding, T.E. *Life and Times of Richard Badiley* p30
53. He commanded the ship in the battle of Kentish Knock
54. Blake transferred from the *Resolution* when it went in for a refit
55. Orders of the Council of State, 29 January 1653, F.D.W. vol. iii, pp418–19
56. Blake–Council of State, 24 November, see note 23
57. Taylor and Chapman were both killed fighting their ships at the battle of Scheveningen. Young and Blake fared better. They returned after the war. Blake commanded the *Gloucester* in the expedition to the West Indies and Young was so far rehabilitated as to command a ship at the battle of Teneriffe. Proof that cowardice or incompetence were not the reasons for their dismissal.
58. See note 29
59. C.J. vol. vii, p221b; Orders of the Council of State, 4 December, F.D.W. vol. iii, pp109–12
60. Nehemiah Bourne–Committee of Admiralty, 19 January 1653, ibid. pp393–6
61. Order of the Committee of Admiralty, 2 February 1653, ibid. p428 shows that all officers are

to be appointed by the State except the boatswain, the carpenter and 1 reformado to act as husband on behalf of the owners

62. Articles of War, 25 December, ibid. pp293–301

63. Oppenheim, M. *Administration of the Royal Navy 1509–1660* p312. The only occasion the author can trace of the death penalty being inflicted was the case of Captain Peter Warren, who was executed for killing one of his crew, and that took place before the issue of the Articles.

CHAPTER 13   REORGANISATION AND PORTLAND   JANUARY–FEBRUARY 1653
pp 164 to 178

1. C.J. vol. vii, p225b, 4 December

2. ibid. and p228a. Also Bodleian Rawlinson A227, Committee of Admiralty Letter Book

3. Resolutions of the Committee of Admiralty, 15 December, vol. iii, pp171–2; Propositions for the Sick and Wounded F.D.W. vol. iii, pp273–6; Orders for Sick and Wounded Men, 20 December, ibid. pp276–7; Committee of Admiralty–Navy Commissioners, 4 January 1653, ibid. pp338–40

4. Council of State–Navy Commissioners, 3 January, ibid. p342

5. Abstract of a Letter from Blake, *Letters* p188

6. Propositions for the Encouragement of Seamen, 20 December, F.D.W. vol. iii, pp273–6

7. Oppenheim, M. *The Administration of the Royal Navy, 1509–1660* p245

8. See note 6

9. Lord General's regiment mentioned 25 November F.D.W. vol. iii, p76. Lord General's and Ingoldsby's regiment, 3 February ibid. p431. 1,200 Orders of the Council of State, 2 February, ibid. pp423–5

10. See note 6

11. *Discourse* pp154–61, for Hollond's view. For discussions see Orders of the Council of State, 4 December, F.D.W. vol. iii, pp109–12; 15 December, ibid. pp168–9; Report of the Committee of Admiralty, 20 December, ibid. pp277–8.

12. Victuallers–Admiralty and Navy Commissioners, 20 December, S.P. 46/114 f42, Council of State–Victuallers, 16 December, F.D.W. vol. iii, p176

13. Orders of the Council of State ibid. pp173–6

14. Copy of the Victuallers Paper, 3 January, SP46/114 f51 shows they were being paid 9d for the extra 4000 for the winter guard

15. Orders of the Council of State, 2 December, F.D.W. vol. iii, pp96–8

16. C.J. vol vii, p225, 4 December

17. e.g. Pett & Bourne–Committee of Admiralty, 16 January, F.D.W. vol. iii, pp383–5; Blake–Secretary of the Committee of Admiralty, 20 January *Letters* pp196–7

18. Oppenheim, p329

19. 13 January, F.D.W. vol. iii, pp373–4

20. Account of Lieutenant Admiral Tromp's Voyage, August 1652, F.D.W. vol. i, pp400–6

21. F.D.W. vol. iv, p367 shows him acting as a Navy Commissioner

22. e.g. Orders of the Council of State, 1 November, F.D.W. vol. iii, p31; 12 November, ibid. pp58–9; 16 November, ibid. p65; Thomas Greene–Navy Commissioners, 20 December, ibid. p280–2; Hatsell–Committee of Admiralty, 14 January, ibid. pp376–8. For Naval stores from Scotland see Orders of the Council of State, 3 January, ibid. pp337–8; Andrew Sandilands–Robert Lilburne, 14 January, ibid. pp367–8; Council of State–Navy Commissioners, F.D.W. vol. iv, pp52–3. For New England, see Order of the Committee for Foreign Affairs, 8 November, F.D.W. vol. iii, p50 and 15 November, ibid. pp64–5.

23. Report on the Ordnance office dated by Gardiner as Dec? 1652, ibid. pp325–7, but it quotes Venn as saying that he was acting for Sir Walter Erle the Lieutenant. Erle lost the office in 1649, so this report is probably much earlier. In 1652 the Lieutenant was Major-General Thomas Harrison. C.J. vol. vii, p124 and 250b, for the discussions. Aylmer, G.M. *The State's Servants* p358, thinks that the abolition of the Lieutenancy was political spite against Harrison.

24. 12 January, F.D.W. vol. iii, p367

25. Blake, Deane and Monck, Committee of Admiralty, 10 February, *Letters* p199
26. 14 January, F.D.W. pp374–5
27. Orders of the Council of State, 24 January, ibid. p406
28. Same, 29 January, ibid. pp418–9
29. 10 February, F.D.W. vol iv, pp34–8
30. ibid. pp20–3
31. Gibson, F.D.W. vol. i, pp14–7
32. Tromp–States General, 22 February, F.D.W. vol. iv, p118
33. F.D.W. vol. iii, pp373–4
34. The *Ruby*'s captain was killed in the battle
35. *Letters* pp206–10
36. See note 32
37. The events of the first day are very difficult to work out. I agree with Powell about the English dispositions. The order of the Dutch attack is more problematical. There is no doubt that Tromp attacked Blake. Many writers make Evertsen attack Penn. His account says that he attacked the English Vice-Admiral, but he also says he and Tromp both attacked Blake's squadron. I have taken that to mean, that he took on Lawson, who was vice-admiral of the Red and not Penn, who was Vice-Admiral of the Fleet. This explanation would go far to obviate the difficulty mentioned by Gardiner because, if Evertsen followed Lawson round Blake's squadron, he would have been to leeward of it. At one point, the Dutch accounts say de Ruijter actually captured an English ship, commanded by a John Bark. There is no English captain of that name but English accounts agree that at one point the *Assistance*, commanded by Captain John Bourne, surrendered to the Dutch only to be recaptured. Bourne was vice-admiral of the Blue, which seems to indicate that de Ruijter was Penn's opponent. Powell does not mention Floriszoon until the Council, but the accounts show that he engaged even before Tromp and ended up far to leeward. His course is uncertain, but I have made him pass between Penn and Blake. He says many of his squadron did not follow him and, if they and de Ruijter had both attacked Penn, that would account for the way in which he was hard pressed in the early part of the battle. Monck's course of action is even more guesswork. My account is based on what was possible, with the wind at North West. The route I have sketched out would bring him into conflict with Evertsen and explain the very heavy casualties on the *Vanguard*.
38. Blake & Deane–Council of State, 27 February, *Letters* p206
39. Letter from on board the *Waterhound*, 21 February, F.D.W. vol. iv, pp88–90
40. Floriszoon's Journal, ibid. pp180–1
41. Evertsen's Journal, ibid. pp188–9
42. ibid.
43. A Relation of the Late Engagement, 20 February; ibid. pp78–84
44. ibid. p80
45. See note 32
46. Evertsen was not actually mentioned but the says he was fighting four miles south of the Isle of Wight, so commanding the northern part of the half moon is a reasonable assumption
47. Evertsen's Journal, 19 February, F.D.W. vol. iv, p190
48. Floriszoon's Journal, 19 February, ibid. pp181–2
49. De Ruijter's Journal, same date, ibid. pp194–7
50. See note 48
51. A Dutch Account, F.D.W. vol. iv, pp69–70
52. See note 39
53. See note 51
54. Tromp–States General, 27 February, F.D.W. vol. iv, p121
55. See note 38
56. See note 54
57. Floriszoon's Journal, 20 February, F.D.W. vol iv, pp183–4
58. Evertsen's Journal, ibid. p190. The English claimed five.

CHAPTER 14   BLAKE ASHORE   FEBRUARY 1653–AUGUST 1656   pp 179 to 191

1. Blackborne–Longland, 14 March 1653, F.D.W. vol. iv, pp227–30
2. Blake and Deane, Council of State, 22 February 1653, *Letters* p204–5. Original among the Marquis of Baths's Mss at Longleat.
3. News from Portsmouth, 27 February, F.D.W. vol. iv, p170
4. Whistler–Council of State, 16 March, ibid. pp231–2
5. Whistler–Vane, 21 March, ibid. pp240–2
6. ibid. pp260–1
7. ibid. pp275–6
8. News from London, 8 April 1653, ibid. pp324–5
9. News from London, 25 March–4 April, ibid. pp233–5
10. Blake–Navy Commissioners, 2 June 1653, *Letters* pp213–4
11. Blake–Navy Commissioners, 2 June, F.D.W. vol. v, pp68–9; Deane and Monck–Admiralty Commissioners, 31 May, ibid. p64–5; Wildey–Same, 2 June, ibid. pp66–8
12. Penn, Granville *Memorials of Sir William Penn* vol. i, p495
13. Lyons–Lord President of the Council, 4 June, ibid. pp496–8
14. The story is not a contemporary one. Early reports were confused, some reporting that it was Monck who was killed, not Deane. The incident is first mentioned in Colliber, S. *Columna Rostrata* p124, published in 1727.
15. Cromwell–Penn, 9 July, F.D.W. vol. v, pp266–7
16. Monck–Same, 5 July, ibid. pp255–6
17. Blackborne–Same, 6 July, ibid. pp258–60
18. Monck–Same, 8 July, ibid. pp262–3
19. Advertisements from London, ibid. pp291–2
20. News from London, ibid. pp339–40
21. Monck–Admiralty Commissioners, 23 July, ibid. pp313–5
22. Blake & Monck–Admiralty Commissioners, 28 June, *Letters* p233
23. Blake–Committee of Admiralty *Letters* p280
24. F.D.W. vol. iv, pp262–72
25. Monck and Blake–Admiralty Commissioners, 4 June *Letters* pp215–6; Tromp–States General, 4 June, F.D.W. vol. v, pp73–5
26. See Scheveningen picture
27. e.g. Joseph Cubitt–Blackborne, 2 August, F.D.W. vol. v, pp367–71
28. ibid. p264
29. Cubitt gives the best account of the behaviour of the captains. See note 27.
30. Beverning–States General, 5 August, F.D.W. vol. v, pp389–90 gives a list of English captains killed and wounded
31. News from London, 29 April 1653, F.D.W. vol. iv, pp384–5
32. This account is taken from Woolrych, A. *From Commonwealth to Protectorate* particularly pp280–7 and 322–3
33. *Clarke Papers* vol. iii Appendix B, pp203–8, gives Mountagu's notes, which show the Machiavellian attitude to the Protector's council in all its starkness

CHAPTER 15   RETURN TO THE MEDITERRANEAN
SEPTEMBER 1654–OCTOBER 1655   pp 195 to 210

1. *CSPD 1654* p200–1
2. ibid. p228, Commissioner Peter Pett–Admiralty Commissioners, Chatham, 29 June 1654
3. Birch, T. (ed) *Letters and State Papers of John Thurloe* vol. ii, p391, RW–M. de Fernes (in Paris), 22 June, (intercepted)
4. The launching dates are drawn from Oppenheim, M. *The Administration of the Royal Navy, 1509–1660* pp330–5. Powell puts all the nine ships in his list below the 4th rate into the 5th rate

(p254). Sir Julian Corbett in *England in the Mediterranean* (vol. i, p283, note) gives only six, dividing them between the 5th and 6th rates. He omits the *Pearl*, *Hope* flyboat and *Merlin* galley, all of which figure in operations. His total is twenty-four but the *Nonsuch*, *Hope* and *Merlin* were probably considered too small to figure in the total. I have therefore adopted Powell's total but described them all simply as 'smaller' ships.

5. *Letters* pp283–4, Blake–Admiralty Commissioners

6. Navy Records Society, vol. 92, Naval Miscellany contains as one item *The Journal of John Weale*. Pack is on p89 and the affair of the lieutenant on p91

7. See for example, letters from Longland to Thurloe of 23 June, in *Thurloe* vol. ii, pp392–3; 7 July, ibid. pp432–3; 14 July, ibid. pp447–8; 21 July, ibid. p477; 28 July, ibid. p494; 4 August, ibid. pp517–8; 11 August, ibid. pp534–5

8. Corbett vol. i, p286

9. Weale, p93. I have preferred his list to Wilson who substitutes the *Merlin* for the *Maidenhead* because he mistakenly refers to the *Dolphin* as a victualling ship

10. ibid. and *CSPD 1654* p572; Wilson–Admiralty Commissioners, 15 November

11. *Weale* p93

12. ibid.

13. ibid. pp93–4

14. ibid. p94 under the date 8 November

16. ibid.

16. See note 12 and *Weale* p95

17. ibid. p96

18. ibid. pp96–7

19. *Thurloe* vol. ii, p603. A Letter of Intelligence forecasts the date. ibid. p634, shows Longland knew that Guise had sailed on 29 September. For Guise's tribulations see Corbett vol. i, pp286–7 and p289.

20. *Thurloe* vol. iii, p12; Longland–Thurloe, 8 December

21. *Thurloe* vol. iii, pp27–8, Letter of Intelligence, 16 December, and ibid. p48, another Letter, 27 December. Corbett vol. i, p291.

22. *Weale* p98

23. ibid.

24. ibid. p96–7

25. *Thurloe* vol. iii, pp232–3, Blake–Thurloe, Cagliari, 14 March 1655

26. *CSP Venetian, 1655–6* p10, p19 and p29

27. *Letters* pp286–8, Blake–Admiralty and Navy Commissioners, Leghorn Road, 19 January 1655

28. The background material, both here and later, is taken from Corbett vol. i, pp294–9

29. ibid. p301

30. *Weale*, pp101–2

31. ibid. p103

32. See note 27 and *Weale* p109

33. *Weale* p103

34. *Letters* pp288–90, Blake–Committee of Admiralty & Navy, 14 March 1655, Cagliari

35. ibid.

36. ibid.

37. *Letters* pp294–6, Blake–Thurloe, Cagliari, 18 April

38. *Weale* p108

39. ibid.

40. *Letters* pp317–18; A Letter from on board the *Plymouth*

41. The *Ruby* was with the fleet the whole time, but the *Diamond* was one of the ships sent to get victuals. However, her instructions do say that she was to take on board any bread collected by the other four ships and bring it to the fleet, so she may have returned.

42. *Weale* pp108–9

43. ibid.
44. There is an excellent description of the process in Howarth, David *The Men-of-War* p94 though he attributes its introduction to Stayner at Teneriffe
45. T.T. E787 No. 8
46. Corbett vol. i, p307
47. ibid.
48. *Weale*, p110
49. ibid. pp111–12 and *Letters* p314, Blake–Navy Commissioners, 13 October 1655
50. *Letters* pp296–8, Blake–Admiralty and Navy Commissioners, off Cadiz, 12 June 1655
51. *Weale* p114
52. ibid. p106, 20 March 1655
53. See note 52
54. ibid.
55. *Weale* p115
56. See note 55 and *Thurloe* vol. iii, p547, Protector–Blake, 13 June 1655
57. *Letters* pp299–300, Blake–Protector, Lagos, 4 July 1644
58. *Weale* p115
59. ibid. p117 and letter in note 57 was from Lagos
60. *Letters* p298, Blake–Protector, 12 June 1655
61. *Thurloe* vol. iii, p547
62. *Weale* p118
63. *Thurloe* vol. iii, p694, Captain Eustace Smyth-Blake, 4 August 1644
64. *Weale* p121
65. ibid. p122
66. ibid.
67. *Letters* pp306–10, Blake–Protector, 30 August 1655
68. Abbott, W.C. *Letters and Speeches of Oliver Cromwell* vol. iii, p311
69. *Weale*, p123
70. The letters Blake complains he had no answer to are dated 4 and 6 July 1655 and listed as numbers 242–50 in *Letters* pp299–305
71. See note 67
72. ibid.
73. ibid. and *Letters* p311, Blake–Stokes, 1 September 1655
74. *Weale* p124
75. *Letters* p313, Blake–Cobham and Blake–Vallis dated 22 September aboard the *George* at sea
76. *Weale* p124
77. *Weale* p125
78. The *Nantwich* was driven off station by the Spanish fleet and came into Plymouth. She was sent out again immediately with letters and fell in with the *Hampshire* on 3 October
79. *Thurloe* vol. iv, p31, Instructions to victuallers, 13 September 1655 and *CSPD 1655* p359, Captain Robert Clarke–Governor of Lagos, 30 September 1655

CHAPTER 16   THE SPANISH BLOCKADE   NOVEMBER 1655–SEPTEMBER 1656
pp 211 to 224

1. Petition to the Admiralty Commissioners, 18 August 1654, BL Add.Mss.18,986 f176; Council of State, Day's Proceedings 13 March 1656, gives the appointment of Prize commissioners; Humphrey Blake was to be Treasurer. *CSPD 1655–6* pp223–4.
2. Resolutions at a Council of War on board the *Swiftsure*. T.T. 669 f19 no. 32; Humble Petition of the Seamen to the Protector, 4 November 1654; T.T. 669 f10 no.33.
3. Council of State, Day's Proceedings, 8 November 1654, *CSPD 1654* p395
4. *Thurloe* vol. iii, p147

5. Gardiner, S.R. *History of the Commonwealth and Protectorate*, vol. iii, pp459–70

6. *CSPD 1655–6* pp137–8, 25 January 1656

7. ibid. pp92–3

8. Gardiner, S. R. *History of the Commonwealth and Protectorate*, vol. iii, p467

9. Mountagu–Thurloe, 2 March 1656, Stokes Bay, *Letters* pp392–4

10. T. Ross–Secretary Nicholas, 11 July 1656, *CSPD 1656–7* pp17–18

11. Nieuport–States General, 4 January 1656, *Thurloe* vol. iv, p388

12. John Crewe–Mountagu, 7 January, Carte 73 f16 (in Bodleian) and Nieuport–States General, 8 February; *Thurloe* vol. iv, p521

13. Blake–Thurloe, Cagliari, 14 March 1654, *Letters* pp291–3

14. Blake and Mountagu–Admiralty Commissioners, 10 March 1656, ibid. p342

15. T.T. E492 No. 6

16. Mountagu–Thurloe, 10 March 1656, *Letters* pp396–7

17. Anderson, R.C. 'Lists of Blake's Fleets' in M.M. vol. 24 No. 4, 1938, pp429–33

18. *Weale* p130–1

19. ibid.

20. Mountagu–Thurloe, 15 April 1656, *Letters* pp399–401. Thomas Pointer–Navy Commissioners, 16 April, ibid. pp431–2

21. ibid. and *Weale* p132

22. Blake and Mountagu–Admiralty Commissioners, Tangier, 9 May, *Letters* p347–9. Mountagu–Thurloe, 29 May, ibid. pp404–8

23. Blake and Mountagu–Admiralty Commissioners, Plymouth Sound, 18 March 1656, ibid. pp346–7

24. *Weale* p133

25. Navy Commissioners–Admiralty Commissioners, 27 September 1654, *CSPD 1654* p557

26. Hill, C. *God's Englishman* pp164–5

27. Mountagu–Thurloe, 29 May, *Letters* pp404–7

28. ibid.

29. Mountagu–Thurloe, Cadiz, 19 May 1656, ibid. pp402–3

30. Protector–Blake and Mountagu, 6 May 1656, *Thurloe* vol. iv, pp768–71

31. The progress of the negotiations can be followed through Meadowe's correspondence in *Thurloe* vol. iv, p598, 681, 682–3, 758–9 and vol. v, p59, 97–8, 112–13 except for the assassination attempt for which see note 29. The loading of the compensation money is in Blake & Mountagu–Meadowe, 11 June, *Letters* p356

32. Meadowe–Blake and Mountagu, 25 May, *Thurloe* vol. v, p59; Meadowe–Thurloe, 16 June, ibid. pp123–4

33. Mountagu–Thurloe, 17 June, Cascais Road, *Letters* pp407–11

34. Thurloe–Mountagu, 6 May 1656, Carte vol. 73 f145

35. Instructions to Captain Lloyd, 28 April 1656, *Thurloe* vol. iv, p744. Tools and ammunition appear to have been carried by the *Cullen*, or a ship that it was escorting. See Longland–Badiley, 1 January 1656/7, *CSPD 1656–7* pp226–7

36. Mountagu–Thurloe, 29 May 1656, *Letters* pp404–8; Blake and Mountagu–Committee of Admiralty, 19 June, ibid. pp361–3

37. Article by Jonathan Israel on Anglo-Dutch rivalry in *History Today* July 1988, pp17–22, written as a trailer for his forthcoming book *Dutch Primacy in World Trade, 1585–1740*, underlines how much English trade suffered from the wars of the Commonwealth and Protectorate

38. Protector–Blake and Mountagu, 9 June; *Thurloe* vol. v, pp101–2

39. Blake & Mountagu–Protector, 1 July, off Cadiz, *Letters* pp366–7

40. *Weale* p136

41. Mountagu–Thurloe, 3 July *Letters* pp413–4

42. Mountagu–Thurloe, 9 July, ibid. pp415–6

43. ibid.

44. ibid.
45. Blake & Mountagu–Committee of Admiralty, 1 July, ibid. pp368–9
46. Journal of Captain Edward Blagg, of the *Fairfax*, 12 June–6 July, ibid. pp440–5
47. Mountagu–Thurloe, 8 July, pp414–5; A Relation of Five Ships of War, 21 July, ibid. pp445–7; Pointer–Navy Commissioners, 24 July, ibid. p439; Mountagu–Thurloe, 31 July, ibid. pp416–7
48. Mountagu–Thurloe, Sallee, 8 August, ibid. pp417–8; Stations of the Fleet, 11 August, ibid. p430, shows the ships to be sent home: those with Mountagu at Sallee and those which Blake took there when the treaty ran into trouble
49. e.g. p132 and p133
50. Mountagu–Thurloe, Oeiras Bay, 11 September, *Letters* pp418–9
51. Stayner–Generals of the Fleet (??), 10 September, ibid. pp448–50, Attribution uncertain
52. Stayner–Generals of the Fleet, 9 September, ibid. pp447–8
53. ibid. and Stayner–Blake & Mountagu, 14 September, ibid. pp450–2; Blake & Mountagu–Committee of Admiralty, 19 September, ibid. p374; Narrative of the Success of the Fleet, 4 October, *CSPD 1656–7* p126
54. Mountagu–Thurloe, 22 October *Letters* pp426–7

CHAPTER 17   TENERIFFE   OCTOBER 1656–SEPTEMBER 1657   pp 225 to 239

1. *Thurloe* vol. v, pp363–4. Protector–Generals at Sea, 28 August 1656
2. *Letters* pp423–6, 20 September, Oeiras Bay
3. *Thurloe* vol. v, pp518–9, Instructions to the Generals of the Fleet
4. *Letters* pp427–9, Mountagu–Committee of Admiralty, 25 October, Stokes Bay
5. *CSPD 1656–7* pp191–4, Council of State, Day's Proceedings, 11 December
6. e.g. *Letters* p440. Thomas Pointer in his letter to the Navy Commissioners of the 8 October anticipates the use of the Canary Islands as a staging post.
7. ibid. pp381–2, Blake–Mountagu, 9 February 1657. Also Stayner's Account which is printed in *Naval Miscellany* vol. ii, Navy Records Society vol. xl, 1910. This is very valuable being an eye witness account for one of the chief protagonists. But it must be remembered that it was not published until after the Restoration when political conditions had changed. In such circumstances memory can be very selective and it has to be balanced by other accounts, especially in the parts which affect his relations with Blake.
8. *Thurloe* vol. v, pp358–61, Papers delivered to the Dutch Ambassador
9. *Thurloe* vol. vi, p5, Maynard–Thurloe, 19 January
10. ibid. p29, Intelligence from Cadiz, 1 February
11. *Letters* pp383–5
12. *Weale* p144; *Letters* pp453–4, Letter from aboard the *Fairfax*, 3 March; ibid. pp383–5, Blake–Committee of Admiralty, 11 March
13. Date from *Weale* p146, details of the council from Stayner
14. *Stayner* pp129–30
15. *Thurloe* vol. vi, pp152–3, Maynard–Thurloe, 30 March, Lisbon
16. ibid. gives *Rainbow*, *James* and *Kent* as being off North Cape (Finisterre) but the *Kent* rejoined the fleet and was replaced by the *Yarmouth*. She did not go to Teneriffe but does not appear to have been under Stokes' direct command.
17. For differing explanations of the delay see *Stayner* p131 and Narrative of the Action at Santa Cruz in *Letters* pp385–8
18. ibid.
19. Firth, Sir C.H. *Last Years of the Protectorate* vol. ii, p250n
20. *Stayner* p133
21. Curtis, C.D. p156
22. Lurting, Thomas *The Fighting Seaman turned Peaceable Christian* for the part played by the

Bristol. The copy I have used is an undated reprint at Gloucester. The editor says that he has made a few verbal alterations which in no way alter the sense.

23. *Stayner* p134

24. This is Powell's view *Robert Blake, General-at-Sea* p302. As he remarks, it is difficult to resolve the conflict of evidence in any other way. However it needs to be said that he has misplaced the position of Fort San Philip, mistaking it for that of San Juan. The ships appear to have been placed in a double line with the larger galleons on the outside and not strung out as in his diagram, so the *Speaker* could have been inside the Admiral and Vice-Admiral and the *Bristol* outside, or vice versa.

25. See note 17 (Narrative)

26. See note 23

27. Clarendon, vol. vi, p36

28. Beadon, Roger *Robert Blake Sometime commanding the Fleets of Great Britain* p255

29. *Weale* p146

30. *Thurloe* vol. vi, p342, Protector–General Blake and Instructions to General Blake

31. *Weale* p150. Stokes–Blackborne, 5 July, *Letters* p462.

32. *Weale*, p149 gives date as 19 June. The incident is mentioned briefly in Maynard–Thurloe, 8 July, *Thurloe* vol vi, pp386–8 and Same–Same, ibid. p401,

33. *Weale* p151

34. Blake–Mountagu, 9 February 1657 *Letters* pp381–2

35. Blake–Committee of Admiralty, 11 March, ibid. pp383–5

36. Maynard–Thurloe, 14 July *Thurloe* vol. vi, p401

37. Clarke–Admiralty and Navy Commissioners, Plymouth Sound, 7 August 1657 *Letters* pp462–3

38. ibid.

39. Hatsell–Admiralty Commissioners, 7 August *CSPD 1657–8* p57

40. Thurloe–(Swift)?, 11 August, ibid. pp58–9

41. Powell gives Will in his appendix pp312–4

42. *Add. Mss. 9300* f359

43. *Add. Mss. 9394* f126

44. ibid.

45. Clarendon, vol. vi, p37

Index

Where ships belong to the English Navy, the year of launching and the number of guns carried are given where they are known. The gun totals are in many cases different from those given in Oppenheim's complete list. He appears to have given the peacetime establishment, but the Dutch War lists show that many of the ships were capable of carrying more guns and I have preferred them. The discrepancies are at their widest with the earlier vessels: e.g. Oppenheim gives the *James* 38 guns, while Dutch War lists have her carrying 66.

Index